THE SOCIALIST REGISTER 1995

WHY NOT CAPITALISM

SOCIALIST REGISTER 1 9 9 5

Edited by LEO PANITCH
Special Coeditors:
ELLEN MELKSINS WOOD
JOHN SAVILLE

First published in 1995
by The Merlin Press Ltd
10 Malden Road
London
NW5 3HR

British Library Cataloguing in Publication Data

The Socialist Register. — 1995
   1. Socialism — 1995
   I. Panitch, Leo
   355'.005

ISBN 0-85036-449-3 Hbk
ISBN 0-85036-448-5 Pbk

Typesetting by
Computerset, Harmondsworth, Middlesex

Printed in Finland by WSOY

TABLE OF CONTENTS

PREFACE

Ralph Miliband, the founder of the *The Socialist Register* with John Saville in 1964, and its co-editor for the subsequent three decades, died on May 21, 1994. His death, after falling ill upon his return to London from the New York Socialist Scholars Conference in April, was unexpected. Despite a close brush with death after a heart by-pass operation three years before, he had resumed his activities with characteristic strength of will and stamina, and celebrated the completion of a new book, *Socialism for a Sceptical Age*, at a festive 70th birthday party in January, 1994. He had been looking forward to a special launch that was being prepared for the publication in June of the thirtieth annual volume of the *Socialist Register*, for which he had written the introductory essay. It was entirely characteristic of him that the final words of his survey of the direction, policy and output of *Register* since its first appearance should have been: 'All in all, I think the publication deserves the mention 'has done well, could do better'; and over the next thirty years it will.'

This thirty-first issue of *The Socialist Register* has been prepared, with the help of John Saville and Ellen Meiksins Wood as special co-editors, with the recognition that we can best honour Ralph's memory by beginning to fulfil that promise. The theme of this year's volume, *Why Not Capitalism*, is taken from the title Ralph originally had intended for his last book, reflecting his concern that the centrality of an anti-capitalist politics for the Left, of a political project fundamentally oriented to transcending the capitalist order, not be displaced. 'Why Not Capitalism' is intended to signal the importance, today more than ever, that the Left develop its capacities to understand and explain the dynamics, contradictions and depredations of contemporary capitalism in its many manifestations around the globe; while, at the same time, undertaking searching reexaminations of the Left's own histories and current practices to the end of reawakening socialist commitment, vision and potential. In this way we may yet be able to challenge the appalling capitalist 'new times' we live in.

It is in this spirit that the opening essay discusses Ralph Miliband's legacy as a socialist intellectual and the contribution he made through his teaching and political writings. This is followed by Ellen Meiksins Wood's essay probing the grounds for the differences between the 'first generation' of the New Left and its successors, and identifying how the former's legacy is more genuinely oppositional and emancipatory as well as more current and relevant than recent intellectual and political fashions. George Ross then traces how the Left's capacity to 'say no to capitalism' has altered in the context of changing historical and material conditions, and analyses in this context the crisis of Left politics and the opportunities it presents. Hilary Wainwright, inspired by Miliband's 'Moving On' essay in the 1976 Register on the British Left's failure to establish an effective political formation in the 20 years after 1956, revisits the problem today, and, drawing on the experiences with the new social movements over the past two decades, identifies the conjunctural conditions now favourable to 'moving on' in creative new strategic and organizational directions. Frances Fox Piven analyses how a globalizing capitalism generates fractious racial, ethnic, religious and gender conflicts, and shows how the class war in America is conducted today through the 'familiar formations of identity politics'. Daniel Singer follows with a survey of disturbing European trends which sharply poses the question of whether the future of Europe is inevitably 'American': and he argues that even a defence of past reforms now requires a radical break with the traditionally moderate tactics and policies of the 'respectful Left'.

K. S. Karol's essay contributes to the theme of 'why not capitalism' by painting a starkly revealing picture of the new bourgeois class made up of nomenklatura and gangsters represented by the Yelstin regime in Russia. And William Graf, in an argument consistent with essays on globalization in *The Socialist Register 1994*, shows how third world states, despite formal 'democratization', are being restructured to play the role of aligning domestic with global markets through 'law and order' enforcements of 'recommodification' practices. The increased use of the concept of the 'underclass' in the core capitalist countries brings to mind the extent to which the conditions and the status of the people so designated are increasingly treated in ways analogous to 'third world' populations. Linda Gordon offers a pathbreaking account of the history of the concept of the 'underclass', and the evolving political practices associated with it in the United States; while Joan Smith uncovers, through an examination of the housing policy of Conservative governments in Britain, the link between the rising problem of homelessness and the New Right's employment of the notion of the 'underclass'.

We turn, in the final four essays, to a direct focus on Ralph Miliband and his work. John Schwartzmantel's reexamination of the concept of 'capitalist democracy' testifies to the acuity of Miliband's understanding of the limited nature of democracy in the contemporary world. The tribute John Saville then pays to Miliband's *Parliamentary Socialism* provides us with a unique perspective of the political and intellectual conditions which Miliband confronted in the 1950s, and the major role his first book played in the revival of socialist ideas through the 1960s and 1970s; it also draws out Miliband's enduring relevance to understanding the evolution of the Labour Party from Gaitskell to Blair. We follow this by publishing here for the first time Ralph Miliband's own tribute to his teacher, Harold Laski, an essay originally commissioned in the 1950s for a Fabian Society pamphlet; this essay not only clearly reveals Laski's influence on Miliband's thought, but it also has a great deal to say of considerable relevance for contemporary problems and debates, not least about the role of socialist intellectuals. We conclude the volume with Marion Kozak's remarkable 'aide memoire' on the birth of *The Socialist Register* itself; drawing on her personal experience as well as Ralph Miliband's papers, her essay provides a highly revealing and insightful perspective on the history of the British New Left and Ralph Miliband's place within it.

Among our contributors, Ellen Meiksins Wood teaches political science at York University in Toronto; and George Ross teaches sociology at Brandeis University in Boston. Hilary Wainwright is political editor of *Red Pepper* and research associate at the International Centre for Labour Studies at Manchester University. Frances Fox Piven teaches political science at the Graduate Centre of the City University of New York. Daniel Singer is the European Correspondent for *The Nation*, and K. S. Karol writes on Eastern Europe and the ex-Soviet Union for *Nouvel Observateur*; both live in Paris. William Graf teaches political science at Guelph University, Ontario; and Linda Gordon teaches history at the University of Wisconsin, Madison. Joan Smith is Reader in the School of Social Sciences, Staffordshire University; and John Schwartzmantel teaches political science at Leeds University. John Saville, co-founder and for many years co-editor of *The Socialist Register* with Ralph Miliband, is Emeritus Professor of Economic and Social History at Hull University. Marion Kozak was until recently Director of the Day Care Trust and is active with other NGOs in London.

I am very grateful to all the contributors, and want to offer additional thanks to Marion Kozak for preparing the selected bibliography of Ralph Miliband's writings which we publish at the end of the volume, as well as to David Macey for his translation of K. S. Karol's essay. At Merlin Press, Julie Millard was once again most helpful, and Martin Eve's encouragement, advice and unfailing support during this sad and difficult year has been particularly invaluable.

I am most appreciative to John Saville and Ellen Meiksins Wood for agreeing to join me as special co-editors for this volume, and for their active part in its planning and realization. Since this has necessarily been a transition year to a new editorial structure for the Register, I am also deeply indebted to them, as well as to Martin Eve of Merlin Press and Susan Lowes of Monthly Review Press, for helping to think through, and see through, this transition. Planning for the 1996 volume is already well underway in the context of this new editorial structure, with two active groups of contributing editors centred at Manchester and Toronto.

The sadness that already attended the preparation of this year's volume was added to by the news of Joe Slovo's death in early 1995. Joe Slovo was a friend of Ralph Miliband's, and a contributor to the Register. In an important article in the 1973 *Socialist Register* on 'Problems of Armed Struggle', Joe Slovo wrote: 'Every political action in South Africa will not necessarily be an armed action. But every political action, whether armed or not, should be regarded as part of the build-up to the conquest of power . . .' His contribution to the victory of the anti-apartheid struggle was immense and we join with the countless others in South Africa and around the world who mourn his death.

The Socialist Register will live on, dedicated to trying to build on a rich legacy so as to enhance the quality of the Left's understanding and analysis and its commitment to strategic renewal and advance. We would like to encourage all our readers to 'register with the Register' by sending their names and addresses to Merlin Press in London or Monthly Review Press in New York.

L. P.

March 1995

RALPH MILIBAND,
SOCIALIST INTELLECTUAL, 1924–1994

Leo Panitch

Ralph Miliband stood as a beacon on the international Left. He epitomized what it meant to be a creative and independent socialist intellectual, and he provided consistent leadership in defining the issues for critical engagement. He ranks among those most directly associated with the emergence of the British New Left after 1956, and for the flourishing Marxist scholarship it spawned in the following decades. As with Edward Thompson in the field of social history, or Raymond Williams in cultural studies, Ralph Miliband took the lead in political studies, clearing the ground and establishing the foundations for, as he once put it, 'what has so long been lacking, namely a radically-oriented, critical and demystifying discipline of political studies'.[1] For those of us nurtured in the fertile and open Marxism that Miliband, like Thompson and Williams, practised, the contemporary spate of charges that economism, determinism or totalitarianism are inherently inscribed in Marxist ideas and practice can only appear as but a reversion to the shabbiest of stereotypes, the crudest of caricatures.

At the same time, perhaps more than any other intellectual of our time, Ralph Miliband consistently devoted himself to demonstrating the necessity for retaining and articulating a vision of an authentically democratic socialist order; and to addressing the possibility for advances towards it through building new socialist movements alternative to both Communism *and* Social Democracy, with a repertoire of socialist practice encumbered neither by Leninism *nor* Labourism. He steadfastly maintained this perspective amidst the political defeats and intellectual recriminations and retreats on the Left in recent years.

I knew Ralph Miliband for 27 years. He was my teacher and supervisor, later briefly my academic colleague, and for the past ten years I had the great privilege of sharing the editorship of *The Socialist Register* with him. We were very close friends. I know now how Ralph himself must have felt when he wrote an appreciation of C. Wright Mills while still mourning 'personally and bitterly' the death of his close friend in 1962. 'I am not

1

minded to write a detached appraisal of his work. But I think I can write about the man he was, and what he was about.'[2] This is what I shall attempt to do here, calling where appropriate on his own words, including from some of the less easily accessible of his writings, and also calling on the insights of a few others who understood and appreciated the person he was.

From Brussels to Highgate: A Youth's Private Pilgrimage

Among his papers, Ralph bequeathed to us a poignant glimpse of the early years of his life and of his parents' enduring influence, in the form of eight pages of hand-written notes he set down in 1983 for a political autobiography he had contemplated writing.[3] He was born in 1924 in Brussels to Polish Jewish immigrants, and, except for a brief visit to relatives in Paris in 1937, it was in Brussels that Ralph spent the first fifteen years of his life. His family's circle in Brussels was that of Jewish immigrants who were 'authentic products of the ghetto': Yiddish was their common tongue (such elementary education as they barely had having been in that language), and most had only learned to speak some broken French. The rise of German fascism, closely observed by these immigrants, merged with their own experience of Polish and Russian anti-semitism to reinforce a culture of isolation, reflecting a sense that 'the world outside the Jews was more or less hostile, suspect at least, not to be trusted or even penetrated.'

Yet Ralph's parents, while very much part of this culture of inter-war Jewish immigrants, refused to be too narrowly constrained by it. His mother's ability to speak excellent Polish was already 'extremely rare in her circle.' And it was again 'most unusual in her circle' that, once she arrived in Belgium as a young unmarried woman after World War I, she taught herself to speak and write French quite well, and that she broke through the barriers that separated Jewish immigrants from the gentile world around them. 'She was a naturally gregarious and outgoing person. ...It may be that it was she who first implanted in my mind the notion that I was destined to be an educated man, some kind of professional, in fact a lawyer.'

But it was his father, a leather worker much more typically 'an authentic product of the ghetto', who awakened Ralph's interest in politics. Ralph's youthful self-image of himself as a lawyer in fact stemmed from his father's fascination with a Parisian (and Jewish) lawyer, Maitre Henri Torres, whose appearance in various great trials the young Miliband followed through newspaper accounts. Indeed, by the age of twelve, Ralph had joined his father in paying 'close attention' to French politics in general, so much so that 'he and I regularly discussed daily events in Paris, changes of ministry, the respective merits of this or that leader.' The fact that it was French rather than Belgian politics that was the object of their attention, had, of course, much to do with Leon Blum's leadership of the

French Socialist Party, and his becoming Premier in the Popular Front Government in 1936.

My father had no strong political convictions but was definitely left of centre, in a loose sort of way, and had for a short time been an active member of the Polish Socialist Party in Warsaw immediately after World War I. The political climate in our house was generally and loosely left: it was unthinkable that a Jew, our sort of Jew, the artisan Jewish worker, self-employed, poor, Yiddish speaking, unassimilated, non religious, could be anything but socialistic, undoctrinally. The right was taken to be antisemitic, the left less so or not at all – after all Blum *was* Prime Minister of France.

Despite recalling his mother's pride in how much he knew about politics and his father's approval of his ideas, Ralph did not, at least in looking back on his youth in recent years, regard himself as having been particularly politically conscious. He could not remember reading a single political work before he was fifteen, although he had consumed much classical French literature by then. It was only as result of wanting to spend more time with his closest friend (later executed at Auschwitz for making Trotskyist propaganda) that he reluctantly joined in 1939, at the age of fifteen, his first political group, the left-zionist youth organisation, Hashomer Hatzair. it was in this context that he 'discovered the Communist Manifesto, though not in any blindingly strong way', and took part in group discussions 'about world affairs, in which the City (of London) and Chamberlain were designated as the chief villains.'

On May 16, 1940, Ralph and his father left Brussels on foot just ahead of the invading Nazis; they walked to Ostend where they had hoped to escape to unoccupied France, but instead boarded the last boat out to Dover, England. Ralph's mother and sister managed to hide from the Nazis with a family of Belgian farmers they had known before the war. Under the protective wing of this family and their neighbours, they were sheltered for the duration of the war, along with 18 other Jews, in a village only a few kilometres from a German military base.

Ralph and his father, having arrived in England on May 19, 1940 were taken to London, where they were at first briefly put up in the home of a Jewish businessman in Chiswick. Then, with the status of refugees, they were lodged with a landlady, the rent for the single room Ralph and his father shared, and a few shillings for food, being paid by the Town Hall out of public funds until they were put to work removing furniture from bombed-out houses. Just how intense a period of political incubation the dreadful years of 1939–40 were for Ralph personally can be gleaned from the description that he set down 43 years later of how in the summer of 1940, only a few months after arriving in England, the sixteen year-old Miliband undertook yet another fateful journey:

I made my way, alone, to Highgate Cemetery on a private pilgrimage to the grave of Marx, which was then still the simple grave in which he had been buried, with the modest stone, instead of the monstrous monument, so clearly Stalinist, which now disfigures the spot. It was a very hot afternoon, the cemetery was utterly deserted, the sun very high in a very blue sky; and I remember standing in front of the grave, fist clenched, and swearing my own private oath that I would be faithful to the workers' cause. I do not recall the exact formulation, but I have no doubt of the gist of it; and I thought of myself as a revolutionary socialist or communist – the exact label was of no consequence. I don't know how faithful I have been to that oath in terms of action: I am sure I should have done more, immeasurably more. But I have not, from that day to this, departed from the view that this was the right cause and that I belonged to it.

It was with distinctive lack of self-delusion that Ralph put this youthful pledge in humourous and honest perspective so many years later. He was on the side of the workers, but:

> On the other hand, and it is a very large other hand, I had no intention of *being* a worker. Here, my mother's ambitions, which I must have assimilated, and her belief that I was destined for higher things, were supplemented by my experience of physical work . . . When London began being bombed in the autumn, we [i.e., Ralph and his father – L.P] took up work, namely removing furniture from bombed houses, an arduous business which was made a lot easier by the fact that the man who led the team of five or six removers and who drove the lorry (all English except us) believed in doing the very minimum possible and would park the lorry off Chiswick High Street as often after lunch as he could, and would lead us all to the cinema, the Hammersmith Gaumont/Commodore for the afternoon, or otherwise pass the time, for instance in expeditions to Kew Gardens. However, the work, when we worked, was hard; and we found out about middle class meanness and snobbery, and kindness; and I found out about the curious combination of kindness, cunning, ignorance, feigned servility and subordination, actual contempt which this particular part of the unskilled working class had for their masters.

> But I remember very clearly the distance I felt existed between them and me, not only on the grounds of Jewishness or being 'Belgian', or refugees, but a budding 'intellectual', to which I had absolutely no title. Why I should have felt that I was superior to them I do not know, and superior in intellectual and political terms. My English was poor though I was learning fast, and my 'status' entirely 'non-intellectual'. But I must have felt the distance in terms of ideology. It never occurred to me to discuss politics with any of them, perhaps because I knew that my views were out of the way and I was very unsure about them.

It was not long before his status as a budding intellectual was to become more securely grounded. Spending as much time as possible in the Chiswick Public Library, where he read the *Daily Worker* as well as other morning papers, and *Labour Monthly* as well as *Keesing's Archives*, he came across the writings of Harold Laski. Seeing that he was connected with the London School of Economics and Political Science (of which Ralph had heretofore never heard), he applied to study with him there and was, astonishingly enough, admitted. Laski's impact was immediate and enduring: 'I was quite dazzled, as a 17-year old student, by his scholarship, his wit, his extraordinary generosity to students, and his familiarity with the great and the mighty.'[4] After three years in the Royal Navy, Ralph returned to his studies at the LSE and became quite close to Laski in the years before his untimely death in 1950 at the age of 56. While still working on a Ph.D thesis on Popular Thought in the French Revolution (he was one of those graduate students who suffered through many long years of struggling to complete a dissertation), he was given a junior teaching position at the LSE. This is where (except for a short stint at Chicago's Roosevelt College where Harold Washington, the future Black mayor of Chicago, was one of his students), he remained until the early 1970s.

The Teacher of Politics

Ralph Miliband was a great teacher, but his long relationship with the LSE was never a very happy one. The LSE was always a far less radical place than its reputation suggested; and faculty positions were often filled in the post-war years with the consideration of changing that reputation somewhere at play. It was Miliband's view that Laski's early death had been 'a grievous blow to the Politics Department at the LSE, from which it never recovered, or I should perhaps say more accurately, from which it has never been allowed to recover.'[5] With characteristic humour, Ralph was wont to compare the conventionally narrow range of views of most teachers of politics in the post-war period to Dorothy Parker's depiction of a play she reviewed as 'having run the whole spectrum of human emotions all the way from A to B.' It was a climate of thought which excluded radical questions 'from serious consideration by serious people, serious being defined, almost, as people who did not ask such questions . . . [A] fellow teacher in politics, confronted with the idea that there was a ruling class in Britain, could retort instantly that there wasn't, and that moreover it was a good one . . .'.[6]

Nor was Miliband the sort of person inclined to bridge his differences with his colleagues under the rubric of a 'community of scholars'. This was a notion of which he was 'extremely suspicious', as he openly put it in his Inaugural Lecture for the Chair of Politics he took up at Leeds in 1972.[7] The reaction of his colleagues to the famous students' revolt at the LSE in 1968 had led him to this view. The principled, yet cool-headed support he offered the students while the School was closed for much of the academic year was matched by the disgust he felt at so many of his colleagues'

> . . . impatience, indignation, anger, fear, contempt, but most notably, what appeared to be a remarkable measure of sheer incomprehension, not least on the part of people whose avocation was supposed to be the study and understanding of social phenomena. Many administrators and teachers, nurtured in a different tradition and climate, simply did not understand what their revolting students were about, and didn't really want to find out. They were content with stereotypes at least as crude as many which students sometimes-manufactured.[8]

Notably, the one criticism of C. Wright Mills that Miliband was prepared to make, in the appreciation he wrote just after Mills' death, had to do with what he regarded as Mills' misplaced faith in the progressive role of the intellectual as 'a free man, in duty bound to help make others free. Such a romantic, naive view is inconvenient; it poses a threat. No wonder he made enemies in the academic fraternity'.[9] Actually, in terms of the enmity they sometimes aroused in the academic fraternity, there was perhaps little to choose between Miliband and Mills. The difference was that whereas Mills was, as Ralph put it, 'on the Left, but not of the Left, a deliberately lone guerilla', Miliband very much saw himself as belonging to an intellectual community. He may have been 'the leading Marxist political scientist in the English-speaking world', as one tribute to him recently averred[10], but the professional associations of political scientists certainly did not constitute his community; the community he felt part of was a community of socialist intellectuals, broadly defined enough to include many people, not least in the labour movement, who had never been inside a university.

Ralph saw his role as developing that community in many ways outside the university, but he was also strongly committed to nurturing socialist intellectual life within the university. When in his interview for the Chair at Leeds, he was asked by the Vice-Chancellor, Lord Boyle (a former Tory cabinet minister), what his ambitions would be for the Politics Department, he answered immediately that he wanted to make it the best socialist politics department in Europe. If Boyle did not recoil in horror at the notion, it was because, being the kind of civilized and broad-minded Tory 'wet' that Thatcher most despised, he could discern the obvious integrity of Ralph's insistence that ' . . . teaching politics, if one is on the left, requires an intransigent probing of all matters which form part of the socialist agenda, an intransigent probing of every formulation, every text and every historical and contemporary figure. After all, it was Marx who said that his favourite motto was 'Doubt all things'.'[11]

Ralph was, in fact, always exceedingly proud of his 'Beruf', his vocation, as teacher. Having himself been nurtured by Laski, whom he regarded, above all, as 'a great teacher of politics', his performance as a teacher mattered enormously to Ralph. The first thing that impressed him about C. Wright Mills was that 'he had succeeded in proving to a new generation of students what most of their teachers had managed to conceal from them: that social analysis could be probing, tough-minded, critical, relevant, and scholarly; that ideas need not be handled as undertakers handle bodies, with care but without passion; that commitment need not be dogmatic; and that radicalism need not be a substitute for hard thinking.'[12] The kind of socialist intellectual community into which Ralph wanted to induct his students stood in sharp contrast to the 'too cosily cloying' notion of the university community which evoked for him 'the sussuration of soft voices saying yeah; of the beery toothiness of the students' bar; or the smarmy solicitude of soulmates'. The community he sought with his students was 'first and foremost, or ought to be, about serious intellectual work; and the first thing that students ought to be told about such work is that it is not only hard and demanding but that much of it is also lonely work. First there must be soliloque, then dialogue.' His expectations of students were high: they needed to 'go away, and read, and wrestle with a problem, and then come back and talk about it.' But he was equally demanding in terms of what was required of the teacher:

> ... [E]veryone pays lip service to discussion and dialogue. But genuine discussion and dialogue and questioning, with no holds barred, and with no pulling of rank, is not easy; it goes against the authoritarian grain which threatens or afflicts every person in authority ... and in teaching, there are particularly attractive excuses ... Of course, it is generally true we know more in our subjects than our students. But whether we always know *better* is very much open to question. If 'better' means we have more insight into the dynamics, say, of a political system, or into police behaviour, then I can imagine many teachers *not* knowing better than many of their students, and even knowing a lot worse.[13]

In Miliband's famous seminar on 'Problems of Contemporary Socialism' at the LSE, he encouraged such a cacophony of student voices that I, at least sometimes, would have preferred a bit more soliloque on his part. But he more than made up for this in his lecture courses. Ralph was an absolutely brilliant orator, and more than one person has commented since his death on what a shame it was that his great powers as an orator were not utilized by the political parties on the Left. But Ralph had no regrets about this whatsoever; and he knew that his talent as a public speaker was hardly wasted on the great many students who crowded together to hear the lectures he planned and crafted so meticulously and delivered with such energy, wit and passion.

My own example is illustrative. I had arrived at the LSE in 1967 as a 22-year-old, enrolled in an utterly conventional public administration programme. (I had made the mistake of saying I wanted to study economic planning on my Commonwealth Scholarship application form.) There I sat, bored and sullen, a student who was nothing but fodder for the upcoming revolt, when a fellow Canadian who had already been around a while took pity on me and told me to come up to the fifth floor to listen to the lectures that became *The State in Capitalist Society*. The main topic that day was not Marx or Mills, but De Gaulle's memoirs and what they unwittingly revealed about the relationship between the state and the capitalist economy and class structure. As he often did, Ralph looked about the packed lecture hall, while embellishing a point with three or four or five metaphors, and he would catch someone's eye and hold it to see if the light had gone on. He caught mine. The light had indeed gone on. I rushed off to the graduate secretary to switch into the political sociology masters programme and was refused: it was too late and in any case too full. Trembling with anxiety, I lay in wait for Dr Miliband at the end of his next lecture to see if he could help. And I immediately discovered how far this hugely generous teacher would go in support of a student who seemed motivated and committed.

It was, I think, his determination to inspire students with a sense that their work really mattered *politically* that made him so effective a teacher. He convinced us that it was not enough to know how to criticise conventional political science and sociology, but that it was a matter of some political urgency to go beyond vanguardist postures and slogans and engage ourselves in constructing a vibrant, unobstructed and accessible Marxist political science. Those of us who went on to do Ph.D. work with him were never just writing a thesis to get a degree and a teaching position; we were writing a book, which, he constantly impressed upon us, had its part to play in furthering the possibility of progressive social change. He was egalitarian with us in the best sense of the term. Arriving for a tutorial with him in his dark office at the LSE, I would be greeted with a genuine welcome and as often as not a proposal that we head down to the Strand to hold our discussion over a coffee and a smoke. 'I can't write your bloody thesis for you, Leo!', he struck out as I whined one day about some impasse I had reached; and I understood immediately that what he meant by this was not just the obvious, but that I had to start to see myself, not him, as having the greater expertise on the subject and the approach. Even if I did not feel that I knew as much as he did, he was telling me that I knew, or could know, 'better'.

My own personal experience was hardly unique. Indeed, mine was one of no less than twenty-five or thirty doctoral dissertations he was supervising at any given time in the late 1960s and early 1970s, a number I have never known equalled in academic life. The reason he was so popular was only partly due to the fact that the LSE attracted so many radical students that the very few radical faculty on staff inevitably carried a heavy burden. It was also due to Ralph's great warmth and humour, his openness and generosity. Nor was it just, or even mainly, the most radical students who studied with him. Because he had no time for dogmatism, he in fact turned many of the militants off, while attracting into the socialist intellectual community many students who had come from quite other directions.

It was perhaps not surprising, given his impatience with the notion of a 'community of scholars', that soon after he took up the Chair at Leeds, he felt unhappy – and just not very good at – administering a department. Starting in the late 1970s he, like a fair number of other European Marxists were also to do, took up a series of one-term teaching posts in North America (Brandeis in Boston, York in Toronto, and the City University of New York Graduate Centre were his main stops). Among the many tributes paid to him as a teacher by his North American students, a letter I received this summer from Mark Neufeld, who took a course with him at Carleton's political economy summer school in Ottawa in the mid-1980s (and now teaches international relations at Trent University), captures especially well what Ralph Miliband was about as a teacher:

> I was finishing up an M.A. at the time, and though I had come to Carleton as a liberal, by that point I was pretty much looking for an alternative. Still, I didn't want to give up my liberal-reformist politics without a fight – and I took that fight into Ralph Miliband's class . . . Anyway, I remember at one point challenging the marxist thesis about the centrality of capital in orienting politics by raising the Galbraithian counter that in advanced capitalist societies, ownership of capital is separated from control, etc. I remember that a number of people in the class jumped on me (and I'm sure I had it coming), urging Miliband to ignore me and get on with more important things. But he was very quick to quiet them, and responded that the Galbraithian view was an important one, and had to be met with reasoned arguments. He then proceeded to do that in considerable detail . . . I was very struck by the degree of respect he showed me. And that was the moment, I think, when I realized (and you have to understand, I was raised in an environment even more hostile to all things marxist than is normally the case in North America) that one didn't have to sacrifice intellectual rigour or moral integrity to work within the marxist tradition.

Political Writings for a New Left

'Intellectual rigour and moral integrity within the marxist tradition.' This defined his politics as much as his teaching. Indeed, of Ralph Miliband it may be said, perhaps even more than of any other of his remarkable contemporaries on the British New Left, that his teaching and writing were but particular facets of an overarching and all-consuming *political* project: the renaissance of a socialist politics in the wake of the intellectual and moral bankruptcy that both the Communist and Social Democratic parties, in their very different ways, had come to represent by the middle of the twentieth century.

The distinctiveness of the British New Left[14] was not only that it predated in its origins the general upsurge of youth radicalism in the advanced capitalist world in the 1960s that reached its peak in the anti-Vietnam War protests, student rebellions and shop-floor worker militancy of '1968', but that it was in its intellectual formation far more consciously, and creatively, Marxist, and much more directly concerned with working class culture and politics. A key moment was the mimeographed publication in June 1956 (equivalent to what would later and elsewhere be called 'samizdat') within the British Communist Party of *The Reasoner* by Edward Thompson and John Saville, followed, a year later (after their suspension and subsequent resignation from the Party) by their founding of the independent 'socialist humanist' journal, *The New Reasoner*. (The masthead quoted Marx: 'To leave error unrefuted is to encourage intellectual immorality'.) Among a remarkable editorial committee (including, among others, Doris Lessing, Ronald Meek, Michael Barratt Brown, and Peter Worsley) the only one who had never been a member of the Communist Party was Ralph Miliband. Miliband had been a rather uncomfortable and peripatetic supporter of the Bevanite Left inside the Labour Party in the early and mid-1950s. With the 'democratic communists' who aligned with Thompson and Saville around *The New Reasoner*, Miliband felt he had finally found a group of true political allies.

One of Ralph's most remarkable qualities was his invariably sound judgement. This was seen in the rather unique appreciation he had at this time of the need to allow for ample space within which a New Left could express its diversity. When in 1959 *The New Reasoner* merged with *Universities and Left Review* (which had emerged in 1957 under the leadership of a group of highly precocious Oxford graduate students, including Stuart Hall from Jamaica and Charles Taylor from Canada) to form *New Left Review*, Miliband had a clearer sense of the troubles that lay ahead, and stood virtually alone among both editorial boards in strongly opposing the merger. Despite (or more likely because of) his ability to get along well with both groups, Miliband understood that 'the two journals represented two very different currents of thought and experience', a distinction he drew in terms of *The New Reasoner* group being intellectuals *of* the labour movement, while the young Oxbridge radicals were intellectuals *for* it.[15] His concerns proved prescient in the crisis-plagued early years of the NLR and the sharp breach that occurred between Thompson and NLR when Perry Anderson took over as editor in 1963.

It was in this context that Miliband proposed in April 1963 that he, Saville and Thompson launch an annual survey of socialist theory and practice which would 'embody the spirit which had informed *The New Reasoner*.' Although Thompson begged off the co-editorship after his harrowing experience at the NLR, it was in the pages of *The Socialist Register* that he conducted his intellectual counterattack on the young turks at the NLR, with Miliband playing an active role as editor in trying to tone down the invective. Miliband, too, could be unforgiving and harsh towards those he felt had abandoned, or were undermining, the socialist project; but this was certainly not the case with the brilliant young comrades at the NLR (Anderson was 24 in 1963, Miliband and Thompson almost 40), and he was very concerned that debates and relations be conducted in a way that prevented (what Thompson, far too pessimistically, believed had already happened) the complete dispersal of the New Left to the point where its enormous potential to establish collective new ground would be lost. Miliband maintained good relations with the group around the NLR, and in these early years Ralph especially helped facilitate the link they made with his friend, Isaac Deutscher.

The intellectual space that was just then beginning to be created by the British New Left did prove to be immense, with a broad and indelible impact on contemporary scholarship, and with considerable effects, especially in Britain, on the cultural and political consciousness of many intellectuals and activists outside of academe. But the idea had been to give rise to a new praxis, to found a new socialist politics. It was to this challenge that Miliband dedicated himself, more insistently and more coherently, than any one else.[16] Indeed, his own considerable contribution to Marxist scholarship was explicitly directed to clarifying what was entailed in realizing that challenge in the advanced capitalist countries.

The first order of business was to address, in the British context, the dominant practice on the Left, above all, as he put it in the third volume of *The Socialist Register*, the fact

> ... that the Labour Party remains the 'party of the working class', and that there is, in this sense, no serious alternative to it at present. This, of course, has always been the central dilemma of British Socialism, and it is not a dilemma which is likely to be soon resolved. But the necessary first step in that direction is to take a realistic view of the Labour Party, of what it can and of what it cannot be expected to do. For it is only on the basis of such a view that socialists can begin to discuss their most important task of all, which is the creation of an authentic socialist movement in Britain.'[17]

Miliband's *Parliamentary Socialism* was published in 1961 – and quickly became widely recognised as one of the seminal texts of the British New Left. Amidst the Labour Party's internal crisis over the leadership's 'revisionist' concern to reduce the Party's commitments to socialist policies, the book proved enormously influential among both students and activists. Miliband's detailed historical account of the politics of Labourism since 1900 afforded a clear perspective on how commonplace, on the one hand, such controversies as the revisionist one were throughout the party's history; while, on the other hand, revealing in the current context the inherent instability of 'that grand reconciliation between the Labour movement and contemporary capitalism which is the essence of revisionism.' Labourism, including most of the Labour left and the trade unions, Miliband demonstrated, had always been dogmatic, not about socialism, but about a conventional interpretation of parliamentary representation. This had insulated the leadership from the mass party and rendered them both unwilling and unable to educate and mobilise for radical purposes their own class and activist base. Moreover, with the aid of his insight that the Labour Party remained a class party even while its leaders 'always sought to escape from the implication of its class character by pursuing what they deemed to be national policies', Miliband presaged the confrontations what were to erupt later in the decade between an 'affluent' working class and the Labour Government. And his study pointed as well towards the intra-party constitutional crisis which would come to characterize – and consume – the Labour Party as an organisation into the 1980s. Indeed, in a critique in 1958 of Robert McKenzie's famous application of the elitist theory of democracy to Britain (Schumpeter, leavened with a lot of Burke and a little Roberto Michels), Miliband had already not only foreseen 'the overwhelming sense of futility and frustration' among party activists that would lead to that constitutional revolt, but he had rehearsed all the key arguments that would be made in favour of intra-party democracy two decades later.[18] But even as he foretold the growing intra-party revolt, his rigorous analyses of the limits of change in the party, articulated with ever greater clarity through the course of the 1960s and 70s, led him to one inescapable conclusion. As he put it in 1966: '. . . it is not reasonable or realistic for socialists inside the Labour Party to believe . . . that they have any serious prospect of shifting the Labour leaders to the left in any substantial or comprehensive sense.' What was now on the agenda therefore was that it was finally necessary for socialists to build towards a mass political alternative to Labourism. Miliband had always argued that the Communist Party was too burdened by its past, too bureaucratic and too ideologically uncreative to be up to the task. And as for the various Trotskyist and other small parties, their sectarianism and isolation were products of their clinging to an insurrectionary model derived from the Bolshevik Revolution, which was entirely incapable of generating mass support from the working classes of liberal democratic, advanced capitalist regimes. But neither was it a matter of simply proclaiming some New Left party when the whole point was that the basis for such a scheme did not yet exist in terms of genuine popular demand for it. This brought him back to the kind of teaching that would broaden the community of socialists. As he put it in 1966:

> The question is not at present one of parties and political combinations, but of a broad and sustained effort of socialist education, cutting across existing boundaries, free from formula-mongering, and carried out with patience and intelligence by socialists wherever in the Labour movement or outside it they may be situated. Such an effort is not an alternative to an immediate involvement in concrete struggle but an essential element of it.[19]

The importance Miliband attached to developing an adequate Marxist understanding of the capitalist state, beginning with his essay on 'Marx and the State' in the second volume of *The Socialist Register* in 1965, was directly related to this. Miliband understood all too well that the failures of the Left on all sides – and including the difficulty of such a new project as he was advancing – had to be understood in relation to the inherent diffi-culty of the task, the greatest obstacle being nothing less than the immense power, material and ideological, of the dominant classes, and the tenacity with which they used that power in defence of their own strategic advan-tages. His most important texts, *The State in Capitalist Society* (1968) and *Marxism and Politics* (1977), were not only directed at advancing political science beyond where pluralist, elitist and Marxist analyses had previously taken it. They were his contributions to the process of delegitimisation of the capitalist system of power; and they were, above all, about challenging people who claimed they wanted to change the system to address the fundamental strategic issues that were entailed in trying to do so.

Without going into a detailed account, it is nevertheless especially appropriate now that a few salient points be stressed concerning this most-discussed body of Miliband's work. The first relates to the accessibility of his writing, the sheer clarity of the prose, the judicious style of argumentation, the marshalling of empirical evidence, the eclectic use of sources and concepts. All of this characterized a text that was indeed unusually 'free from formula-mongering', as was vitally necessary for socialist education to be broad and sustained. The charges that were levelled against *The State in Capitalist Society* for being 'pre-theoretical', trapped within the elite-pluralist framework that was ostensibly the book's object of critique, reflected an impatience not only with this style of writing, but with this stage in the evolution of theory. Yet it was an absolutely necessary step if more people than those who were already cloistered within a Marxist framework were to be addressed by the new theory of the state. In any case, the criticism that Miliband was trapped by elite-pluralist concepts was certainly much overdrawn. It was only with *The State in Capitalist Society* that a student reared in British and North American political science had the sense that one finally could go beyond just criticising the dominant paradigm and move to an alternative theorization. Miliband left us in no doubt that this theorization had to be a Marxist one; but he also demonstrated that it could be the kind of independent Marxism that did not cut itself off from the non-Marxist intellectual world, indeed that it would be best if one actively tried to incorporate the best insights of other approaches into the Marxist theorization.

A second point that needs to be made is that the theoretical and political significance of the famous debates between Miliband and Poulantzas should not be misunderstood as reflecting incompatible positions. In particular, the parcellization of the theorists into instrumentalist and structuralist, while useful in constructing a snappy-looking course outline, proved especially misleading. This is not to say that the differences of method, focus and interpretation were not substantive. Yet they should not obscure what was common to the project, which was to provide a nuanced counterpoint to the notion that the modern state in the West had freed itself from the determining power of capital, rather than, to the contrary, having become an ever more integral element in modern capitalism's development and reproduction. Both theorists acknowledged the state's autonomy from immediate pressures from capitalists, but understood such autonomy as one of the key conditions for efficient and stable defence of the system, in the context of the contradictions generated by class conflict and the competitive nature of the economy and of the capitalist class itself. Since they were both motivated by the hope that a realistic view of the capitalist state would help in clarifying socialist strategy, their work was above all an invitation for further analysis of the variations of 'relative autonomy' as a means of assessing in different states and conjunctures the limits beyond which reform could not go without creating a crisis of capitalist confidence and a crisis of accumulation.

If they had stopped here, the new theory of the state might have had defeatist implications, but by the late 1970s, with Miliband's *Marxism and Politics* and Poulantzas's *State, Power, Socialism*, they also had turned their attention to moving beyond classical Marxism's contradictory and brittle conceptualisation of the institutional framework of a democratic socialist state. In Miliband's critique of the concept of the dictatorship of the proletariat and of Lenin's democratic centralism, as well as in his creative extension of the notion of structural reform (a concept first formulated by Gorz in *The Socialist Register* in 1968), a crucial step was taken in the new Marxist theory of the state. Miliband was trying to formulate a vision of what kind of state a new socialist politics should aim for, and how it might be realized through a strategy of administrative pluralism ('dual power') which would be anchored in civil society as well as the state. When Poulantzas followed with his own trenchant critique of the utopian notions of direct democracy within the Marxist tradition and his insistence on thinking through the place and meaning of representative institutions in socialist democracy, this was very much consistent with, and complementary to, the position Miliband had advanced. That this development in the new Marxist theory of the state hardly went far enough, Miliband knew very well. Right up to his death, Miliband was bothered that he had not done enough to 'address the question of socialist construction with anything like the rigorous and detailed concern which it requires.'[20] For without developing 'a clear indication of what was being struggled for', the promise of the New Left to found a new politics would not be realized, however great its impact as an intellectual current.

A year before *Marxism and Politics* was published in 1977, Miliband already had expressed his frustration, in his important essay 'Moving On', that 'twenty years after 1956, the main problem for the socialist left in Britain is still that of its own organisation into an effective political formation, able to attract a substantial measure of support and hold out a genuine promise of further growth.'[21] The great tragedy was that rather than moving on in the direction of socialist advance that Miliband had in mind, the British intellectual left, like much of intellectual left elsewhere, increasingly lost its bearings amidst the resurgent capitalist reaction of the 1980s.

A considerable intellectual reaction had emerged as well against the new Marxist state theory, not least on the part of those who sought to deflect capitalist reaction by reverting to a defence of the social democratic welfare state. This involved a challenge to the notion of *relative* autonomy, stressing once again the state's independence from determination by the capitalist economy and class structure. The great irony of all the variants of the state autonomy approach (Skocpol, Nordlinger, Korpi, etc.) was that they emerged just as limits of even the *relative* autonomy of the state were severely tested. The instability of Keynesian policies and corporatist structures became more and more manifest in a new era of capitalist crisis from the mid-1970s on. By the early 1980s, with the rise of the Thatcher-Reagan type of regime, governments and bureaucrats proudly enveloped themselves in an ideology that proclaimed the necessity of the state's subordination to the requirements of global capital markets and even to the norms and opinions of capitalists themselves. Through the course of the decade, moreover, as social democratic regimes (including even Sweden's) found their freedom of manoeuvre restrained by the new limits to capitalist growth, growing capital mobility and a renewed ideological militancy on the part of capitalists, they soon abandoned all pretext that the mixed economy had not all along been a capitalist one and that the welfare state had not always been dependent on and necessarily contained within the limits of capital accumulation. The old 'post-capitalist' 'mixed-economy-revisionism by now had no purchase on reality, yet even it had some plausibility in the 1950s. By contrast, rarely has an academic theory been less apposite to its times that the one that tried to make the case for state autonomy in the 1980s.

Miliband was relatively non-plussed by this development and even went some way (too far in my view) towards accommodating critics like Skocpol.[22] But whereas he was quite tolerant of the academic drift (he had never had any illusions about the 'community of scholars'), he was angered by a similar drift in the socialist intellectual community, especially on the British Left. This was seen in his famous critique of 'The New Revisionism in Britain' in the 25th anniversary issue of *New Left Review* in 1985. He did not deny that there were 'many important insights, many very necessary corrections and critiques of traditional and complacent socialist notions . . . which must be taken with the utmost seriousness by anyone concerned with socialist advance' in the arguments made by Hobsbawm, Hall, Laclau and Mouffe and others around working class conservatism, recomposition and decline, the importance of the new social movements as agents of social change, or the attention that needed to be paid to civil society, as opposed to 'statism'. But what was insupportable was that these points were often made in a way that glided over – amidst an obsession with, and false polarization of, new versus old agencies, or civil society versus the state – many of the central issues that any serious socialist strategy still had to address.

The argument he advanced in this regard is so important, and so indicative of Miliband's passion and insight as a socialist intellectual, that it deserves to be quoted at some length.[23] First, on where any socialist agencies, whether social movements or working classes, or whatever, were starting from:

The new revisionism consistently underestimates or even ignores the fact that the kind of change implied by the notion of socialism is a very arduous enterprise, not only because the working class may not support it, but because the dominant class is against it, and would be even if the working class were to be fervently for it. The 'dominant class' is not a figure of speech: it denotes a very real and formidable concentration of power, a close partnership of capital and the capitalist state, a combined force of class power and state power, armed with vast resources, and determined to use them to the full, in conjunction with its allies abroad, to prevent an effective challenge to its power. The new revisionism does not seem to me to take this power seriously enough: most of the relevant literature is remarkably short on the factual acknowledgement and analysis of its nature and meaning, and its implications for a realistic socialist strategy.

Second, on the question of agencies of change:

. . . the primacy of organized labour in struggle arises from the fact that no other group, movement or force in capitalist society is remotely capable of mounting as effective and formidable a challenge to the existing structures of power and privilege . . . [I]n no way is this to say that movements of women, blacks, peace activists, ecologists, gays, and others are not important, or cannot have effect, or that they ought to surrender their separate identity. Not at all. It is only to say that . . . if, as one is constantly told is the case, the organized working class will refuse to do the job, then the job will not be done; and capitalist society will continue, generation after generation, as a conflict-ridden, growingly authoritarian and brutalized social system, poisoned by its inability to make humane and rational use of the immense resources capitalism has itself brought into being.

Third, on the question of the state in socialist construction:

The power of the dominant class and its allies can be overcome: but overcoming it requires an effective state. To say this is not statist, elitist, undemocratic, male chauvinist ('the state is male'), or to be unaware of the dangers the labels point to. But the way to obviate these dangers is not to devalue and deny the role of the state, but to seek to combine state power with class power from below, in a system of 'dual power' which brings into play an array of popular forces, parties, trade unions, workers' councils, local government, women's groups, black caucuses, activists of every sort, in a democratic exercise of power and maximum self-government in the productive process and every sphere of life. But the state must have an important role in the whole process . . . not only to contain and subdue reactionary resistance to socialist advance, but to fulfil many different functions, including arbitration between the diverse and possibly conflictual forces subsumed under the rubric 'popular power' . . . It is upon that state and its diverse local and regional organs that will fall the task of providing the *ultimate* protection of political, civic and social rights; and it is the state that will be the *ultimate* recourse against manifestations of sexism, racism, discrimination, and abuses of power which will hardly be unknown even after capitalism has been transcended.

What particularly angered Ralph about the new revisionism in Britain was the way it sought to make its case through interventions of a denigrative kind *vis à vis* the Bennite Left in the Labour Party, especially for their persistence in advancing unpopular socialist positions. Miliband was hardly one to harbour a naive view of the capacity or prospects of the Labour Left. As he put it in 1976: 'My own view, often reiterated, is that the belief in the effective transformation of the Labour Party is the most crippling of all illusions to which socialists in Britain have been prone.'[24] He did not change that view, but he recognised that the new activists in the Labour Party, many of them influenced by the intellectual currents of the New Left, had issued the most serious challenge to traditional Labourism in the party's history. He especially was irked by caricatures that ignored the importance Benn and many of the new activists placed on turning the Party's focus towards popular mobilization and socialist education, and that misunderstood or misrepresented the whole point of trying to make parliamentary leaders accountable to socialist policies adopted at party conferences – which was precisely to be able finally to get on with such education and mobilization as would create support for such policies. Yet such caricatures and misrepresentations became as commonplace in *Marxism Today* as they were in *The Guardian* (indeed, the two fed on each other's misrepresentations). When confronted with the kind of jaded comment by one of the founders of *Universities and Left Review* that derided Benn for taking up 'the cause of socialism at the very moment when . . . it was ceasing to be a working class faith,' Miliband's response was harsh: '. . . no one in the Labour Party who has ever held Cabinet office has been as explicit, specific and thorough as Benn (Nye Bevan not excluded) in the denunciation of the economic, social and political power structure in Britain. This hardly places him above criticism. But denigration is something else, and is best left to the enemies of socialism.'[25]

Miliband was not spared the denigration himself. A few months after his critique of the new revisionism appeared, a letter to the editor appeared in *The Guardian* by John Keane, in response to an op-ed piece Miliband had written calling for a new socialist party in the wake of the defeat and marginalisation of the Labour Left. 'Readers of [Miliband's] theoretical works will know that he is an old-fashioned class reductionist and no friend of democratic pluralism. In practice, his class and party-centred perspective would reproduce the worst features of vanguardist politics: especially its authoritarianism, machismo, implicit racism, and pro-Soviet prejudices.'[26] It was a sad commentary on how far the level of intellectual debate in Britain (and not only in Britain) had sunk in certain circles that Miliband, who famously stood in the state debate *against* the reduction of state power to class power, and who had undertaken (beginning with his to well-known essay on 'The State and Revolution' in *The Socialist Register 1970*) the most consistent criticism on the British Left of the undemocratic facets of Lenin's writings and practice, should have been so traduced in this fashion by one of the new 'civil society' theorists.

Even leaving aside the venality of the attempt to tar Miliband with racism, etc., it was no less scurrilous to taint him with pro-Soviet prejudices: here was a Marxist who had never joined a Communist Party, or any vanguard party, who had opposed the invasion of Hungary as a young man,

and who in his maturity had not only opposed the Soviet military inter-
vention in Afghanistan but had used it as an occasion, (in his 'Military
Intervention and Socialist Internationalism', the lead essay in *The Socialist
Register 1980*) not just to deplore all such military interventions by
Communist regimes (including the Vietnamese in Cambodia) but to
undertake what has been called the 'first notable attempt' to theorize the
international relations between unevenly developed socialist countries.[27]
Miliband's long-standing personal litmus test for whether the reform of
Soviet-style regimes was genuine was whether he would be allowed to start
an association for the abolition of capital punishment in such regimes. ('Do
you know why they have no cafés there?' he asked me on his return from
a visit to Russia. 'Central Planning, of course,' I replied. 'Don't be silly',
he said. 'Cafés are where revolutions are hatched.')

To appreciate just how unfair Keane's attack was it is worth recalling
that Ralph chose the following sentences to conclude his most important
book, *Marxism and Politics:*

> Regimes which do, either by necessity or choice, depend on the suppression of all
> opposition and the stifling of all civic freedoms must be taken to represent a disastrous
> regression, in political terms, from bourgeois democracy, whatever the economic and
> social achievements of which they may be capable . . . [T]he civic freedoms which,
> however inadequately, form part of bourgeois democracy are the product of centuries of
> unremitting popular struggles. The task of Marxist politics is to defend these freedoms
> and to make possible their enlargement by the removal of their class boundaries.[28]

It was Ralph's commitment to this kind of socialism that sustained him
to the end of his life. In 1981 Ralph helped found the Socialist Society as
an organisation devoted to socialist education and research. Unlike some of
the other intellectuals involved, Ralph helped build the organization, and
was a regular and punctual attender of steering committee meetings, no
matter how frustrating they sometimes were. He also brought together a
small socialist brains-trust which met regularly with Tony Benn, and was
active with Benn and Hilary Wainwright in setting up the Chesterfield
Socialist Conferences and the Socialist Movement that developed out of
them. Yet this was only a continuation of the kind of work Ralph was
always involved in, from the Centres for Socialist Education in the mid-
1960s to the Marxist study centres he founded when he moved to Yorkshire
in the 1970s. His commitment to developing the socialist intellectual
community outside the cloisters of academe had never weakened.

Meanwhile, he continued to produce a body of work through the 1980s
(especially *Capitalist Democracy in Britain* in 1982 and *Divided Societies*
in 1989) which patiently, even-handedly and cogently addressed those
central themes of class and state which the new revisionists glided over.
And even in ill health, his unremitting dedication to advancing the socialist
case was evident in the energy he summoned up to work on his last book,

which he explicitly undertook, as its title, *Socialism for a Sceptical Age*, makes clear, to counter the view that the socialist cause was irretrievably dead and gone at the end of the twentieth century. He was particularly concerned to sketch out the political and economic institutional framework which would distinguish socialist from capitalist democracy, and to try to outline the kinds of structural reforms that would be required to advance towards such a socialist democracy. This is not to say he was anything but sober about current prospects. Indeed, even before he delivered his last book to the publisher he began to plan a new book which would seriously address 'the fundamental challenge' that the growth of ethnic, nationalist and religious racism, not least in the ex-Communist countries, 'poses to anyone on the progressive side of politics, and particularly to the socialist Left.' These words are from a lecture delivered in Amsterdam in February 1993[29]:

> Marx and later Marxists [were] far too optimistic in relying on the class location of wage-earners to produce a 'class consciousness' that would obliterate all divisions among them. This quite clearly greatly underestimated the strength of these divisions; and it also failed to take account of what might be called an epistemic dimension, meaning that it is a great deal *easier* to attribute social ills to Jews, black people, immigrants, other ethnic or religious groups than to a social system and to the men who run it and who are of the same nationality, ethnicity, or religion. To acquire *this* class consciousness requires a mental leap which many people in the working class (and beyond) have performed, but which many other people, subject to intense obfuscation, have not . . . [C]lass location produces a consciousness which is much more complex and wayward than Marxism assumed; for it leads to reactionary positions as well as progressive ones . . .

These were sober reflections. But they did not induce despair, as his last words in closing this lecture reveal:

> In the long term, the hope that ethnic and national racism might be effectively subdued and turned into no more than a minor nuisance, must rest on the coming into being of societies in which men and women would be assured of a secure material existence, with the guarantee of essential civic and political freedoms, where cooperation and friendship would be genuine rather than rehetorical principles of social organisation. Communist regimes failed to create these conditions; and so, in different ways is capitalism unable to create them . . . A radically different social order seems nowadays remote: but the notion that such an alternative belongs to the realm of fantasy, and that there is no point in striving for it, is a gratuitous surrender to the many voices which preach the conservative message that there is no alternative to the here and now . . . For the Left the struggle against racism in all its forms is not only an absolute obligation in itself; it is also an intrinsic part of the struggle for a radically different social order.

Many have marvelled over, or grumbled about, Ralph Miliband's refusal to join the retreat of the intellectuals over the past decade. Those of us who knew him well were not surprised. So much of the despondency and sheer confusion of our time has had to do with the tendency – long present on the Left – to mix up our own mortality with a timetable for the achievement of socialist goals. Ralph was too modest to have ever shared in such 'chutzpah'. He put it clearly in the opening chapter of *Socialism for a Sceptical Age*:

> For my part, I think of socialism as a new social order, whose realization is a process stretching over many generations, and which may never be fully 'achieved'. Socialism, that is to say, involves a process of striving to advance the goals that define it.[30]

Ralph Miliband's respect for and confidence in future generations was captured, very personally and very poignantly, in the eulogy his son Edward delivered at his funeral on May 27, 1994:

> There is sometimes a general presumption that intellectuals and academics, occupied with thinking, writing and teaching, do not have time for such mundane things as their children and that when they do, it is only to force feed them with their latest ideas. In Ralph's case, nothing cold be further from the truth . . . I never heard the words 'Not now, I'm too busy' pass from his lips . . . He might be up against a deadline, but our needs trumped all others . . . When we were young children, he was an absolutely amazing storyteller. We sometimes joked that he was passing up the chance of undreamt sales – undreamt of, at least, by a socialist academic – by not going into print with the stories he used to tell us about the adventures of Boo-Boo and Hee-Hee, two sheep on the Yorkshire Moors . . . Ralph relished our political views and encouraged them. Indeed, I remember on more than one occasion, him leaping to the defence of the 12-year-old in the corner, who was arguing with a rather surprised friend or academic who happened to come round to dinner . . . Ralph's respect for our point of view was unflinching.

This is the kind of person Ralph Miliband was. It is one of the problems of socialist advance that intellectuals of his like are so hard to come by.

NOTES

This essay considerably expands on a lecture delivered to the plenary session in honour of Ralph Miliband organized by the Caucus for a New Political Science at the 1994 Annual Meeting of the American Political Science Association, New York City, September 3, 1994, an abbreviated version of which was published in *Studies in Political Economy: A Socialist Review*, No. 45, Fall 1994.

1. 'Teaching Politics in an Age of Crisis', Inaugural Lecture to the Chair of Politics, Leeds University, October 7, 1974, in *The University of Leeds Review*, Volume 18, 1975, p. 145.
2. Ralph Miliband, 'C. Wright Mills' in G. William Domhoff and Hyt B. Ballard, eds. *C. Wright Mills and the Power Elite*, (Boston: Beacon Press, 1968), p. 3. Miliband's essay on Mills first appeared, both in *New Left Review* and *Monthly Review*, in 1962.
3. The following quotations in this section are drawn from these notes, entitled 'Political Autobiography: 1st draft' and dated April 7 and May 22, 1983.
4. 'Harold Laski: An Exemplary Public Intellectual,' *New Left Review* 200, (July/August 1993), p.175.
5. 'Teaching Politics', *op. cit.*, pp. 129–30.
6. *Ibid.*, pp. 136–7.
7. *Ibid.*, pp. 139–40.
8. *Ibid.*, p. 145. Ralph especially liked to tell the story, in this context, of how the famous LSE economist, Lord Robbins, at the time Chairman of the LSE Governors, retorted to a group of students who were heckling him that they would not 'fare any better in Russia'. For Ralph this remark demonstrated 'an extraordinary failure to realize that, for the militants, Russia was not a model, but an anti-model, a prime example of what socialism is not.'

9. 'C. Wright Mills', *op. cit.*, p. 7.

10. Robin Blackburn, 'Ralph Miliband, 1924–1994', *New Left Review* 206, July/August 1994, p. 15.

11. 'Teaching Politics', *op. cit.*, p.145.

12. 'C. Wright Mills'. *op. cit.*, p. 3.

13. *Ibid.*, pp. 140–141.

14. See the excellent recent study by Lin Chun, *The British New Left*, (Edinburgh University Press,1993).

15. See Miliband's 'Thirty Years of *The Socialist Register*', and John Saville's 'Edward Thompson, the Communist Party and 1956', both in *The Socialist Register 1994*; cf. Lun's *The British New Left*, esp. pp. 10–16 and 60–64.

16. Lin Chun's study of the British New Left stresses 'its leadership role in advancing a Marxist scholarship and radicalising the national culture', but she is in no doubt that 'in comparison with the old left, a major failing of the New Left was its lack of any organisational strength . . . New Left people, with only one or two outstanding exceptions, at no point showed any intention of creating an alternative organisation to the stagnant left-wing bodies'. In this context, she goes so far as to contend that 'Miliband was almost alone in arguing that giving up the old left parties ought to have posed the whole question of 'in what other existing or soon to-be-created organisation would it be possible for Marxists to further the socialist cause'. But there was no adequate perception that such a new organisation was needed, and where there was such a perception of it, 'there was no clear view as to what it should specifically stand for, in programmatic and organisational as well as theoretical terms'. *The British New Left*, *op. cit.*, pp, xvi–xvii and fn. 8.

17. 'The Labour Government and Beyond', *The Socialist Register 1966*, p. 24.

18. See *Parliamentary Socialism* (Merlin, London 1965), esp. pp, 344–49; and 'Party Democracy and Parliamentary Government', *Political Studies*, Vol. VI (1958), esp. pp. 170–4.

19. 'The Labour Government and Beyond', *op. cit.*, p. 25.

20. 'Thirty Years of *The Socialist Register*', *op. cit.*, p. 6.

21. 'Moving On', *The Socialist Register 1976*, p. 128.

22. See 'State Power and Class Interests', in R. Miliband, *Class Power & State Power: Political Essays*, London: Verso, 1983; and 'State Power and Capitalist Democracy', in S. Resnick and R. Wolff, eds., *Rethinking Marxism: Essays for Harry Magdoff and Paul Sweezy*, (New York, Automedia, 1985).

23. The quotations in this paragraph and in what follows are from 'The New Revisionism in Britain', *New Left Review* 150 (March/April 1985), pp. 8, 13, 15–16.

24. 'Moving On', *op. cit.*, p. 128.

25. 'The New Revisionism in Britain', *op. cit.*, p. 16.

26. *The Guardian*, August 8, 1985.

27. *The British New Left*, *op. cit.*, p. 179, fn.78.

28. *Marxism and Politics* (Oxford University Press, 1977), pp. 189–90.

29. This lecture was posthumously published as 'Ethnicity and Nationalism: A View from the Left' in *Socialist Alternatives*, Vol. 3, No. 1, 1994, pp. 1–15.

30. *Socialism for a Sceptical Age*, (Cambridge: Polity Press, 1994,) p. 3.

A CHRONOLOGY OF THE NEW LEFT AND ITS SUCCESSORS, OR: WHO'S OLD-FASHIONED NOW?

Ellen Meiksins Wood

1956, 1968 and 1989: these are, on any conventional reckoning, major milestones in the odyssey of the post-war Western Left. They are likely to figure as epochal moments in any typical history: from Khrushchev's 'secret' speech at the 20th Party Congress and the invasion of Hungary, through the 'revolution' of May '68, to the collapse of Communism and the destruction of the Berlin Wall; from a 'New Left' seeking a third way beyond Stalinism and social democracy, through anti-war and student movements, Western Maoism, Eurocommunism and the new social movements, to the politics of identity and discourse; from a socialist-humanist Marxism, through Althusserianism, post-structuralism and post-Marxism, to post-modernism and beyond.

The narrative of formative episodes in the biography of the Western Left is generally situated in the context of another, over-arching history: the rise of 'welfare' and 'consumer' capitalism bringing the 'masses' and specifically the working class under its hegemonic spell, the changing structure (or in some versions, the virtual disappearance) of the working class, the consequent decline of working class militancy (not to mention the failure of even an 'economistically' militant proletariat to fulfill its historic mission as the agent of a socialist revolution), and hence the increasing separation of left intellectuals from the labour movement or, indeed, any political movement at all.

Where, then, does the New Left belong in this story? Its historical coordinates are clear enough: at least in Britain, it emerged at the point where the anti-Stalinist revulsion after 1956 converged with the rise of 'welfare' and 'consumer' capitalism, which seemed to give a new importance to cultural struggle. Histories of the New Left have further broken down this formation into two more or less distinct generations, a 'first' and a 'second' New Left, the latter more distant than the former from traditional forms of activism and class politics, more unambiguously committed to purely intellectual and cultural practice.[1] Nevertheless, the era of the second New Left was also a period in which the long-term secular decline of socialist militancy and even class struggle seemed to be undergoing a reversal. The late sixties and early seventies appeared to be a decade of renewal, with dramatic outbreaks of student rebellion, a resurgence of working class militancy and even hopes of socialist revolution, associated with a resurgence of radical thought, including a revival of revolutionary Marxism by the second generation of the New Left in Britain.

Yet this period of resurgence was in turn followed by an equally dramatic era of 'retreat', a decisive, and many would say irremediable, decline of the labour movement, and a corresponding shift among left intellectuals. Looking back from the vantage point of the post-Communist era, historians of the Western Left are likely to see this retreat as a resumption, if not a completion, of the longer secular downturn of working class politics. In many if not most scenarios, the working class has taken its final exit, replaced by a plurality of agencies and struggles in the 'new social movements', and finally a shift from these movements to the 'politics of identity'. Agencies still attached to a broad emancipatory project have now given way to new forms of particularism or outright despair. Seen from this angle, the collapse of Communism is not only a world-historic episode in the history of the Left since the decline of Stalinism. It is also a climactic moment in the history of capitalism, the extension of its hegemony beyond its own long-standing borders to a 'new world order', which must – according not only to right-wing observers but to increasing numbers on the left – surely sweep away any residues of the old 'essentialist', 'reductionist' and 'totalizing' project of traditional socialism that may have survived in the New Left and its successors.

In these accounts, then, the history of Western left intellectuals from the fifties through the eighties appears to be one long story of reactive adjustments to changes of directions in working class politics, culminating in (at least according to some versions of this story) the more or less final triumph of capitalism. After a brief renewal of both working class militancy and Marxist theory, the process set in train by 'Western Marxism' has moved on, beyond the early philosophical and cultural responses to the failure of proletarian revolutions and Stalinist deformations, ending in a final and complete accommodation by the Left to the realities of capitalist advance and working class retreat.

I want to suggest a different periodization. In this one, the logic of intellectual trends on the left since the sixties is not so directly connected to working class politics. It has to do with some major epochal transformations and also with the sociology of the academy. In this alternative periodization, the rupture between the first and second New Left is a pivotal – or at least symptomatic – moment; and my chronology brings into sharper focus the depth of that rupture, as well as the significant continuities between the *second* New Left and what went after, up to and including today's most current fashions. Finally, the implication of this alternative chronology is that the first New Left is not only more genuinely oppositional and emancipatory than the current intellectual and political fashions but in some respects also more *current*.

I

The term 'New Left' has been applied to a fairly broad range of political formations in various countries, commonly associated with the radicalism of the late 1960s. But to the extent that all these formations had something fundamental in common, what made the New Left 'new' was above all its dissociation from the traditional forms of 'old' left politics, both Stalinist Communism and social democracy. More particularly, the various New Lefts shared a commitment to emancipatory struggles apart from – or at least in addition to – traditional class struggle, especially the student, anti-Vietnam War and black liberation movements.

In Britain the development of the New Left was marked by institutional milestones in the form of influential journals whose changes of content and style record the trajectory of this movement through its various permutations. This literary record therefore provides a particularly useful framework for tracking the relevant history. It is true that the British New Left was in some important respects distinctive, especially because here the radicalism of the sixties, while converging with the international wave that culminated in the 'revolution' of 1968, was directly connected to, and continuous from, an earlier and rather different 'New Left', composed largely of dissident Communists with strong and abiding roots in the labour movement. But if this means that the British experience cannot be generalized without great caution, it also means that the history of the New Left in Britain provides a particularly well documented record of the transition from 'Old' Left to 'New' and, in the public debates between one generation and the next, eloquent testimony to the changes in the Western Left since 1956.

In 1959, *The New Reasoner*, founded by Communist dissidents John Saville and E. P. Thompson in 1956–7, joined by Ralph Miliband who had never been a member of the Party, merged with *Universities and Left Review*, created in 1957 by a group of very young Oxbridge radicals, notably Stuart Hall, Charles Taylor, and Raphael Samuel. The fruit of this union was the *New Left Review*. The two rather disparate founding projects were brought together not only by what they had in common but by what essentially divided them. Both were committed to the kind of cultural struggle which was felt to be especially urgent in the conditions of 'consumer capitalism'. Yet they came to this common project not only from different generations but from substantially different directions, in the hope, no doubt, of converting their differences into complementarities.

Raymond Williams, who was brought into the planning of the new journal very early, makes an interesting witness because he never neatly fitted into either group and for that reason could be seen as bridging them. Looking back on his experience some years later, he spoke of various differences between the two:[2] the ULR people were less interested in the history and traditions of the international left than in the rapidly changing society of Britain, and more interested in a changing cultural experience than in political activism. The *New Reasoner* group was less attuned to immediate cultural changes in Britain and more steeped in the traditions of both international Marxism and of the labour movement, including the native British radical tradition. Williams situated himself somewhere in between. While he regarded the *New Reasoner* as a 'much more solid journal', and while in his own 'experience and style' (not to mention age) he located himself within the older generation, he found himself drawn to the interests of the younger generation, their preoccupation with a changing cultural experience. In retrospect, however, he judged himself wrong in having thought that a cultural and educational programme was enough, to the exclusion of engagement with 'tougher political problems'. More significantly, he concluded that the New Left and especially the younger generation, in its preoccupation with all that had changed in Britain with the advent of consumer capitalism, seriously underestimated all that had remained the same, miscalculating the power of the capitalist state and overestimating the possibilities of cultural politics. If the older generation was not entirely immune to this weakness, its engagement in traditional Marxist arguments may have offered some protection. Elsewhere (I shall come back to this), Williams also demonstrated another major difference between himself and the younger generation, refusing its tendency – also resisted by Thompson and others – to treat the working class as passive victims, irredeemably 'hegemonized' by TV and mass consumption.[3] At any rate, his judgment from the start seems to have been that the merger never really took hold.[4]

The product of this uneasy merger, the *New Left Review* under the editorship of Stuart Hall, was itself soon to fracture, at first more or less along the fault lines between the two founding projects. The result was the departure of Hall and Taylor; but the crisis did not in the end consolidate the ascendancy of the other, senior partner. On the contrary, control of the *Review* passed to another younger generation; and a wholly new team – Perry Anderson, Tom Nairn, Robin Blackburn *et al*. – soon displaced both of the founding projects and their leading figures.

This editorial succession, specifically the passage of editorial control from the *New Reasoner* generation to Perry Anderson *et al*., is generally identified as the transition from the first to the second New Left; and it is this transition that will form the background to my discussion here. I am conscious that to focus on this editorial history is to neglect a wide range of 'New Left' activisms which flourished in Britain at the same time: CND, anti-racist and women's movements, and so on. The new NLR could hardly be regarded as a journal of these or any other movements and was, in fact, remarkably detached from any such political organizations. My object, however, is not to offer a comprehensive history of the New Left but to trace some important intellectual developments of which the history of NLR is symptomatic. It also needs to be said that the filiations and divergences between the various strands of the New Left are not unambiguous. The new NLR team, for example, was certainly young; yet despite the well-known breach between Anderson and E. P. Thompson (which spawned an influential debate about the history of Britain), Stuart Hall might have been excused for thinking that Anderson and co. had more in common with Thompson and Saville than with himself, more in common with *The New Reasoner* than with ULR. Certainly they proved, among other things, to be more interested in the Marxist tradition than in popular culture or consumption patterns. Nonetheless, it will be argued in what follows that the rupture signalled by the accession of the new editorial team was real and deep, symptomatic not simply of a generational transition from one phase of a single movement to another but of a larger epochal shift in the history of the post-war Western Left, which may be disguised by the common 'New Left' rubric. What is at issue here is not simply the history of one particular formation but the development of the Western Left at least from 1956 until today.

II

Let me begin by looking at some recent interpretations of the New Left in Britain. In a review of Lin Chun's book on the British New Left, Gregory Elliott describes the mission of the first New Left thus: 'a transformation of the British labour movement' which involved 'an adequate analysis of contemporary welfare capitalism (the "affluent society"); a critique of the culture of post-war Britain (the "consumer society"); and an exploration of the nature of a future post-capitalist order (socialism as a "whole way of life").'[5] The second new left – in particular, the second generation of the *New Left Review*: Anderson, Nairn, Blackburn *et al.* – did not, suggests Elliott, represent as complete a rupture with the old guard as the new generation liked to believe, but it did set itself apart in at least one major respect, eschewing 'what it regarded as the defining characteristic – and abiding vice – of its precursor: populism'. '[W]hereas the first New Left had regretted, and sought to bridge, the mutually injurious gulf between culture and politics, 'theory', and 'practice', intellectual and manual workers, their successors made, as it were, a virtue of necessity.'[6] Turning from 'popular' culture to 'high culture' (and, Elliott might have added, from the study of 'popular struggles' to a preoccupation with 'high politics'), this second New Left began its intellectual convergence with Continental Marxism as well as with the cultural-political configuration culminating in the events of 1968.

This climactic year, argues Elliott, turned out to be not so much a revolutionary rupture for the Left as the 'year of the New Right'. Eventually, the New Left found itself increasingly 'on the defensive, bereft of any viable domestic – or international – alternative to a Labourism in disorderly retreat before the Thatcherite offensive'.[7] The New Left may have represented, as Lin Chun suggests, a transition from the old left to new oppositional forces and theories, new forms of struggle of and for women, anti-racism, ecology and peace; but the 'new social movements' briefly occupied the Left's centre stage only to be superseded by 'some "old" (or at any rate, regressive) ones', 'the assembled ranks with an appetite for the shlock of the new, busy enjoining the British labour movement to lie down and die before the glossy French magazines'.[8]

In general, this seems to me an acute and illuminating account. But some questions need to be raised about the suggestion (if I have understood it correctly) that both generations of the New Left were responding to the effects of 'welfare' and 'consumer' capitalism on the working class, although the second generation, in its flight from 'populism', accepted these realities by making a virtue of necessity. This suggestion seems to accord with those accounts of the post-war Western left, in Britain and elsewhere, which treat the various shifts of left intellectuals as responses to the cycles of working class militancy. The second New Left, it appears, adapted itself more completely to the realities of working class decline.

The history of the Western Left would then go something like this: within the long-term trend toward cultural and ideological struggle in response to the decline or failure of revolutionary class politics, there was a sharp hiatus in 1956, with an opening for a new kind of Western left, followed by two distinct but connected phases corresponding to the trajectory of the labour movement – the resurgence of the late sixties and early seventies, followed by a more decisive turn away from old left positions some time in the late 1970s with the retreat of the labour movement, and a final break with old verities about the conditions and agencies of struggle, and especially away from class politics of any kind.

Connecting the 'retreat of the intellectuals' to a declining labour movement is, again, a common theme in histories of the post-war Western Left, though there are, of course, variations on this basic theme. For example, on the further left, there is less indulgence toward the New Left's odyssey. The 'upturn-downturn' thesis of the Socialist Workers Party in

Britain (the largest of the neo-Trotskyist groups) suggests that the move away from class politics by many left intellectuals corresponds to the 'downturn' of working class militancy in the late seventies, after an upturn in the previous decade; but the SWP is inclined to judge this shift less as a necessity turned into a virtue than as an excessive and regrettable failure of nerve in a difficult period of 'downturn'. The first premise of the argument nevertheless remains the same: people who in principle embraced class politics and other old-left commitments responded to the realities of consumer capitalism and/or the disappointing failures of the working class by shifting to other – especially ideological and cultural – terrains of struggle.

There is, of course, much to be said in favour of accounts like this. In relation to the long-term trends, there can be little doubt that the history of the labour movement since World War II, or perhaps even since the 1920s, has encouraged a search for alternative revolutionary agencies and forms of struggle. And with respect to the phases in the development of the Western Left since 1956, there has, since the resurgence of the sixties and early seventies, certainly been a notable convergence of decline in labour militancy with the 'retreat of the intellectuals'. But there are some aspects of such explanations that seem to me problematic, especially as they relate to the history of the New Left and its successors. First, these explanations may be misreading the connection between working class politics and intellectual trends on the left; and second, far from exaggerating the rupture within the New Left, they may underestimate the break between the two generations, as well as the continuities between the second New Left and developments since the mid-seventies. Seen from a different perspective, the history of left intellectuals does not correspond so neatly to the rises and declines of working class politics; and the second New Left may have less – or at least no more – in common with the first than with the post-Marxisms and post-modernisms which emerged from the 'retreat'.

To bring this alternative history into perspective, we may begin with the judgment rendered by Ralph Miliband on the merger that founded the *New Left Review*. Miliband was almost alone in objecting to the merger. The two journals, he maintained, represented two very different currents of thought and experience. The editors of the *New Reasoner* were intellectuals *of* the labour movement, while the others were intellectuals *for* that movement. This judgment, which lay behind the departure of Miliband and Saville to found the *Socialist Register*, was to prove prophetic and seems to me to capture the essence of a historic rupture in the history of the post-war Western Left.

As it turned out, Miliband might have painted the contrast even more starkly than he did, because it would soon become clear that the detachment of the second New Left from the labour movement was even greater than he had suggested; and this applies not just to the intellectuals of *Universities and Left Review* but also the second generation of *NLR*, among others. The second New Left did, to be sure, proclaim its commitment to the labour movement; and it showed a greater interest in economic questions than had either partner in the original merger. But a shift away from working class struggle was underway from the beginning, though it was to go through various stages. As early as 1964, Peter Sedgwick identified the first phase of that shift: 'NLR', he wrote, 'is now committed, at least on paper, to an activist and Marxist philosophy, in which struggle is acknowledged as the engine of social change, and economic levers are seen as operating at a more fundamental level of potency than cultural influences. Only the forms of struggle which are picked out for attention and commendation are not those of an industrial working-class movement; they are predominantly either agrarian or technocratic, depending on whether an underdeveloped or an advanced society is under scrutiny.'[9] Marked by its 'gallicized syntax' and its Olympian tone, Sedgwick suggested, NLR under the new regime had severed any even notional 'umbilical link between itself and extra-intellectual sources of action in British society'.[10] The freedom from those traditional ties expressed itself first in its preoccupation with the 'Third World'. In the years after Sedgwick wrote, this detachment would increasingly take the form of a self-proclaimed mission to import into Britain the most up-to-date (and scholastic) varieties of Continental Marxist theory. The new NLR project thus represented not only a detachment from any British political movement but also from the native tradition of radical thought and even from the important body of cultural criticism which was flourishing in post-war Britain.

The displacement from 'extra-intellectual sources of action in British society' was not simply geographic. It also signalled an increasing theoretical distance between NLR and *any* 'popular' movements. If, as Sedgwick suggested, NLR Mark II, even in its earliest days and at the height of its preoccupation with 'Third World' struggles, directed its attention 'not down to the grass-roots, but upwards',[11] there was no inconsistency between that project and the turn to high politics and culture with which it came to be associated as it became the major vehicle for the transmission of Continental Marxism to a benighted and 'empiricist' British culture. What Greg Elliott has described as the second New Left's repudiation of the first generation's 'abiding voice', its populism, can be read as a loss of interest in popular struggles in general, and the labour movement in particular. It can also be read as reflecting a growing conviction that the central terrain of socialist struggle was from now on intellectual.

Notwithstanding the friendly relations among at least some members of the first and second New Left, the break between these two generations should not be underestimated; and I shall return to a consideration of its implications. I shall argue that this intellectual and political rupture was not just the product of a generational shift but was rooted in one of the greatest epochal transformations in modern history. But I want to turn first to the corollary of this discontinuity: the continuities between the second New Left and what came after. To state the point starkly: the major strand of continuity between current fashions and the second New Left (in sharp contrast to the first) is rooted not only in a common emancipatory project but in some of the *less* democratic impulses of the 1960s left. The corollary of this historical connection is that current fashions have more to do with the agenda of the 1960s than with the realities of the eighties and nineties.

III

There is one continous theoretical strand which can be traced more or less without a break from the sixties up to now. Among the diverse movements we tend to lump together as the 'revolution' of the sixties, there emerged one major and long-lasting theme: an emphasis on the autonomy of ideological struggle and the leading role of intellectuals, in default of the working class. This tendency was not, at least in principle, inconsistent with support for popular struggles, especially in the 'Third World'. Dissatisfaction with the working class in advanced capitalist societies was, for example, sometimes expressed in a transfer of revolutionary faith to 'the South', the 'Third World', or peasant revolutions, and a keen interest in thinkers like Fanon; but even here, there existed a variety of 'Third Worldism' (to be distinguished from other varieties, belonging to an older left tradition, as in the journal, *Monthly Review*) marked by a strong tendency to promote students and intellectuals to the vanguard of history, as the leading agents of human emancipation – perhaps through the medium of 'cultural revolution'. A doctrine like Maoism, which for some represented an extension of traditional Marxist theories of class struggle, for others became a warrant for putting student radicals in place of revolutionary classes.

But with or without this kind of 'Third Worldism', there emerged a current of thought in which the labour movement was replaced by 'ideological class struggle'. Rebellious students and their intellectual mentors, armed with theories ranging from Mao and Fanon to Sartre and Althusser, were thought to represent the transmutation of theory into a 'material force', whose apotheosis came in 1968. This intellectual self-glorification binds some strands of yesterday's student radicalism with today's intellectual fashions which focus on *discourse* as the constitutive practice of social life and tend to regard the academy as the central arena of emancipatory politics. From that point of view, there is a direct evolutionary line from Maoism to post-modernism, and from 'cultural revolution' to textual deconstruction.

This evolutionary path poses problems for any attempt to draw neat connections between intellectual retreat and the decline of working class militancy. Some of the problems are plainly chronological. We can acknowledge the long-range secular trends in Western socialist thought – the turn away from 'economistic' preoccupations which in the broadest terms unites the early forms of 'Western Marxism' with the current fashions in discourse theory – and their association with a long-term decline in revolutionary working class politics. But there are some important discrepancies in the attempt to establish more fine-grained connections, between the retreat of the labour movement in the late seventies and eighties and the definitive shift away from traditional socialist preoccupations toward the politics of discourse and 'identity' signalled by the emergence of 'post-Marxism'. The suggested correspondences between working class accommodations to capitalism and intellectual adjustments to the deficiencies of the labour movement are difficult to square with the chronology of post-Marxist theory.

The theoretical trends associated with the student movement of the sixties no doubt began with attempts to find revolutionary substitutes for a quiescent, or at least 'economistic', working class. But the very specific intellectual developments that gave rise to post-Marxism and its successors were taking place at a time – after 1968 – when advanced capitalist countries had just experienced a surge of working class militancy. In the years after 1968, 'a new wave of working-class struggle and socialist politics surged forward in the heartlands of the capitalist world,' writes Lin Chun. 'Large-scale workers' strikes in Italy (and the continued electoral advance of the Italian Communist Party), industrial militancy in Britain, and the high point of the labour movement in Japan were a few striking examples. The Portuguese revolution (1974–5) reopened the question of the possibility of a socialist revolution in post-war western Europe'. In Britain, whichever party was in power, 'factory occupations and other forms of workers' struggles reached a scale that had not been seen in this country since the 1920s', including the miners' strikes of 1972 and 1974,[12] and so on. This was, as Lin Chun points out, also a moment when Marxist theory enjoyed a revival, and socialist intellectuals were not as isolated in the academy as they had been in previous decades.

Any decline of working class opposition in the decade following the recession of 1975–6 in Britain cannot, then, explain, for instance, the apparently sudden U-turn executed in the mid-seventies by some of the most extreme structuralist Marxists – not only heirs to the Althusserian legacy which had been conveyed to Britain by the *New Left Review* Mark II, but also adherents of Maoism.[13] No such decline can explain their turn, almost overnight, from the most uncompromising insistence on the centrality of class struggle to a denial altogether of its 'effectivity' (and, indeed, of any 'privileged' connection between the 'economic' and the 'political'), from the most doctrinaire structuralist theoreticism to the most dogmatic (if still abstractly theoretical) empiricism and the reduction of all history and social process to contingency. The most efficient explanation of such apparently sudden and extreme reversals – and at such an odd moment – is that they were not as sudden and extreme as they appear. It may be that the logic of the second phase was already very much present in the first, and that what looks like a U-turn is more like a flip of the coin.

Other less dramatic but, in retrospect, even more significant theoretical moves were being made in the 1970s. Theories emerged which, if not yet ostensibly repudiating Marxism, the traditional preoccupation with political economy and history, or the politics of class – indeed still affirming its centrality – were converting class struggle into a purely ideological battle conducted largely by intellectual proxy. It was not long before the same theorists gave birth to post-Marxism, and this development too makes more sense as an elaboration of themes already present in the brand of Marxism to which its adherents had earlier subscribed.[14] At any rate, it would be difficult, quite so soon after the surge of 1968–1975, to regard these intellectual developments as responses to the decline of working class militancy, unless the Owl of Minerva had taken flight with uncanny prescience and alacrity.

Something no doubt happened in the seventies. But a slightly longer historical perspective brings into focus the continuities that cut across the apparent rupture in the middle of that decade. No appeal to the 'retreat' or 'downturn' after the surge can explain a development already well established in the 'upturn' phase.[15] An answer can, however, be found in the student movement of the previous decade. There had, of course, existed not just one student movement but a whole range of political and cultural groups and projects, from revolutionary socialism to fundamentally apolitical 'counter-cultures'; but at the very peak of the 'upturn', in the midst of all the revolutionary fervour, all the activism, all the democratic aspirations, all the acts of courage, indeed even in the midst of a renewed optimism about the resurgence of working class militancy, one theoretical principle was establishing itself which would prove especially tenacious: the autonomy of political and ideological struggles.

The early student movement, especially in the US, turned to thinkers like Herbert Marcuse, whose philosophy was certainly predicated on the absorption of the masses by the hegemony of consumer capitalism. But even more telling is the fact that the autonomy of politics and ideology was a leitmotif even – or especially – in some of the ostensibly most revolutionary manifestations of late-sixties radicalism, those most likely to proclaim the importance of class struggle. This was most notably true of Maoism, with its extreme voluntarism and its conviction that revolutions can be made by sheer political and ideological will unfettered by material constraints. This tendency, both in its militant activism and in its sometimes wild irrationalism, differed sharply from the philosophical turn to culture by 'Western Marxists' earlier in the century. But for all the rhetoric of class struggle, the theoretical developments of the sixties provided a warrant for a view of socialist transformations as 'cultural revolutions' – whether Maoist or not – in which intellectuals and students are the principal agents, at best acting in alliance with, or even on behalf of workers and/or peasants, and increasingly as autonomous revolutionary agents in their own right.

Louis Althusser played a central role in the theoretical evolution of this trend, although his own relation to it was ambiguous. He seems never to have accepted an alternative to the working class as revolutionary agent, and his view of the '68 'revolution' was ambivalent at best; but he did contribute greatly to the theoretical process of establishing the 'autonomy' of ideology and politics. His wish to counter the economistic reductionism of Stalinist Marxism is not enough to explain what he was about. At least part of the explanation must lie in his own flirtation with Maoism as an alternative to Stalinism. At any rate, whatever his own political views may have been, it was the theoretical 'autonomy' of 'instances' that remained as his principal legacy to student radicals.

The second New Left in Britain certainly identified itself with the revolutionary socialist end of the student radical spectrum, aligned, if anything, with the neo-Trotskyist revival which occurred in the late 1960s. But it is at least worth noting that, of the two main neo-Trotskyist groups, the International Socialists (IS, later the SWP) and the International Marxist Group (IMG), it was the latter that attracted some of NLR's leading figures, notably Robin Blackburn (future editor of NLR), with its greater emphasis on Third World struggles, anti-imperialism, student radicalism and cultural politics, as against the more 'orthodox' commitment to working class struggle which characterized IS. Nor, incidentally, were Blackburn and others immune to that brand of Maoism which promoted the centrality of student revolutionaries, and with it the autonomy of ideological and political struggle. Lin Chun, writing of Blackburn's advocacy, together with Alexander Cockburn, of 'Red Bases' on campuses, quotes him as saying, 'those who reject the strategy of the Red Base . . . will be in serious danger of becoming the objective allies of social imperialism and social fascism'. Her comment on this is that, 'Neither Blackburn nor Cockburn rejected the classical notion of the proletariat as the major leading agency of change, but the implication of their "Red Base" theory seems to contain something of the opposite.'[16]

Seen in this perspective, May '68 is indeed the emblematic moment of the new-model Left, but in its aspect as a 'cultural revolution' more than as an alliance of student radicalism with working class militancy. The dramatic events of the late sixties were certainly marked by a momentary convergence, at least in some countries, between working class militancy and a radical impulse of a different kind, though elsewhere such a convergence hardly took place, as in Germany, while in the US the gulf between students and workers could hardly have been more striking than in the Vietnam war. At any rate, even where there was a remarkable moment of unity, a divergence was not long in coming. That this divergence was in process before any decisive downward trend in working class militancy suggests that it may not have been simply a retreat by socialists, and their evolution into post-Marxists, in response to the deficiencies of the labour movement. It suggests instead that, among the various emancipatory impulses that made up the student movement, there existed a political tendency whose belief in class politics was always subordinate to faith in the revolutionary efficacy of intellectuals, radical students, and cultural revolution. If anything, the surge of militancy after 1968 seems to have accelerated rather than retarded the divergence, while the elevation of intellectual practice in the theories of the western Left had a momentum of its own.

A comparison of 1968 and 1972 is suggestive – and here the differences are as much national as temporal. If Paris '68 represents a movement in which students and intellectuals play a prominent role in alliance with workers, the British miners' strikes of 1972 and 1974 are hardly representative of working class retreat, but they do epitomize another kind of divergence from student radicalism or cultural struggle. These were outbreaks of class militancy belonging entirely to organized labour and in no way congenial to the aspirations of intellectuals as the vanguard of revolution, cultural or otherwise. It is hard to know what to make of the fact that post-Marxism was gestating in Britain just when militancy of this kind had experienced a resurgence; but the chronology becomes somewhat less mysterious if the convergence of the British New Left with the forces of May '68 is understood less as endorsing class struggle, even with an intellectual vanguard, than as asserting the autonomy of politics and ideology, promoting not the revolutionary agency of workers but that of intellectuals and students. The varieties of Marxism which flourished at the same time were those most congenial to this view of revolutionary agency.

If there is an epochal rupture in the evolution of the Western left since 1956, it occurs at the point when a section of the left intelligentsia stopped thinking of itself as an ally in popular struggles, or even as a vanguard, or even as a critic from the philosophical sidelines, the point at which people stopped thinking of themselves, to use Miliband's formula, as intellectuals *of* an emancipatory movement, and started to think of themselves as intellectuals *for* that movement, or, to put it more strongly, when they started thinking of themselves as the movement itself. This rupture more or less coincides with the generational shift from the first to the second New Left. What we are seeing today is that development taken to its ultimate conclusion, and the end-result is a fairly extreme kind of intellectual substitutism.

IV

Explanations for these developments are no doubt to be found not so much in the history of the labour movement as in the sociology of the academy. Both, of course, are ultimately rooted in the evolution of post-war capitalism; but the connections between the two processes – between the decline of class politics and the autonomization of intellectual activity – are rather more mediated than the 'upturn-downturn' or 'surge-retreat' explanations imply. This is not the place to venture any systematic explanation, but one or two points are worth noting. The most obvious point is that the post-war period of economic growth, and the sixties in particular, saw a massive expansion of post-secondary education in the capitalist world, though to varying degrees and with varying effects in different countries. There is an almost perfect correspondence between the explosion of numbers and the emergence of student radicalism, as the conservatism of the fifties was followed by the militancy of the sixties.

Historians of the student movement generally seem to agree that the sheer growth in numbers was unquestionably significant; but it is not so easy to determine where exactly that significance lay – whether, for example, rapid expansion led to a deterioration of conditions in the university, so that students found themselves in over-crowded and under-resourced institutions; whether the growth of a hitherto miniscule privileged group evoked an experience of relative status-deprivation as it became a less distinctive mass, an experience compounded by a disproportion between the rising numbers and the resources to accommodate them; whether, on the contrary, the relevant factor was a revolution of rising expectations; or whether the emergence of a mass student body simply dissolved traditional solidarities between students and ruling elites, reinforcing a general reaction against authority common to students and workers.

The suggestion has, for example, been made that the student movements of 1966–68 were a result of the complex problems caused by a 'proletarianization' of the intelligentsia in the West, as their numbers dramatically increased, their social status declined while their moral authority generally remained intact.[17] 'We are no longer assured of becoming future rulers . . .', wrote the students of the Sorbonne in 1968. 'We are from now on workers like others.'[18]

It is no doubt true that in some places – notably the urban universities of France and Italy – expansion produced overcrowded institutions, inadequate resources and a lack of contact with professors. Perhaps even in the US, where university campuses (not least, the centre of student radicalism, the University of California at Berkeley) were typically well-endowed oases sheltered from the disorders and discomforts of urban life in advanced capitalism, there were some legitimate complaints about the inaccessibility of senior professors and the inordinate responsibilities devolving on their teaching assistants. Yet the students' claim to proletarian status was always a bit of romantic self-dramatization on the part of an albeit enlarged privileged minority.

Still, some national distinctions can be drawn. For example, the argument that student unrest in the sixties had something to do with the declining status of the intelligentsia may have a certain plausibility in France – the site of the archetypal student 'revolution' – where intellectual life had long been closely tied to rule, where state-office had long been regarded as the highest career in a tradition reaching back to the absolutist state, and where education in elite academies prepared the country's governors, creating (as indeed it still does) virtual dynasties of high office-holders. Against that background, the massive expansion of higher education – without commensurate resources to accommodate the growing numbers or high places to absorb more aspirants to office, not to mention long-term shifts in the centre of gravity from the state to capitalist enterprise – might have been experienced as a loss of status; and this might not only have evoked a demand for material improvements but may also have displaced to other spheres the claims and aspirations of intellectuals.

Elsewhere, conditions were not quite the same. In Britain, the role of intellectuals was traditionally different than in France. In any case, there has been a tendency to exaggerate the growth of post-secondary education in the 1960s, which still left Britain with a shamefully low proportion of its population in higher education. (In fact, one of the paradoxical features of the Thatcher era was a real explosion in the post-secondary student population, which, in the economic aftermath of Thatcherism and in conditions of structural mass unemployment, really does begin to look like the disadvantaged proletariat that some sixties radicals claimed to be.) Still, there was substantial growth especially outside the established elite institutions; and while this surely represented an expansion more than a contraction of opportunity, it nevertheless created the conditions for a 'mass, oppositional intelligentsia in Britain – one unintegrated into the traditional "intellectual aristocracy" ... and disinclined to relate to its society "as if" (in [Perry] Anderson's words) "it were an immutable second nature"".[19] With the growth of polytechnics, there also emerged a new layer of students and lecturers, often with class origins and career paths different from those of traditional academics in the universities (sometimes, for example, becoming researchers for trade unions). But if these institutions did perhaps fit more exactly the model of the under-resourced proletarianized academy, their students were less rather than more likely to be attracted to the student politics of 'cultural revolution'; and they may have looked to some observers on the left as if they might develop into Gramsci's 'organic intellectuals' of the working class.

In the US, where the proportion of the population in higher education has long been exceptionally large, university students were (and, up to a point, remain) an advantaged group, whose 'life-chances' in the 1960s were certainly privileged. In fact, career prospects for students could hardly have been better than they were in the sixties. Nonetheless, the Vietnam war produced exceptional tensions, at a time when the expansion of higher education had created a mass of students far larger than the British, and even less integrated into any kind of 'aristocracy'. There were, of course, other distinctive circumstances too, particularly the racial conditions that had produced the civil rights movement. And all of this occurred in the wake of a particularly virulent strain of Cold War politics, with its own particular resonances in the university, which gave rise to the Free Speech Movement, often credited with setting off the international wave of student radicalism.

The American case, for all its specificities, reveals the complexities and paradoxes of the student movement with particular clarity. If the first wave of student activism began here, with the Free Speech Movement in 1960, it may conceal as much as it reveals to treat this movement as the opening salvo in a decade of student radicalism. As a response to the Cold War witch hunt perpetrated in particular by the House Un-American Activities Committee, the Free Speech Movement represented the end of the old left as much as the launch of the new.[20] It was in a sense a bridge between old and new forms of radicalism, temporarily uniting Spanish Civil War veterans and trade union activists with academic liberals and student radicals; but it also marked a breach. After this, there was a major change of terrain and agencies, as student radicalism began to turn inward.

The Free Speech Movement was still connected to old forms of radicalism outside the university, to both the veterans of anti-Fascist struggles and the labour movement. In the wake of the FSM, the campus became for many the main arena of struggle, with students as principal agents and their grievances as primary motivations. Some of the most notable leaders were, to be sure, civil rights activists, involved, at some risk to themselves, in voter registration drives and marches in the Deep South, especially in 1964; and the impulses which drove the kind of extra-campus activism displayed during the Vietnam war were never completely exhausted, still faintly in evidence perhaps more recently, for example, in opposition to US imperialism in Nicaragua and El Salvador. But the student movement in its other, inward-turning aspect followed its own historical trajectory; and it has left a different and more lasting legacy.

The difficulty of disentangling the various strands of student radicalism is, of course, compounded by the convergence of traditional left politics with new forms of 'counter-culture'. There is no need here, however, to explore the connections or the contradictions between these often very different motivations or the diverse movements that together constituted student radicalism. We need only acknowledge the existence of certain impulses in some elements of student radicalism which have less to do with opposition to capitalism than with submersion in it. It is not simply that – as critics have often liked to say – music and drugs were just another outlet for consumer capitalism. The point is rather that to talk about the growth of student numbers as a proletarianization of intellectuals tends to obscure the degree to which that growth testified to the expansion of capitalist prosperity. This explanation masks the extent to which the culture of the sixties Left was determined not by the experience of capitalist decline and depression which had shaped the old left but, on the contrary, by an ascendant capitalism. It also disguises the degree to which a university education was becoming for the first time, and particularly in the US, an inevitable and universal rite of passage for all members of the 'middle class' – an initiation that for some involved the breaking of taboos before assuming once and for all the obligations of the dominant culture.

The relevant process here may not be proletarianization but bourgeoisi-fication – perhaps a loss of status as students ceased to form an aristocracy, but nonetheless a gateway to privilege. The university itself now also offered a particularly attractive bourgeois career. The expansion of the university meant, after all, not just a growth in student numbers but new job opportunities for its graduates, an explosion of university teachers which was to last just long enough for veterans of the sixties to become the lecturers of later decades. Those theoretical currents that in the sixties had celebrated ideological struggle, cultural revolution and the world-historic agency of intellectuals and students were bound to hold special attractions for many in this social layer. The expansion of this academic bourgeoisie may also have tended to magnify out of all proportion the importance of intellectual fashions which, while looming very large in the eyes of academics, left the rest of the world untouched (a tendency more pronounced today than ever). At any rate, whether or not these currents represented the best, or even the most important, tendency in sixties radicalism, they were always likely to be the most intellectually – or acade-mically – long-lasting. They were certainly the most flattering to intellectual pretensions, the most conducive to academic productivity and the least susceptible to the vagaries of history and material constraints.

This tendency is, of course, not all that remains of sixties radicalism, and one point in particular needs to be added to any assessment of its legacy. In the vast expansion of post-secondary education, there were qualitative as well as quantitative changes in the demographic profile of the student body. Although changes in its class composition were, and still are, notoriously slow, there was one significant demographic revolution, with the most far-reaching effects: the growth in the number of women. In the US, for example, the number of women receiving college degrees doubled between 1960 and 1968, and by the late 1960s almost half of all women high-school graduates went on to higher education.[21] This, needless to say, gave a huge boost to the women's movement, producing a new generation of activists as well as a whole range of new intellectual practices. But if the women's movement has remained as the sixties' most consistently activist legacy, it is especially ironic that it has also produced some of the most inaccessible and exclusionary discourses in today's academy.

V

The history of Western intellectuals clearly has a logic of its own, determined by their own situation, their own material conditions, their own relations to the state and capital, and not just by upturns and downturns in working class activity. There is, presumably, nothing particularly controversial about this observation; but it also means that any periodization of the Western Left must take all this into account. A different periodization implies different axes of division between one phase and another and among the varied tendencies within each phase. The convergence of so many strands in the emancipatory projects of the Left – the labour movement, the civil rights movement, the anti-war movement, the women's movement, the environmental movement – complicates the picture, but some broad trends are clear enough.

One point again stands out: whatever the immediate causes of the student revolt and whatever deprivations may have played a part in it, the movement occurred not in the context of economic decline or stagnation but in a moment – and as a result – of capitalist prosperity. The intricate mechanisms by which material prosperity produced widespread rebellion may not be easy to trace, but a recognition of this simple fact brings into focus the sharp generational rupture between the first New Left and those that followed it.

Greg Elliott describes the second British New Left as founded on a similar social base as their predecessors: 'the enlarged stratum of intellectual and cultural producers generated by post-war capitalism – a category swelled by the massive expansion of tertiary education in the 1960s'.[22] Without making too much of the (not insignificant) difference between the enlargement of the 'stratum of intellectual and cultural producers' before the 1960s and the growth of the tertiary sector which occurred in that decade, I do think that (apart from various differences in age, personal experience, background and experience) some important distinctions need to be made between the first New Left's leading lights – people like E. P. Thompson, John Saville and Ralph Miliband – and the second generation: Perry Anderson, Robin Blackburn, *et al.*.

The difference between Ralph Miliband, Edward Thompson, or John Saville and the next generation of New Left luminaries was not just an age difference of, say, twelve to twenty years. That relatively small generational difference reflected a much larger historical shift, maybe one of the most significant epochal shifts in modern history. One clear dividing line between these generations is World War II (in which Miliband, Thompson and Saville all served), preceded by the Spanish Civil War which was the formative event for so many Western socialists. This means that the first generation, in one way or another, directly experienced the historic trauma of Fascism and the struggle against it, as well as the social interactions, the contact with people of all classes, the political experience and expectations generated by the Second World War.

There was no comparable formative experience in the political development of the second generation. Even the Vietnam war, opposition to which was a critical moment in the development of the second New Left, is as important for what it did *not* mean to them as for what it did. After all, besides its geographic distance, this was a war to which students and intellectuals related largely by their absence from it. At any rate, it may help to place the differences between the two generations into perspective if we consider that the only life-experience that shaped the second generation as World War II had shaped the first was their experience as university students.

In some ways even more important is the fact that the first and second generations stood on different sides of the great divide between the Depression and an ascendant capitalism. The difference between those two generations is the very large difference between those who grew up in the Depression and those who came to political consciousness in a time of rising prosperity. The historical memory of the first generation would continue to shape their conception of capitalism, its possibilities and limits, just as Fascism – together with the class divide between ruling class appeasement and socialist resistance – would remain for them the most vivid expression of capitalist decline. For the second generation, capitalist productivity and growth, conjoined with 'bourgeois democracy' in advanced capitalist countries, would serve as the normative guide.

It may seem odd to make this claim about the second generation, a group of young intellectuals whose theoretical and political agenda grew out of a preoccupation with capitalist *decline*, in a country that seemed to them exempt from any rising economic tide. Perry Anderson himself has written that the new editorial group found its bearings, its own editorial programme, at a time when 'the national crisis of British capitalism was unmistakable', and that NLR's project was to comprehend that national crisis.[23] The series of articles written by Anderson and Nairn in 1964–5, analyzing the various elements of Britain's crisis, the inadequacies of British capitalism and its attendant culture, set the agenda which established the new identity of NLR. Yet if the dominant theme in the new NLR programme was capitalist decline, it is just here, in the 'Nairn-Anderson' theses, that the assumptions of NLR II about capitalist progress are most clearly visible. The analysis of Britain's 'present crisis' makes it clear that the defining idea of this second New Left, the idea that determined its self-proclaimed identity, was a conception of capitalism in which that 'crisis' was *exceptional*, testimony not to the inherent contradictions of capitalism in general but to the specific *imperfections* of Britain as a capitalist economy and its *deviations* from the capitalist norm. This was combined with a view of capitalist democracy according to which Britain's failure to transform its political and cultural superstructures, and especially its failure to modernize its state by means of 'bourgeois revolution', was at the root of its economic debility.

Nothing could be further from the formative experience of the first generation. The ensemble of Depression, Fascism and Second World War surely shaped the consciousness of the first New Left as profoundly as, say, the French Revolution and Napoleonic wars had determined the intellectual life of another generation. It is hard to imagine an intellectual history of the late 18th and early 19th centuries that remains silent on the cultural and ideological effects of the latter events, but some histories of the New Left have accomplished something like a silence of that magnitude. Yet the epochal difference that divides the first and second generations of the New Left is if anything underlined by the failure of recent commentators to take note of it. That failure testifies to a historical amnesia so profound that it has afflicted historians and their subjects alike.

Contextual differences, then, had a great deal to do with the distinctive attitudes that set the first New Left apart from their successors. Not least among these attitudes, especially in Britain, was the first generation's continuing attachment – often organizational but always in principle – to the labour movement. Their conception of capitalism entailed a particular view of the agencies best suited to transform it; and, while the realities of modern capitalism and modern means of communication had, in their view, placed cultural struggle very high on the socialist agenda, the objective was to transform not to replace the working class. People like Thompson (and, for that matter, Raymond Williams) remained vehemently opposed to conceptions of hegemony depicting a working class irredeemably mesmerized by consumer capitalism and the mass media, and requiring substitution by free-thinking intellectuals. The continuities between the cultural preoccupations of the first and second New Left should not disguise the rupture between their respective conceptions of socialist agency and the relationship between intellectuals and the working class.

It is also worth noting certain significant differences between British Marxist intellectuals and their counterparts elsewhere in Europe. If the British Communist Party never became a mass party like others in Europe, it was nevertheless grounded in a uniquely long-established and strong labour movement. By contrast, the mass parties of Italy, France or Spain had less well established traditions of organized labour. They did, however, gain a powerful impetus from the anti-Fascist struggle. Perhaps because so many Communist intellectuals in these countries had been drawn to Communism not so much by any attachment to the labour movement or even any prior ideological commitment to socialism but by the fight against Fascism – and perhaps because of other more long-standing differences in the position of intellectuals, notably in their relation to the state – their relationship to the working class was also arguably different, certainly as regards their conception of the task confronting left intellectuals in advancing the socialist cause. It is possible to argue that the intellectual's aspiration to primacy was embedded in the culture of the Continental Left much earlier, and more organically. To put the point briefly and baldly, it is hard to imagine anyone accusing, say, French left intellectuals at *any* time of 'populism'.

This means that the autonomization of politics and ideology, together with a detachment from the labour movement, represented a sharper rupture for the British Left than for some others. It also means that the adoption of Continental Marxism by the second New Left, in its *NLR* incarnation, represented a significant *political* break, marking a more decisive shift away from the labour movement and class politics than is immediately apparent in its revival of Marxist theory. That shift was, it could be argued, right from the beginning encoded in NLR's anti-'populism'; and it is one of the major paradoxes of the second New Left that this transformation took the form of a renewed commitment to revolutionary Marxism.

The ambiguities in the project of the second New Left seem to have been apparent to its predecessors. Here, for example, is what E. P. Thompson had to say about the political implications of Western Marxism:

There is no mark more distinctive of Western Marxisms, nor more revealing as to their profoundly anti-democratic premises. Whether Frankfurt School or Althusser, they are marked by their heavy emphasis upon the ineluctable weight of ideological modes of domination – domination which destroys every space for the initiative or creativity of the mass of the people – a domination from which only the enlightened minority or intellectuals can struggle free. . . . it is a sad premise from which socialist theory should start (all men and women, except for us, are originally stupid) and one which is bound to lead on to pessimistic or authoritarian conclusions.[24]

Even Raymond Williams, in spite of his differences with the first New Left, had something not dissimilar to say about his own attitude to the choices confronting British Marxists in the 1950s and thereafter, as he looked back in 1977 at the development of the post-War Left in Britain. He rejected, he says, the rhetorical populism which complacently ignored the implications of 'consumer' capitalism and the 'powerful new pull' it exerted upon the people. At the same time, he continued:

because I saw the process as options under pressure, and knew where the pressure was coming from, I could not move to the other available position: that contempt of the people, of their hopelessly corrupted state, of their vulgarity and credulity by comparison with an educated minority, which was the staple of cultural criticism of a non-Marxist kind and which seems to have survived intact, through the appropriate alterations of vocabulary, into a formalist Marxism which makes the whole people, including the whole working class, mere carriers of the structures of a corrupt ideology. . . .[25]

Against this trend, Williams insisted that 'there were still, and still powerful, existing resources':

To stay with the existing resources; to learn and perhaps to teach new resources; to live the contradictions and the options under pressure so that instead of denunciation or writing-off there was a chance of understanding them and tipping them the other way: if these things were populism, then it is as well that the British Left, including most Marxists, stayed with it.[26]

There may be some ambiguity here about whether Williams would, in the 1960s, have included the new editorial board of the *New Left Review* among those Marxists who 'stayed with it'. Nevertheless, there can be little doubt that, as Greg Elliott has emphasized, they themselves defined their own project as a significant departure from the old Marxist 'populism'. They certainly took upon themselves the task of importing those 'Western' or 'formalist' Marxisms which Thompson and Williams associated with the 'writing-off' of a thoroughly hegemonized working class and with the transfer of socialist agency to enlightened intellectuals. In this respect, the renewal of Marxist theory which the second New Left did so much to promote had as much in common with the project of their post-Marxist successors as with that of their first New Left predecessors.

VI

The *New Left Review* has never explicitly 'written off' the working class, and it has continued to advance the Marxist tradition in various ways. Its editorial programme has, to be sure, continued to display a declining interest in 'popular' culture, 'popular' struggles and the labour movement in particular.[27] It has also remained to a great extent insulated from a substantial section of British left intellectuals – those polytechnic lecturers, other academics and trade union researchers whose interests have been more consistently articulated by an organization like the Conference of Socialist Economists and a journal like *Capital and Class*. At the same time, while its theoretical project, its conception of socialist agency and the role of intellectuals, has certainly had important affinities with 'post-Marxist', post-structuralist and post-modernist currents, the trajectory of leading NLR figures has remained distinctive. For example, the focus on high politics and culture which has marked NLR II from its earliest days, together with the Andersonian analysis of British capitalism and the antiquated British state, has found a new expression in a preoccupation with constitutional and electoral reform (many leading figures in Charter 88, the current movement for constitutional reform in Britain, cut their teeth on the Nairn-Anderson theses). Early critics like Peter Sedgwick, who remarked on the lack of concern evinced by the new NLR for the fate of political democracy in the regimes they singled out for praise, might be surprised at the current enthusiasm for 'democratic' constitutional reform; yet Sedgwick might have found the displacement of 'popular' struggles by constitutional change a predictable outcome of what he saw as a tendency on the part of the second New Left toward an elitist, Fabian-style reformism.[28] Be that as it may, the characteristic preoccupations of this second New Left may also have sheltered NLR from the more extravagant – and ultimately more anti-democratic and regressive – manifestations of today's intellectual culture. Certainly NLR's continuing interest in politics and economics (and an abiding attachment to the 'Enlightenment project') have precluded anything more, at best, than a profound ambivalence toward the latest irrationalist tendencies in post-structuralism and post-modernism (though NLR's book-publishing partner, Verso, seems more attuned to current fashions).

Others on the left in Britain and elsewhere have, of course, taken much further the logic ascribed by Thompson to 'Western Marxisms'. Not the least of the many ironies in the history of the Western Left is the extent to which European Communism became a breeding ground for the 'retreat from class'. The CPGB's fashionable (but now defunct) journal, *Marxism Today*, for example, became a major vehicle for the autonomization of ideology, 'culture' and intellectual practice in general. To situate these intellectual developments in their historical context, it is probably worth adding that this journal enjoyed its brief vogue – and suffered its demise – in the hands of British Communists who stood on the same side of the historic and generational divide as the founders of NLR Mark II, though Martin Jacques and co. went immeasurably further than Anderson et al. in accepting the triumph of consumerism and even Margaret Thatcher's 'people's capitalism'.[29]

The autonomization of cultural and intellectual practice has now been pushed to its outer limits by left academics. Productive activity has finally been displaced by 'discourse' as the constitutive practice of social life, the material reconstruction of society has been replaced by the intellectual deconstruction of texts, and the terrain of left politics has been purposefully enclosed within the walls of the academy, while historical causality has been completely dissolved in post-modern fragmentation, 'difference' and contingency.

This story has its own chronology. In this chronology, as we have seen, there is an epochal rupture not in the mid-seventies but earlier, at the point when a section of the left intelligentsia aspired to become the movement itself. The line from there to here – from, say, Maoism to post-modernism – cuts across the epochal phases of working class politics, a course of development chronologically coeval with the career-span of people who were students in the 1960s and who today are senior academics. The attempt to detach intellectual and cultural practice from material and historical constraints has run the full course from Maoist voluntarism to post-modern contingency, between two poles of that curious but not uncommon paradox, the irrationalism of intellectuals.

The implications of these intellectual developments have been disguised by the fact that their exponents have often claimed to speak for the truly democratic and emancipatory impulses of the 'new social movements' or the 'politics of identity'. The paradox here is not simply that 'theory' has been separated from 'practice', or that the Left has become more 'academic' than ever. It is rather that left academics have adopted modes of intellectual activity that seem deliberately exclusionary; and the waters are further muddied by the fact that the more inaccessible the fashionable discourses become, the less available they are to all but a small minority of initiates, the more they proclaim their celebration of 'popular culture'. If the old anti-populism grew out of a conviction that the working class had been effectively submerged in the culture of capitalism, that anti-populism has now come full circle. The very same conviction on which it was based has now produced a new and perverse kind of populism. The hegemony of consumer capitalism is now irrevocably conceded, sometimes embraced and even celebrated, at the same time as it is invoked to justify the identification of 'politics' with the academy's most exclusive and arcane discursive practices. Even in the women's movement, which once broke down so many barricades, there now exists a form of post-modern academic feminism which is shoring up one of the most stubborn roadblocks standing in the way of its own emancipatory project, the class barrier which has often divided feminists from working class women.

The readiness with which some British left intellectuals in the eighties (most notably in *Marxism Today*) accepted the claims of Thatcher's 'people's capitalism' – its boasts about extending the benefits of consumerism, shareholding and home-ownership to the working class – illustrates how divorced the new inverted (or anti) populism could be from the realities of capitalism as it now is, and how thoroughly unprepared it would be for the prolonged and structural crisis that was just around the corner. Even at the height of Thatcherism this judgment seemed at best a little premature and overblown, and at worst patronizing, vastly exaggerating the extent and duration of the material benefits accruing to the great majority and underestimating the very strict limits of that 'revolution'. Today, as Thatcher's chickens have come home to roost with a vengeance, that judgment seems not only naive but in questionable taste.

But this is only one – and not the most extreme – example of the extent to which the Left today is ill-equipped to confront the problems of the here and now. If a growing consumerism was the defining characteristic of earlier decades, the capitalism of the nineties, while still, of course, consumerist, has its own distinctive form. It is more specifically defined by things like structural mass unemployment, growing poverty and homelessness, 'flexible' labour markets, and changing patterns of work in the form of casualization and low-paid part-time jobs, or overwork for the remaining few in 'downsized' enterprises, together with the global imposition of market imperatives increasingly immune to cushioning by the old forms of state intervention.

The new capitalism has its expression, too, in the altered prospects and aspirations of university students. Lin Chun and Greg Elliott both conclude their discussions of the British New Left with a reference to Jonathan Ree's comment in 1974 that 'the socialist intellectual youngsters occupy the buildings, while the socialist intellectual oldsters occupy the chairs'.[30] For Lin Chun, this is a comment on the confinement of modern radicalism in the West to the academy, both then and now. For Greg Elliott, Ree's observation highlights the difference between then and now. 'Updated for New Times,' he nicely observes, 'Ree's verdict might read: the post-modernist intellectual oldsters occupy the chairs, while the environmentalist youngsters are preoccupied with making ends meet.'

And that about sums it up. Some of yesterday's militant youngsters are today's post-modernist chair-holding oldsters. If their high aspirations yesterday to change (if not to rule) the world have failed to materialize, their hopes of a comfortable career have at least been fulfilled. Their – I should say our – students today can barely hope for a decent job, never mind think about leading a cultural revolution. If there ever was a proletarianization of students, this is it, as overcrowded and underfunded universities house students many of whom (especially in North America) are already part-time wage-earners, and for whom a university education has become both more economically essential and increasingly irrelevant, a necessary but far from sufficient condition of life-time employment.

The current theoretical fashions are very far removed from these realities. They are not about the new world order since 1989, nor even about the long-term trends in capitalist development since the late 1970s. What passes for the very up-to-date looks less like a confrontation with the eighties and nineties than the agenda of the sixties running its course. At the very time that capitalism exerts its totalizing logic on the whole 'new world order', the most fashionable left intellectuals, cultivating their varied and fragmented patches of discourse and difference, claim the supremacy of their discursive practices while ruling out any form of 'totalizing' knowledge that might be adequate to comprehend the operations of the capitalist system. They even deny its systematic totality, its very existence as a system, while still, paradoxically, accepting, at least by default, the universality and eternity of 'the market'. As the expanding logic of that 'market' creates increasing strains along the fault lines of class, we are enjoined to pursue the fragmented 'politics of identity', with little hope of anything more than the most particularistic and local resistances within the interstices of capitalism.

To confront today's realities requires striking out in new directions. At the same time, while the new conditions of contemporary capitalism require new analyses, we should not make the mistake, as Raymond Williams tells us the younger New Left did, of underestimating everything that has not changed in the capitalist system. If, as now seems very likely, the rising tide of capitalist prosperity in the fifties and sixties proves to be an aberration, it also seems likely that in our present condition we shall get more guidance from those who remember the thirties and forties than from those whose ideas are deeply rooted in an ascendant capitalism, or from their post-modern successors who have yet to catch up with the present, let alone look to the future.

NOTES

1 Perhaps the earliest account of this distinction is Peter Sedgwick's 'The Two New Left's', originally published in *International Socialism* 17, August 1964, and reprinted in David Widgery ed., *The Left in Britain, 1956–1968* (Harmondsworth, 1976). References here will be to the latter edition. The most recent major study of the British New Left, which also speaks of two generations, is Lin Chun's *The British New Left* (Edinburgh, 1993).

2 Raymond Williams, *Politics and Letters* (London, 1979), pp. 361–66.

3 See Sedgwick, pp. 137–8.

4 Williams, *Politics and Letters*, p. 363.

5 Gregory Elliott, 'Missing Ingredients', *Radical Philosophy* 68, Autumn 1994, p. 46.

6 *Ibid.*, p. 47.

7 *Ibid.*, p. 48.

8 *Ibid.*

9 Sedgwick, p. 148.

10 *Ibid.*, pp. 147–8.

11 *Ibid.*, p. 145.

12 Lin Chun, p. 109.

13 The most dramatic example is provided by Barry Hindess and Paul Hirst, whose trans-formation I have discussed in *The Retreat from Class* (London, 1986), pp. 79–84.

14 See, for example, Ernesto Laclau's 'Fascism and Ideology', in *Politics and Ideology in Marxist Theory* (London, 1977), a critique of Nicos Poulantzas's *Fascism and Dictatorship* (published in 1974), in which Laclau already goes some distance in estab-lishing the autonomy of ideology. I have discussed his argument in *The Retreat from Class*, pp. 47–53.

15 I originally made some of these points in a response I was invited to make to a critical review of my book, *The Retreat from Class*, by Alex Callinicos in the SWP theoretical journal, a review in which the 'upturn-downturn' thesis figured prominently. My reply appeared in *International Socialism* 2:35.

16 Lin Chun, pp. 106 n. 106 and 96.

17 See, for example, Boris Kagarlitsky, *The Thinking Reed: Intellectuals and the Soviet State, 1917 to the Present* (London, 1988), p. 97.

18 Quoted in *ibid.* p. 97 (my own translation).

19 Elliott, p. 47.

20 Some of the connections, personal if not ideological, between the Old Left, particularly Spanish Civil War veterans, and the Left of the sixties, are traced in Peter N. Carroll, *The Odyssey of the Abraham Lincoln Brigade* (Stanford, 1994). See also David Lance Goines, *The Free Speech Movement* (Berkeley, 1994).

21 Johanna Brenner, 'The Best of Times, The Worst of Times: US Feminism Today', *New Left Review* 200 (1993), p. 107 n. 13.

22 Elliott, p. 46.

23 Perry Anderson, *Arguments Within English Marxism* (London, 1980), pp. 137–8.

24 Thompson, *Poverty of Theory*, pp. 377–8.

25 Raymond Williams, 'Notes on Marxism in Britain since 1945', *New Left Review* 100 (November 1976–January 1977), p. 87.

26 Williams, 'Notes on Marxism', p. 87.

27 Although my own tenure on the editorial board of *New Left Review* fell within the period of 'downturn' or 'retreat', the journal's charter continued to proclaim that 'a revolution in social and political life will only be achieved by the conscious will and aspiration of the majority of the producers. The central contingents of that majority continue to be the body of workers engaged in the fundamental processes of the generation of material wealth, in the advanced capitalist economies of today.' I once did a quick survey of articles for the period 1984–1988, in preparation for a 'perspectives' meeting to which I submitted an internal document, outlining some concerns about the *Review*'s editorial direction. For all that the relevant period fell within the 'downturn' phase, it nonetheless embraced some fairly important moments in the history of the British labour movement, the miners' strike of 1984–5, Wapping, etc. I quote here from my document: 'Out of 184 articles, there has been *one* minor piece on the miners' strike, an anecdotal, experiential account of the strike as it affected one community. There has been nothing more on this event or about any other major industrial dispute in Britain or elsewhere, whether empirical, experiential, or analytical. Only one or two articles have appeared concerning anything remotely resem-bling the issues of immediate concern to workers: one on the labour process debate, and another on the Swedish wage-earner funds. Apart from that, there has been one article relating to the composition of the working class – i.e. on white-collar workers; one on the general prospects of European labour parties; and one historical article on the by-gone

days of labour in the great city. That is the sum of our coverage of workers' struggles, the issues which engage them, the condition of the working class under Thatcherism, the attack on trade union rights in Britain, the comparative state of working class struggles internationally, the changing composition of the working class, the assumptions about transformations in the nature of capitalism and the working class within it on which post-Marxist arguments are founded, and so on.' It seemed to me then, as it does now, that this editorial deficit had roots much further back.

28 Sedgwick, pp. 148–9.
29 For a devastating analysis of one year's issues of *Marxism Today* (1988), see John Saville, '*Marxism Today*: An Anatomy', *Socialist Register* 1990, pp. 35–59.
30 Lin Chun, p. 195; Elliott, p. 48.

SAYING NO TO CAPITALISM AT THE MILLENIUM

George Ross

Saying No to capitalism has traditionally been the point of departure for socialist movements – including social democracy and the universe of groups to its left, 'the Left' of this essay. Doing so credibly has involved connecting fundamental critique of the capitalist system with an alternative vision of socialism. The act of saying No to capitalism has been historically and materially conditioned, varying with the stage of capitalism. Since World War II capitalism has changed tremendously, moving from the post-war boom to today's crisis and reconfiguration. In each moment of this evolution the Left has had to reconsider its ideas and practices. At present, the Left's ability to say No is in crisis. The circumstances of the Left's existence have changed dramatically, as have the questions the Left must answer. This essay tries to analyze the sources and nature of this crisis and the opportunities that it presents.

I The Odd Couple – The Socialist Left and Social Democracy in the Post-War Boom

> . . . a 'reformist' strategy, if it is taken seriously and pursued to its necessary conclusion, must lead to a vast extension of democratic participation in all areas of civic life – amounting to a very considerable transformation of the character of the state and of existing bourgeois democratic forms.
>
> Ralph Miliband, *Marxism and Politics*[1]

The centre piece of modern socialist politics has been a multiform discourse constructed over a century of struggle. The framework of this discourse is a class analytical map of capitalism privileging the position and agency of workers. The immediate purpose of socialist politics was to limit the harshness of capitalism. Its deeper purpose was to strengthen workers' commitment to basic change, while also gathering support from groups outside the working class. The direction of such change was to be towards socialism, defined fluidly as what capitalism was not and implying drastic limitations on the scope of the market, if not its total elimination, plus the extension of full democratic decision-making into those areas

50

where capitalism, even in its liberal democratic political formulations, did not allow: matters of economic allocation, the nature of the workplace and the distribution of life-chances through unequal advantages granted by inheritance and unfair distribution of opportunities.

More specifically, however, the complicated task of saying No to capitalism depended upon what capitalism actually was at any particular moment. The political economy of post-war capitalism thus established the logics that controlled the behaviours of both Left and social democracy in the post-war boom and thereafter. Social democracy remained the dominant branch of the broader socialist movement in the period, and its growing integration into this system made it particularly vulnerable to Left critique. The act of saying No to capitalism from the mid-1940s through the end of the post-war boom was thus overdetermined by symbiotic relationships between the Left and the social democrats. For the Left, criticizing social democracy became the most important focus of its critique of capitalism itself.

Post-War Social Democracy

The nature of social democracy in capitalism's Cold War years is well understood. Almost all social democratic movements converted to a strategy of promoting Keynesian welfare states. This required, first of all, nested compromises between labour and monopoly capital aimed at conciliating capital's competitiveness and profit with limited redistribution and democratization. Minor shifts of income and wealth through taxation were small, if always contested, prices for capital to pay. New deals in the workplace gave higher wages and greater employment security to some workers in exchange for quiescence about technological change. Next, public policy was set to stimulate demand to generate near-to-full employment, moderate the business cycle and allow mass production capitalism to tap a predictable and growing consumer market. The expansion of social programmes also moderated capitalism's otherwise harsh allocation of misfortunes while providing a degree of counter-cyclic income stability. Built into all this was often some form of neo- or meso-corporatist collaboration between trade unions (tied to social democrats in one way or another), capital and the state to promote price stability, the Achilles heel of attempts to manage demand.

The general deal was productivist: economic growth was the key to everything else. Facilitating, fine-tuning and sharing the fruits of this growth were the central policy matters. At the heart of things was the expansion of Fordist consumer durable and producer goods corporations employing large numbers of semi-skilled manufacturing workers. The major beneficiaries, besides monopoly capital, were unionized workers who gained greater employment security, improving consumerist living standards and optimistic prospects for the immediate future in exchange for collaboration in productivity growth. Male blue collar workers were the base of social democracy electorally, organizationally and often financially. The power of this base and the success of the system enticed other social groups, particularly the growing public sector new middle strata, into political alliance.

There were great national variations in the model. In Northern Europe the elements were most fully combined. In Sweden, export-oriented large corporations, high levels of unionization and an intelligent social democratic party allowed innovations to come earlier and go further.[2] In the UK, decentralized trade unionism with considerable power over the evolution of the Labour party produced incomplete reformism and inability to sustain effective neo-corporatism. In Germany, sectoral meso-corporatism brought only partial social democratization. In Latin European countries, where social democratic hegemony was contested by strong Communist movements, developments were different, even though the outlines of the social democratic post-war compromise inevitably seeped in, as they did in North America, despite the absence of serious social democratic movements.

During the glory days of post-war compromise the nation state could hope to regulate national economic flows, controlling capital movements, exchange rates, fiscal policies and the strength of demand. A changing capitalist state became a central agent in the accumulation process, moving tax revenues and national savings and using state agencies to promote economic policy goals. Many important social choices, including extensive efforts to structure and 'frame' the market itself, could be made through political processes, most often centralized at national state level. The political struggle of organized groups, including those of workers, could influence these processes, generating a range of 'public goods.'

There was an international price to be paid for social democratic success. The Bretton Woods monetary and financial regimes which coordinated international trade were run by the Americans. These regimes, which facilitated 'good' national trade, monetary and fiscal policies and punished bad ones (high inflation, excessive deficits), policed reformist governments to keep them within acceptable limits. The Americans also used their power to promote ever-broadening free trade. NATO and its complex security arrangements were the final major pillar of American domination. The post-war boom thus became largely dependent upon and incorporated within the Cold War, with social democrats enlisted on the American side.

The Left's Tasks During the Post-War Boom

In these nested national and international contexts the general tasks of the Left seemed clear. First, it was necessary to expose the shortcomings of social democracy. The message was that social democracy, despite vague invocations of socialist utopianism, was not socialist at all. Claims that post-war arrangements were steps towards a different, non-capitalist alternative were hollow. At best, social democracy was tinkering with a capitalist order that otherwise seemed destined to go from strength to strength. The Left could thus warn that social democracy was unlikely to succeed at democratizing capitalism or even at changing it very much. Capital constrained its options, and these options, in turn, controlled the bulk of the workers' movements. In this context, the Left had to keep the flame of socialism alive until illusions of social democratic success had been shattered. 'Saying No to capitalism' was a plausible Left endeavour at this point because social democracy continued to claim, in transparently false ways, that it was doing the same thing.

These critical tasks were complicated by the divisions within the Left. The Left had always been populated by argumentative intellectuals and activists with a passion for doctrine and the rhetorical voluntarism that small group life can nurture. In this post-war period democratic Socialists, Marxist-Leninists, anarchists, various 'western Marxists' and the warring tribes of Trotskyism were quite capable, on their own, of a high level of cacophony. In addition, since Communist parties were also part of this Left, the Soviet model, with its vanguardist substitutism and denial of democratic rights, became a more important factor in Left discussion than it should have been. The Soviet model was also the cause of incessant and often destructive internecine divisions between pro-Soviets and anti-Soviets, like the Trotskyist movement, within the Left. It also erected additional barriers to communication with parts of social democracy's base.

The post-war boom period was not continuous and the life of the Left-social democrat 'odd couple' was divisible into two moments. During the first, from the late 1940s into the early 1960s, social democracy struck its new deals with capital, and the post-war consumerist boom gathered steam. The second, stretching into the 1970s, saw the explosion of many of the contradictions of this new capitalism and a renewal of Left hope. The valence of the relationship between the Left and social democracy was different during each.

The first of the Left's tasks as the post-war boom took hold was to debunk the intellectual claims made for the new capitalism, many from social democracy. Beginning in the 1950s there was an onslaught from progressive 'social science' drawing all manner of conclusions about capitalist economic, social and political success. Among major claims were that the 'economic problem had been solved' (Galbraith) and that solutions to major distributive problems were thereby at hand. It was also announced that the monopoly corporation had become 'soulful.' No longer a profit maximizer, it was instead a trustee of the public interest. Then a panoply of arguments declared the end of class as the central social cleavage in parliamentary democratic systems, in ideology and in the workplace. Perhaps the most articulate summary of most of these arguments came in Anthony Crosland's tour de force, *The Future of Socialism*, the most prophetic recasting of social democratic tenets in English. Crosland saw the post-war boom as an indicator that capital had found the secret of perpetual expansion, that workers were declining in importance as the white collar middle class grew and that new, and no longer *socialisant*, forms of redistributive politics could become social democracy's programme. Crosland was clear in ways that official social democratic positions were not. To him saying No to capitalism was no longer a useful thing for social democrats to do.

In this context the Left persistently denied these extravagant claims.[3] However, it was less successful at combining such denial with analyses of what precisely was new in the new capitalism. Indeed, Left intellectuals and activists, with notable exceptions, became so engaged in exposing the fact that capitalism still had nefarious consequences, that exploitation continued, that inequalities were harsh and that class remained important that they neglected to explore fully the logics of the changes that had occurred. It was perhaps natural, when memories of the Great Depression, Fascism and World War II were so fresh, to write off changing post-war economic and social circumstances as temporary aberrations before the return of the old system. The Left was nonetheless late in acknowledging the very real modifications in class structure and the sociology of politics which was occurring.[4]

The Left's analyses of the international politics of the Cold War, nuclear threat and decolonization were much more robust. New declensions of the Marxist theory of imperialism were of enormous help in illuminating events and persuasive enough to penetrate broader political and intellectual circles. Thus they provided meaning and purpose to peace movement activities and labour action. The period was contradictory, however. Because of the importance of the Soviet experience in Left discourse the Cold War became a manichaean affair in which a logic of 'the enemy of my enemy is my friend' textured Left appreciations. The power of Communist parties within Left debate contributed to this. Often there were problems distinguishing socialist internationalism from the great power manoeuvrings of the USSR. It also fed an unfortunate tendency to accept the self-definitions of Third World socialist and liberation movements at face value. Non-Communist Leftists were not as sharply critical on fundamental issues of human and democratic rights as they might have been.[5]

Important implications for action followed from the Left's positions. Thus it supported militant workers' movements and urged them to resist the sirens of neo-corporatism. It denounced many of the policy lines chosen by the social democrats. It defended peace, denounced the arms race and supported anti-imperialist struggle. These were considerable accomplishments. Resisting 'happy days' rhetoric and uncovering the logics of international policies were in themselves important ways of saying No to capitalism, but the Left was least successful in elucidating the socialist alternative. The outlines of a socialist future were much less well portrayed than the substance of social democratic betrayal.

The second moment, which began in the 1960s, brought to be the fore many of the contradictions upon which the post-war boom had been built. The period revealed the absence of any 'invisible' hand stabilising the various neo-, meso- and pseudo- corporatisms by which relationships between labour, capital and the state had come to be structured. In many places relatively full employment led workers to push for higher income to sustain the consumerist lifestyle which they had been encouraged to adopt. Where workers and their allies were powerful politically, they also demanded substantial expansion of social protection and welfare state programmes. And where growth involved industrial restructuring, as it did in most European economies, strong working class movements used their power to protect themselves. Finally, restructuring and expansion drew new social groups into the labour force who often rebelled against intensifying Fordist work disciplines.

These contradictions were unsettling. Governments faced increasing levels of workplace struggle and growing inflationary pressure. Inflation threatened international trade positions, prompting devaluations or stop-go policies which stimulated more problems and further destabilized the international trading system. The deeper trends were more ominous. The social-democratic deal with monopoly capital depended upon national insulation from international economic settings which was thinning because the international dimensions of the post-war boom were changing. The deterioration of US economic power in the face of successful catchup strategies of European and Japanese capitalisms undercut American capacities to sustain the Bretton Woods financial and monetary system. A combination of new competition in markets that the US had earlier dominated, the decline of US trade advantage, the rise of US transnational corporations and the costs of American military expenditures abroad changed the logics of American monetary hegemony. Earlier the US had underwritten an international monetary and financial order that it perceived to be in its medium-term interests. Henceforth it would exploit the vulnerability of others to compensate for its own problems. These logics led to the abandonment of gold standard and the Bretton Woods system by the Americans in the earlier 1970s.

These trends were hugely compounded by the Vietnam War. The costs of the war for the American treasury, the Johnson administration's unwillingness to raise taxes plus demand-side pressures on international markets created by the war injected substantial new inflationary trends into world capitalism. Exporting the costs of war and inflation accentuated already existing trends towards inflation and domestic distributive conflict. Quite as important, Vietnam demonstrated that there were political limits to US Cold War foreign policy.

All this was striking confirmation of Left warnings about the ultimate instability of the post-war order, but it was only the beginning. The 1960s saw a widespread reawakening of social protest as a way of doing politics. The Vietnam War became the centre of a transnational movement that shook the American empire to its core. Workers mobilized and struck with unprecedented strength, often overwhelming employer and government efforts to contain them. Such was the case in the UK during the late 1960s shop-stewards movements (under a Labour government), in France in 1968, in Italy's 'hot autumn' of 1969 and, in less spectacular ways, in other places (including the US). Student mobilizations, often occurring as complements to worker action, were equally spectacular and very often announced in strong Left vocabularies, a discursive success of great comfort to the Left.[6]

Class conflict had 'returned,' class was clearly an essential dividing line and younger generations of intellectuals and the proliferating new middle strata were lining up alongside workers. The power of this return of class-oriented protest not only confirmed the Left's positions and projected the Left into much greater prominence in progressive political discussions. It also had a profound effect on social democracy, reinvigorating ideas about planning and redistribution that had been neglected or abandoned. The Left thereby gained new power in the British Labour Party, the French Left unified tactically in 1972 around the most stringent left programme that anyone had seen in decades, Italians theorized and practised the beginnings of a 'historic compromise' and a Spanish Left steeled by decades of anti-Fascist struggle prepared for a new era. The Swedish social democrats decided to push their 'third way' further to the Left through greater industrial democracy and the socialization of profit through wage-earner funds. Even in areas which had weak or non-existent social democratic formations (like Canada and the US) there was a distinct new reformist tinge.

The late 1960s and early 1970s looked to be a critical point when the symbiosis between social democracy and the Left might change its nature. Long-standing Left arguments were taken more seriously. Perhaps the most interesting dimension of this was the rapid return of *socialisant* and

Marxist intellectual and political discourse. There were many examples of Left success in academic debates – a good index of discursive change – in economics, sociology and political science, although nowhere greater than in new efforts to conceptualize the capitalist state. Here distinguished Left contributions intervened to raise a whole new set of issues about the relationships between economic dynamics, social forces and the use of state power in ways that had direct political implications.[7]

At this time the Left shifted its discussion towards transcending capitalism and defining a democratic socialist order. The French Communists abandoned their *miserabiliste* traditionalism and developed a reformist version of State Monopoly Capitalism theory positing a democratic transition to socialism, for example. The Italian and Spanish Left developed their Eurocommunist visions. Convincing new ideas came from the independent Left, too.[8] Common to all participants in the debate was a conviction that a strategy of 'revolutionary reformism' was conceivable. In such a strategy progressive forces would first establish beachheads in the capitalist state through political struggle, defined largely to include articulated mobilizational and electoral activities. With careful forethought these beachheads, rather than forestalling further changes (as social democratic reformism did), could be used to empower popular forces further in their struggle for further reform. The underlying logic in the strategy was to target and unleash ever-expanding processes of democratization. 'Decapitalizing' the capitalist state, piece by piece, could create a snowball of change that would lead to the transcendence of capitalism.

II The Odd Couple Divorces: New Social Democracy and the Implosion of the Left

In recent years, it is the very notion of socialism as a comprehensive reorganization of the social order which has come under fire, often from people who have remained more or less committed to the progressive side of politics. Each in its own way, post-Marxism, postmodernism, post-structuralism and related currents of thought, has served, whatever the intentions of its protagonists, to strengthen the recoil from general notions of human emancipation, particularly Marxism

Ralph Miliband, *Socialism for a Sceptical Age*[9]

Almost as quickly as it had begun, the post-war boom ended. By the early 1980s it was clear that hopes for 'exiting the crisis from the Left' had been dashed. Indeed, as more farsighted advocates of revolutionary reformism had anticipated, Left failure to seize the occasion allowed capitalism to exit crisis from the Right. The economic and political circumstances that ensued pushed social democracy towards renunciation of any reference to socialism. Social democracy's shift logically implied the break up of its symbiotic coupling with the Left.

New Capitalism

The virtuous cycle of post-war economic growth had ended by the mid-1970s. In fact, capitalism was in transition to increased internationalization in a chaos of oil shocks, stagflation, increased competition, deindustrialization in traditional sectors, low investment, monetary chaos, low productivity growth and rising unemployment. The new dynamics of accumulation had devastating effects. National level Keynesian welfare states and social democratic policies no longer functioned. Globalization, in particular of the movement of capital, helped reverse trends towards political regulation and brought a decisive shift towards the 'marketization' of decision-making, away from conscious political choice. Moreover, the nature and content of dramatically reduced state activity changed. In the new context, the state became a mediator between internationalized capitalist economic flows over which it had declining control.[10] Conscious political intervention did not disappear, of course, but it refocused, in 'supply-side' ways, on the promotion of international competitiveness for each country's 'own' companies.

The transition was devastating for the working class. As capital ranged over the entire planet, labour markets became global. However, working classes remained national, at least in terms of collective identity. Simultaneously the longer term restructuring of production and expansion of the service sector led to massive development of new middle strata and a striking feminization of the labour force. The changes further undercut the power of many, if not most, union movements. High unemployment, 'flexibilization,' and changing labour-market structures had terrible effects. In Europe, official unemployment figures of about 10% masked much higher real levels; there was an explosion of 'junk jobs' and other forms of precarious employment. It became customary to speak of a 'two-thirds, one third society' in which the bottom third was substantially excluded.[11] The 'contingent worker' appeared. Neo-corporatist arrangements, the backbone of post-war social democratic regulation, were dismantled, unions' membership declined and their efforts at mobilization became more difficult.[12]

Industrial restructuring within specific advanced capitalist societies had its own decomposing effects on the traditional bases of social democracy.[13] The supply-side outlook of firms and governments brought mechanisms and techniques to seduce and prod labour to focus more on life at firm level than on national matters. Collective bargaining was decentralized towards the firm, for example, while various organizational efforts to create firm-oriented worker consciousness – work-teams, quality circles, official works' councils, expression groups, merit-based individualized salary scales, and/or simple propaganda barrages – were generalized.[14] One consequence of such decentralizing tendencies was that the focus of workers' 'consciousness' became less national and more localized or regionalized.

New Social Democracy

By the 1980s the response of social democracy to these changes had taken a 'post-workerist' form.[15] Faced with the economic rebalancing of national and international the emerging social democratic project gave increasing priority to the regeneration of national economic capacities in the face of a rapidly shifting and threatening international economic environment. In part this involved 'deregulating' – minimizing various national rigidities and market imperfections to encourage capital to adapt and innovate rapidly. These measures were almost always accompanied by monetarist macroeconomic policies. The coming of costly high unemployment helped to increase running budgetary deficits, despite the new neo-liberalism of macroeconomic policies, and this led to constant pressure to squeeze down welfare state expenditures.

Rather than abandoning state intervention the new social democrats reconfigured it. The political levers which remained available to national governments were converted to a quest for 'competitiveness.' The state should quit shaping and reshaping economic sectors and markets and turn to fostering environments in which firms, henceforth the key actors for national destinies, made decisions to enhance their international competitive positions. The interventionist and *dirigiste* state had to be dismantled through privatizations and the 'marketization' of areas which had earlier been considered public services and/or 'natural monopolies' – transport systems, energy and telecommunications networks, post office etc. This involved ending arrangements protecting firms against the cold winds of the international market. It also meant extensive state investment in research and development and targeted educational spending to upgrade human capital.

This complex set of changes had an important impact on the way new-style social democracy actually *did* politics. New social democratic movements were increasingly dominated by a caste of policy intellectuals and high administrators who promised that their particular national capitalism would be better managed and coordinated, more rational and successful when central political tasks were given to people like themselves. They were also resolutely 'modernist' in an economic sense, promising the kind of state-of-the-art, 'international best practice' capitalism which, they argued, narrowly self-interested capitalists and a political Right tied to conservative social interests were unable to produce. But they claimed to be modernists 'with a heart,' concerned with preserving those aspects of the national welfare state which were consistent with economic constraints and promised new 'flexible' social programmes to help specific groups most directly threatened by rapid economic restructuring.[16] In most places this claim appealed to populations who did not approve of dismantling the welfare state. These claims combined into a package which contrasted strongly with earlier social democracy. If earlier appeals had enjoined class collaboration to promote capitalist profits that might then be redistributed into high wages and collective goods, new appeals were for general social cooperation and solidarity in a national crusade for success in the international market.

The new social democracy was thus vastly less workerist and class-oriented than its predecessor, seeking power not by representing a class and its organizations but by attracting votes from those constituencies who desired to civilize and humanize capitalism. Political scientists used to portray social democracy as anchored on a workerist left but dragged towards 'catch all' politics by the logic of electoral competition. The new social democracy, in contrast, began slightly on the reformist side of the political centre and was a 'catch-all' operation from the outset, with workers simply one constitituency among others. Finally, its political strategies and tactics were driven by modern electoralism: polls, advertising, television, focus on personalities, etc.

For some time in the 1980s the best examples of the new socialism were found in Latin Europe. France was most revealing. The French socialists brought with them a radical reformist programme of nationalizations, planning, redistribution and measures to strengthen labour when they won elections in 1981. After a brief eighteen months and a very difficult introduction to the realities of globalizing capitalism they completely shifted gears. Short-term austerity programmes led to efforts to restructure French industry. Public sector firms led the way to rapid labour shedding and rising unemployment. Policies were introduced to shift the share of wages in national income to profit, encourage the stock market and pursue a resolute monetarism, all in the interest of establishing new conditions to compete in Europe and internationally.[17]

The Spanish socialists pursued a similar path, if anything much more vigorously. In power beginning in 1982 they opened up their economy to the harsh winds of the European Community and dismantled the old 'rust belt' industries where Spanish labour's base largely resided and which even Franco had been afraid to touch. They too turned towards a harsh monetarism and invited capital to seek profit by whatever means. Labour was marginalized and, on occasion, beaten back during strikes.[18] Spain's growth levels rose, but official unemployment rates climbed to 20%. For socialist elites, the idealism of opposition to Francoism became a hard-nosed managerial Europeanism, cloaked in the argument that the new policies were the unavoidable route to consolidating Spanish democracy. Since the socialists' opponents were tainted by direct filiation with the authoritarian old regime, a decade of electoral success ensued. The PSOE had even more space to reconfigure its approaches than the French had, and made no bones about the personalism and electoralism of their political operations.[19]

Many purist analysts initially doubted the exemplarity of these Latin European experiences. After all, none of the Latin socialist parties had really emerged from the earlier social democracy, they had never managed a Keynesian welfare state during the post-war boom, and none had ever had strong links with an organized working class and experience with neo-corporatist practices. The sinuous evolution of the British Labour Party was less dramatic, but its conclusion in the Kinnock, Smith and Blair leaderships confirmed the general trend.[20] The fate of Swedish social democracy, the last best hope of genuine social democrats, demonstrated the breadth of the pattern.[21] By the later 1980s the famous Swedish 'third way' had begun to move to Latin rhythms. Large multinationals, for long happy with an export-led strategy based on production in Sweden itself, began to relocate off-shore. They also took to attacking neo-corporatism through the dismantling of 'solidaristic wage bargaining.'[22] At the same time rapidly rising budget deficits and inflation levels led a social democratic government to take decisive steps to austerity, dismantling neo-corporatism, welfare state cutbacks and rising unemployment. By the mid 1990s, with the change still far from completed, Sweden's unemployment rate was at the European average of 10%, its budget deficits huge, and it faced gigantic new constraints as a new member of the European Union.[23]

Left Crisis, Left Opportunity?

The lip-service allegiance of post-war social democracy to a general socialist discourse had produced the symbiotic coupling of Left and social democracy after 1945. Today's social democracy has abandoned discourses of class conflict constructed around the primacy of workers and their organizations, statist and *dirigiste* policy programmes (including efforts to create welfare state programmes), redistributive economic policies and even vague commitments to transcending capitalism towards 'socialism.' Most social democratic parties are now appealing opportunistically for votes from whatever constituencies can be detected 'out there' by opinion polling. Their goal now is less to democratize capitalism than to bring elites to power with relatively free hands. What gave the earlier Left its place on the political map was that it shared a general political and moral discourse with social democracy. Because the 'new' social democracy no longer partakes of this discourse, the Left has lost its traditional moorings. On the other side of the ledger, it is now freer to define its own course.

Parallel changes *inside* the smaller world of the Left itself render the situation even more complex. The evolution of the working class is the most important of these. The socialist movement in general had always counted on the working class as base and hope. For the Left this had involved trying to build on the deeper meanings of anti-capitalist radicalism that it was certain lay in the working class.[24] The end of the post-war boom revealed that workers, both as base and hope, were not what they once had been, either in size or nature. Simultaneously the social importance of the new middle classes was growing.[25] All this made it very difficult for the Left to sustain the idea of workers as any kind of 'universal class,' at least within the specific national confines of advanced capitalist societies.

The changes undercut trade unions, the major organizational forms possessed by workers. The weakening of unions encouraged renewed employer anti-unionism and in a few places, the UK in particular, there was a massive onslaught against the legal and political positions that unions had acquired over decades. Unions were often pushed into very difficult corners to survive, including 'concession bargaining' with employers. To protect themselves, unions and their memberships accentuated boundaries between 'insiders' and 'outsiders,' even when these outsiders were workers as well. In politics, the exchange relationship between workers and social democrats cracked. In the earlier post-war period social democrats had promised policies that would enhance workers' income, job security and life chances. Changes in capitalism and social democracy meant that such promised benefits were less and less forthcoming. Workers came to be a less predictable electoral base for social democrats, and unions often began to take their distance from former partisan allies.

As the twentieth century moved into its last decades the internationalization of capitalism denationalized labour markets apace. In addition the socialist and workers' movements in the twentieth century had slowly but surely been nationalized, and their ideas, resources, policy programmes and outlooks focused upon the national arenas. It was understandable that national union movements sought to protect the threatened positions of their own members nationally, since their organizations were profoundly national. In a context of growing liberalization of elite values, this made them look like 'special interests' rather than the bearers of progress. The situation has become a trap for those on the left tempted by *ouvriérisme*. It is unquestionably very important for the Left to defend the gains workers have won over the years, but accepting the definitions of such struggles advanced by unions has opened the Left to the 'special interest' accusation as well.

The Left's next internal problem flows from the contradictory nature of the student and intellectual mobilizations of the 1960s and 1970s. The *marxisant* discourses initially announced by student rebels proved misleading. Beneath the surface of student movements, in fact, was an unstable amalgamation of new middle strata counterculturalism and *gauchiste* utopianism. As the student rebellion ran its course the protest began to focus upon new issues, generating the new feminism, enviromentalism, and the 1980s peace movement. If some fragments of these newer movements claimed to be anti-capitalist, in most cases they saw their struggles as transcending 'older' debates about capitalism altogether. The *gauchiste* dimensions of the student movement, which had allowed student activists to announce themselves as 'true revolutionaries' often attached to Third Worldist vanguards (the Cubans, Chinese, Vietnamese and a few others), had very short half lives. Strident Marxism and the formation of sectarian collectives, often including missionary efforts to convert the workers on various factory floors and dabbling in terrorism, had been abandoned by the early 1970s.[26]

That the coming of new social movements brought an onslaught against the Left from intellectuals is evident from the flowering of literature about the 'New Social Movements.' One important school of thought around the French sociologist Alain Touraine claimed that the NSMs were the harbingers of new forms of protest appropriate to a post-industrial society in which new middle strata replaced workers as the location of progressive action.[27] Habermasian analyses made NSMs the vanguard of struggle to sustain the 'life world' against colonization by 'the system,' while classifying workers' organizations as part of the latter.[28] Post-modernists and post-structuralists denounced the Left's efforts at 'meta-analysis' of the social world as totalitarian.[29] More generally, activists and intellectual interpreters of the NSMs rejected the Left's claim that anti-capitalism defined progressivism.

The collapse of the Socialist bloc in 1989 made a huge third contribution to the Left's new setting. 'Real, existing socialism' in its sclerosed Brezhnevite forms had been in decline for a considerable time before the events of 1989, as had the appeal of the Soviet model to the Left in advanced capitalist societies. Still, with all of its problems, the model had exercised a powerful influence inside the Left historically because of the activities of Communists inside the Left and Trotskyist counter-discussions. Beyond this, the defence of existing socialism had been conflated with progressive anti-imperialist positions before and during the Cold War. Finally, whether the Left liked it or not, the Soviet model and socialism *tout court* had been successfully amalgamated in the general political discourses of capitalist societies. The Left put on a brave face, or a self-critical one, after the ignominious collapse of the Soviet model, but the damage was great. On the other hand, the removal of the Soviet albatross from the Left's shoulders was an opportunity.

III Saying No to Capitalism Today: Questions in Search of New Answers

> . . . socialism is part of the struggle for the deepening and extension of democracy in all areas of life. Its advance is not inscribed in some preordained historical process, but it is the result of a constant pressure from below for the enlargement of democratic rights; and this pressure is itself based on the fact that the vast majority located at the lower ends of the social pyramid *needs* these rights . . . to resist and limit the power to which they are subject . . . This, however, is not enough. Socialism seeks not only the limitation of power, but its eventual abolition as the organizing principle of social life. There is a profound sense in which democracy, equality and socialization must be taken to be means to an end which ultimately defines socialism, namely the achievement of a greater degree of social harmony than can ever be achieved in societies based on domination and exploitation. . .
>
> Ralph Miliband, *Socialism for a Sceptical Age*[30]

The situation of the Left today is very difficult. The discursive setting that established symbiosis between the Left and social democracy has disappeared. The coming of new social democracy has disoriented workers and others. When queried about promises of hope in difficult times, social democrats paraphrase Margaret Thatcher. 'There is no alternative' to pro-capitalist austerity and monetarism. Many ordinary workers have accepted this new package, along with a large part of the intelligentsia. Others gravitate towards national populist anger. The socialist Left that remains is greatly reduced in size and beleaguered by other 'progressives' who ridicule the very idea of socialism.

We are not yet at the end of history, however. Capitalism still secretes misery. In the 'West' one sees Brazilianized 'two-thirds' societies where 'insiders' fight tooth and nail to protect their positions at the expense of internal 'outsiders' whose exclusion from the surrounding setting of wealth and prosperity grows more intolerable by the day. Resource shortages and elite neo-liberalization have generated ever more ferocious attacks on industrial relations systems and welfare states. In the 'south' unregulated, low-wage, sweatshop exploitation and social degradation are rife, often in political settings where basic rights are denied and redress of popular grievances impossible.

Recent capitalist development has thus been busily preparing new recipes for social instability and rebellion around the globe. Nonetheless nothing guarantees that instability and rebellion will generate socialism or even be progressive. Only solid political work by the Left can promote such outcomes. Herein lies the opportunity contained in the Left's crisis. The first step toward seizing the opportunity is to face the most important questions about the Left's new setting.

How to Understand the New Capitalism?

Capitalism continues to produce muzzled democracy, inequality, economic harshness and exploitation, but it *has* changed in major ways since the end of the post-war boom. The Left's first task should be to decode these changes. Mapping the new capitalism, uncovering its particular logics and the social relationships that it is creating are fundamental building blocks. One of the Left's great strengths throughout the post-war period was that it was better able to illuminate the deeper nature of capitalism than could those with commitments to the system. The influence of Left perspectives on imperialism and international relations, on the capitalist state, on ideology, on the nature of work and on the contradictory nature of the post-war boom were out of all proportion to the Left's size. New critical perspectives on the post-1989 world could be tremendously important in an intellectual universe otherwise dominated monotonically by technocrats and neo-liberals.

What do we need to know? An exhaustive list would be very long, but some matters stand out. At the top is understanding the internationalization of capital. Among other things we need to consider is the possibility that the interests of capitalism as a system and those of leading capitalist nation states have diverged somewhat. The new capitalists have enhanced capacities to move exploitation around the globe with almost as little regard for the political and social stability of 'advanced' societies as they have had for those of the South. The geography of the international labour market has also been transformed, making it necessary to understand the real meanings of the 'global city,' the development of new technoproductive regions both in the North and South and the logics of 'Brazilianization' in the North.

We need as well to know a great deal more about transnational class and economic actors. Nothing would help class analysis more than a convincing reconfiguration of international social forces. Is there something that can be labelled a 'cosmopolitan bourgeoisie?' How is it articulated to other fractions of the bourgeois class? To what extent have this class and the transnational market actually placed constraints on national decision-making? What are the structures of the transnational working class and how is it segmented? What does 'competitiveness' really mean in these circumstances?

Old concepts for designating those areas of the globe that are 'not us' are obsolete. This is not because global inequalities have disappeared, or even been attenuated, but because it no longer makes much sense to employ the simple dichotomies of the past. Inequalities have been redistributed between and among 'the others', and formerly third world interests are more fragmented. Even if some regions, like Africa, are worse off than ever, 'north-south' divisions, interests and relationships have become more complicated. We need a geography of these complexities and their implications.

Without overemphasizing the importance of ideas, it is also likely that good critical Left intellectual work might enhance prospects for new progressive coalitions. Even on our preliminary list there are questions to which sound Left answers might enhance new social movement sympathies for the socialist cause. New patterns of gendering are an essential dimension of the transnational labour market. Shedding some light on the global structure of the changing gender division of labour and its connection to capitalist evolution might well create greater rapprochement between the Left and feminists. The environmentally destructive dynamics of the new capitalism are also huge. Charting them well might bring fruitful new contacts with environmentalists.

National vs International Strategies?

Although the Left has been linked transnationally through numbered internationals and dense networks of informal contact, it has rarely been capable of serious transnational action.[31] The reasons for this are not hard to find. Today labour and other markets are now international and segmented in new ways that disrupt the unity of national working classes. The problems to be understood and faced are huge. Capital traditionally 'whipsawed' different unions, sectors and regions within nation states to gain advantage. The coincidence of national boundaries and capitalist economies gave workers opportunity to use national political and legal arenas for struggle against this. Capital is now much more able to use its transnational mobility to engage in social dumping to encourage social policy 'races to the bottom' in the heartlands of strong labour movements.

In this context reliance on national resources to the exclusion of new Labour internationalization will help capital, divide national labour movements from one another and render transnational solidarity even less likely.[32] If the working class is now international in important objective ways, then strategic steps must be devised to internationalize its capacity to struggle. This is easier said than done, however, for two reasons. Many of the societies that now participate fully in the new transnationalized capitalist labour market are not democratic and deny workers their basic rights. Furthermore, in these societies it may well be in the interests of local workers to undercut those in advanced societies in order to benefit from the trickle down fruits of capitalist development. It is not always easy, therefore, to find eager transnational colleagues, even if unions and workers in the 'West' (who have analogous differences of interest from the others) decide to seek them out. The second problem arises because the best investment of a Western labour movement's resources remains national. Pressure on national governments is still the most effective means of getting concessions and of moving national governments to act in labour's favour in the international arena. Transnational action, if collectively central for workers as a larger group, can thus appear as a high cost luxury from the point of view of national movements.

Transnational solidarity is thus a real challenge, as well as a great opportunity. Paradoxically, the way to develop it may begin by drawing a clearer picture of what progressive policies can still be undertaken at national level through national pressure. This involves finding different answers to the claims of neo-liberals and new social democrats that nothing can – or should – be done at this level at all. Such a picture would give the Left a better understanding of genuine international constraints and what might simultaneously be done internationally to cope with them. For the Left and labour energetically to promote human rights, greater democracy and civilized labour standards transnationally would be a dramatic gesture. It is important as well to develop international Left and labour programmes establishing proper limitations on the movement of capital. Acting to initiate and sustain transnational efforts to stimulate demand would also be significant. These are all 'reformist' proposals. But the issue of saying No to the new capitalism is complicated and initial steps will seem modest.

Offensive or Defensive?

The most important self-assigned business of the Left historically has been to criticize the broader progressive world for its inadequacies in saying No to capitalism. This placed a premium on being strong and strident. When it was doing its work properly the Left was deconstructing the efforts of social democracy and connecting this deconstruction with arguments about how better to denounce and transcend capitalism. However, given its symbiotic ties with others, the Left was never very good at recognizing defensive historic moments, when the Left's enemies had a powerful upper hand. Clearly, however, there have been periods in the history of the socialist movement when it has made sense to protect historic gains against external threat. Everyone can recall cases when Left sectarianism was hugely costly – the refusal of Communists to cooperate with Social Democrats against the rise of Hitler comes to mind.

The geometry of today's situation is more complex. Now few outside the Left, strictly defined, are concerned with saying No to capitalism at all, even in ineffective ways. Perhaps this should mean a change in the Left's understanding of its role or at least enhanced sensitivity to the fluctuations of its environments. It can no longer be sure that pushing others to be more radical is consistently the right thing to do, and it must hone its capacities to distinguish between when advance is possible and when defensive action is appropriate. This is important because a case can be made that, for the time being, progressive forces and subordinate classes are in a strongly defensive period. One would have to be remarkably unobservant to miss the fact that many of the things that T.H. Marshall saw fifty years ago as the product of ineluctable expansion towards generalized 'social citizenship' are under siege. Legal protection for workers to organize and bargain, universal programmes of social protection, equal access to decent education, entitlements to a decent minimal standard of living are all threatened in many of those societies we have perhaps too quickly labelled 'advanced.' Moreover, these days the threats come as easily from social democrats as neo-liberals. The destruction of such past victories would be a defeat for those who benefit from them directly and reduce their ability to move forward in the future. It would be an even greater loss for those in other parts of the globe who have not yet achieved them. With the changes in social democracy and the defection of much of the new middle strata from progressive politics there are few good candidates but the Left to lead the defence of such things.

Nevertheless, as the Left correctly pointed out when such victories were being won, they were insufficient. In the intervening years these criticisms have become even more justified. The Left thus must find ways to defend past victories *and* criticize the inadequacies of present programmes in the optic of saying No to capitalism, proposing viable alternatives and modifications to what exists in the name of a reformism opening to socialism. Threatened existing social programmes often involve unwieldly, patronizing bureaucracies. Their universality, where it exists, is often one of *noblesse oblige* – universally dependent and weak clients faced by condescending agents and experts, characteristics which enhance their vulnerability to attack. The principles of universal education guaranteeing equal opportunity, universal health care, disability protection, a decent living standard at all stages of life and other such things cannot be relinquished by the Left. But the programmes as they stand cannot be defended intact, lest the Left contribute to, rather than transcend, existing problems. The Left thus needs to sharpen its ability to make innovative proposals built on the principles of universality and equality. But these proposals must also make existing programmes more flexible, decentralized and above all democratic (in particular in ways that will minimize bureaucracy). To the degree to which such proposals, if enacted, would provide better social protection *and* promote greater democratic empowerment they would indeed be saying No to capitalism in quite a concrete way. But to do this the Left has to be willing to dirty its hands more in the elaboration of 'revolutionary' reformist policy proposals.

The Left and Other Movements?

The Left's relationships with the new social movements raises profound questions. In its defence the Left did not ignore issues of central concern to NSMs. Rather it tended to incorporate them into its own socialist discourse, redefining them in the process. More often than not the result was that these issues were subordinated by the Left to 'more important' matters of class and class conflict. Women's issues were a case in point. Whatever the initial form of their expression, the Left had usually translated them into the concerns of women *workers*. Similarly, environmental matters were often subordinated to the Left's productivism. Issues involving the so-called private sphere were either collectivized or dismissed as petit bourgeois individualism. Peace issues were often subordinated to Cold War mapping of international class struggle. The reasons for the general approach were obvious. The socialist movement, including social democracy, had established hegemony over the definitions of radicalism.

Over the years the Left's propensity to translate the concerns of others into its own terms became rebarbative to NSM practitioners, to the point where the NSMs often classified the Left and the broader socialist movement as part of the enemy. Then, as social democracy shifted away from socialist discourse and the Left imploded, new social movements added a conviction of Left irrelevancy to its animosity. The socialist movement had lost its ability to arbitrate the definition of progressive behaviour in its own terms. The culmination of this, reached by the 1980s in most places, was open competition between the Left and the NSMs, and among the movements themselves, about whom and what were genuinely progressive. With no larger hegemonic movement to decide such things there could be no real decision.

This situation creates basic dilemmas for the Left. The highly competitive political market for the definition of what is progressive means that the Left's 'products,' class analysis and socialist goals, no longer have the comparative advantage they once had. Henceforth Left ideas will win or lose on the strength of the compelling nature of the case the Left can make for them. The invocation of traditional symbols and an appeal to scriptures will no longer work. In the new setting the Left will nonetheless have to engage in coalitional practices with social movements which do not share its commitment to socialism. The lingering tendency to compose a laundry list of various rebellious groups – the Left + social democrats + unionists + feminists + anti-racists + environmentalists + others may work for organizing demonstrations, but believing that all of these groups are 'really' socialist is a dangerous illusion. Many are not socialist at all. The absence of unifying notions of progressivism plus the place of NSMs in parliamentary democratic systems establishes a situation in which most NSMs will seek out 'pluralist' political deals from the establishment to benefit their own bases and causes rather than undertaking the more difficult tasks of cooperating with others. The Left has to seek coalitions in an ecumenical way. But it also has to think through the nature and logics of such coalitions. And, finally, the *only* way that the Left will succeed in influencing the outlooks of such coalition members in socialist directions will be to convince them that the interests of women, environmentalism, people of colour and others really do lie in transcending capitalism. This will not happen simply because 'history is on our side.' The analyses, ideas and ability to convince others on such matters remain to be constructed.

Socialism, Equality and Individuals

Finally, history has presented the Left with a basic problem in its political philosophy. What should be the contemporary meaning of equality? The socialist movement, writ large, settled for answers to this question that are no longer completely adequate. Whether in matters of education, treatment in the workplace, the nature of social programmes or private life the movement's response was that equality meant universality of treatment. Everyone should be approached in the same ways.

Such an outlook, part of the long democratic revolution, was laudable in the context of societies in which barriers to universality of treatment were endemic. Beneath this lay an assumption that everyone really would be the same if only the effects of evil social structures could be eliminated. It followed that removing such effects through political change would allow such cooperative and altruistic human similarity to blossom. All this was a far cry from Marx's own sense that socialism would liberate individuality in the multiplicity of ways it might be constructed in a social setting free of class power. Still, huge contributions to democracy, social advancement and human dignity were brought by this definition of equality. The definition nonetheless bore an artificial homogenization of genuine, differences among people. It also played into the consolidation of bureaucracies charged with the creation and administration of universality.

Saying No to capitalism in the name of a socialism that promises uniformity and standardization is a losing argument. Arguments for socialism must be able to claim credibly that there are other and better ways to sustain individual self-fulfilment than those proposed by capitalism. The Left needs to reconfigure the notion of equality to embrace human differences in point of departure and outcomes. It follows from this that individuals' desires for biographical and group distinctiveness are not simply artifacts of capitalist consumerism and competition. Capitalism does cultivate egoism and the desire to dominate through the accumulation of purchasable differences. But freedom involves the space to create and tolerate real differences. The Left's arguments must propose new egalitarian ways towards such an end. Decentralization, enhanced participation, new forms of education that promote diversity, genuine life-long learning and level playing fields, recognition of a wide range of lifestyle choices, different options in social policy and more effective democratic determination over such policy choices should be a part of the new egalitarianism.

Moving On

There are many other questions that the Left will need to face, plus great disagreement with those that I have here highlighted. But the very fact that we can at this point agree that questions of such a basic nature now need to be posed indicates how deep the Left's present crisis is, how long it will take to resolve and how complicated its resolutions will be. It also points to the huge field of opportunity awaiting the Left. As we all know, and as Ralph Miliband constantly reminded us, capitalism is an inherently contradictory and unstable social order. It will continue to have its own deepening crises. And it will also continue to elicit rebellious responses from those it oppresses. The Left's task is to provide plausible and practical understanding to help workers and others find progressive ways to rebel. Without such help, there is a strong chance that future rebels will not be able to say No to capitalism effectively. As Miliband underlined, the erosion of beliefs that a 'comprehensive alternative to capitalist society' is possible

> . . . is a matter of immense importance. For, in suggesting that there is no real alternative to the capitalist society of today, it plays its own part in creating a climate of thought which contributes to the flowering of poisonous weeds in the capitalist jungle . . . racism, sexism, xenophobia, anti-Semitism, ethnic hatreds, fundamentalism, intolerance . . .[33]

Providing such help means that the Left must be capable of confronting and surmounting the present crisis. Crises are beginnings as well as endings.

NOTES

Thanks to Jane Jenson for great help.

1. *Marxism and Politics* (Oxford: Oxford University Press, 1977), p. 188–189.
2. Greater divergence existed in the rest of Scandinavia and in other smaller Northern European societies, even if many of the elements were put into place.
3. My own memories of Ralph Miliband's famous 'problems of contemporary socialism' at the LSE from 1962–1964 are of an intellectual collective prodded by Miliband to confront all of these arguments, from the Left, in an open-ended and tolerant way. The subsequent Left intellectual and political production of generations of Miliband's students demonstrates how effective this seminar, and its later complement, the LSE master's programme in political sociology, turned out to be.
4. Miliband was a notable exception here. *Parliamentary Socialism*, his first book, published in 1961 (London: Allen and Unwin), explored the 'relative autonomy' of the linkages between the Labour Establishment and British capitalism and elucidated the complex social mechanisms that led Labour to behave as it had done since the war. To Miliband it was not simply cravenness and bad ideas that led to compromise, but institutions and their workings.
5. Ralph Miliband was a persistent exception here as well. Although after 1989 he began to rethink his own experience with such matters, during the post-war period he was as careful as any major Left intellectual to sort out genuine socialist internationalism from pro-Soviet and anti-democratic cant. Stories of Miliband standing up in the midst of Soviet and Cuban 'high masses' and, in stentorian tones, telling important leaders the truth about their own behaviours are legendary. Miliband's own injunctions about distin-

guishing military intervention from socialist internationalism are worth citing. '. . .(Socialist military intervention) has generated great uncertainty, confusion and division. And it has commonly led to the adoption of positions which are not based on any obvious socialist principle but rather on antecedent sympathies or antipathies, according to which a particular intervention is approved or condemned . . .' in Miliband, *Class Power and State Power* (London: Verso, 1983), pp. 230–1.

6. The work of intellectuals like Miliband in universities was of particular importance to the socialist radicalization of student rebels, particularly in Anglo-Saxon settings where the cogent presentation of alternative, often Marxist, ideas sweeping away the bland arguments in vogue about growing social and political consensus was a breath of fresh air. This work was particularly appreciated by students when the intellectuals in question were open and sympathetic towards the actions of student rebels and willing to break with the self-protective professional conventions of the academy. Ralph Miliband was one of these rare such individuals.

7. Ralph Miliband's *The State in Capitalist Society* (1969) was the most important contribution to this debate. That the 'state' was a complex entity separable from government and the workings of the economy, but ultimately linked as a pivot in the maintenance of capitalist democratic societies, and that it deserved new analysis may seem obvious in retrospect. It was most certainly not so at the time, however, either among 'bourgeois' specialists or Left analysts. Miliband's book spoke directly and clearly to both. Like *Parliamentary Socialism*, it stressed the need to ground theory in empirical investigation and eschewed the formalistic structuralism found in the works of Nicos Poulantzas. The exchanges between Miliband and Poulantzas helped launch the broader debate on the capitalist state. The 'theory of the state' debate which raged through academe made Ralph Miliband one of the most-cited of political scientists, as confirmed in a survey done by the American Political Science Association in the 1970s.

8. Among the most important of these contributions were Miliband's *Marxism and Politics* (Oxford: Oxford University Press, 1977) and Nicos Poulantzas' *State, Power and Socialism* (London: Verso, 1978). Ironically, after their earlier debate, these two new works showed that their authors had come to share many assumptions and outlooks.

9. *Socialism For A Sceptical Age* (Cambridge: Polity Press, 1994), p. 69.

10. Fritz Scharpf's magnificent *Crisis and Choice in European Social Democracy* (Ithaca: Cornell University Press, 1991) analyzes the impossible policy dilemmas posed for social democratic governments in the new circumstances.

11. See Göran Therborn, 'The Two-Thirds, One-Third Society,' in Stuart Hall and Martin Jacques, eds. *New Times* (London: Lawrence and Wishart, 1989). Gösta Esping Anderson's *Three Worlds of Capitalism* (Princeton: Princeton UP, 1990) traces labour market changes of this kind in a comparative way.

12. The degree of union movement decline varies from country to country. For some figures, see Jelle Visser, *European Trade Unions in Figures* (Boston: Kluwer, 1989).

13. For European data see Guido Baglioni and Colin Crouch eds. *European Industrial Relations* (Beverly Hills: Sage, 1990).

14. There is a gigantic literature on such matters. See, among other things, Rober Boyer, ed. *The Search for Labour Market Flexibility* (Oxford: Clarendon Press, 1988); Richard Hyman and Wolfgang Streeck eds. *Industrial Relations and Technical Change* (Oxford: Blackwell, 1988); Michael Piore and Charles Sabel, *The Second Industrial Divide* (New York: Basic, 1984); Steven Wood, ed. *The Transformation of Work* (London: Unwin, 1989).

15. Richard Gillespie, in concluding his edition of a group of articles on European social democratic renewal, announced '. . . the existence of a European 'wave' of social democratic programmatic renewal effort during the 1980s, the sweep of which was if anything broader that the previous renewal wave in the 1950s.' p. 174 in *West European Politics*, 16,1, January 1993, Special Issue on Rethinking Social Democracy in Western Europe,

edited by Richard Gillespie and William E. Patterson.

16. Education and retraining programmes are a favourite new policy area, as are income maintenance and 'social reinsertion' programmes for those who must be sacrificed to enhance factor mobility.

17. The fascinating story of the French Left's first years in power, including the 'great shift' of 1982–83, is told from a number of policy points of view in George Ross, Stanley Hoffmann and Sylvia Malzacher eds. *The Mitterrand Experiment* (New York: Polity-Oxford, 1987). Among the useful French sources see Roland Favier and Pierre Martin-Rolland, *La Décennie Mitterrand*, 2 volumes (Paris: Seuil, 1991, 1992) and Serge Halimi, *Sysyphe est fatigué, les échecs de la gauche au pouvior* (Paris: Robert Laffont, 1993).

18. On Spanish labour see Robert Fishman, *Working-Class Organization and the Return to Democracy in Spain* (Ithaca: Cornell University Press, 1990); See also Richard Gillespie 'The Break-up of the 'Socialist Family': Party-Union Relations in Spain, 1982–1989', *West European Politics* 13/1 (January 1990). Richard Gillespie, *The Spanish Socialist Party* (New York: Oxford UP, 1989).

19. We could also include the Portuguese Socialists, who followed a route like the Spanish. The Italian Socialists, given the Italian political system, followed a sinuous route of national coalition-building which led their leader, Bettino Craxi, to become Prime Minister. As we now know, the operation was premised on a corrupt clientelism which has destroyed the party's credibility and may put Craxi and his lieutenants in prison.

20. The strength of the Left in the broader orbit of British Labour, plus the powerful pull of workerism in British social democratic culture, was what made Labour's movement towards 'modernization' so complex. Ralph Miliband was a central figure in organizing alternatives to this evolution. The Socialist Society, which he and others founded in the early 1980s, became a remarkable centre for Left debate, later eliciting the Chesterfield conferences. Miliband's 1982 book *Capitalist Democracy in Britain* (Oxford: Oxford University Press) was an important benchmark for the Left in this long, and ultimately losing, struggle.

21. The illustrative material could be endless, including, among others, the German and Austrian, Dutch and Danish Social Democrats. Closer to North American home, albeit on a provincial level in Canada's federal system, the experience of the Rae New Democrat government after 1991 is classic.

22. For an excellent review of this see Andrew Martin, in Peter Gourevitch et al *Unions and Economic Crisis* (London: Allen and Unwin, 1984). On employer attacks see Peter Swenson *Fair Shares* (Ithaca: Cornell University Press, 1990). On broader economic policy matters see Jonas Pontusson, *The Limits of Social Democracy* (Ithaca: Cornell University Press, 1992).

23. Good sources for general comparative considerations of these matters are Frances Fox Piven, ed. *Labour Parties in Postindustrial Societies* (Cambridge: Polity, 1991) and Perry Anderson and Patrick Camiller, eds. *Mapping The West European Left* (London: Verso, 1994).

24. One of Ralph Miliband's strengths was the distance that he kept from *ouvriérisme*, even if this connected with one of his few weaknesses, a similar distancing from the political economy of class analysis altogether. Unlike the workerists who saw in the life of trade-unionism and the spontaneous expressions of working class culture direct emanations of rebelliousness and a desire to transcend capitalism, Miliband saw workers in ordinary circumstances as quite conservative. Miliband was primarily interested in the sociology and practice of politics. Beyond this his convictions were that capitalism was a social system that inevitably created its own persistent oppositions from workers and others. What counted, to use a term that he employed frequently, was the 'desubordination' of different social groups which varied in time and which the capitalist state and capitalist politicians spent their time trying to minimize. At certain points, however, efforts at

containment were insufficient, and then significant change became possible. Here Miliband's conception of the Left's role entered, for it was the Left's task to keep alive and promote ideas about the nature and direction of such change – towards socialism – so that they would be available at precisely such moments. For a more general survey of this perspective, see Ralph Miliband, *Divided Societies* (Oxford: Oxford University Press, 1989).

25. Here Miliband's great colleague and rival, Nicos Poulantzas, was for once more acute in his analysis than Miliband himself. Poulantzas was convinced of the growing political importance and complex identities of what he labelled the 'new petite bourgeoisie.' To Poulantzas, the 'desubordination' of these groups visible in the 1960s and 1970s was of a very different type from that of workers, and in many cases contradictory to it. See Nicos Poulantzas, *Classes in Contemporary Capitalism* (London: Verso, 1975).

26. Many ex-revolutionaries then connected with the 'new social movements' while others became apostate Left intellectuals, making new, media-sponsored careers denouncing their earlier selves, along with 'master narratives' and various other mortal dangers stemming from the hubris of the Enlightenment. The French 'new philosophers' were the most outrageous practitioners of such apostasy, but they were far from alone.

27. In the eyes of Touraine and his followers the movements of which social democracy and the Left were components were attached to the earlier social forms of industrial society and destined to decline. See Alain Touraine et al. *The Workers' Movement* (Cambridge: Cambridge UP, 1991).

28. Habermasian celebrators of NSMs proudly announced that the movements had transcended earlier fixations on capitalism, the market and the 'material' more generally. Claus Offe had the rare perspicacity, however, to note that the positioning of NSMs between Left and Right was problematic, depending a great deal on how both poles reacted to new sources of protest. See Claus Offe in *Social Research*, Summer, 1985.

29. The most valiant effort to avoid the excommunicative reductionism of Tourainians and Habermasians and the relativism of post-modernists while connecting 'old' with 'new' forms of protest, that of Ernesto Laclau and Chantal Mouffe, *Hegemony and Socialist Strategy* (London: Verso, 1985) attacked the Left for its attachment to metanarrative while reinventing its own vague metanarrative about the forward progress of democracy.

30. *Socialism for a Sceptical Age* p. 57.

31. The major exception was the Comintern where, in fact, national Communist parties were subordinated to the objectives of the Soviet Union.

32. There are very good empirical illustrations of this. Labour's inability to generate more effective transnational cooperation within the European Community/Union after 1985 undoubtedly helped make the consequences of the '1992' programme and its sequels even more neo-liberal than they might have been.

33. *Socialism for a Sceptical Age* p. 70.

ONCE MORE MOVING ON: SOCIAL MOVEMENTS, POLITICAL REPRESENTATION AND THE FUTURE OF THE RADICAL LEFT*

Hilary Wainwright

Introduction

A paradox highlights the problem facing the radical left in Britain to-day. Historically the British working class movement has been one of Europe's strongest: the earliest, the most densely organised, one of the most militant and associated throughout its history with a rich variety of wider democratic movements and co-operative experiments. Yet the British state has remained one of the most undemocratic in Europe, retaining close protective bonds with the financial heart of British capitalism. It is as if some resilient, invisible membrane has separated the labour and other democratic social movements from unsettling the real centres of economic power in Britain. No doubt the membrane has many constituents but one is certainly the highly mediated, indirect way in which extra-parliamentary radicalism is represented – but in effect diffused – by the Labour Party. The membrane is held in place by the majoritarian, first-past-the-post electoral system which makes it very difficult for minorities on the left, reflecting radical social forces, to thrive and gain a voice of their own.

The problem of how to create such a voice; how, in other words, to establish a socialist organisation in Britain 'able to attract a substantial measure of support and hold out genuine promise of further growth',[1] was one of Ralph Miliband's theoretical and practical preoccupations. It was one I shared with him. The idea was not and is not some grandiose fantasy of replacing the Labour Party. The aim is rather to create an independent, insubordinate challenge and spur to the left of Labour.

In 'Moving On' in *Socialist Register* 1976 Ralph looks back over the period since 1956. He concludes that in the intervening twenty years the radical left in Britain made no progress towards establishing such 'an effective political formation'. 'A lot has happened in the Labour movement in these years, and much of this has been positive.' 'But,' he insists: 'in

*I want to thank Leo Panitch and Aleks Sierz for their very helpful comments and suggestions in editing this essay.

organisational and programmatic terms there has been no advance.'[2] Ralph had a rare ability to see and report the left's weaknesses with cool clarity and without despair. In 'Moving On' as in all his political writings, he addressed these difficulties all the better to overcome them.

He analysed the enormous problem posed by the Labour Party. Electorally it is the party of the majority of the working class and the only left party with any 'mass' membership; yet at the same time it is irretrievably tied to the reproduction of British capitalism, albeit in an ameliorated form. Ralph describes how this difficulty is compounded by the debilitating but deeply and widely held illusion that the Labour Party could become an instrument for socialism, an illusion which imprisons the left of the party in permanent subordination.

He then describes the predicament of the Communist Party of Great Britain with its significant base in the trade unions, but its inability to gain any electoral representation. He challenges its defensive acceptance of the Labour Party's irrevocable domination of the labour movement. He is contemptuous of its attempts to inflect the Labour Party leftwards while at the same time denying any belief that 'the Labour Party will be transformed into the kind of socialist organisation required to assume the leadership of socialist advance in Britain.'[3] The CPGB was a party doomed to remain marginal.

Finally, Ralph addresses the question of why the groups on the radical left – most notably at that time, the International Socialists and the International Marxist Group – whose growth was in part a response to exactly the failings he had analysed of the Labour and Communist Parties, had not fared better. As he remarks, 'a good deal depends on the answer.' After considering the explanations the groups themselves suggest – ruling class hegemony, the reformism of existing working class parties and their leaders – or the explanations which highlight the sectarian, internally rigid organisation of these groups, he focuses on the inappropriateness of their Bolshevik perspective. 'It is *this* which produces their isolation' and what he describes earlier as their 'lack of implantation.' (And this isolation in turn disposes them to a dogmatic and sectarian style.) By Bolshevik he means an underlying understanding of socialist change based on a revolutionary seizure of power on the Bolshevik model of 1917. He argues that in the context of a parliamentary bourgeois democratic regime, a strategy of socialist advance has to include a real measure of electoral legitimation.

So his essay ends with a statement of the need for a new kind of party: one which aims to achieve representation within existing political institutions but which is also involved in many different forms of action, pressure and struggle. He does not in this essay emphasise or explore the distinctiveness of such a party, with its strategic perspectives fitting into neither the parliamentary nor the Bolshevik models that have underlain the division within the socialist movement over the last 50 years. He returns to this theme in his last book *Socialism for a Sceptical Age* in ways which I will discuss below.

In 1995, nearly a further 20 years on from Ralph's survey, has the radical left in Britain moved on? Has it come nearer to defining the kind of 'political formation' that could be effective for a strategy for socialist transformation in Britain in the 21st century? Has it begun to prepare at least the elements that might constitute it?

Twenty years of change

Four very different kinds of changes have occurred in the past twenty years which influence both the character and the potential for a political organisation to the left of the Labour Party a political formation with both parliamentary representation and a significant active base in society. At the risk of opening a Pandora's Box of questions, which I have no chance of answering in this essay, I want to emphasise that these changes have also influenced the vision and perspectives of the radical left.

First, there has been the rise of 'new' social movements on the left - indeed several waves of them. These have been an expression of thoroughgoing frustration with the existing parties and political system. There is nothing unique to the past twenty five years or so in the mere fact of movements forming around new issues of social justice, emancipation, democracy and peace. What has been distinctive about the movements which have waxed and waned repeatedly since the late 60s is their sense of themselves as more than protest movements or efforts to extend the agenda of mainstream parties. I am thinking of the student, feminist, lesbian and gay, ecological, peace and solidarity movements and also many community based groups, alternative or 'counter-cultural' projects and networks, organisations of ethnic minorities and radically-minded parts of the trade union movement. They have in common an explicit sense of themselves as direct agencies of social and political transformation, with their own methods and understandings of political power. From their origins they have turned their backs on the politics of passing the buck: in other words asking others, MPs, councillors, parties, to act on their behalf or 'take their problem to the relevant authorities.' Instead they have experimented with a politics of doing it themselves. In the course of their struggles they may make a variety of alliances with conventional political parties, but in doing so they are usually assertive of their autonomy and their distinct sources of power and knowledge.

The historical timing of these movements is significant here: they emerged at a time when Labour and Social Democratic Parties – the expression of earlier movements' faith in the power of the vote and parliamentary representation – were in office and had had several previous periods in office. Thus the new radicalism of these movements has been shaped more or less explicitly by experience of both the benefits and the limits of social changes which earlier reformers had believed could be achieved by social democratic governments and their benevolent experts.

Secondly and at the same time, processes of international economic competition and political realignment have meant that both political power and political culture have become increasingly international, and for Britain, European. This has steadily, sometimes imperceptibly, eroded the sovereignty of the British nation state and the foundations of all its peculiarities – for example its centralised character and its disproportional, first-past-the-post electoral system. The external forces of erosion have been periodically hastened by internal pressures from the nations and regions of the United Kingdom. This internationalisation and regionalisation has also widened the horizons of the radical left in Britain. Strategic thinking is influenced increasingly by a growing awareness of the paths pursued by the left on the continent. Also, as the importance of Britain and Europe diminishes on a global scale with the industrialisation of the East and South, experiments in the industrial South, most notably in South Africa and Brazil, are providing new models – precarious and tentative – of the role of popular movements in social transformation and in producing innovative forms of radical political agency.

Thirdly, profound changes have taken place in the Labour Party which are likely to alter radically the way the Labour left, who had hoped that the party would one day be theirs, see their future. Some of these changes are common to social democratic parties throughout Western Europe, for instance the promotion, even in opposition, of an explicitly market-led economic strategy and a weakening of previous commitments to public expenditure and intervention. Some of the changes are specific or at any rate particularly marked, in the British circumstances of four successive election defeats. The strategic thinking of the party's leadership ever since the second of these defeats has been premised on the notion that the trades unions and the Party's left are to blame for Mrs Thatcher's first and second general election victories, in 1979 and '83. Hence, the logic goes, Labour's comeback as a party of government depends on establishing the party's independence from the unions and eliminating from the party all trace of the radical left. While loyalty to the party and its recently elected leader, Tony Blair, as the only alternative to the Tories is strong, dissent over this particular project of supposed modernisation is widespread. It is not restricted to the left itself but also includes party members who, whatever their own beliefs, are loyal to the Labour Party's founding claim to be a broad church. For the time being, at a moment when getting rid of the Tories provides a unifying discipline, this dissent is subdued. But a sign of this instability behind the Labour Party avocado stage sets has been the hostile response to the leadership's rewriting of the party's aims and objectives, followed by a debate in which Tony Blair has been given wary and conditional support. The expression of this pent up dissent in the event of a Labour government will be a central factor influencing the future of the left.

Fourthly, the collapse of the Soviet bloc produced a final crisis in the already confused and divided Communist party of Great Britain, leading to the demolition of what had proved to be, in spite of its merits in particular struggles, a dead end for activists, especially trade union activists, committed to building a left independent of Labour. The end of the Cold War and the way it ended, has had wider reverberations for the radical left. Amongst this left that believes in change that goes to the roots of capitalist society, there has long been an underlying divide. There are those for whom socialism was a project brought about from above, an elitist project carried out by a leadership with the support of the people, on behalf of the people, to meet their needs in a rational way. Such a vision has been most closely associated with the Communist Party: Eric Hobsbawm's *Age of Extremes*[4] expresses its character and faces up to its failure with a breathtaking historical sweep. But it also has had a variety of champions on the Labour left.

On the other hand is the tradition of socialism from below, a prolonged and uneven process of collective self-emancipation in which democratic state power would play a role that was framing and supporting more direct forms of economic and community democracy and self-management. Throughout the 20th Century this tradition has been subordinate, though with moments of heroic expression and daring experiment. These range from the writing and political leadership of Rosa Luxemburg, through the workers councils of 1920s Northern Italy, to the workers councils of Hungary in 1956 and many of the activities of the student revolutionaries of Paris 1968 and more mundanely, the experiments of Ken Livingstone's Greater London Council in the 1980s. Subordination has also allowed this tradition to survive on a somewhat vague promise. It has inspired many cooperative and decentralised initiatives, but in general it has not had to address in a sustained manner the problems of its faith in the capacities of the majority of people and its objectives of eliminating injustice and oppression of ruthless and powerful enemies. The end of the Soviet bloc and the patent failure of socialism as social engineering from above requires exponents and practitioners of this tradition to face up to the realities of dealing with power.

In this process they will be aided by a further consequence of the end of the Cold War. Political debate is slowly releasing itself from sterile polarities: reform versus revolution, parliamentary versus extra-parliamentary –

and related to this, reform of the state and constitution versus popular struggle, individual versus collective, state versus market. A shift from such polarities had already begun under the impact of social movements, especially feminism.

I will argue that these changes are producing a conjuncture in which the radical left can move on and is tentatively doing so. Moreover, an arduous and sometimes apparently futile process of preparation has been going on over the last twenty years, trying not so much to found a new organisation, but to create and maintain connections of solidarity and intellectual engagement amongst those on the left whose political commitment does not end with the Labour Party. It has been and continues to be a process which does not lay down the form that a popularly based organisation of the radical left might take. Rather it has modestly helped to gather, and nurture, practical and intellectual resources to grasp the opportunities to create such an organisation when they arise[5]. This process has built on the work of the 'old' new left in the previous twenty years.[6] Ralph was a central figure in both phases. In the course of this essay, I will attempt to draw some lessons from my own involvement in the work of the last twenty years.

New movements and old parties

The foundational change affecting prospects for a new political agency for the left has been the emergence of social movements with a strong sense of themselves as bringing about radical social change through directly challenging the institutions they experience as oppressive. The signs of this were apparent as Ralph wrote, but their significance only became clear in Britain in the eighties – and even now it is a little hazy. Their organisational forms do not have the visibility, formality or longevity of the traditional organisations of the left with which Ralph's 1976 survey was concerned. They are fluid, diverse and often highly localised. I am not assuming that these movements are in their entirety on the left. But a left has been shaped by them and, in Britain, seeks change through them rather than through any of the parties of the left. Moreover in Britain at any rate, this is not a phenomena limited to a single generation or two: 'the class of '68' for example. The movements of squatters, ravers, anti-road protesters, travellers and organisations of the unemployed that have coalesced with others on the left against the Criminal Justice Bill, now meet regularly to develop what they explicitly describe as a 'Do-It-Yourself (DIY) politics'.

Before reflecting on their distinctiveness and on how far they do represent a moving on, it is important to clarify that the description 'new' does not imply that these movements are counterposed or invariably separate from workers' organisations originating in earlier decades. In Britain a complex lattice work of connections has grown up in which feminists, eco-, peace or anti-racist activists, for example, have had considerable influence on both the policies and ways of organising of the trade unions and vice versa. This process has been uneven and primarily at a local and regional level, but its significance is that the politics of the social movement left is backed by some of the sources of power of the 'old' labour movement; and on the other hand the labour movement has, through the work of these new movement activists, reached constituencies beyond the scope of its traditional, often inflexible and inward-looking, procedures.

One example of these interconnections is the tradition of women's support groups in strikes of mainly male workers. It started with feminists and pro-trade union women in the communities surrounding the Oxford car factories in the early 1970s who organised to counter right-wing housewives seeking to undermine the strikes of car workers resisting new more exploitative work systems. It reached a peak with the extra-ordinary alliance of women in the mining communities, urban feminists, lesbian and gay activists, black groups and rank and file Labour Party and trade union activists, that came together to support the miners in 1984/85. Other examples are the ways in which socialist feminists have worked with trade unions like the shopworkers union USDAW, parts of the textile unions, and the T&GWU to reach out to home workers, especially women, who are best reached through community organising. Further connections include the links the peace movement made and continues to make with some workers in the arms industry; the links between radical scientists and trade unionists over health and safety and the environment, and more recently, local trades councils in towns like Coventry working with animal rights activists against the export of live animals.

In his last book *Socialism For a Sceptical Age* Ralph did address the emergence of new social movements. He recognised that many on the left in the past 25 years or so have found involvement in social movements to be both far more politically effective and more personally satisfying than life in existing political parties. Moreover he acknowledged that movement criticisms of left parties were generally valid and that new movements had been highly successful in forcing upon these parties 'questions they had in an earlier epoch tended to relegate to the periphery of their concerns, or to ignore altogether.'[7] But he insists that, be this as it may, 'parties of the Left do remain of primary importance as a potential, if not actual, instrument of socialist advance.' In defence of this conclusion, he notes the ways that movements wane when the issues that brought them to the fore lose their mobilising force. He points to the experience of the US, a country without a socialist party where, even though there is no shortage of grass roots movements, conservatism holds sway and has been hugely successful in warding off any serious challenge from the left.

After an assessment of the present state and future potential of left parties and movements in the post-Cold War world, he concludes that the radical left's best hope lies with strengthening the left in social democratic parties. He says: 'Ultimately, the best that the left can hope for in the relevant future in advanced capitalist countries (and for that matter elsewhere as well) is the strengthening of left reformism as a current of thought and policy in social democratic parties.'[8]

This appears to represent quite a significant shift from the position he arrived at in the conclusion to the second edition of *Parliamentary Socialism* in 1972. Here he analysed how the lack 'at present' of any effective challenge to an overwhelming preponderance of the Labour Party 'as "the party of the left" helps to explain why so many socialists at the grass roots of the party, the trade unions and even the Communist Party, cling to the belief that the Labour party will eventually be radically transformed.' He ends sternly with both a reprimand and a prescription: 'But the absence of a viable socialist alternative is no reason for resigned acceptance or the perpetuation of hopes which have no basis in political reality. On the contrary, what is required is to begin preparing the ground for the coming into being of such an alternative . . .'[9]

I don't think his argument in *Socialism for a Sceptical Age* is in fact a rejection of this earlier position. It is a particular way of addressing practical and immediate questions of governmental power – a pressing problem after 16 years of brutal Conservative rule. But it can still incorporate the idea of an independent party of the radical left. Ralph's notion of strengthening left reformism depends on the vitality of the left outside Social Democratic Parties as well as, perhaps even more than, inside them. Indeed Ralph notes that 'the emergence of new socialist parties in many countries is one of the notable features of the present time . . . Their growth is essential if the left is to prosper.'[10] He was thinking presumably of the Socialist People's Party which regularly wins between 12 and 17% of the vote in Denmark; the Left Socialists in Norway, a decisive influence in the campaign for a 'no' vote in the referendum on membership of the European Union; the United Left in Spain, formed out of parts of the defunct Spanish Communist Party, the left of the nationalist movements and the independent left from the 1980s to campaign against Spain's membership of NATO; the Green Left in Holland, another product of several left parties, working in close alliance with a variety of social and trade union movements. Above all he was thinking transatlantically of the Workers Party of Brazil, a relatively new party based on the militant workers, peasant and urban social movements of modern Brazil: a party which fights and sometimes wins elections at every level (with the exception, after high hopes, of the top elective job of President) but whose driving strategy for social change rests on grass roots organisation amongst the movements that are its base.[11]

The notion of alliances and coalitions is essential to these new left formations. Their implicit conception of alliances works in two directions: first, sideways, as it were, to other political parties and secondly, outwards to autonomous movements and campaigns. First, an element in their strategy as parliamentary parties involves alliances with – or conditional support for – other parliamentary parties, most notably Social Democratic Parties, to pursue legislative support and gain public resources for radical policies often initiated by movements outside conventional politics. As Ralph says, these parties are not likely to supplant Social Democratic Parties but to act as a spur and a challenge.

In Northern Europe, under proportional electoral systems, it is often the case that Social Democratic Parties have depended on the support of either liberal or centre right parties in order to govern. There is growing pressure on them, to look to their left and consider a federal coalition – already a reality in several regions – with the party on their left, for instance in Germany, the Greens. Similarly in Holland and Denmark at a local level there are many examples of the radical left governing in coalition or giving conditional support to a social democratic majority.

An important example of a relatively open and publicly valued process of negotiated and conditional alliances between a party of the socialist left and a social democratic government is emerging in South Africa in the relation between the South African Communist Party (SACP) and the moderate leadership of the ANC. The relationship no doubt is fraught with tensions and is probably dependent for whatever stability it has on the many decades of common struggle through which all those involved have come. Nevertheless its development could provide important lessons for the North. Central to the SACP's influence is its base in the ANC and trade union movements that became so powerful in South African society in the course of the struggle against apartheid.

This experience illustrates the other direction in which the notion of alliances is so important to the new parties of the left: alliances between parties and autonomous social movements.

Here too Ralph recognised a new possibility, an opportunity for 'moving on'. 'In Marxist thought,' he reminds us, 'dual power has always been taken to mean an adversary relation between a revolutionary movement operating in a revolutionary situation, and a bourgeois government under challenge from that movement. It is, however, possible to think of dual power in different terms: as a partnership between socialist government on the one hand and a variety of grassroots agencies on the other.'[12]

To be effective such a partnership could not be one that was formed the day after an election victory. Consequently this idea must apply to the relation between socialist parties and grass roots movements long before the former achieved office. The exemplary case of such partnership would be the Brazilian Workers Party and its close relation with a variety of autonomous movements and campaigns including the radical trade union movement (CUT).

These two conceptions of alliances (both with other political parties and with autonomous social movements) are implicit in the activities of new left parties in Western Europe. They point to a form of party that is modelled on neither existing Social Democratic or Labour Parties nor of Communist Parties of the past. Certainly, when I talk here of moving on towards an organisation of the radical left in Britain, I am imagining a party which, though in part born out of struggles within these traditional parties – and the lessons drawn from their failures – has a distinctive character that is greatly influenced by both the agendas and the implicit methodology of the new movements – the feminist, green, anti-racist and 1980s peace/anti-Cold War movements in particular.

Questions of political methodology

The influence of these movements on the programmes of all parties on the left, old as well as new, is well known. Less analysed but equally important is the question of methodology: principles of organisation, approaches to power, views of knowledge and of whose knowledge matters. In Britain, where the space for the new left to develop politically has been notably cramped, the explicit development of a new political methodology is a vital condition for moving on. So I will summarise my own assessment of important elements of the methodological differences.

My argument is that in practice, though not yet in any systematic theory, these movements from the late sixties onwards have been pioneering a new and distinct form of political agency in often instinctive revolt at the pompous irrelevance of conventional politics to the problems of everyday life. It is not that everything they do is entirely novel or notably coherent. It is rather that across the movements that have developed independently of established political parties, certain common themes can be identified in the ways that they organise, develop policies and more generally mobilise new sources of power. These themes seem to me to come from a common experience of both the limits of government in parliamentary democracies (and the state that ruled in the name of socialism in the East) and the personal and environmental costs of an overarching emphasis on the priority of economic growth – whether under private ownership or public.

The theme on which I will elaborate, because of its fundamental character – it is not of course the only methodical theme – concerns the character and organisation of knowledge. Discussions about knowledge are not normally the stuff of politics. But state and party institutions are under-

pinned by presuppositions about the character of knowledge and its organisation – for example what constitutes valid knowledge; what knowledge
matters to political decisions; who carries or holds politically significant
knowledge. Normally these presuppositions are just part of the culture of
an institution that people inherit and duly reproduce or more or less unconsciously modify. But when these institutions fail to live up to the
expectations of significant numbers of people and/or break down, and
when people organise radically to transform them, a counter culture
emerges, and the old presuppositions are laid bare. Thus as the traditional
parties of the left (the main subjects of Ralph's 1976 survey) failed
adequately to respond to the new and radical demands of feminism,
ecology, sexual liberation, radical trade unionism and the anti-Cold War
politics of the peace movement, competing conceptions of knowledge
became important in political debate. This is one aspect of the widespread
interest among movement and left activists, at different times in the critical
theory of Marcuse and Habermas, in the 'post-modernism' of Foucault and
Derrida and more recently the critical realism of Bhaskar. Unfortunately,
however, these philosophical debates have rarely been explicitly anchored
in questions of political agency. Indeed some tendencies of post-
modernism have in effect denied the efficacy of purposeful political
activity.[13] Without entering into these debates on this occasion[14] I will
indicate the importance of the challenge of recent social movements to
presumptions of traditional parties of the left to be able to centralise and
codify the knowledge necessary for social change. I will also highlight the
importance of this for questions of political organisation.

The old methods of Social Democratic and Labour Parties on the one
hand and Communist Parties on the other, differ in important ways, and
historically there are many varieties of each. But they share similar roots
which have produced features common to both. Both kinds of parties, for
instance, have traditionally tended either to take social movements under
their wing: 'our womens/peace/tenants movement', 'This Great Movement
of Ours' or, if the movement is too stroppy to be embraced, to give them
leper status and treat them as 'outside our/the movement' – and
presumably irrelevant and doomed. Their underlying assumption is that
power for change lies overwhelmingly through steering the nation state, in
the case of social democratic parties, or in effect, becoming the state in the
case of Communist Parties.

My purpose is to highlight the way that a common focus on the nation
state (i.e. a single focus of popular sovereignty) and with it, the party, as a
single focus of the power to transform, has been underpinned by assumptions about the character of social and economic knowledge. The
understanding of knowledge that shaped state action and especially the use
to which social reformers desired to put the state was based on the model

of the natural sciences. It was an understanding which first developed alongside the ideal of the nation state in the 18th and 19th centuries. This model aspired to formulate general laws describing regular conjunctions of events or phenomena. These laws then provided the premises from which social as well as natural science was thought to be able to make certain predictions and gain evermore perfect knowledge as the discovery of further generalisations progressed. Historically this positivistic model had a progressive impact, countering the reactionary influence of religious faith and superstition on medical, physical and social intervention. It has now been criticised and surpassed in many different ways. For my concern with the *politics* of knowledge the crucial point is that when applied to the study and reform of society, it assumed that general 'scientific' laws were the only valid form of knowledge, hence dismissing the practical, often tacit, uncodified and sometimes uncodifiable knowledge of the majority of people. This in turn favoured a social engineering approach to the process of social change: change from above by those who know the mechanics of society.

In the early 1980s in Britain and in a more sweeping form in the former Soviet bloc in the early 90s, free-market ideology rose from the intellectual grave to challenge this from the right. The theoretical case for the free-market elaborated and propounded most effectively by Frederick Hayek throughout his long life, challenged the possibility of democratic collective intervention in the market. This attack on what Hayek saw as invariably a disastrous social engineering was based on a theory of the economic uses of knowledge which celebrated the intimate knowledge of the individual consumer or entrepreneur. My argument concerning the importance of recent democratic social movements is that in their practice they hold out an alternative to the engineering model of social change – and all the mechanistic ways of organising and 'intervening' which flow from it – *from the left*. Hence a critical theorisation of the innovatory features of their practice provides tools for a more convincing reply to the right than could be made in the past. Their practice combines both a striving towards purposefully bringing about an intended social outcome, with a recognition of the practical, sometimes uncodifiable and hence non-predictive character of much socially and politically important knowledge. Their forms of organisation are frequently shaped specifically for the purpose of socialising, sharing the kinds of 'inside' knowledge unavailable to centralised state and party institutions. It is collective and not individual-istic.

This does not imply an uncritical acceptance of whatever practical knowledge is offered by a movement's membership on the spurious grounds that knowledge from experience has its own inherent truth, 'I am a woman; the knowledge that comes from my experience as a woman is

valid; therefore whatever I say about women's oppression must be true.'
But central to the debates in these movements has been the problem of
collectively arriving at some agreed solution that is based on taking
seriously, without critically accepting, everyone's practical knowledge and
drawing on appropriate historical and theoretical knowledge. The methodology developed from this gives the lie to the right's presumption that the
choice is between state and market; the fantasy of a central brain versus the
pragmatic reality of atomised economic man.

Robert Michels in formulating his ' the iron law of oligarchy' provides,
albeit unintentionally, the best description of how the social engineering
model of social scientific knowledge underpinned the methods of the traditional parties of the left. Writing about the Social Democratic Party in
Germany before World War I, he formulated his law before the founding
of the Third International. But much of what he says about the parties of
the Second International is apposite to the Third. He believes that in any
political organisation, however formally democratic, there is an
unavoidable degree of specialised expertise owned by a professional elite
which, whatever the procedures for accountability, becomes autonomous
from 'the masses', grass roots or base. These, as the term 'the masses'
implies, are understood as undifferentiated in their interests and passive in
their knowledge. Michels assumes that they are capable only of knowing
with which elite their interests lie, and lack the expertise to know, even
partially, how those interests might be met.

Michels took as a 'given' – in accord with the philosophical orthodoxy
of his time – the exclusive importance of scientific or professional
knowledge and the incompetence or ignorance of the masses. 'In all the
affairs of management for whose decision there is requisite specialised
knowledge . . . a measure of despotism must be allowed and thereby a
deviation from the principles of pure democracy. From the democratic
point of view this is perhaps an evil, but it is a necessary evil. Socialism
does not signify everything by the people, but everything for the people'.[15]
Several important assumptions lead Michels to this conclusion. First is the
idea that the only knowledge relevant to the efficacy of the party is a
technical, positivistically construed scientific knowledge that is inaccessible to the ordinary member and, once learnt by an official of the party,
sets him or her apart from the members. Possession of knowledge in
Michels' terms 'emancipates (the officers) from the masses and makes
them independent of their control'.

Second, there is the assumption that facts and values are entirely
separate: that the members are capable simply of establishing the party's
values. The party then appoints or elects an official to collect the appropriate facts, which is a purely technical matter and depends on specialised
knowledge. Parties based on these assumptions have structures for

involving the members in taking decisions of principle – assumed to be entirely separate from questions of implementation. They also have an extensive staff which works with the executive to implement and elaborate these policies. A gulf develops between the members and the leadership because the former have little basis on which to judge the appropriateness of the executive's work from the standpoint of the principles in which they believe. Where they believe the executive to be wrong they have little basis on which to argue for an alternative. They are in effect politically deskilled.

Michels also assumed that a socialist party's energies must unavoidably be fixed on a single goal, around a single locus of power: the goal of capturing the wheel of state power to steer it towards socialism. Organisation, it was assumed, is 'the only means for the creation of a collective will'. And organisation, according to Michels, is based on 'the principle of least effort, that is to say, upon the greatest possible economy of energy'. The metaphors for the kind of party this produced were, not surprisingly, military and mechanical: the party is divided into the 'rank and file' and the 'officers' – an efficient party is also an effective 'electoral machine'. Michels' client party is also an effective 'electoral machine'. Michels remarks, from his observations, that 'there is hardly one expression of military tactics and strategy, hardly a phrase of barrack slang which does not recur again and again in the leading articles of the socialist press'. Efficiency in capturing state power required that the specialised elite ruled as standardised an organisation as possible. Corners of autonomous activity undermined the party. Centralisation made for economies of effort.

Given the underlying political culture which he describes, the iron law of oligarchy does indeed hold. He was writing, however, from within this culture. Having the perspicacity of a trained sceptic he identified its fundamental features, of which many a party cadre, believing the party's democratic rhetoric, would hardly have been conscious. He treats these features as the unavoidable 'givens' of socialist political agency.

Existing new left parties in Europe illustrate radically distinct principles from those of traditional Communist or Social Democratic Parties on all these issues of underlying methodology. First, there is a recognition of sources of knowledge of social needs and possible solutions not encompassed by the kinds of scientific – or 'top down' – knowledge available to a state or party leadership. The second principle involves a recognition of diverse sources of power to change. This stems from the understanding which activists in recent movements have of the power to bring about social change; a view based on an alertness to their own complicity in reproducing and therefore potentially in transforming social institutions. As a result they have identified spheres of everyday life – sexual and familial relations, food consumption and distribution, housing arrangements, transport, work – where non-compliance or experimentation with alternatives can be a source, however limited, of political power, especially if it is exercised in combination with more traditional sources – strike action, political representation, demonstrations. This leads at best to a recognition of quite different political functions requiring quite distinct ways of organising: the organising necessary to build and spread a grass roots movement or to sustain a co-operative business alongside for example, the organising necessary to achieve political representation. So for instance in the Dutch Green Left, the obligations of party membership are based on the assumption that many party members are active in movements that are autonomous of the party, something the party supports. Moreover, on the party's election list and among their MPs are people who are known mainly as leaders of local movements rather than as party spokespeople, thought they support the party's aims.

Knowledge and power are closely related instruments for any effective agency or process of social change. These parties have experimented with new methods of organising which recognise that they have no monopoly of the knowledge and power necessary for changes they desire. The newer parties such as the German Greens (1979) and the Dutch Green Left (1989) see themselves as political voices for movements which are independent but in close association with the party.

Crucial to these new ways of organising is the influence of the movements themselves – including a degree of learning from their failures and limitations. This is why, of all the various changes over the last two decades, I consider the emergence of the new movements as fundamental to the possibilities of 'moving on'. When Ralph wrote in 1976, the old models had reached an impasse, but no new principles of political organisation had emerged. One still cannot talk about a clear and proven new model of left political agency anywhere, least of all in Britain. On the continent, especially Northern countries, the new left parties are an accepted part of public political debate. But even there the impact of the new politics is not assured. Its development depends on the strength of movements outside the political systems. Old methods have a subtle, unconscious pulling power, drawing supposedly innovating organisations back into well established grooves, especially when the objectives of these organisations include public office. This has been a recurrent source of division in the German Greens for instance. They introduced a variety of measures, for example that people should only hold positions of leadership for a limited period (the principle of rotation); that there should always be several spokespeople; that all leading bodies should be made up of at least 50% women. The old methods appear to present the easiest route, especially when, as with West Germany's parliamentary state, they are backed by enormous resources; or as in Britain, where in the past beguiling short cuts to office via taking over sometimes hollow structures of the Labour Party, tempt social movement radicals to devote themselves to committee room manoeuvring. On the other hand occasionally, for example in London in the late 70s and early 80s, it was of great importance for the whole of the radical left that some activists *were* prepared to devote several years to the plotting and manoeuvring – as well as some very creative policy work – necessary to win control of the London Labour Party and hence the Greater London Council. Perhaps this will be a permanent tension, inherent in the very nature of political organisations whose source of radicalism rests on the knowledge and power of grass roots movements but whose stability and lasting, cumulative political impact requires at least a foothold within the existing political system.

Challenges to national sovereignty; openings for the left

But National state institutions and the parties that cleave to them, particularly those of the British state, are being shaken by economic globalisation and political reconfiguration. In the case of Britain, this is an erosion taking place from Europe and from the nations and regions of the UK; it is taking place through institutional changes from above and cultural shifts and organisational innovations from below. Over the past twenty years or so these international developments have stimulated ambitious initiatives from movements on a European scale, whether of an economic kind: workplace trade union leaders developing organised links with equivalent leaders on the continent in industries as diverse as pharmaceuticals, cars and chocolate; or involving previously unorganised workers like the European network of homeworkers; or of a directly political kind, for instance the powerfully pan-European peace movement of the 1980s. Moreover the regional, national and continental challenges to the unitary and centralised British state are opening opportunities by which these movements and other radical social forces could gain more radical political representation.

As processes of globalisation have become apparent, movement forms of organisation have proved more able to mobilise effective kinds of international knowledge and power than political parties whose strategies for change have been exclusively focused on national state power. This comparison should not be exaggerated, because the overwhelming political reality that has accompanied globalisation is the victory of neo-liberalism. Those challenges that have in any way dented the right, however, owe much to the distinctive organisational reach of recent social movements.

A good example of the ability that radical movements have developed to think and organise strategically on an international scale is the peace movement of the early 80s. For a brief but vital moment it influenced the course of European history, in particular the way the Cold War ended. My argument here is not that this movement brought about the end of the Cold War. It was the process of implosion and conscious democratic reform in Gorbachev's Soviet Union that was the prime historic moving force which led eventually to the fall of the wall. But if the hawks in the Western alliance had been unchallenged in the period when Gorbachev called Reagan's bluff and responded to the West's 'Zero Option' – exchanging the scrapping of cruise for that of SS20s – with his offer to dismantle SS20s and negotiate a nuclear free Europe, perestroika and glasnost would probably not have had the time and space to gather the momentum they did. The pan-European peace movement, with its East-West networks; its ability to mobilise simultaneously across Western capitals; its ability to gather, piece together and publicise strategic intelligence on NATO, had an impact on West European public opinion which politicians could not ignore. The West's initial offer of the 'Zero Option' was itself an attempt to defuse the popular anxiety about the siting of cruise missiles across Western Europe. It was made in ignorance of the changes taking place in the Soviet bureaucracy and on the assumption that the Soviet response would be inadequate. The peace movement knew differently. Their contacts gave them an inside knowledge – some would say also a little influence – which gave them greater insight into the momentous processes that were underway.[16]

They did not pack up the camps that surrounded the missile sites, or lift their pressure on all political parties to see the Zero Option through. The result was that the NATO powers, contrary to the initial personal preferences of Thatcher and Reagan, responded favourably to Gorbachev and entered into serious negotiations one of whose by-products was the precarious and unstable path of perestroika. If the peace movement had been powerless and the hawks had had their way, Gorbachev would probably have been rebuffed. As a result, the ending of the Soviet bloc would very likely have been much longer and more drawn out and marked by the kind of violence and state resistance that suppressed the students at Tienanmen Square. In this sense the European peace movement of the 80s influenced history in a way that no national party was able to. Its full goals – the dismantling of Cold War institutions in the West as well as the East – are as yet unfulfilled, but its distinctive political capacities helped to create the international conditions that favoured the generally peaceful way in which the people of the Soviet Union and Eastern and Central Europe brought down their side of the Iron Curtain.

In any cool assessment of the importance of recent grass roots movements for socialist change, these periods of sustained activity and partial success must be balanced by a recognition of how quickly movements can lose their breath, disperse and all but disappear. It is also important to remember how at times of visibility movements have often depended on representatives within the political system, either from 'movement' parties or supporters in traditional parties. For instance, the Dutch and German peace movements – the strength of both of which had a decisive impact on NATO – were significantly aided by the parliamentary work and voices of the Greens, the Dutch Left and left MPs in the social democratic parties of both countries.

The problem of political visibility

Why should representation matter? After all, the strength and persistence of the peace movement in the 1980s shows that some modern social movements have many of the advantages of political organisation that one associates with a party: continuity, memory, cumulative understanding and resources, sustained visibility. The quick-footedness, self-confidence and political maturity of the 1980s peace movement, for instance, owes something to the lasting roots which earlier movements, of feminists, students, anti-nuclear, radical trade union activists had put down. Significant groupings of people who became politically active in the 60s and 70s and who in earlier generations would have been the cadre of Communist or Social Democratic Parties instead devoted their political energies to long term if sporadic independent organising, educating and agitating. Even their personal networks provided a kind of framework for passing on traditions.

A major contribution to this continuity was provided by the infrastructure and communication network of CND. Although CND was only one part of this very widely based movement, its longevity across generations of the radical left and its political visibility make a revealing study in any discussion of the problems of visibility and sustainability facing any notion of an organisation to the left of the Labour Party.

CND was founded in the late 50s in response to the agreement of the then Conservative government to allow US nuclear missiles (the Thor missile) to be sited around the country. It is still going strong with 50,000 members in 1995. Periodically it has brought together the predominantly middle class non-conformist British left, regardless of party. In doing so it has acted as a form of political displacement for a limited but significant section of the British left, a political home for many of the disaffected. It has much of the infrastructure of a party – hundreds of branches; a centre which briefs and informs the members; an annual conference; frequently high profile leaders and something of a common culture. It has even managed to gain political representation and the visibility that flows from it, by making sure that MPs who supported it were very closely identified with the cause, Michael Foot in his early political days being the classic example. At the same time as unintentionally and informally serving a wider political function for the disaffected left, it very strictly limited its formal concerns to nuclear disarmament. This is probably a factor in its longevity and its high visibility. Different parts of the left came together because they agreed on one central issue: banning the bomb. The intense ideological debates took place in the pub and on the demonstrations. Also, under Britain's present political system it is probably only by being, or presenting itself, as a single issue campaign that a movement can gain sustained political representation and hence visibility.

In these ways CND is the exception that proves the rule that without parliamentary representation a social movement can easily become invisible. Normally a left movement that has broad political goals has no direct access to the political system. Not only does it therefore lack political visibility but it tends to become abstract and overly propagandistic in its appeal. Political representation acts as a focus and a pressure on an organisation to translate its aspirations into specific proposals about the exercise of power. Moreover the experience of trying (whether through the New Left Clubs of the 1950s or the Socialist Society in the 1980s and the Socialist Movement in the 1990s) shows the difficulties of establishing lasting local, regional structures amongst the independent activists of the radical left in Britain, where such structures cannot feed into a political organisation with a national public presence able to reach out and gain popular support.

Organisation on a purely extra-parliamentary basis is extremely difficult to sustain. Given the fact that the media reflect the parliamentary and majoritarian definition of politics in Britain, an extra-parliamentary left, even with a few sympathetic Labour MPs, is in effect organising in the dark. It takes a great effort of will to keep up one's own forms of communication when the movement gains little validation from the wider society. An example would be the fate of the left that came together during the 1984–85 miners strike and later led to the creation of the Socialist Movement. During the strike there was a tremendously active and creative coalition involving, especially at local level, just about every social and trade union movement and almost all the organisations of the left. Efforts were made to build something from this: for example a Socialist Conference attended by nearly 2,000 people was held in Chesterfield in 1986 attracting significant national publicity. These conferences have continued, and a movement has been partially institutionalised, even to the extent of launching an independent magazine for the wider left, *Red Pepper*. Moreover, in most towns and cities there is an active radical left that comes together across party and organisational boundaries around major issues of the day. It is tempting to think of this network of disparate activists as a party in waiting; in reality it is a coalition of the disenfranchised with as yet no very clear definition of its future. Moreover, involvement in these and other somewhat precarious projects of the radical left is far far smaller than on the continent where it has its own political presence. In sum, the marginal fate of the radical left in Britain is a telling witness to the limits of extra-parliamentary movements in parliamentary democracies.

In recent years, however, both the internal and external challenges to the existing British state have increased the possibilities of direct political representation for the radical left.

Already in Scotland the level of political debate and negotiation provides something of an inspiration and encouragement to democrats and pluralist socialists south of the border. All parties bar the Tories have highly developed proposals for a Scottish Parliament involving proportional representation and positive discrimination to remedy the disadvantages facing women. The Labour Party in Scotland, reluctantly and still with a few laggards, has had to accept that it cannot rule the roost of the left. A left exists independently and in electoral competition with Labour. Such a left is in part represented by the Scottish National Party (SNP), a party whose present leadership and the majority of its membership are well to the left of Labour, though it is first and foremost a nationalist party. Scottish Militant, a small but very active party formed, as its name implies, by Scottish members of the Trotskyist, 'entrist' group Militant when they were expelled from the party, has also built a small electoral base through the leading role it played in the campaign against the poll tax and on other problems facing working class communities in Scotland.

Developments in Ireland also shake the status quo of Britain's unwritten codes of oligarchic rule. Although there is unlikely to be any lasting democratic settlement until after the next general election, debate and negotiations are driving towards a written constitution. The associated constitutional issues of bills of rights, electoral systems, degrees of decentralisation and the ending of the hold of Westminster are all becoming central to public debate. The cultural and information flows between Eire, Northern Ireland, Scotland, England and Wales make it impossible to innoculate the English mainland against the democracy bug, especially, when the mainland carries independent campaigns like Charter 88, Liberty and the Electoral Reform Society or politically allied groups like the Labour Campaign for Electoral Reform.

The pressure for electoral reform is strongly reinforced from Europe. Membership of the European Union requires Britain to introduce a proportional electoral system for the European elections by 1996. Constitutional conservatives in both major parties will have great difficulty preventing such a reform from attracting public interest and spreading to the elections for Westminster, especially with the all-party − bar the Tory minority − agreement for a proportional system in the Scottish Parliament, to whose creation the Labour leadership is committed. The extent of public disaffection with existing political parties, and the general sense of not being represented – both well-documented in opinion polls – is also likely to lead to a spread of interest in a more proportional electoral system once people have had a taste of the extended choices for which it can allow.

A further institutional pressure stemming from Europe is (paradoxically, given the concern over the democratic deficit in Brussels) the way that it provides an alternative source of resources and political platform to Westminster. It thus strengthens decentralising pressures against party leaderships seeking to tighten central control and helps to pluralise British politics. An example of the former is the way that radical employment, social or ecological projects in many British cities – previously funded by left wing local authorities – have been able to get money from the European Commission which is not available from the government. This experience has helped to nurture the seeds of regional consciousness and militancy in different regions of the UK as well as fuelling national consciousness in Scotland and Wales.[17]

Another pluralising mechanism can be seen in the way that the emergence of the European Parliament as an increasingly serious political platform upsets the ultimately centralised character of the Labour Party (the power of the parliamentary leadership through its extensive capacities for patronage). Members of the Labour Group of the European Parliament, which increasingly offers a career structure of its own, are not beholden in any way to the Westminster leadership. Neither does Walworth Road, the Labour Party's HQ, have anything like as much influence over the choice of candidates for European constituencies. They have the independence to develop their own line. A recent example was when nearly half of the Labour MEPs publicly challenged Tony Blair's attempts to eliminate a commitment to common ownership from the Party's constitution. Several of them, most notably Ken Coates, went on to argue the relevance of common ownership for a European economy. Such a rebellion would be unthinkable among MPs. It gave a considerable fillip of confidence to activists in the constituencies and unions who wanted to challenge the direction of the new leadership.

Another source of the political and intellectual confidence of the left MEPs is the fact they have allies to their left in votes and campaigns in the European Parliament. The experience of working with the new left parties on the continent has begun to break down the fear of such parties that has long been a feature of the political monoculture of the British labour movement – in which any talk of left alternatives to Labour is viewed as a betrayal. It has even enabled left Labour MEPs to observe that the existence of an electoral and extra-parliamentary competitor to the left of social democracy usually strengthens the hand of the left inside these social democratic parties and more generally adds to critical and left influences on the whole political culture. Such thoughts have historically been inimical to Labour Party thinking. Labourism involved a political logic which transfers, inappropriately and indiscriminately, the imperatives of industrial unity – 'one out all out'; the importance of unity for the effectiveness of strike action – to politics, a sphere where a more pluralist ethos would be more appropriate to the lively political culture of the left. Here Tony Blair's leadership – despite his claim to modernise – deploys this anti-pluralist ethic of old Labour as a bulwark to the leadership's power. In this organisational sense he is just the latest chip off old Labour's block.

How might the break up of Labour's monoculture develop and allow democratic expression of the views and activities of the radical left?

Labour's options and the end of the left's illusions

The former Cambridge economist and adviser to Labour in the 1960s, Nicholas Kaldor, once remarked that if post-war regulations over the movement and conduct of finance were lifted there would never again be a Labour government. What he did not anticipate was Labour learning to live with financial deregulation and operating monetarist policies along with some mild social reforms. The Spanish and French Socialist Parties responded to the mobility of capital in this way, and Tony Blair's Labour Party shows every indication of governing in the same way.

Its rhetoric proclaims a passionate and no doubt sincere concern with social justice and the righting of sixteen years of Tory wrongs. Labour's new leadership is determined, however, not to make specific policy commitments beyond those that have been proved by the opinion polls to be uncontroversial. This is not inertia or unconscious cowardice but electoral strategy. It hopes to glide into office on fair winds released by the collapse of the Major government, steering according to the lights of middle England. Any specific commitment of which the public is yet to be convinced is a hostage to fortune, an electoral gaffe. At times this can make Labour spokespeople appear evasive and totally unconvincing. If it were not for the extent of the failure, the corruption and the divided state of the government, one would seriously doubt the tactical wisdom – not to mention deeper strategic disagreements – of this approach.

My purpose here, however, is not to second-guess Labour's electoral advisers but to explore the likely dynamic of Labour politics in the event of a Labour government – either a Labour majority or a coalition with the Liberal Democrats. To consider likely developments in depth we need to ask a question to which many loyal but independent minded activists have assumed, as they gave support to Tony Blair, that there is a positive answer. Is there any possibility that the softly, softly, no commitments tactics are simply that: tactics to get into government? Once in government will Tony

Blair implement a programme of radical reform on which his research team has been working discreetly in the meantime?

Certainly there is no lack of alternative policies which are quite compatible with the modernisation of Labour. The most coherent are provided by Will Hutton, *The Guardian's* Economics Editor in his latest book *The State We're In*[18]. This is in effect a manifesto for modernising British capitalism. Hutton argues that the economic weakness of British capitalism lies in its financial system with its high profit targets and its short-term horizons. He also argues that this has been sustained by and has symbiotically reinforced Britain's unmodernised, undemocratic political system. He argues for a radical, republican overhaul of the City and industry which would involve a regionalised Bank of England, a German model of workers rights vis à vis management and regulatory measures to ensure the greater availability of finance for long term and socially useful investment. He also argues for a thoroughgoing democratisation of every state institution aimed at the sharing of sovereignty between local, regional, national and continental levels of government and civic associations, and at the dethroning of the executive and particularly the Treasury. He further urges that Britain should play a leading role in establishing stable democratic international economic institutions. It is not socialism, but, if it were to be implemented by Labour, it would be very widely supported within the party.

The problem, however, for a party that has gained office by stealth as Labour seems intent on doing, is that it will not have built a public awareness, the groundswell of popular pressure that would put the City and similar entrenched interests on the defensive. Putting Will Hutton in the Cabinet or employing him as an adviser would not be a solution. For the problem is not simply of devising the reforms but, given their challenging character, the current condition is winning public understanding and confidence in the reforms. This requires a pre-election campaign of persuasion and consciousness–raising which at the time of writing Tony Blair seems to be avoiding like the plague.

In the absence of a strong public campaign on these kind of reforming economic and social policies, a majority or even more so, a minority Labour government is likely to come into serious conflict with many of its own supporters in the trade unions, in parliament and amongst the public more generally – people will expect that a Labour government will mean the end of the absolute rule of the market and a noticeable improvement in the lives of millions of people. These are the kinds of circumstances in which Left Labour MPs are likely to vote against the party whip and ally themselves with extra-parliamentary campaigns rather than fall in behind government action.

In fact, in the event of a minority Labour government, a well organised, politically coherent band of Left MPs could have as much bargaining power as the Liberal Democrats. The Socialist Campaign Group of MPs (the most organised group of left MPs) has not been notable for its coherence in the past five years or so. But recent new recruits from the 1993 election appear to be joining with others to make it a more effective body. However, the variables involved in the event of some kind of Labour government make it too complex to predict the form that divisions in the party, and most significantly the unions, might take.

But several points can be made with certainty which return us to some of the reasons behind Ralph's conclusion that by 1976 the left had not moved on. First, most radical socialist members of the Labour Party, including MPs, have few if any illusions about turning it into a socialist party, whether with one, two or three more heaves. That does not mean they will walk away from it in disgust when a Labour government fails to introduce radical economic reform – though some certainly will. They feel the party or at least parts of it are as much, if not more, 'their party' as the leadership's – and they will fight for their right to remain in the party on their own terms. The constitutional reforms in the late 1970s and early 1980s, especially mandatory reselection of MPs, has had the effect of strengthening the bond between effective and conscientious MPs and their constituency party. Most of the Campaign Group MPs fit into that category. Before any rebellious stand they will work to bring significant sections of the party with them. But they too are under no illusions about where power in the party lies.

The late Richard Crossman, left of centre member of Labour Cabinets in the 1960s, political diarist and political theorist, once made a classic comparison between the 'dignified' elements of Britain's unwritten constitution disguising the realities of power and a similar mystification in the structure of the Labour Party. 'In order to maintain the enthusiasm of party militants to do the organising work for which the Conservative Party pays a vast army of workers,' argues Crossman, 'a constitution was needed which apparently created a full party democracy while excluding (these militants) from power'[19]. With the constitutional reforms of the late 70s and early 80s 'these militants', with support from thousands of trade unionists, threatened to intrude into the party's centres of power. Some accommodated to this power; others have been rudely pushed back. But many of them have seen through the constitution's dignified appearance and become fully aware of their position. They know that they may have a power base in the party but that this is not realistically a spring board for the centres of party power. More likely it is a way outwards and sideways to the left and movements outside the party and a platform to communicate to the wider public. This is how they use it.

The other notable way in which the left in the Labour Party have moved on from the state of affairs that Ralph described in 1976 is that they no longer conduct themselves as subordinates. In terms of the power structure of the party they are under no illusion that they are in a subordinate position, but they have no hesitation in drawing on other sources of power to win political victories independently of Labour's front bench. Tony Benn sets the example. He constantly runs his own campaign on matters of government abuses of power regardless of the Party leadership. On the basis of considerable popularity, reluctant respect and interest from the media he sometimes wins and almost always strikes a noticeably insubordinate note of opposition. Other MPs, Jeremy Corbyn and Chris Mullin for instance, are associated with impressive victories in the Courts over the appalling miscarriages of justice and helped free the wrongfully convicted Birmingham Six and Guildford Four, where the powerful opposition came from a persistent extra-parliamentary campaign.

These features of the radical Labour Left also reveal something about the left outside Westminster and frequently outside the Labour Party: that diffuse though it is, it has the potential to provide a power base of its own. Whether on the issue of cruise missiles in the 80s, the Gulf War in the 90s; over the poll tax, education, hospital closures, the rights of the disabled, or the Criminal Justice Act, movements have been organised independently of the Labour Party – or of any party. Most of the activists who come together in these movements and regularly participate in local networks of the left are in no hurry to join or form a party. Whether Labourist or Leninist, parties do not have a good record as far as most of the left in Britain is concerned. But this does not mean these activists limit themselves to 'single issue' politics. Amongst many of them there is a strong desire to make connections across issues and localities and to define a shared vision based on common wealth, common land, equality, justice, sustainability and do-it-yourself politics.

A minority of left activists have joined the Green Party. And in recent years, following a split with the more parliamentarist – moderate – group of well known personalities, this party is open to close collaboration with others on the radical left, inviting left Labour MPs and independent socialists to speak at their conference and collaborate in their campaigns. A smaller minority has joined the Socialist Workers Party, which though energetic and persistent has not, for all its longevity, managed seriously to grow or extend its impact beyond the campuses and occasional workplaces and union branches. It includes many serious and effective socialists, and it is likely to grow as individuals leave a Labour Party whose leadership intends to drop the party's founding socialist commitment. But as an organisation it has not really moved on from the isolated and often sectarian position Ralph describes in his 1976 survey.

In sum then, and trying with difficulty to be as cool in my assessment as Ralph was in his, I would argue that there *has* been progress in the last twenty years towards 'an effective political formation' of the radical left. But it has been uneven and incomplete. It cannot be measured by membership cards, numbers of branches, election victories or the size of the 'troops' on the ground. The progress has been in the growth of a self-confident left without illusions about Labour (inside as well as outside the Labour Party) and able to reach out to and ally with movements independent of Labour; in the methodological foundations for a political organisation that is rooted in the daily life and struggles of working people but has representatives in the political system; in creating coalitions of like-minded radical leftists across formal party divides. It is too early to tell how these changes will combine with others to produce the political agency we need. After all, it has been done successfully elsewhere in Western Europe. The British left, more particularly the English left, tends to be a little slow. But with the British state, the symbol and part cause of our inertia, under pressure from all sides, and with the chance to add to that pressure ourselves if and when Labour is in office, we might catch up. Perhaps too, if we are attentive to the experiences and lessons of others, we can gain from being late.

NOTES

1. See Ralph Miliband, 'Moving On', *Socialist Register* 1976, ed. Ralph Miliband and John Saville. Merlin Press, London p. 128.
2. Ibid.
3. Ibid. pp. 133 & 134.
4. Eric Hobsbawm, *The Age of Extremes,* Michael Joseph, London 1994.
5. For myself this is a process which began by attending the Conferences of the Institute for Workers Control in the late 60s and early 70s, usually in Birmingham, Nottingham or Sheffield. These brought together from all over the country local left wing working class leaders of an independent turn of mind, those intellectuals from the 'old' new left engaged with grass roots politics, and activists from the new student movement and even the emerging women's movement. Then in 1981 came the 2,000 strong conference following the publication of *Beyond the Fragments* which I co-authored with Sheila Rowbotham and Lynne Segal. Following this, in 1982, came the foundation of the Socialist Society committed to socialist education, research and propaganda of a radical kind, independent of party. In 1986, in the aftermath of the miners strike, when there was the strong pressure for a left movement that was not tied to the increasingly hostile inner life of the Labour Party but on the other hand did not involve withdrawal from the party, the Society jointly with the Campaign Group of Labour MPs to organise a Socialist Conference in Chesterfield. This became an annual event and led to the formation of the Socialist Movement, which in 1994 helped to launch *Red Pepper* as an independent magazine for the radical left.
6. For example the New Left Clubs in the late 1950s and early 1960s associated with the *Universities and Left Review.* Then in 1967, the Convention of the Left organised by Raymond Williams.
7. Ralph Miliband, *Socialism For A Sceptical Age,* Polity Press, Cambridge 1994.
8. Ibid. p. 148.
9. R. Miliband, *Parliamentary Socialism*, Merlin Press London 1972.

10. *Socialism For A Sceptical Age,* p. 148.
11. For the history of the Workers Party see M. Keck, *Workers Party and Democracy in Brazil,* London 1991.
12. *Socialism For a Sceptical Age,* p. 184.
13. Critical theory, especially the work of Marcuse, was especially influential with the student movements of Germany, Britain and the US in the late 60s. Critical theory's focus on themes such as bureaucracy, authoritarianism, information technology and sexual repression resonated with the movement's own interests. In the 1980s post-modernism, with its focus on the symbolic, was a strong influence on many people associated with for example, feminism and sexual liberation, many of whose activities were also concerned with the symbolic, as well as the material. However, the denial by many post-modern theorists of any reality beyond discourse, could not resonate with those social movements activists whose collective effort was aimed at transforming power structures that existed independently of themselves. Here critical realism, a philosophical development influenced by the movements as well seeking to act as an 'underlabourer' for their politics, is closer to the movements methods. It can sustain philosophically the presumption of most social movement activists of a real world independent of their knowledge of it – the object of their efforts of transformation. But in contrast to many forms of positivism and crude determinism, it does not reduce this reality to one structure or one level of reality. For useful commentaries on these different traditions see W. Outhwaite *New Philosophies of Science,* London, 1987 and *Jurgen Habermas,* Polity Press, Cambridge 1994; D. Harvey *The Condition of Postmodernity* Blackwells, Oxford 1990 and R. Braidotti *Patterns of Dissonance*; A. Sayer *An Introduction to Critical realism* Verso, London 1994 and R. Bhaskar, *Reclaiming Reality,* Verso, London 1991.
14. In *Arguments for a New Left; Answering the Free Market* I do assess central contributions to these debates from the point of view of strategies for democratic social change.
15. Robert Michels, *Political Parties,* Dover Publications, New York 1959.
16. For the full story see Chapter 8 of my *Arguments For A New Left,* Blackwells, Oxford. 1994. And also for the views of many of the leading participants, East and West see M. Kaldor ed. *Europe From Below* Verso. London 1991.
17. Looking ahead to the days when such regional and city autonomy exists in Britain: strong city and regional layers of government provide favourable conditions for parties of the new left – on the continent it is at these levels that new left parties are strongest. Another lesson from these continental experiences is that it is at this level that the partnership between political representatives of the left and democratic civic activity has strongest day-to-day reality. Also, it seems that at a local level voters are more prepared to experiment with choosing a party to the left of the mainstream.
18. Will Hutton, *The State We're In,* Jonathan Cape, London 1995.
19. Richard Crossman in his Introduction to Bagehot's *The English Constitution*, Fontana 1963.

GLOBALIZING CAPITALISM AND THE RISE OF IDENTITY POLITICS

Frances Fox Piven

For more than a century, the Left has been guided by the conviction that industrial capitalism would inevitably homogenize social life, and thus lay the basis for a universalizing politics. Capitalism meant the expansion of a bourgeoisie whose search for profit would steadily penetrate the social life of traditional societies, and eventually reach across the globe, in the process wiping out 'all fixed relations and their train of ancient and venerable prejudices and opinions.' Meanwhile, industrial capitalism would also nourish an ever-larger working class based in the mass production industries that would bind diverse people together in class-based solidarity. And this class would reap the harvest of capitalist destruction and possibility, for it would become the carrier of an emancipatory creed uniting all humankind. Capitalism itself, by obliterating ancient differences and polarizing humanity into two great classes, would pave the way for the universalizing mission of the proletariat.

This model now seems shattered. Capitalism has indeed penetrated societies and spanned the globe. In this sense, it is homogenizing social life. But instead of universalizing popular politics, capitalist expansion is weakening and conceivably destroying working class politics. The advance of international markets and technological change are eviscerating the mass production industries, at least in the mother countries, diminishing the working class numbers and organizations which once gave life to the idea of the proletariat as the hope of humankind. And the new mobility of capitalist investment is also reducing the autonomy of the nation state, with a crushing impact on existing forms of working class organization and influence.

Moreover, instead of wiping out all ancient prejudices, a globalizing capital is prompting a rising tide of fractious racial, ethnic, religious and gender conflict. It is contributing to an identity politics which expresses not only the ancient and venerable prejudices and opinions which were presumably to be swept aside, but the apparently inexhaustible human capacity to create new prejudices and opinions, albeit often in the name of an imagined ancient past. We can see this most awesomely in the conflicts between Hindus and Muslims, Sikhs and Hindus, Hindus and Kashmiris in India; between Xhosa and Zuli, Christians, animists and Muslims in Africa; or between Germans and Turks, French and Algerians, Serbs and Muslims and Croats in Europe; or between Chechens, Ossetians, Abhkazians and Russians; or between Jews and Blacks, Gays and fundamentalists in the United States. Even the Cossacks are on the move again, demanding recognition, in the words of their supreme leader, 'as a distinct people' with 'our territory, property and traditions all restored.'[1] Two decades ago, even a decade ago, such proclamations from the past would have seemed exotic. Now they seem unremarkable. No people, no place, is immune from the tide of identity politics.

As always, intellectual fashion refracts these real world developments, and perhaps contributes to them as well. After all, the old idea that industrial capitalism nourished universalizing classes was itself an intellectual construction, with large consequences in energizing and guiding the development of working class politics. Left intellectuals took for granted the idea that class mattered in politics, that the social structure of modern societies generated broad collectivities, bound together for political action by common interests, a common experience, and perhaps common visions of emancipation. Now, however, those premises seem hopelessly out-of-date, overshadowed by a stream of theorizing which emphasizes the fractured and evanescent nature of political identities constructed and reconstructed by actors more influenced by cultural orientations than by the constraints of socially structured class divisions.[2] In a way, this sort of perspective with its emphasis on the fluidity of culture seems a poor fit with the apparent rootedness and hardness of the inherited ethnic and religious identities which underly many contemporary conflicts.[3] Nevertheless, the new intellectual fashion challenges the old confidence in class in favour of an emphasis on culture as a force in its own right. So does Samuel Huntington's view that the grand axes of conflict in the world are no longer between princes or nation states or ideologies, but rather between religious cultures.[4]

A good deal of the recent discussion of identity politics takes the form of arguments about whether to be for it, or against it.[5] The dispute is in one sense pointless. Identity politics is almost surely inevitable, because it is a way of thinking that reflects something very elemental about human experience. Identity politics seems to be rooted quite simply in attachments to the group, attachments that are common to humankind, and that probably reflect primordial needs that are satisfied by the group, for material survival in a predatory world, as well as for recognition, community, security, and perhaps also a yearning for immortality. Hence people construct the 'collective identities' which define the common traits and common interests of the group, and inherit and invent shared traditions and rituals which bind them together. The mirror image of this collective identity is the invention of the Other, whoever that may be, and however many they may be. And as is often pointed out, it is partly through the construction of the Other, the naming of its traits, the demarcation of its locality, and the construction of a myth-like history of struggle between the group and the Other, that the group recognizes itself.[6] All of this seems natural enough.

If identification with the group is ubiquitous, it is also typically the case that groupness and Otherness are understood as the result of biological nature. Perhaps this is simply because nature provides the most obvious explanation of groupness that is available to people. Even when groups are demarcated by their religion or culture, these mentalities are often regarded as traits so deeply rooted as to be virtually biological, inevitably passed on to future generations. Moreover, the pernicious traits attributed to the Other can easily be woven into explanations of the travails that people experience, into theories of why the rains don't come, or why children sicken and die, or why jobs are scarce and wages fall. This sort of racial theorizing makes the world as people experience it more comprehensible. Even labour politics, ideas about a universalistic proletarian class notwithstanding, was riddled with identity politics. Thus Hobsbawm makes the sensible point that the very fact that 20th century political movements proferred religious, nationalist, socialist and confessional credos suggests that their potential followers were responsive to all these appeals.[7] Politicized workers were bonded together not only and perhaps not mainly by common class position, but by the particularisms of maleness, of whiteness, and of diverse European ethnic and religious identities. In short, features of the human condition seem to drive people to identity politics and, if it is not an inevitable way of thinking, it is surely widespread.

But if identity politics is ubiquitous because of what it offers people in protection, comfort and pride, it has also been a bane upon humankind, the source of unending tragedy. The fatal flaw in identity politics is easily recognized. Class politics, at least in principle, promotes vertical cleavages, mobilizing people around axes which broadly correspond to hierarchies of power, and which promote challenges to these hierarchies. By contrast, identity politics fosters lateral cleavages which are unlikely to reflect fundamental conflicts over societal power and resources and, indeed, may seal popular allegiance to the ruling classes that exploit them. This fatal flaw at the very heart of a popular politics based on identity is in turn regularly exploited by elites. We can see it dramatically, for example, in the unfolding of the genocidal tribal massacres in Rwanda, fomented by a Hutu governing class which found itself losing a war with Tutsi rebels. And of course the vulnerability to manipulation resulting from identity politics is as characteristic of modern societies as tribal societies.

Thus identity politics makes people susceptible to the appeals of modern nationalism, to the bloody idea of loyalty to state and flag, which is surely one of the more murderous ideas to beset humankind. State builders cultivate a sort of race pride to build allegiance to an abstract state, drawing on the ordinary and human attachments that people form to their group and their locality,[8] and drawing also on the animosity to the Other that is typically the complement of these attachments. The actual group that people experience, the local territory that they actually know, comes to be joined with the remote state and its flag, just as the external enemy of the state comes to be seen as the menacing Other, now depicted as a threat not only to the group and its locale, but as a threat to the nation state. I hardly need add that this melding of identity politics with state patriotism can stir people to extraordinary acts of destruction and self-destruction in the name of mystical abstractions, and the identity politics that energizes them. Napoleon was able to waste his own men easily in his murdurous march across Europe because they were quickly replaced with waves of recruits drawn from a French population enthused by their new attachment to the French nation. And World War I showed that modern states could extract even more extraordinary contributions of life and material well-being from their citizenry, as Europeans seized by nationalist passions joined in a frenzy of destruction and death in the name of state patriotism.[9]

In the United States, popular politics has always been primarily about race, ethnicity and religion. Perhaps a population of slaves and immigrants of diverse origins, captive and free, provided some objective basis for the cultivation of identity politics, constructed by ordinary people themselves, and of course by political and economic elites who have never been slow to see that division ensured domination.[10] From the colonial era, public policy engraved distinctions among whites, blacks and native Americans by enshrining elaborate racial hierarchies by law, by prohibiting sexual liaisons across racial lines, and by punishing with particular ferocity the insurrections in which humble people of different races joined together.

The institutions of the American South, especially the post reconstruction South, are illustrative, for they can be understood as a vast complex of social arrangements which, by strictly segregating Afro-Amercians, and specifying their obligations of deference, made factitious racial differences real. Similar practices by industrialists had similar if less total consequences in inscribing difference. Employers deliberately drew from diverse ethnic groups for their workforce, and then artfully arranged job assignments, wage scales and residential quarters in company towns so as to maintain and underline those differences. Or note the strident

emphasis on ethnic, religious, and later racial identities in the organizations, the mobilizing strategies and the policy outcomes of big city politics.
The labour movement was riddled by these influences and, if it was
sometimes strengthened by the gender, racial and ethnic solidarities that
flourished within it, particularistic identities also blinded workers to their
commonalities, making them vulnerable to employers who pitted one
group against another, and leading them also to engage in terrible episodes
of labour fratricide. Needless perhaps to add, this history still marks
American politics today.

All this notwithstanding, identity politics can also be a potentially liber-
ating and even equalizing development, especially among subordinate
groups, and the more so in a political culture already dominated by identity
politics. This possibility has sometimes been difficult for liberals honed on
ideals of universalism to appreciate. Certainly it has been difficult for a
Left preoccupied with class to appreciate.

Contemporary complaints about identity politics would be more understandable if they were aimed at elites who help foment and manipulate
divisions. Instead, however, they are often directed at the subordinate
groups who assert fractious identities. It may well be, however, that
identity politics is especially necessary to lower status peoples, to those
who are more insecure, and who are more likely to be deprived of recognition and respect by wider currents of culture and social interaction.
Subordinate groups try to construct distinctive and sometimes defiant
group identities, perhaps to defend themselves against dominant definitions, at least when they are allowed the cultural space to do so. Moreover,
the construction of distinctive identities may be a necessary prelude to self-
organization and political assertion, and particularly so in a political
culture organized by identity politics. Indeed, in the cauldron of an
American politics based on difference, immigrants who had previously
recognized only a village or a locale as their homeland invented new
national identities the better to survive and do battle in contests among
nationalities. For them, the construction of new identities was a vehicle of
at least psychic emancipation, and sometimes of political empowerment as
well.

The black movement of the post World War II era, which is often
(unreasonably) blamed for heightened identity politics, is a good example
of the emancipatory construction and assertion of group identity. The
celebration of Blackness was in the first instance reactive to the racism of
American society: to the experience of racial subordination and terror in
the South, to the extreme subordination imposed by the North whose
cultural imagery at its most benign featured minstrels in blackface,
Sambos, and so on. Blacks reconstructed their identity in the face of these

imposed identities, and this was almost surely essential to the rise of a movement demanding racial liberation – and to the substantial achievements of that movement in dismantling the caste arrangements which had engraved racial identity politics.

However, these achievements set in motion a train of repercussions that were not simple. The new assertions of Black pride and the political demands that pride fuelled provoked alarmed and angry reactions from other groups whose own identities depended on the subordination of blacks. And of course political elites, especially but not only Republican party operatives, who stood to benefit from the politics of backlash, worked to sharpen these reactions, making such code words of race hatred as 'quotas,' or 'law and order,' or 'welfare dependency,' focal to their popular appeals. Still, the very emergence of far-reaching race conflict reflected the fact that subordination had come to be contested. Blacks were no longer allowing others to define their identity, repress their interests, and stamp out their aspirations. That was an achievement.

The rise of gender politics followed a similar course. While women do not have what is recognized as a distinctive language or turf, the understanding of gender has in other ways been prototypical of the understanding of group identity. Gender identities are closely similar to racial identities, because the traits which were thought to be feminine or masculine, and the social roles to which women and men were consigned, were always understood as the natural consequence of biological difference. Necessarily, therefore, the emergence of a liberatory movement among women was preceded and accompanied by an effort to cast off this inherited identity and construct new identities that disavowed biological fatalism or, in some variants, celebrated biological difference. Indeed, Zaretsky writes of 'the profundity and the intensity of the identity impulse among women that emerged in the early seventies.'[11] The most salient issues of the women's movement – the struggle for the Equal Rights Amendment, for reproductive rights, and the campaigns against rape and sexual harassment – are closely reflective of this effort to reconstruct the meaning of gender by challenging the biological underpinnings of traditional meanings. The mounting of such a challenge to the most ancient of subordinations, and a subordination rooted in understandings of nature itself, is surely a stunning accomplishment.

As with Blacks, the consequences were not simple. Liberatory reconstructions of gender struck at deeply imprinted understandings, threatening and arousing people still embedded in more traditional relationships, including many women embedded in traditional relationships. And as had been the case with conflict over racial identities, the contest over understandings of gender became the focus of elite manipulations in electoral politics. By 1980, the Republicans had taken notice, and in an effort to turn the widening anxieties provoked by gender conflict to electoral advantage, struck support for ERA from their platform, and initiated a campaign that culminated in the odd spectacle of American Presidents – leaders of the richest and most technologically advanced nation in the world – casting themselves as leaders of a holy war against abortion.

While identity politics may always be with us, the contemporary world appears to be engulfed by particularistic conflicts of rising intensity and destructiveness, in a pattern reminiscent of the rising tide of nationalist furies of the late 19th century. The main reasons for this, then and now, can be traced to the transformation of world capitalism. First, in the contemporary period, capitalist expansion is at least partly responsible for the weakening or collapse of nation states, with horrific consequences for ethnic and religious conflict. Second, economic restructuring is enfeebling existing forms of working class political organization which in the past sometimes restrained particularistic conflicts in the interests of class solidarity. Finally, even while the restraining capacities of governments and working class organizations are diminishing, capitalist restructuring is aggravating group conflict, by accelerating the migration of peoples, by intensifying competition for scarce resources, and by creating the widespread economic and social insecurity which always accompanies large-scale change, and particularly so when the changes for many people are for the worse.

Of course, not every instance of the weakening or collapse of central governments that had previously restrained group conflict can be traced to the current global capitalist transformation. Ancient animosities can erupt whenever central governments no longer hold them in check. The withdrawal of the British Raj unleashed bloody conflicts in India which persist to this day, and the withdrawal of the colonial powers from Africa also spurred tribal conflicts. But other instances of central government collapse cannot easily be disentangled from the changes wrought by world capitalism. Waves of anarchic warfare in the developing world are at least partly the result of saddling third world governments with debt through the imposition of neo-liberal credit policies.[12] The fall of the Yugoslavian government, and the ethnic wars that resulted, was similarly at least partly the result of the shock therapy administered by the IMF. And other Eastern European governments were undermined by the spread of a consumer culture which fuelled popular discontent with state provision. (The Eastern European revolutions, says Benjamin R. Barber, were less over the right to vote than the right to shop.[13])

Other consequences of capitalist tranformation for the intensification of identity politics are more direct. In a sense, the old prediction has proved true; the bourgeoisie is on the move with a series of universalizing projects which promise utterly to transform the world, penetrating and homogenizing social life across the globe. But instead of nourishing a growing proletariat, a missionary capitalism is destroying the working class formations of the older industrial order, at least in the rich countries of the West.

I do not want to overstate the unifying influence of the labour movement at its peak. I have already pointed out that worker mobilizations were riven by the particularistic divisions of race and ethnicity, and sometimes gender. Nevertheless, the promise of the labour movement was that class solidarity would override particularisms, and even that proletarian internationalism would override state patriotism. And in instance after instance, where the successful use of the strike power demanded it, labour did indeed override the divisions of identity politics, even in the United States. Now that moderating influence has weakened.

The basic lines of capitalist restructuring and the impact on organized labour are familiar. First, the expansion of global trade, itself promoted by the internationalizing of markets in finance and production, as well as by improvements in transportation and communications, has lead to the intensified exploitation of labour and resources across the globe. From Indonesia to China to Haiti, previously peripheral peoples and places are being incorporated into capitalist markets, with the consequence that organized workers in the mother countries find themselves competing with products made by low wage workers across the globe, including workers made docile by coercive authoritarian governments.

Second, the power constellations patterning the policies of national governments have shifted. Organized labour has lost ground dramatically to new supra-national institutions created by capital. It is true, as Panitch says, that the nation states are major authors of these institutions, and also continue to serve important functions for internationalizing capital.[14] Nevertheless, once in existence, international organizations and networks, including multinational corporations and international banking organizations, together with their domestic corporate and financial allies who freely use the threat of disinvestment as leverage in their dealings with governments, become major constraints on the policy options of the state. Constraints on the state are also constraints on the ability of democratic publics, including the organized working class, to exert influence through electoral-representative arrangements. The trade unions and political parties constructed by organized workers in the mother countries gained what influence they had through their leverage on governments, where strike power, trade union organization and working class voting numbers made them a force with which to be reckoned. If capitalist internationalism circumscribes what national governments can do, it inevitably also circumscribes working class political power.

Third, as a consequence of both internationalism and the shifting power constellations within nations, the economies and polities of the mother-counties of industrial capitalism are being restructured, with dire consequences for the old working class. This process is most advanced in England and the United States where unions are weaker and welfare state protections less adequate. The old mass production industries which created the industrial working class are being dismantled or reorganized and decentralized, with the consequence that the numbers of blue collar workers are shrinking. And as communities disperse and the mass media supplants the local pub, the old working class culture also crumbles. Those who remain have become excruciatingly vulnerable to the threat power of a mobile capital, unable to resist shrinking wages and benefits, and the worsening terms of work, including speedup, and forced overtime for some, and involuntary part-time or temporary work for others, all of which undermines union organization. At the same time, capitalists have launched a specifically political project to dismantle the institutional supports created by working class politics, by attacking unions, and slashing welfare state income and service protections which shielded workers from the market, and by discrediting Keynesian macro-economic political regulation.[15]

Finally, a capitalist class on the move has launched an ideological campaign to justify and promote its expansionary mission. International markets exist, but they have also been cast as a superordinate order, operating according to a kind of natural law, penetrating national economies more deeply than they actually do, and beyond the reach of politics. In fact, this neo-laissez faire doctrine cloaks the capitalist class with the mantle once claimed by the proletariat. Capital is forging the way to the future, it is the great force for progress, the hope of humankind. And as with 19th century laissez faire notions to which this doctrine owes its main tenets, the ideology is touched with fanaticism, with a zealous utopianism that ignores the actual needs of the human subjects of any world order. Of course, this ideological campaign is as persuasive as it is because international markets are also real, and the palpable evidence of capital and goods mobility lends the sweeping doctrine of neo-laissez faire a certain material reality.

In all of these ways a universalizing capitalism has weakened the old industrial working class as a political force. No wonder unions and labour parties that were the instrument of this class have also lost their ideological footing. The imagery which gave working-class politics is élan, the idea that the future belonged to the workers, and that workers acted for all humankind, has collapsed. That universalizing myth now belongs to a capitalist class on the move.

The surge of identity politics is not just the result of a collapsing central governments or a receding class politics. It is also the result of the massive dislocations of people set in motion by capitalist restructuring. More and more people are being drawn into the orbit of capitalism. Considered abstractly, that process is universalizing. In the actual experience of people, it has had the effect of heightening particularistic identities and conflicts. Gellner, writing of an earlier phase of capitalist transformation and the nationalist furies it helped to set loose, showed how an 'explosive blend of early industrialism (dislocation, mobility, acute inequality *not* hallowed by time and custom) seeks out, as it were, all the available nooks and crannies of cultural differentiation, wherever they be.'[16] The pattern is being repeated in the contemporary era. In other words, instead of wiping out the 'train of ancient and venerable prejudices,' the advance of global capitalism is whipping ancient prejudices to fever pitch.

Identity politics is pervasive, and probably inevitable. But group conflict is likely to rise under some conditions, and subside under others. One important source of disturbance has to do with the large-scale migration of people spurred by capitalist penetration of subsistence agricultural economies, with the consequence that conflicts over land escalate, and people no longer able to survive in agriculture migrate to urban centres.[17] At the same time, the spread of consumer culture also attracts people from the periphery, while the development of globe-spanning circuits of communication and transportation facilitates the recruitment of cheap labour to the metropole.[18] 'Every migration,' says Enzensberger, 'no matter what triggered it, what motive underlies it, whether it is voluntary or involuntary, and what scale it assumes, leads to conflicts.'[19] Or as Jean Daniel, editor of *Le Nouvel Observateur*, warns about population movements and the 'unprecedented' mingling of peoples, we should remember that 'Babel . . . was a curse.'[20]

If unfamiliar proximity is likely to intensify group consciousness and fractionalism, this is especially so when outsider groups are seen as competitors for limited jobs, neighbourhood space, honour and influence. In his last book, Ralph Miliband wrote that intra-class conflicts among wage-earners involving race or gender or ethnicity or religion can reasonably be understood as the effort to find scapegoats to explain insecurity and alienation.[21] If he was not entirely right, he was surely at least significantly right. Group conflict is far more likely when people feel growing uncertainty about their own future and as is true in many instances, are experiencing real declines in living standards. When times get harder, and competition for scarce resources intensifies, theories about the Other, and how the Other is to blame for these turns in events, being ubiquitous, are readily available. And, of course, such interpretations are more likely to be seized upon when alternative and perhaps more systemic explanations of the troubles people face are not available, or when such explanations yield no practicable line of action. No wonder there has been a spread of an identity politics, often a hate-filled identity politics, in the metropole. As Vaclav Havel says, 'The world of our experiences seems chaotic, confusing . . . And the fewer answers the era of rational knowledge provides . . . the more deeply it would seem that people, behind its back as it were, cling to the ancient certainties of their tribe.'[22]

Finally, as so many times before, the group divisions of identity politics are being worsened by political elites who seize the opportunity for gaining advantage from popular division. In particular, politicians on the Right – Le Pen's Front National in France, the Christian Right in the United States, the Freedom Party in Austria, the Falangists in Spain, the Lombardy League in Italy, or the Republicans in Germany where half a million immigrants arrived in 1992 alone – work to stoke the anger against outsiders. They draw popular attention away from the economic transformations underway, and try to hold or win anxious voters by directing resentment against outsiders. Or, as a retired Russian officer commented to a *New York Times* reporter about the conflict between the Tatars and ethnic Russians, 'Half the population is building mosques, the other half is building churches. And the bosses are building big brick houses for themselves.'

Once again, the United States is at the forefront. Last October, *BusinessWeek* editorialized about the 'unprecedented widening of the income gap between winners and losers in the workplace.' *BusinessWeek* worried that the losers might ignore its advice that 'Growth is the single most important salve for the high-risk, high gain society' and seek scapegoats, such as 'elitist big business.'

There are of course reasons for *BusinessWeek's* concerns about the resurgence of class politics. Big business is politically mobilized as never before, having developed over the past two decades a range of vehicles to do ideological and policy warfare, from big think tanks, to revived trade associations, to new associations of peak corporations. Reflecting both these developments and the changed international economic context in which they have unfolded, enormous changes have taken place in the American class structure, as the rich have gotten much richer, the poor much poorer, and most people have gotten poorer as well. National wealth increased, but the vast majority of wage earners lost ground, with the consequence that more people are working, working longer, and harder. The U. S. Census reported that between 1973 and 1989, the real income of male high school graduates dropped by a third; the income of those who didn't make it through high school dropped by 40 percent. And the palpable evidence of economic trauma also grew, in the form of visible poverty and pathology, of beggars and spreading homeless encampments in all of the major cities.

Still, *BusinessWeek* needn't worry, at least not so far. Americans are being led by their political leaders to other scapegoats, and certain conditions prepare the way. For one thing, organized labour is on its back, its membership at 11 percent of the private sector labour force, down from 30 percent only two decades ago. For another, economic changes are not the only shocks to the American psyche. Cultural changes which undermine the established bases of identity are contributing to widespread unease. Contested racial boundaries and, not less important, changing sexual and family mores are eroding a world in which whites were in command, men were men, women were women, and the rules for mating and family life were clear. Needless to say, in a society in which the culture of group identity figures so largely, changes of this sort generate a distinctive terror. In this sense, the numerous commentators who blame the black movement and the women's movement for the rightward shift of the past two decades are not entirely wrong. In a world of identity politics, mobilization by the Other is always a provocation.

Thus economic and cultural change are combining to generate popular anxiety and anger. But the economic transformation, its impact on hard-hit groups, the measures that might moderate the transformation or its impact, do not figure much in American political discussion, except sometimes in the speculations of pundits trying to account for electoral discontent. Instead, public anger has easily been routed into the familiar channels of identity politics, as issues like immigration, crime, and welfare, all code terms for Afro-American and Latino minorities, (with welfare a code evoking wanton women besides) dominate the political discussion. Republican and Democratic leaders alike are following the precedents of American history. Hemmed in by a politically mobilized and aggressive capitalist class, party leaders promulgate arguments which account for the felt problems of ordinary people by singling out the Other. Political discourse is dominated by a narrative in which immigrants, or criminals, or welfare recipients, are variously pointed to as the source of America's problems.

The focus on welfare is a good illustration. As these thing go, welfare (or AFDC) is a small programme. Yet to listen to all of the talk, including talk about 'reforms' that would slash millions of children and their mothers from the rolls, one would think that this small and benighted programme is a main reason for high taxes, spreading poverty, out-of-wedlock births, and just about everything else that people find upsetting. The argument works as well as it does because it meshes with American racism and chauvinism, (and also because people are prepared for it by a history of welfare practices which denigrate recipients by keeping them so miserably poor that they are inevitably outsiders, and by stripping them of any procedural rights).

Interestingly, the old intellectual justification for identity politics is also having a modest renaissance. As economic hardship spreads, theories about the genetic roots of economic success and failure are once more respectable, as signalled by the reception given *The Bell Curve*, the racist tome by Charles Murray and Richard Herrnstein. Their argument is a justi-fication for the most extreme sort of identity politics, proposing as it does that an innate and biologically determined intelligence influences economic and social circumstances, making it more likely that some people end up poor (and deviant), and others end up rich. In other words, the argument goes, class itself, and especially the widening class polar-ization of the contemporary period, is rooted in biology.

Still, all is not hopeless. The de facto bipartisan coalition now directing American popular politics may be overreaching. At the very least, there are signs that the Republican initiatives in particular may have triggered a fight, maybe even the opening salvo in a bigger war against congressional moves to accelerate economic polarization with a three/fifths vote rule on tax cuts and a balanced budget amendment. Together with their promised funding cuts, these measures will seal off the tax and expenditure advan-tages of the well-off so they are impervious to the currents of democratic politics, while slashing programmes that reach wider publics, beginning with the programmes that reach the poor.

This is boldly and clearly class legislation. But the groups that are moving to resist are not the familiar organs of the working class. Rather, in the past few months the civil rights and advocacy organizations created by the black movement and the feminist movement have been spurred into action, goaded by estimates of the impact of the more outrageous proposals of the new congress on their constituencies. In other words, if this is a class war, one side is moving into battle in the familiar formations of identity politics.

Of course, the Republicans are likely to prevail, at least in the short run, especially since a weak-kneed and business-oriented Democractic admin-istration seems to be conceding much of their programme. Nevertheless, there may be a public battle, where until now there has been little resis-tance to business aggression from any quarter. Some will see in this kind of battle the dim outlines of a reconstituted working class mobilizing along the lines of its diverse identities to resist a capitalist class assault. I think that is partly true, maybe even more true than not.

Still, the other part of the truth is the politics of identity.

NOTES

1. Quoted in Fred Weir, 'Riders on the Storm,' *In These Times,* May 16, 1994.
2. For similar observations, see Ellen Meiksins Wood. 'Identity Crisis,' *In These Times,* June 13, 1994.
3. Of course, inherited identities may serve merely as the raw material from which contemporary identities are constructed, a point made by Zygmunt Bauman, among others. See 'Europe of Nations, Europe of Tribes,' *Sociologisk Rapportserie,* no. 2, 1993, Department of Sociology, University of Copenhagen.
4. See Samuel Huntington, 'The Clash of Civilizations?' *Foreign Affairs,* summer, 1993, and Samuel Huntington, 'If not Civilizations, What?' in *Foreign Affairs,* November/December 1993.
5. See for example Todd Gitlin who faults proponents of identity politics for fracturing the commitment of the Left to universalism, leading to 'paranoid, jargon-clotted, postmodernist groupthink, cult celebrations of victimization and stylized marginality.' 'From Universality to Difference: Notes on the Fragmentation of the Idea of the Left,' *Contention,* Vol. 2, no. 2, Winter 1993, p. 21.
6. Weber discussed racial groups as subjective constructions, resulting from common political actions, or common experiences in antagonism to members of an obviously different group. See *Economy and Society,* Berkeley, University of California Press, 1922, vol. 1, p. 387. See also Stuart Hall, 'Ethnicity: Identity and Difference,' *Radical America,* Vol. 23, no. 4, October 1991.
7. On the overlap and tension between the appeals of national identity and class in working class political mobilization, see Eric Hobsbawm, *Nations and Nationalism since 1789,* Cambridge University Press, 1990.
8. On the relationship between the development of the nation state and nationalism as ideology, see John Breuilly, *Nationalism and the State,* University of Chicago Press, 1982.
9. Hobsbawm defines nationalism as a principle which holds that the duty of the citizen to the nation overrides all other obligations. See *Nations and Nationalism,* p. 9.
10. Wacquant points out that 'the symbolic work necessary to establish race or class as salient subjective principles . . . can be successful only to the extent that it corresponds to the material differences inscribed in objectivity.' See Loïc J. D. Wacquant, 'The Puzzle of Race and Class in American Society and Social Science,' *Scholarship and Excellence,* Benjamin E. Mays Monograph Series, Vol. 2, no. 1.
11. Eli Zaretsky, 'Responses,' *Socialist Review,* Vol 23, no. 3, 1994.
12. See Manfred Bienefeld, 'Capitalism and the Nation State in the Dog Days of the Twentieth Century,' *The Socialist Register,* London: Merlin Press, 1994. Hobsbawm and Bauman both argue that, in general, the assumption by supra-national agencies of functions once performed by nation states may so eviscerate the idea of nationhood as to encourage the proliferation of claims by upstart 'nations.'
13. 'Jihad Vs. McWorld,' *Atlantic Monthly,* March, 1992.
14. See Leo Panitch, 'Globalization and the State, *The Socialist Register* 1994.
15. These developments are clearest in the United States. However, see the Organizations for Economic Cooperation and Development, *The OECD Jobs Study,* Paris, 1994, which recommends broadly the same directions for Europe.
16. Gellner, *Nations and Nationalism,* p. 112.
17. The *New York Times* reported that the number of intrastate and interstate refugees in the world had reached 49 million. See August 8, 1994.
18. On the push and pull factors in migration, see Amartya Sen, 'Population: Delusion and Reality,' *New York Review of Books,* September 22, 1994.
19. Hans Enzensberger, *Civil Wars from L.A. to Bosnia,* The New Press, 1994.
20. See Jean Daniel, 'God is Not a Head of State,' *New Perspective Quarterly,* Vol. 11, no. 2,

spring, 1994.
21. Ralph Miliband, *Socialism for a Sceptical Age*, Cambridge: Polity Press, 1994, p. 22, 192–3.
22. 'The New Measure of Man,' *New York Times*, July 8, 1994.

EUROPE IN SEARCH OF A FUTURE*

Daniel Singer

Must western Europe follow in the footsteps of the United States? Is our future inevitably American? The question was raised, spectacularly, at the end of 1993 during discussions over 'culture' as part of the Gatt negotiations. Must our images, our heroes, our models, even our dreams be shaped by the American media? asked the passionate advocates of the so-called cultural exception. Actually they won the day. Culture, you may recall, was at the last moment removed from the Gatt deal; the European Community was thus able to preserve some quotas on the import of American films. The victory, as could be guessed, was very provisional. Indeed, this *kulturkampf* revealed, as we shall see below, that what is crucial for the independence of western Europe is not so much its capacity to shelter behind protective walls as its ability and will to build a different society.

In a western Europe having rediscovered mass unemployment, the question is now put back on the historical agenda in dramatic fashion. The United States is given as an example to follow by the international establishment. With its 'working poor', its 'labour flexibility', its absence of a national health service and its growing gap between the haves and the have nots, the model may be unattractive, but in the new deregulated world, in which capital can move freely in search of cheap labour, Europe is told that it has no choice. It must now start dismantling its welfare state in earnest.

Such a prospect poses a problem for the Left in western Europe. It may have swallowed a great deal and carried an ideological retreat tantamount to surrender. Yet even this is not enough. To follow the American pattern, to imitate the Democratic Party, the European Left must break its organic links with labour unions, accept the total deregulation of the labour market and the rapid removal of all the social conquests won by the working people in the period of postwar prosperity. The Left would now be allowed into office not as the reformist manager of capitalism but as a tough champion of austerity. The leaders may be eager but, judging by the

*A version of this text was given at the Nillercomm lecture at the University of Illinois, Urbana in March 1995.

117

popular protests in Italy provoked by a frontal attack on pensions, they may not be able to deliver.

On the other hand, any attempt to defend the achievements, on which the success and popularity of social-democracy rested, would require a highly radical line and mass mobilisation, breaking altogether with the moderate policy pursued hitherto by the respectful Left. Just to ensure full employment today would demand a total revision of economic and social policies. The left-wing parties, when in office, have contributed to their present predicament, accepting among other things the complete lifting of restrictions on the international movement of capital. The last few years have seen a drastic reduction of the powers of the individual nation states to manage their own economy. A leftish government coming into office in Rome or London today would have incomparably less room for manoeuvre than the French Left had – though it did not use it – in 1981.

Yet, if the medium-sized European nation state can no longer go it on its own, the European Union as such could protect itself and stand up to the United States. I will argue that it will only have the drive to do so if it consciously tries to forge a society fundamentally different from the American. But this issue of the field on which the battle should be waged raises for us another series of problems: does the medium-size nation state still offer the initial terrain for the radical transformation of society and, if it does, how fast must it attract support from other countries, and thus spread, to survive?

Finally, I shall have to admit the rather rhetorical use of the term American to describe our future. The United States is taken in this context as the most advanced (and hopefully the last) stage of capitalism now spreading all over the globe. There is no curse condemning Americans to live for ever in a socially unjust society. All that I will argue is that, as the attack on welfare state capitalism intensifies, it is in western Europe, because of its historical background, that the battle crucial for our historical future will be fought first, at the turn of this millenium.

Shaping our dreams

The struggle for the survival of a European film industry was instructive because it was at once vital and phoney. It was vital because what was at stake was the imposed uniformity of our images and, beyond, of our cultural representation. It was phoney because, while directors, actors, critics and their associates fought for their very existence, the real conflict was between merchants who, when they hear the word culture, reach for their pocket calculators. Behind the high-sounding slogans – resist the American invasion and Joan of Arc to the rescue, on one side, down with protectionism, people have the right to choose, on the other – you could detect the calculations of the accountants. To make matters still more ridiculous, the Americans talked as if western Europe were some kind of Zhdanovian fortress protected by high walls against the wicked products of Hollywood. In fact, at the time, three-quarters of the film revenue earned within the European Community went to American companies. Audiovisual exports from the US to the EEC amounted to $4 billion compared with shipments of $250 million in the opposite direction. What was being questioned was not the dominant position that the American industry had already acquired in the European market. It was Hollywood's inexorable drive towards a quasi monopoly.

Two major obstacles were involved. One was the subsidy granted to the domestic film industry, notably in France. The American objection was that all films were taxed to provide the subsidy, but only French films got it. The television quota system was potentially a more serious hurdle. It was based on a directive known as 'television without frontiers', and provided that a majority of programmes on each television station must originate within the Community (now the European Union). It is this provision which survived as 'cultural goods' were threatened. Actually it was never strictly applied in all the countries. With the expansion of cable, the spread of satellites and Europe's continued deregulation, the powerful vested interests are once again on the offensive.

During the 1993 polemics, Regis Debray quoted the words of a Time Warner executive speaking on a French television channel: 'You French are best at making cheese and wine, or in fashion. Filming is our speciality. So let us get on with film-making and you keep on with the cheeses'. Debray summed it up, tongue in cheek: 'let us shape the minds and you stick to stomachs'.[2] Not so fast. Our collective stomachs are financially too precious to be left to the French, as was shown in the bitter Gatt battles over agriculture. But the control of the mind, the monopoly of the image, is even more important.

The trouble here is that we are not dealing with films as a form of art, but with films as merchandise, as a commodity. The United States is better at manufacturing, packaging, advertising and selling cultural goods. It has advantages in size and scope, in language and experience. This applies not only to films but to mass-produced TV programmes that, having covered their costs at home, can be dumped abroad at prices the local competition cannot match. Yet what is at stake is more than profits alone. When Rambo is splashed all over China, when the recent American soap operas and sitcoms dominate the screens of western Europe and the older versions the poorer half of the Continent, one wonders whether mastery of the image has not become both the instrument and the symbol of leadership in the new world order.

Should Europe copy the Americans in order to resist them? Judging by some of the European co-productions aimed at the lowest common denominator and dubbed in English so as to broaden the market, the remedy is worse than the disease. Yet, even if the European producers were commercially successful, this would in no way solve our problem, since what matters is the nature of the product and not the language or the nominal nationality of the producer. Universal is owned by Matsushita, Columbia by Sony, Fox by ex-Australian Rupert Murdoch and MGM by Crédit Lyonnais, and all this in no way diminishes the extent of American cultural domination. Similarly, the real masters of European TV (like Silvio Berlusconi, the tycoon turned politician, or Martin Bouygues, whose father, with money made on public works, bought France's biggest channel, TF1), whatever they may say for immediate commercial gain, have nothing against the American system, on which their fortune rests. By contrast, the real opponents of cultural imperialism have nothing against American art. They are fighting against the commercialisation of creativity, the imposed uniformity, the manufacturing of culture, which American big business has raised to a fine art but of which it is not the only practitioner.

Genuine artists manage to create against the odds. It is easier for writers or painters than for film makers, because less initial outlay is needed. Such genuine creators exist on both sides of the ocean. Whatever their success, they go against the trend of the machine of commercial mass culture, which codifies our desires, stifles our dreams, shrinks instead of widening our consciousness. The 'anti-imperialist' battle is thus our common struggle against commercial conveyor belts and culture treated as a commodity. This dictates the way for European resistance. Since culture will not cease to be a commodity in a world of merchandise, the road to independence leads through a radical transformation of society, a difficult search for a world in which artistic creation will no longer be dominated by the tyranny of the market but will not be subjected to the dictatorship of the state either (a categorical imperative since the Soviet experience).

A tall order, especially with the wind clearly blowing in the opposite direction. In the meantime all we can do is to multiply islands of free creation and pockets of resistance, slow down the advance of the juggernaut of conformity, relying on the gut resistance to GATT culture, to the resistible reign of merchandise. Ultimately, Europe's independence is linked to the nature of its society and this lesson is valid not only for culture.

A historic compromise

One cannot grasp the gravity of the current crisis and the dilemma it sets for social-democracy, taken here in the now accepted meaning of reformist management of capitalist society, without looking back, however briefly, at the half century of postwar development in western Europe, with its thirty years of exceptionally fast growth, followed by the two decades of the still unfinished restructuring.

The first thirty years will go down in history books as a period of unprecedented expansion and deep change of the social landscape, particularly rapid in countries where the industrial revolution in the 19th century had not gone as far as in Britain or Germany. Those were the years of the vanishing peasantry, with fast rising agricultural productivity and mass migration to town. But this was not enough to satisfy demand: immigrant workers and women joined the labour force *en masse*. Except in Britain, the national product was rising at an average 5% a year. Living standards, measured in material terms, nearly trebled within a generation, as western Europe was catching up with America, copying its pattern of consumption.

The image of Europe during this period of exceptional prosperity is, obviously, too bright. It does not take into account the inequalities of development, the urban overcrowding, the strains and stresses of this social upheaval. The French students' and workers rising of 1968 or the Italian 'Hot Autumn' the year after cannot be understood without the awareness of the deep discontent below the glittering surface of the so-called *consumer* society. Nevertheless, in terms of material goods and even of social welfare the progress was undeniable. This is why the period can be described, retrospectively, as the golden age of social democracy, taken here in its narrow current meaning. And the scope for reforms within the system was great.

Real wages were rising. Unemployment was kept around 3% of the labour force. A minimum wage was introduced, coupled in many countries with a sliding scale linked to inflation. Some controls were introduced into the labour market. The network of social security spread and a public health system was extended to the whole population. Reformism was the fashion even where the governments were neither Labour nor social-democratic. The Gaullists described planning as 'an ardent obligation', while German Christian Democrats talked of a *social* market economy. Governments were trying to run the economy by Keynesian methods and their propagandists proclaimed that capitalism had found the secret of eternal growth.

The mood was contagious. Towards the end of the period – after Khrushchev's indictment of Stalin and the invasion of Hungary in 1956 and, twelve years later, the entry of Soviet tanks into Prague – when it became plain to everybody that the Soviet Union presented no alternative, even the Communists, led by the Italians, accepted the idea that what was at stake from now on was a further improvement of the system and not its abolition. History, however, has its ironies. By the time they had accepted this 'historical compromise', this *compromesso storico*, the foundations on which it rested had begun to collapse. The mid-seventies actually mark the beginning of a new historical period in which the achievements of social-democracy come under mounting attack.

As if guided by conditioned reflexes, the Left stuck to the centre of the stage. Its protagonist, however, moved sharply to the Right. The years that followed, particularly the 'eighties, saw serious defeats of the labour movement which, so far, has not adjusted itself to the continuing restructuring of the labour force (the shrinking of its strongholds in the mines, in steel, in shipbuilding; the rise of the white collar workers, coupled with the mass inflow of women etc). These were also the years of rapid deregulation, with particular emphasis on the opening of frontiers and the full liberation of capital movements. In western Europe the resulting reduction of the powers of the nation state – hitherto the instrument of Keynesian intervention – was not compensated by any corresponding strengthening of a European state, of a federation with its capital in Brussels.

Finally, this was a period of privatisation, of mounting criticism against the welfare state and, altogether, of a fantastic ideological swing to the Right. Private became beautiful and public nasty, both by definition. Free enterprise and profits acquired a new virtue. So did inequality. Huge salaries and even bigger incomes from investment were first presented as a 'necessary evil', then as the rightful reward. Last but not least those have been the years of a relentless rise in unemployment.

But it is only in the current decade, in the 'nineties, with the long depression that has only now ended, that the crisis of social-democracy has come to a head. For a long time we were told that the restructuring was temporary, that it only affected old industries and that the expanding services would absorb the surplus labour. Now, reality can no longer be concealed: unemployment has come to stay. It may decrease slightly during the boom, but it is much higher at the end of each cycle than it was at the end of its predecessor. At about 12% of the labour force – and the figures for the jobless are everywhere underestimated unemployment is the major preoccupation of the people in western Europe. Yet every suggestion that one should drastically reduce working hours or reorganise society so as to eliminate this calamity are met with the same response from the OECD or the IMF, from the international establishment or from the domestic ones: follow the American example.

A nightmarish model

What we are now being offered as a model is not some new version of the American dream. Quite the contrary. The United States is given as an example, because the rate of unemployment there is about half the West European average, but the advocates of the American solution do not hide the price that has to be paid. In the USA the gap between the privileged few at the top and the deprived many at the bottom of society is not only big; it has been growing fast in the last twenty years. So has the number of people living below the level of subsistence and, having a job is no protection: the 'working poor' are the latest American invention. Throughout the postwar period the country had little social protection by European standards, and even that limited welfare is now being drastically reduced. It is a nightmare rather than a dream that Europe is offered as a model.

Russia and its 'empire of evil' used to be described by the Reaganites as a hell from which there is no exit. Since the collapse of the Berlin wall, it is capitalism, invading the whole planet, that is being painted as omnipresent and eternal. Capital and commodities (though not labour) flowing virtually freely within this global system, Europe allegedly has no choice. It can no longer afford the 'luxury' of a significant minimum wage, of permanent jobs, of a health service for all, of a welfare state instead of charitable institutions. It must conform or collapse, follow in American footsteps because there is no other way out. The fiction of a capitalism with a human face must now be abandoned. Its basic principle is the survival of the 'fittest'. It's back to the asphalt jungle, with charity as an outlet for the bleeding hearts.

The snag for Europe's social-democracy is that this line implies an open offensive against both its myths and its actual achievements, against the very reason for its existence. Admittedly, the social-democratic leaders have in recent years performed a spectacular ideological retreat. On property, profits, equality the Left now accepts ideas that the Right did not dare to proclaim a quarter of a century ago. In countries of open political consensus, like Britain, Maggie Thatcher preached the new gospel and successive Labour leaders learnt to recite a bowdlerised version of the same prayer. In the countries of southern Europe, where the Left was supposed to stand for a radical transformation of society, these were the years of "normalisation", of the conversion to consensus politics. True, in France, General de Gaulle had prepared the ground with the institutions of the Fifth Republic. Yet it took François Mitterrand and the Left in office to persuade the French people (provisionally?) that there is no alternative, that society, and therefore life, cannot be radically altered by collective political action. In Spain, Felippe Gonzales performed the same function. But the problem today is no longer the acceptance of the existing system. The difficulty for the respectful Left is that it must combine consensus politics with a frontal attack against the vital interests of the working people. The Italian case, with the sudden rise of TV tycoon Silvio Berlusconi, leaning heavily on Gianfranco Fini, the neo-fascist from whom you would buy a second-hand car, is thus worth examining, because Italy seems to link past and present, the normalisation with the attempt of the bourgeoisie to prepare itself for the new phase in European history.

This is not the place to study the specifications of the Italian situation: the yawning development gap between North and South, which explains the emergence of the *League*; the weakness of the relatively young state which helps to understand the pervasive nature of corruption; the possession by one tycoon of half the country's television or the presence of a 'fascist with a human face'. Whatever the peculiarities, a big puzzle remains. The capitalist establishment does not particularly like fascism. It calls it to the rescue only if it faces a terrible danger, if society is in total disarray and a radical Left is ready to take over. Nothing of the kind was happening in Italy. The Left was no threat. Its strongest section, the ex-Communist PDS (Democratic Party of the Left) would not frighten a fly: during the electoral campaign in March, 1994, it claimed to have the backing of the City, the blessing of Nato, and hailed Aurelio Ciampi, the former governor of the Bank of Italy, as its model statesman.

There are, thus, two possible explanations. One can be called accidental. After the fall of the Berlin wall, the establishment thought it could afford a smooth transition. When it allowed the judges of Milan to act, however, it unleashed a Frankenstein. Hell broke loose and the establishment was compelled to improvise to put the pieces together. Still mistrusting the Left, it put its money on Berlusconi and Fini. But it is already trying to restore a more traditional order. The other explanation postulates that Italy is, possibly, a forerunner, setting the pattern for other countries of western Europe. It assumes that all the changes are advance preparations for potential threats. The establishment knew what austerity measures would have to be introduced, what sacrifices demanded from the poorer sections of the population in order to keep Italy in the top European league, fulfilling the obligations of the Maastricht Treaty. It therefore, decided to introduce in advance an authoritatian regime, including a party ready for anything, if needed. Even if the second interpretation is right, big business may now be shifting positions. Berlusconi's frontal attack on the welfare state, taking pensions as its first target, provoked a massive popular response, strikes and the biggest *demo* Rome has seen since the war, enough to provoke second thoughts about general strategy.

Italy's rulers must now decide whether they want to take the risk of confrontation or whether they can rely on the Left, essentially the PDS, to get the same medicine absorbed more slowly but without shocks. In more general terms, the west European establishment must choose between class conflict and class collaboration for this new phase of intensified offensive against the conquests won by the labour movement in the postwar period. The leaders of the official Left have hitherto shown an eagerness to work within the system and to prop it up. What they are now being asked to do, however, is qualitatively different. To perform the function the Democratic Party plays in the States, they would have to break and organic ties that still link them with labour unions and disown the heritage on which their postwar success depended. The welfare state now has roots within society, and the Italian popular response to the open attack against pensions gives an idea of what the resistance might be. True, after his presidential victory Bill Clinton was hailed as hero to be imitated by the Labour Party in Britain, the Socialists in France and the PDS in Italy. The decomposition of the Democratic Party has tempered the zeal of political climbers, particularly in countries, like Germany, where the party links with the labour movement are strongest. Whatever the temptation of office, the leaders of the respectful Left must now be aware of the risks of political suicide.

Yet, to move in the opposite direction and try to defend old conquests against the new offensive would carry the movement well beyond the conceptions of its current leadership. There is no scope now for a moderate defence of the welfare state. Just to stick to the central front, the search for full employment implies a radical revision of the organisation of labour both at the level of the factory, the shop or the office, as that of society at large. To impose it, a mass movement from below would be needed, and it would be rapidly driven to tackle the vital issues that were at least put on the historical agenda in the sixties and then, though unsolved, were simply pushed aside: what kind of growth? for what purpose? in whose interest? within which social, international and ecological context? Inventing what forms of democracy at all levels so that people should really take part in shaping their work and their fate?

Even if we assume, in a moment of optimism, that the movement is boldly trying to tackle such questions, can it find answers within the now bursting frontiers of the nation state?

Europe and the Nation State

To argue that a nation state the size of Britain, France or Italy can no longer provide the ground on which the radical transformation of society is at least initiated is to abdicate; it is to rule out such a transition for a forth-coming historical period. The European Union, after all, is not, or rather not yet, a state with power to be seized in Brussels, while it is idle to expect the mood of the people to mature simultaneously in all the member countries. I nevertheless disagree with the left-wingers who pleaded in favour of the Maastricht Treaty, arguing that Europe will be the field for the crucial class struggles of tomorrow. If you don't fight against the established order on your home pitch, you will not be magically radicalised by the transfer of the confrontation to a bigger ground.

But you will not become radical either simply by sticking to narrow frontiers. There was a time when in the British Labour Party it was enough to be 'anti-European' to have a leftish reputation. The attitude was the more absurd since it was obvious that the policies of a prospective Labour government would be too mild to clash with the liberal framework of the then Common Market. The conversion to 'Europe' of a Labour Party drifting further and further to the Right is thus natural. The debate over the capitalist integration of western Europe is losing at least some of its ambiguity.

The Left-wing critics of the Maastricht Treaty (or of Nafta) must be extremely careful to distinguish their opposition from that of the jingoist challengers of the Treaty. They have to stress that their opposition is essentially tactical, that sovereignty is not one of their shibboleths, that they will be ready tomorrow to reach agreements with the unions or workers' councils of Alcatel, Siemens or Fiat, whereas they reject the deal reached by their bosses to-day. They must emphasise their internationalism not only to preserve the Left's principles and identity, but also for strategic reasons. If the nation state still provides scope for initial action, it does not do it for long. The breathing space must be counted in weeks and months rather than years. A left-wing government coming into office and trying to introduce policies running against the trend would be under immediate attack in this deregulated environment, where almost all money is potentially hot money. Therefore, it must have an internationally minded platform (involving, for instance, a reduction of working hours, the transformation of the Social Chapter in the Treaty into an instrument of genuine defence of workers' rights, a programme for the reshaping and strengthening of the welfare state, and so on), one that can mobilise the working people in the other member countries, allowing it to extend the confrontation from the national to the European terrain.

Historians who examine our age may be puzzled by the one-sided nature of the struggle so far. The Left dropped any reference to the class nature of the conflict at the very moment when the Right, headed by Reagan and Thatcher, embarked on an episode of naked class war. Similarly, while employers have been busy building a Europe of big business, designed to stimulate their profits, the labour unions have been paradoxically parochial. Nobody would now envisage a trade union limited, say, to Lombardy or Yorkshire or Michigan. A purely national union in Europe is fast becoming equally absurd. The differences in wages and social benefits between countries within the European Union are such that the employers don't even have to move overseas to start their strategy of the lowest common denominator. The Left, if it wants to survive, has internationalism thrust upon it. Necessity, alas, is not always the guarantee of a progressive solution.

Since a Europe *from below* is unlikely to be built in the immediate future, is it impossible to envisage an independent European Union built *from above* by the capitalist state? I shall have to give the reasons for my negative answer in shorthand. For unification you need a unifier, a country which could perform the role Prussia had played within the German *Zollverein*. There were three such candidates. First, the United States, which pushed Europe towards integration, then decided it would be a dangerous rival and gave up. Next came General de Gaulle, whose dominant figure concealed for a time the fact that he had the trappings of power, not its substance. Finally, there was and there is Germany itself. As long as it was divided and considered that it needed an American nuclear umbrella to protect it, Germany could not be the leader of a coalition standing up to the United States. This handicap should have vanished together with the Berlin wall. But, though the united Germany is undoubtedly the crucial power in Europe, the Europe is not moving beyond the American orbit. The desire to see the United States assuring the capitalist world order seems stronger than the inner contradiction. This is why the old slogan stressing the alternative – United Socialist States of Europe or Europe of the United States – remains valid for the foreseeable future.

Americanisation is a bit of a misnomer. In a sense, ever since the war, Europe, emerging from ruins, has been 'catching up with America', imitating its pattern of consumption and, hence, its way of life. americanisation here means the form of exploitation destined by the United States for the privileged parts of the world as capitalism spreads across the globe. In other words, to reject our American future is to question the inevitability of capitalism.

Actually, it is nowhere written that the United States is bound to be capitalist for ever. True, there was a time when one assumed that the break with the old system would first occur in countries like France and Italy, with their big Communist parties and a radical tradition. Nobody would now venture such orders of priority. The odd lands out have been 'normalised'; and it is in countries where its link with the labour movement is strongest, like Germany, that the Left may find it most difficult to accept the new strategy. Besides, with the economy becoming really global, to think of 'socialism in a single country' becomes totally absurd.

In the current conjuncture, however, because of its social democratic developments and left-wing heritage now coming under attack, western Europe is more likely in the next few years to provide the state for a crucial confrontation. It is there that the regime is getting close to the end of its tether. It is there that rising unemployment shows the basic contradiction between our technological genius and the absurdity of our social organisation. It is there, as mentioned earlier, that the questions – raised but unanswered in the 'sixties about the nature of our production, the purposes of our consumption, the pattern of our social organisation – that these questions will have to be tackled.

Rimbaud wrote about the need to reinvent love. Socialism, too, will have to be reinvented or, rather, brought up to date to meet the needs of our epoch. Nobody now thinks in terms of seizure of the Winter Palace. The best one can hope for is the beginning of a movement from below destined for a distant seizure of power. Even if people are no longer fooled by the idea that history has come to a stop, they must still be convinced once again that life can be altered by collective action. To begin with, the protection of past conquests will require wide coalitions and defensive tactics. Yet, if the defence is not to lead to surrender, it will have to turn into an offensive, offering alternative solutions. Thus, it will be difficult to rally the people for long around the welfare state as it is. It will be necessary to suggest a different version, run by the people and in their interests, and therefore the vision of a different, self-managed society. All this will take time. Yet simultaneously, we are racing against the clock, because Nature abhors the void and, if the Left does not provide rational solutions, the Extreme Right may well usher in the reign of Unreason. From Antwerp with its Vlaams Blok to Rome with its neo-fascists, the ghosts from the past remind us of the dangerous future.

THE YELTSIN REGIME

K.S. Karol

Translated by David Macey

Who holds power in Russia? The question seems ridiculous. Since 12 December 1993, the country has had an ultra-presidential constitution and its architect, Boris Yeltsin, supposedly rules virtually unopposed. For a number of reasons that are the subject of fierce controversy in Moscow, he cannot do so. Various explanations have been put forward: his health, his lack of judgement when it comes to choosing his collaborators, or his inability to decide on the right policies. Some are already laying bets that he will not last until his mandate expires in June 1996; others, like Gennady Burbulis hope that he will complete his mandate 'with dignity' and then leave the stage. But does Boris Yeltsin himself have any intention of doing so?

The Russian President has surrounded himself with a much larger staff than that of the Central Committee of the defunct CPSU. The President's administration employs 40,000 people and has an annual budget of three billion roubles. It pays the salaries of deputies and senators, the judges of the Constitutional Court and the state prosecutors. Running this little empire is no easy task, particularly in that those who belong to it are not bound together by any party discipline or solidarity. The 'old democrats' who brought Boris Yeltsin to power can be counted on the fingers of one hand. They have been replaced by so-called administrators recruited on the basis of whom they know. Access to 'Tsar Boris' counts for much more than an individual's place in the hierarchy. Those who get to the 'Tsar' first win their case. Better still, they can have a dacha if they need it, or a luxury flat in Moscow. They can travel in planes belonging to the presidential flight and enjoy other privileges, some of them paid in coin of the realm. In 1994 Yeltsin rewarded the Duma for its 'good behaviour' by giving every deputy a holiday bonus of two million roubles; very few of them refused the tip.

Yuri Petrov has long been the most influential man at court.[1] He was Boris Yeltsin's assistant and then his successor on the CPSU secretariat in Sverdlovsk before becoming the President's chief of staff. Worn out by the campaigns waged against him by the 'democrats', who resented his friendship with Fidel Castro, he opted for the less important but much more promising post of Director General of the State Investment Corporation in 1992. Since then Boris Nikolaevich's timetable has been drawn up for him every morning by Victor Ilyushin, another former member of the Sverdlosk secretariat who has worked with Yeltsin since 1977.[2] One other man has unrestricted access to the presidential office: General Alexander Korjakov, who is responsible for his security.[3] The former KGB major has not left Yeltsin's side since he became his bodyguard in the late 1980s. He now runs a security service that does not report to any ministry and which has been likened to a presidential mini-army. Korzhakov holds a lower rank than General Barsukov, the Kremlin's military commander, but that does not prevent him from playing a much more important role. The President has surrounded himself with a Pretorian Guard because, as he indicates in his memoirs, his relationships with the minister for National Defence and with the Security Services have not always been idyllic. He has recently been defending Defence Minister General Pavel Grachev tooth and nail. Grachev is very unpopular with the army and is suspected of being corrupt: it is said that Yeltsin is afraid that his possible successor might be less accommodating.[4]

This list of the men who rule the roost in the Kremlin wold be incomplete without the name of another veteran of the Sverdlovsk CPSU: Oleg Lobov, who has become Secretary General of the National Security Council.[5] Originally modelled on the American NSC, the Council is no longer a consultative body that advises the President and has become a sort of super-government made up of a handful of very influential ministers who decide the fate of the country. This small committee has been compared to the old Politburo and, as in the Brezhnev period, it meets behind closed doors and is accountable to no one. Within this context, Oleg Lobov appears to be a more important leader than Prime Minister Chernomyrdin, to say nothing of the presidents of the upper and lower houses, who are mere figureheads.

Be that as it may, more than half of Boris Yeltsin's most eminent collaborators are former apparatchiks from Sverdlovsk. This fact is very much part of the Soviet tradition: it was normal practice for a Secretary General of the CPSU to staff the Kremlin with his own men, who were known, outside the walls of the Kremlin, as his 'mafia'. Some see this continuity in Moscow as a comical paradox. For the West, Yeltsin is the man who 'killed the communist monster'; Russians have the impression that he is in fact the 'saviour of the CPSU's cadres', as they still hold key positions both in the centre and on the periphery. Having put their party cards in their back pockets, these privileged members of the 'old regime' can now govern with a clear conscience and under a different name. Their detractors are, nevertheless, wrong to conclude that nothing has really changed in Moscow. It is true that much of the old Nomenklatura is still there, but the rules that once governed recruitment and internal promotion no longer exist. They vanished the day the CPSU was dissolved, and nothing has been put in their place. The new government is not based on a Party-State, and that is an improvement, but it has done nothing to stimulate political life or give it a new basis. On the contrary, it is now openly preaching depoliticization and argues that it is essential if society is to be stabilized. The presidential team's new doctrine has much in common with that adopted by the CPSU in its final days, when it relied solely upon the apathy of the population to keep it in power. Political activity is no longer illegal, but there is so little of it that it is difficult to understand what it consists of.

In this connection, electoral arithmetic is of no help. Counting how many 'communists' have handed in their party cards and how many claim to have kept them is a pointless exercise. Two sociologists who work for the weekly *Argument i Faty* have, however, attempted to do so in order to demonstrate that the influence of the CP remained astonishingly stable between November 1917 and December 1993, and has always hovered at between thirty and thirty-five per cent of the vote. In the election to the Constituent Assembly in November 1917, Lenin's list did indeed win thirty per cent of the vote; in 1991, Yeltsin's four communist opponents won thirty-five per cent between them. In the latest legislative elections (1993), the CP and its ally, the Agrarian Party, won twenty-two per cent of the vote. The other Communist Parties –there are four – called on their supporters to abstain, but would probably otherwise have taken a further ten per cent (the turnout was very low). Taken as a whole, they probably still represent the strongest party in Russia, but it is estimated that they have no more than 550,00 members in a country with a population of 150 million. Gennady Ziuganov's communists are recruited mainly from medium-sized towns and rural areas.[6] In the autonomous republics of the Caucasus, they won as much as seventy-two per cent of the vote (but not in Chechenia, which refused to take part in the elections). In Moscow and St Petersburg, however, they won only twelve and nine per cent respectively, and that is not enough to influence developments in the metropolitan areas which, in the eyes of the world, are the very incarnation of Russia.

Although biased and partial, the data are enough to demonstrate the fragility of the 'eternal red nomenklatura' thesis. The Nomenklatura has shattered into fragments, and the dividing lines are roughly the same as those that have appeared in the economy. The 'nomenklaturists' have made sure that they have dominant positions in what is now known as 'finance capital' and 'industrial capital', but they have abandoned the strictly political realm. That is regarded as a no man's land that no force is likely to occupy in the foreseeable future. And this may be the specifically

Russian feature of post-communism; in the other Slav republics – the Ukraine and Bielorussia – different developments have led to a democratic handover of power.

The 'nomenklaturists' who once ran the economic ministries and big factories throughout the entire USSR are in an ideal position to profit from the sudden and chaotic dismantling of the centralized administrative system. What have they replaced it with? They very quickly set up joint stock companies and firms of every possible – and imaginable – kind. They are based on Western models, but are free of the minimal controls that exist in the West, even in deregulated economies. If we look at the structure of any new trading company in Russia, we will find that it is either allied with or owned by a bank. Behind the bank, we will find a group of companies and, behind them, a holding company or a financial-industrial group. The president of the bank is in most cases the manager of the conglomerate. Thanks to their contacts in the Western world, Russian bankers learned very quickly that it is possible to multiply their money effortlessly and at no risk to themselves by means of purely financial deals. They make colossal sums by gambling on interest rates, speculating on the weakness of the rouble and investing their capital abroad. In November 1994, the Kremlin issued a decree banning the purchase of property in the West without prior authorization from the National Bank of Russia. This provoked great mirth in Moscow society: 'the Kremlin has just learned from its vigilant counter-espionage service that, for three years now, our wheeler-dealers have been buying more apartment blocks than anyone else in Western Europe, Florida, California and even the Seychelles.' Russia's financial giants, who are worth trillions of roubles, invest almost nothing in Russian industry because they know that its productivity is poor and precarious. This has greatly disappointed Yegor Gaidar, who promoted radical economic reforms in 1991.[7] One can well understand his disappointment: his government did the impossible to create 'Russian finance capital' *ex nihilo*. He played that card for doctrinal reasons, hoping to place drastic limitations on the State's economic role and assuming that the banks would pump prime the 'free market'. Something went wrong with the equation.

Being a third-generation 'nomenklaturist', Yegor Gaidar knew all about the official economy and nothing at all about the shadow economy that had been developing since at least 1970. He therefore failed to foresee that, by giving existing banks the green light, he would trigger an extraordinary proliferation of two to three thousand banks of all kinds. They are subject to no controls. Many are not registered with the Ministry of Finance and they are involved in all kinds of speculation. The wheeler-dealers of the 'grey economy' initially had an estimated capital of seventy billion 'old regime' roubles (at a time when the dollar was worth five roubles on the black market, and not four thousand, as at the end of 1994). Many of them were intelligent men and, in their own way, they were brave. They defied the laws of a totalitarian regime by organizing a whole parallel trade system with the help of corrupt officials and, of course, the criminal underworld. It is not surprising that, when the free market came into being, they should have abandoned their favourite activity (commerce) and gone into banking. In Yeltsin's Russia, no one asks anyone about how they made their fortunes. Indeed, such questions are regarded as 'totalitarian'. There was therefore no legal obstacle to prevent 'the bosses who lay down the law for thieves' – *vory v zakonie*, as they say in Russian – from transforming themselves overnight into respectable bankers and businessmen. According to official statistics, twenty-two per cent of these parvenus have done lengthy vocational courses in prison, and twenty-five per cent have had more or less serious dealings with the police. But money can open any door, even the door that leads into the Kremlin's offices and that is so well guarded by General Alexander Korzhakov.

We know, however, that the ways of the 'shadow economy' and the underworld have always been rough and even violent. They soon permeated into the new financial world. Before long anyone who wanted to recover a debt or settle a more dubious score was recruiting henchmen and taking direct action. A law passed as early as 1992 authorized the formation of 'agencies to protect people and their property', and these spread like mushrooms after a shower of rain (there are reported to be over twenty-six thousand in Russia). It goes without saying that they have the right to arm their recruits, who are also numbered in their thousands. As a result Russia, which was once regarded as a country with a poor criminal culture where people were killed with knives, has taken a qualitative step forward into sophisticated crime. Scores are now settled not only with fire arms of all calibres, but even with bazookas and surface-to-surface missiles.[8] Moscow and St Petersburg already figure amongst the most violent cities in the world.

So-called 'popular' privatization, which took the form of distributing vouchers to the population at large, has made these bloody gangland killings more serious still. Investment funds have begun to buy vouchers, and to send sackloads of them to towns where factories are about to be privatized. To cite only one example which caused a scandal, one such fund bought Severryba, a huge fishing company in Murmansk, for a song – ten million roubles or so. Its real value is estimated at five billion dollars. Such purchases are planned like military operations. *Razviedchiki* (reconnaissance patrols) are sent out in advance, and are then followed by shock troops who take out the potential competitors. If *Izvestia* is to be believed, the mafia bosses have gained control of the entire aluminium industry. It is, after hydrocarbons, Russia's second biggest exporter.

On 14 June 1994, Boris Yeltsin signed Decree no. 1226, which provides for 'exceptional measures to protect the population from banditry and organized crime.' It allows suspects to be held for questioning for thirty days. Premises can be searched without a warrant and unannounced checks can be made on bank accounts. The Duma refused to endorse this 'liberticide' decree, but the President stood firm. The problem is that nothing has happened since then. And yet in Moscow it is increasingly a matter of common knowledge that the crucial financial sector is falling into the hands of the mafia, and that the situation is dangerous. Having relied solely upon 'the power of money' to introduce the market, the government is now powerless against the criminals who are running the economy. The West, which was initially very tolerant of Russia's *nouveaux riches*, is in its turn beginning to have doubts about their 'dirty money'. There is more and more talk of the 'threat posed by the Russian mafia', which could become even larger than the international drugs mafia, and that is saying a great deal. It has therefore been suggested that the Russian government should do something, if only to give Russian banks a minimal credibility abroad and to save what can still be saved of an economy that has been selling everything off for three years. But how is the government to go about doing this? There is talk of setting up a Russian FBI, but such a body is unlikely to become operational in the months to come.

The approach of the 1996 elections makes things more complicated still. The court in the Kremlin would not survive Boris Yeltsin's defeat, and it is not a body that is designed to hand over power should it be defeated. A good part of the present elite would be likely to find itself in Lefortovo prison, so flagrant are the abuses of power and the accumulation of illicit wealth. Vladimir Chumeiko,[9] who is already wanted for embezzlement, has suggested that the elections should be postponed for two years, but this proposal has been violently rejected by the opposition and by most of the public. Being a cautious man, Yeltsin did not support the proposal, but he is capable of doing so as 1996 comes nearer. What is more, the opposition is sadly lacking in charismatic figures, and it is well known that it is divided.

Given this void, analysts think that a candidate supported by the big banks, such as Yuri Lukyov, the mayor of Moscow,[10] would stand the best chance of winning the election. His only dangerous rival would be Prime Minister Viktor Chernomyrdin, who can rely on the financial support of Gazprom, which has a monopoly on gas exports and handles billions of dollars. But, blinded by 'the power of money', the same analysts failed to predict the breakthrough made by Vladimir Zhirinovsky's far-right party in the 1993 legislative elections, and fail to take into account military candidates like the eminently charismatic General Alexander Lebed, who might be able to win on a 'law and order' platform without any help from the banks.[11] Russia is, as Solzhenitsyn has said, ruled by an oligarchy which lives from day to day. Its policies serve only its own interests, and it is allowing the country to go to the dogs. That, however, has not resigned it to accepting what can only be a negative verdict from the electorate.

It is in this context that we have to situate the war that was launched against Chechenia on 11 December 1994. It is not for me to explain here the complex history of the small Caucasian republic (population: 1.2 million) that declared itself independent at the end of 1991. From then onwards, it was 'a small thorn in the foot of the Russian elephant', as the saying goes. Russia seemed to be willing to live with it. The National Security Council's sudden decision to use extreme military measures to extirpate the 'Chechen thorn' was totally unexpected by the public. That the 'war party' – Generals Grachev, Korzhakov and Lobov – was convinced that a Blitzkrieg in Chechenia would restore the Russian President's tarnished reputation and allow him to regain his lost popularity, provides only a partial explanation. They were also relying upon the anti-Chechen xenophobia of sectors of the population that are already furiously hostile to the Caucasians because they are supposedly all in the mafia. The enemy was, then well chosen. Unfortunately for Yeltsin and his allies, the enemy also proved to be capable of stubborn resistance and very difficult to defeat. A war which, according to General Grachev, should have lasted for a few hours threatened to set the whole Caucasus ablaze and last for years.

For many in both Russia and the West, the invasion of Chechenia has revealed the dictatorial nature of the Yeltsin regime. In a democracy, a President – even one with extensive powers – cannot declare war without consulting his government and without getting the go-ahead from his parliament within a reasonable space of time. In Russia, Yeltsin acted like an all-powerful Tsar, and provoked protests even from those who, like Gaidar, Burbulis and Poltoranin, were prepared to guarantee the democratic nature of his regime only a year before. What is more, many military men – and important ones at that – are becoming rebellious because they take the view that the army should not be used on Russian soil against a population that is, officially, Russian. This makes for a highly explosive mixture, and suggests that the tragedy that is being played out in Chechenia will have its epilogue in Moscow. The Russian army does not have a Bonapartist tradition and is afraid that internal divisions might lead to a fratricidal war. Even so, the prestige of 'dissident' generals like Boris Gromov, former commander in chief in Afghanistan,[12] or Alexander Lebed, who commands the Fourteenth Army in Dniestr region is infinitely greater than that of the generals in command of the Chechen expedition. The latter have been discredited both by their military incompetence and their politics. It is therefore not impossible that the entire army will rally to generals hostile to Yeltsin, and that would signal the end of his reign.

Western attitudes towards Boris Yeltsin are a perfect illustration of the saying that 'Victory has a host of fathers, but defeat is always an orphan.' Once his Blitzkrieg in Chechnia was halted, neither Washington nor Bonn looked so favourably on Yeltsin. Nor does the London-based *The Economist*, which constantly sang his praises for so many years. On 7 January 1995, the cover of the famous British weekly that is the Bible of the neo-liberals, featured a photograph of a rather doleful Russian President and the legend: 'The Wrong Man for Russia.' This sudden change of heart was not the result of humanitarian concerns, nor is it a protest against the bloodbath in Grozny. It is the result of some very down to earth thinking: this man is surrounded by a clique that is out of control; he is becoming bogged down in the Chechen quagmire, and might turn his back on 'reformist' policies overnight. And so, they begin to dig out the CIA's confidential reports on the President's entourage, which is dominated not by 'real reformers', but by apparatchiks and military men. Now all the individuals mentioned by the CIA – from General Korzhakov to Viktor Ilyushin – have long been familiar figures in Moscow and elsewhere. It was with their help that Yeltsin dissolved the Supreme Soviet on 21 September 1993 and then shelled it on 4 October of the same year. Russian's democratic experiment ended then, with the blessing of the West. And the West would have done the same if the invasion of Chechenia had ended with a rapid victory.

Yeltsin was forgiven everything because, as he himself put it when he was in Washington, he had 'killed the communist monster' and because he was going to bring the lost Russian sheep back into the capitalist fold. But as we entered 1995, doubts were arising as to his ability to keep that promise because all he has created is a market with a high crime rate, and that is not what serious Western investors want, and because he is politically unpredictable. That is why Moscow's 'democrats', who remain faithful to the market at all costs, are being strongly advised to find another candidate for the Russian Presidency and to drop 'the wrong man for Russia.' There is no proof that if the right candidate did come to power with the help of the West, he wold be acceptable to the Russians. Indeed, the odds are that he would not.

One of Moscow's most important bankers, Vladimir Gussinski, who became a billionaire in the space of three years, has argued that dynamic businessmen like himself – five per cent of the population – must be put in command if the remaining ninety-five per cent is to work efficiently.[13] He is saying aloud what the neo-liberal shock-therapists are thinking to themselves. That is why they had no qualms about robbing the entire population of its savings and handing them on a plate to the sharks of the Nomenklatura and Russia's Wild West in January 1992. The Supreme

Soviet protested against this unauthorized redistribution of wealth, but was accused of wanting to restore the old regime and was then dispersed by gunfire. Since then, social inequalities in Russia have reached Latin American proportions, and even the ultra-rich (five per cent of the population) do not find this climate of general lawlessness to their liking. Vladimir Gussinski for example, has chosen to seek shelter with his family in London. In a society ruled by the law of the jungle, everyone defends themselves as best they can, falling back on their clan or family, or relying on their own resources. Hence the increase in centrifugal forces, Chechenia being only one example amongst many. The Chechens – and the other people of the Caucasus – have undeniable historical claims on Russia, but they would not have taken such a savagely intransigent form if Russia had offered them a decent life and civilized relations. Boris Yeltsin has failed to understand this basic political truth. In October 1993, it took only five tanks, and five very well paid tank crews, to launch an assault on Moscow's White House. But he does not have enough tanks, or enough money to pay their crews, to restore order in the Caucasus, or in Moscow, when the time comes. The blame for his disaster lies with Yeltsin and his team. There is no doubt about that, but the West – G7, the IMF and the World Bank – are also partly responsible for encouraging them to take a road that leads only into the abyss.

Paris, December 1994

NOTES

1. Having succeeded Boris Yeltsin as the head of the CPSU's regional secretariat in Sverdlovsk in 1986, Yuri Petrov became the USSR's ambassador to Cuba in 1990. On his return to Moscow, he took up the post of head of the President's administration in 1991. His pro-Castro statements unwittingly triggered a campaign on the part of the 'democratic' press, which accused him of being pro-communist. On Petrov's sixtieth birthday in May 1992, Yeltsin himself suggested that he should choose another post that would leave him less exposed to press criticisms.
2. The forty-eight year old Viktor Ilyushin comes originally from the Urals and has spent almost his entire career in Boris Yeltsin's shadow. He started his career in a modest post in the party apparatus in Sverdlovsk and then served as Yeltsin's 'aide' in Moscow in 1991–92. Since May 1992, he has been 'the president's principal collaborator', but that does not make him his chief of staff.
3. Not a great deal is known about General Korzhakov, whose entire career has been spent in the KGB. When Boris Yeltsin came to Moscow in 1985, Korzhakov was only thirty-five and held the rank of major. When Yeltsin fell from grace two years later, the young officer remained in touch with him and has been very generously rewarded for his loyalty since 1991. In 1992, Korzhakov, promoted to the rank of general and now in command of the President's mini-army, was accused in the press of having asked journalists for large sums of money in exchange for arranging an interview with the President. This scandal, like so many others, was quickly hushed up.
4. The forty-seven year old General Pavel Grachev was appointed Defence Minister in May 1992. At that very time Bolduriev, the President of the State Control Commission, was severely attacking him over the corruption prevailing amongst Russian troops stationed in

Germany. Grachev therefore owes Yeltsin everything, and yet in 1993, he hesitated for a long time before obeying the President's written orders to attack Parliament with his tanks. Since then the two men, who live in the same building and share a taste for vodka, seem to have grown very close, but we do not know who the dominant partner is.

5. The fifty-eight year old Oleg Ivanovich Labov was born in Kiev but worked in Sverdlovsk for a long time, and is the only real politician in Boris Yeltsin's entourage. During the anti-Gorbachev putsch of August 1991, Yeltsin even entrusted him with a mission to go to the Urals and form a government there. Lobov later became Deputy Prime Minister, and has been Secretary General of the National Security Council since 15 April 1993.

6. The fifty-year old Gennady Ziuganov is from Orel, one of the central-Russian cities that have remained very loyal to the Communist Party. Before becoming a CPSU official, he taught mathematics and did not hold an important post until 1990. He became a member of the Politburo of the Russian CP, which was founded at the end of the Gorbachev era. Elected to the Supreme Soviet, he left the White House before the events of 4 October 1993. As the coordinator and then the leader of the new Communist Party of the Russian Federation, he refused to boycott the elections in December 1993, and his success strengthened his position. He is not, however, popular with everyone within the CP leadership, or even within his own parliamentary group. He is thought to take too concil-iatory a view of the Kremlin and to be too timid in general. Ziuganov claims that his cautious line will win him the next legislative elections, but he does not appear to wish to be a candidate for the Russian presidency.

7. The thirty-nine year old Yegor Gaidar is the grandson of a 'red commissar' and the son of an admiral, and won a certain audience as an economic analysist working on *Kommunist* and *Pravda*. In late 1991, Yeltsin put him in charge of the economy. It was therefore Gaidar who applied the 'shock therapy' that was supposed to reform society. Removed from his post by the Supreme Soviet in December 1992, he was given the position of deputy Prime Minister on 14 December 1993 – a week to the day after the dissolution of the Supreme Soviet. After the events of October 1993, he launched his 'Russia's Choice' movement in the hope of winning the elections with a large majority. He won only fourteen per cent of the votes cast. He still remained loyal to Yeltsin, and it was only when the Chechen adventure got under way that he distanced himself from him.

8. This detail about scores being settled with bazookas and surface-to-surface missiles seemed to me to be exaggerated, but it appears in an article about crime in Russia published in *Izvestia* on 20 October 1994.

9. Currently president of the upper house, the fifty-year old Vladimir Chumeiko was involved in a very compromising scandal involving the import of 'table football' games from Switzerland in 1993. Although duly paid for, they never reached Moscow. Yeltsin had to relieve him of his post as Deputy Prime Minister, but he was restored to grace when the Supreme Soviet was abolished. Very closely involved with Russia's financial sharks, he has suggested that the presidential elections due to be held in June 1996 should be postponed, hoping that this will save Yeltsin and perhaps even allow him to stand himself.

10. Yuri Lukyov, fifty-eight, 'inherited' the position of Mayor of Moscow in July 1992 after the resignation of Gavril Popov, who had been elected by universal suffrage and who was critical of Yeltsin's new nomenklatura. Well regarded by the 'business community', Lukyov did not stand in the 1993 parliamentary elections and has therefore not been adversely affected by the defeat of the 'democrats'.

11. Born in Novocherkask, the capital of the Don Cossacks, the forty-four year old Alexander Lebed won his general's stars with a paratroop regiment in Afghanistan. In June 1992, he took command of the Fourteenth Army in Transdniestria and gained immense popularity when he succeeded in bringing the war between the Moldavans and the Russian population to an end. While paying tribute to his qualities as a paratrooper, Yeltsin remarks in his memoirs that the general is very 'sharp-tongued'. General Lebed, who is also famous for his sobriety, did not mince his words when he criticised both the Russian

President – a 'useless specimen' in his view – and the war in Chechenia.

12. The fifty-two year old Boris Gromov was the Soviet Army's commander in chief when it pulled out of Afghanistan, and he is no political novice. In 1990, he was Deputy Minister of the Interior, and in 1991 he stood for the Vice-Presidency on the ticket of Nikolai Ryzhkov, then Mikhail Gorbachev's Prime Minister. Under Yeltsin, he became Deputy Minister for national Defence. he was relieved of his functions in January 1995, but that has not led him to leave the army.

13. The forty-two year old Vladimir Gussinski, an obscure theatre director from the provinces, founded the 'Most' bank in 1992. He enjoys the protection of the mayor of Moscow and has become spectacularly rich through speculative property deals and thanks to murky banking operations. In the hope of becoming Russia's Berlusconi, he launched NTR, the country's first private television station, and the daily *Sevodnia*. His ambitions eventually began to alarm the Kremlin, which disarmed his 'army' of bodyguards (between one and three thousand men) and thus forced him into exile in London.

THE STATE IN THE THIRD WORLD*

William Graf

Theories of 'the' state, in particular 'the' Third World state, have fallen far from their erstwhile theoretical pre-eminence. Caught up in the postulated dual 'impasse' of development theory[1] on the one hand, and of the state in international relations theory[2] on the other, and eroded by a growing corpus of sub-state, and indeed extra-state theories, the theory of the Third World state has not fared well in the first half of the neo-classical nineties.

Nor has the discourse in which the Third World state has been framed. If the mainstream development literature of the 1960s and 1970s presupposed a 'modernizing' or 'developmental' state and the Marxist approaches of the same period invoked the 'strong,' 'overdeveloped' and (relatively) 'autonomous' postcolonial state; and if the eighties produced rather more ambiguous concepts such as the 'rentier state,' the 'peripheral state' or the 'bureaucratic-authoritarian state;' then in the nineties the imagery has turned relentlessly negative as expressed in such coinages as 'vassal state,' 'predator state,' 'vampire state,' 'receiver state,' 'prostrate state,' and even 'fictitious state,' 'show of state' or 'collapsed state.'

The changing imagery of the Third World state reflects the new reality, particularly for states in Africa and large parts of Latin and Central American, Asia, and the Middle East as well as those Eastern European states that have now been downgraded from the Second to the Third World. Despite the formidable heterogeneity of this 'South' and the susceptibility to charges of ethnocentrism and simplification to which one exposes oneself in trying to deal with it as one undifferentiated whole, the states, or most of them, do, I think, share a common reality in their subordinate situation – their peripheralization or marginalization – within an increasingly globalized and polarized world capitalist system. This justifies the blanket term 'Third World;' and it is with this rapidly changing and evolving entity that the present contribution is concerned.

*A first draft of this contribution was presented to the December 1994 British International Studies Association conference in York. The comments and criticisms there were most helpful in preparing this version. John McMurtry, Jorge Nef, Craig Benjamin and Leo Panitch have also contributed their thoughts and suggestions for which I am grateful

140

Globalization and Neo-liberalism

The hegemonic vision of world society for the Millennium has clearly emerged in the notion of globalization. In contrast to the still aggressively anticommunist 'New World Order' that opened the nineties, the 'kinder, gentler' – and more self-evidently hegemonic – 'globalization' of the dominant international discourse is a 'postcommunist' and even 'postimperialist' statement of a world becoming more and more unified in a progressive neo-classical and neo-liberal system proclaiming free choice, free enterprise and free labour. The end of the state-socialist challenge to hegemonic capitalism lends force to the powerful underlying myths of globalization – that it is desirable, that it is dynamic, that it is inevitable, and that, anyway, it is the only game in town.

From out of the surfeit of recent literature on globalization one central leitmotif clearly emerges: it is in its core profoundly and relentlessly anti-state. The overinflated, centralized and bureaucratized state is the universal villain in the neo-liberal world-view. At the state's doorstep is laid blame for the world economic crises of the mid-seventies and early eighties. Its suffocating grip is said to have held in check the many creative, entrepreneurial forces waiting to emerge. The state is everywhere depicted as an institution to be overcome, decentralized, devolved and otherwise reduced in role and status.

In its stead, the market becomes the central institution in the neo-liberal vision. To use Charles Lindblom's still-relevant terms, the 'authority relation' of the state is replaced by the 'exchange relation' of the market as the primary mechanism of social control.[3] Or as Peter Self suggests, neo-liberalism is, at its core, 'government by the market' wherein government appears as 'a pale auxiliary of the market system.'[4] In other words, the market is viewed not merely as a means of allocating goods and services, but as a form of social regulation. It becomes in many ways the leading principle to guide individual and collective action, corresponding with Lockean and Adam Smithian laissez-faire liberal ideology of two hundred years ago and with what became the dominant world-view in the mid-nineteenth century.[5] (The difference is, of course, that the initial liberal project also represented a historical struggle for greater individual freedom in society against the privilege and arbitrary power of the landed aristocracy, and mid-nineteenth century liberalism underpinned an industrial revolution, while today's neo-liberalism is the core of the ideological project of big, entrenched and transnational capital.) This restoration of market pre-eminence and its internationalization presents market capitalism, or the generalized use of commodities, as the optimal strategy for economic progress and efficiency. Within it, business and commercial groups in individual states, as well as wealthier, industrialized, and indeed post-Fordist Northern states are strengthened vis-a-vis labour, the poor and the South respectively.

Globalization thus represents a (unilateral) abrogation of the Keynesian pact or the postwar social contract between capital and labour in the advanced capitalist states – but not in the peripheral areas, where Keynesian welfare capitalism has never made it onto the agenda – according to which labour accepted capital's right to ownership and overall economic direction in exchange for social benefits, an expanding welfare state and a guaranteed level of employment security. As global economic growth slowed in the seventies, as regional capitalist competition grew within the changing international division of labour, and as a growing chorus of new social movements and other oppositional groups sought to renegotiate or even abrogate the deal, however, capital and 'its' states in the OECD area developed and are carrying out a project of dissolution of the Keynesian bloc. The 'borderless' international economy that capital has created can, piece by piece, simply declare the Keynesian compromise to be at an end, and insist on reducing wages and benefits by delinking them from productivity increases and allowing them to fall to their 'market' value. Job security is declared obsolete and unemployment is allowed to rise to a 'natural' level. Internationalized production eclipses Fordist mass production, at least in the less profitable sectors, which it consigns to the less-developed regions of the globe, and concentrates on 'post-Fordist' high-quality, high-technology production as well as selected sectors of still-profitable Fordist production. The 'Third Industrial Revolution' facilitates these processes by differentiating the production process, segmenting markets, globalizing finance, implementing flexible manufacturing systems, transnationalizing intra-firm management, and creating new 'circuits of power' through international regimes.[6]

Trade, rather than domestic mass purchasing power, becomes the driving force of the new global economy. Sales abroad, in fierce and unrelenting competition to drive down costs and therefore prices, is its distinguishing characteristic – a strategy that seems particularly dysfunctional when one considers that only about one-quarter of global trade can be considered as GATT-governed, unimpeded free trade.[7] In this 'race to the bottom where each state competes against every other state to make itself more attractive to global commerce and the ambulatory well-off,'[8] part-time, low-wage employment (the 'McDonaldization' of the work force[9]) becomes the norm for most, while a comparatively small, more specialized, higher-paid technocratic and managerial elite enhances its relative influence in the economy. For all, job insecurity and constant competition for fewer positions is the norm. Workers – like nations – who are no longer central to this internationalized division of labour, can be left to fend for themselves, without state 'interference,' in an increasingly Darwinian struggle for survival and dominance.

Of course, the perception of such harsh, debilitating effects is mitigated by the belief that economic rationality, methodological individualism, deregulation, privatization of state-owned industries, rollback of the state and elimination of barriers to trade will, in the long term, produce dynamic economic expansion across all sectors (after eliminating the weak or obsolete industries and trades) and all global regions, with resultant benefits to all. For Robert Reich, who can be said to represent the 'social democratic' or still somewhat socially oriented tendency in this school, the challenge is for each state to adapt to the new exigencies. Since there are no longer any national economies or national industries or national companies, 'all that remains behind are people who share a political system . . . Each nation's primary political task is to cope with the centrifugal forces of the global economy.'[10]

Recommodification and Democratization

From the perspective of the Third World state, the phenomenon of globalization can, I think, be usefully cast in terms of a primarily economic dimension, *recommodification,* and a very closely related, mainly political one, formal-liberal *democratization.*

The former concept, *recommodification,* I borrow and develop from Claus Offe's important analysis of the welfare state which, a decade ago, he saw as threatened by the power of capital because it was implicated in a 'primary contradiction' from which it could not extricate itself: on the one hand, the capitalist economy, with the profits, revenues, etc. that it generates, was historically necessary to make the welfare state work in the first place; but state intervention increased the scope of decommodification (or autonomous, unregulated spheres of social action). However, decommodification, while it brought greater social peace and increased mass purchasing power, was in the longer term also a limitation on capital's sphere of action, flexibility and profitability and hence a threat to its power. Capital's (logical) response was to recommodify, a process which 'seeks to decrease the scope and importance of decommodified political and administrative power by resuscitating 'market forces,'[11] mainly by means of wresting functions and powers from the state and 'privatizing' or abolishing them.

Subject to some obvious qualifications mainly related to scale and sovereignty, the recommodification process has many parallels in the international order. From about the early 1950s onward, the Third World had managed, through collective actions and the selective use of relevant fora such as UNCTAD or the UNGA, to carve out for itself certain spheres in which it was at least partially protected from imperialist penetration and the international market. The Keynesian or social democratic strategy that led to the assertion of a New International Economic Order aspiring to establish floor prices for commodities or at least partly curb multinational corporations' powers;[12] or the Bandung movement toward implementing collective policies aimed at overcoming underdevelopment; or the limited privileges and special advantages that the Third World countries had obtained within the international trading system, notably the Generalized Scheme of Preferences;[13] or in particular the Non-Aligned movement (G–77) which sought to keep the South relatively free from Cold War entanglement and at times threatened to evolve into an anti-imperialist and thus anti-North movement – all these in some measure were about creating a 'decommodified' sphere for the Third World, beyond the direct reach of international capital, and as such represented a challenge to Northern hegemony, albeit mainly a potential rather than imminent challenge. And all have, in greater or lesser degree, been undermined, countered and rolled back within the framework of neo-liberal globalization. The reassertion of Northern power is perhaps best symbolized by the wholesale elimination of special trade concessions in the wake of the 1994 GATT agreement as well as the 1992 Rio Conference which, among other things, imputed much of the onus for pollution to the Third World with its blame-the-victim assertion of the principle that poverty is a major contributor to environmental degradation.

In the globalized international political economy, trade has clearly emerged as the main instrument of recommodification, of deepening the subjection of the South to the dominant capitalist order. The neo-liberal doctrine of free trade, which historically has always been the ideology of the economically powerful, negates practically all forms of extra-market action and pressures the economies of the periphery to make accommodations with, or adapt to, the central global accumulation processes.

The imperative for 'freer' trade reinforces the recommodification offensive against the Third World state. Economic planning is banished to the realm of the past, and with it subsidies and price controls. In their place are substituted the laws of supply and demand. State-sponsored industrialization and economic diversification are likewise replaced by export-led development based on the principle of comparative advantage. Applied to the South, comparative advantage signifies further economic specialization in the production of raw materials and/or cheap labour within the framework of the New International Division of Labour. In place of indigenous ownership and control – the 'indigenization' drive of a decade ago – comes unrestricted foreign investment.

The institutions and 'regimes' of the international economy, particularly the World Bank and International Monetary Fund, act to enforce this recommodification process. They have instrumentalized the debt crisis of the 1980s as perhaps the major disciplining mechanism of the nineties. Conditions for debt postponement and, especially, new loans are tied to integration into the new world economy in a variety of ways, so that, in Robert Cox's words, 'governments' accountability to foreign creditors [comes] to outweigh accountability to their own citizens,'which requires them to ensure 'freedom for transnational movements of capital, facilities for the development of international production, devaluation of national currencies, raising of domestic prices, and allowing increased unemployment.'[14] Conditionalities imposed on new loans to Third World countries, particularly in the form of Structural Adjustment Programmes (SAPs) have been especially effective in this respect, in that they have induced debtor countries to divert resources from domestic production of goods and services to production for export in the manner described above. More recently, the GATT Uruguay Round, the WTO it established, and the enhanced global trade regime it foreshadows will surely increase the transnational corporations' powers and reduce the sovereign space of Third World countries.[15]

Basing himself expressly on the World Bank ethos of the late eighties, Richard Sklar, a senior American Africanist, writes that 'The spirit of capitalism in Africa has now emerged from a long shadow of ideological distrust, attributable mainly to its historical association with colonial rule. Its growth will surely invigorate the African bourgeoisie and shape its nature as African societies begin to free themselves from oppressive statism.'[16] What counts, in this Sklarian prescription, is to create an 'enabling environment' for capital – presumably international capital, since not only is African capital in short supply, what there is of it is largely held abroad as flight capital. Making the system work is then merely a matter of honest administration, stability, law and order, and an adequate infrastructure. These assumptions in turn fit neatly into the neo-liberal concept of democratization which will be examined presently.

Sklar's plea is, I think, one of the most succinct, and indeed eloquent formulations of the neo-liberal, anti-statist recommodification project as applied to the Third World (although substantially there is nothing in it that one does not encounter in the World Bank literature). It is also, in all its important elements, wrong: there is little 'spirit of capitalism' in Africa, where pre-colonial societies were characterized by collectivist and cooperative forms of social organization rather than rugged individualism; the economies are not growing, but shrinking – what is growing is foreign capital penetration; to talk of a vigorous African bourgeoisie is patently absurd; and making capitalism work in Africa, or anywhere in the South for that matter, clearly requires much more than a wider infrastructure and honest administration. But the strength of neo-liberal orthodoxy lies not in its correspondence with actual reality in the Third World, but in its potent ideological force as both a reflection of the current widespread scepticism – on both left and right – about the efficacy of the state, and as the theoretical core of world hegemonic discourse.

I argued earlier that this global recommodification process is closely connected with the prescriptions for formal-liberal *democratization*. The term 'democratization' has to be prefixed with this rather awkward combination of adjectives in order to distinguish it from the post-1989 international movements for greater emancipation and participation at the grassroots. The literature on the new social movements, popular uprisings, and participatory action research, as well as on the 'indigenous voice', discusses that form of democratization. Here I mean the hegemonic variant of democratization which is prescribed *for* the Third World.

Democracy, in this sense, turns out to be the political form most compatible with recommodification and the new globalism. If the bureau-cratic-authoritarian type of regime with some measure of relative autonomy was long thought to be more appropriate to ensure the maintenance of international order, now the exigencies of the era of structural adjustment and conditionalities are thought to require a (liberal-)democratic facade to compensate for the delegitimating effects of shrinking state services and intra-societal polarization. Jan Black shows that, in Latin America, military withdrawals from power coincide with declining GNPs and that 'redemocratization' is also accompanied by growing indebtedness and serious erosion of national economic sovereignty.[17] In other words, the call for democratization of the South, at this particular juncture, represents an admission that 'development' has actually failed, since the once-prevalent 'modernization' theory saw rapid development – with its improved standards of literacy, education and material well-being – as prior to democracy; but as a consequence of neo-liberal globalism the former is a 'chimera' and 'democratization is now advanced as a condition for development and no longer as its delayed product.'[18] To want to impose democratization on the South in this way thus signifies (a) that rapid development is no longer on the agenda for the South, so that (b) at least non-antagonistic relations can be established that reinforce the North-South status quo, while (c) imported liberal-democratic structures forestall the threat of indigenous popular democracy which would be anti-imperialist and hence, in some measure, anti-North.

A formal-liberal variant of democracy is clearly what is envisioned for the South, one that 'signifies conservatism without stagnation and reform without revolution,'[19] since this allows for (and justifies) both tolerance of social inequality and a separation of economic from political democracy. What is democratized, is the form, not the substance of democracy, which in Latin America and Africa especially, allows the military to remain 'more or less on call.'[20] Indeed, the African and South American transitions from military rule of recent years have been decreed and carried out by the military elites themselves, albeit with some prompting from advanced capitalist powers and international agencies, thus ensuring that the same social structures, income differentials and power distributions are carried over into the civilianized regimes.

All this helps to explain why the main source of pressure for formal-liberal democratization largely emanates from outside Third World societies.[21] It is therefore not surprising to learn that recently democratized regimes in Latin America 'are weak civilian regimes, with limited political agendas, narrow support, significant exclusion of popular sectors from the political arenas, [in which] external constituencies, both economic and military, enjoy *de facto* veto power and hold the key to regime support.'[22] Gills and Rocamora perhaps best capture what is at issue here with their concept of 'low-intensity democracy,' which they see as a kind of 'half-way house' between the earlier unstable democratic regimes and the more recent 'counter-productive' military dictatorships. Low-intensity democracy offers a 'stability that pre-empts more radical change by incorporating broad popular forces in electoral participation', because these conservative civilian regimes 'can better pursue painful and regressive policies' than can more authoritarian governments.[23] Thus, the 'democracy' that neo-liberalism envisages is essentially a weak and literally decontextualized replication of the structures of Western liberal democracy, and political liberalization amounts to a complementary strategy, along with recommodification, to maintain a hegemonic structure of domination.[24]

Two further concepts infuse and augment the neo-liberal democratization project, namely 'civil society' and 'good governance.' Although both have intellectual pedigrees going back at least to Aristotle (in the latter case) and Hegel (in the former), their 're-functioning' into components of the globalization orthodoxy only became possible with the collapse of state-socialist Communism. The demise of an anti-capitalist alternative has enabled the West to impose expressly political conditions, in addition to longstanding economic ones, on Third World aid and loan recipients, while the implosive nature of Communism's collapse lent force to the contention that *all* forms of socialism were inefficient, bureaucratized and undemocratic. 'Good governance,' as a form of commodified regime management, and a renewed 'civil society' as a countervailing force of multiple extra-state groups thus link economic and political liberalism into an ideologically effective support for neo-classical globalism.[25]

Seen in this way, civil society (which resembles the 'political culture' approach of modernization theory), with its voluntarist ethos and emphasis on groups and associations as the primary movers in social progress, is both an alternative to the state, in particular in the economic sphere, and a substitute for it, particularly in the decommodified spheres of welfare, education and health. And good governance by analogy advocates economic efficiency via privatization of state services and enterprises in the spheres of parastatal management, public projects and intra-societal redistributive measures – but *not* in the areas of infrastructure, law and order, or incentives for private enterprise. Competitive elections are a major mechanism for restoring good governance and encouraging civil society, as are separation of powers, pluralism and public service account-ability, which together amount to the replication of the democratic capitalist systems of the West. Every new association formed, every state function dismantled, is heralded as a victory for pluralism and democracy.

The two concepts are thus entirely consonant with, and indeed largely rooted in, World Bank and IMF prescriptions. They coincide with donors' and lenders' concepts of a Third World able to accept and administer aid on Northern terms and conditions as well as to repay debts and obligations fully and punctually. They are also, in the context of the North-South 'dialogue,' key elements in the anti-state discourse of neo-liberalism. Civil society is to be liberated from the fetters of state power, while good gover-nance does away with large state sectors and functions. The more the state can be discredited in this way, the more justified is the devolution of its powers 'downwardly' into the private sectors and 'outwardly' into the transnational sectors of capital. Of course, the reality is that, in the Third World, where very little organized economic activity has existed outside the state, 'civil society' develops *within* the ambit of the state. As Bjorn Beckman points out, civil society is 'situated in rules and transactions which connect state and society,' particularly in the 'public service nexus.'[26] The reality is also that good governance translates unambiguously into a formal liberal democracy that vindicates adaptation and subordi-nation to the globalized world order.

Market and State

For the peoples of the Third World, the neo-classical projects of recom-modification and democratization have little to do with their own historical or socio-economic situation, except of course in as much as they are induced to conform to them or have them imposed upon them. These projects are formulated by, and fit the special conditions of, the advanced capitalist countries whose agenda they mirror. At the periphery these projects are experienced as the simultaneous processes of selectively dismantling all or part of certain institutions and functions of the state and internationalizing the political economy. But while all this dismantling and internationalization is accomplished more or less explicitly, the neo-liberal project *implicitly* proceeds to re-mantle the state, as it were, in order to ensure its own realization. For instance, the institutions of the peripheral capitalist state – analogous to those of advanced capitalist states[27] – that promote debt management, accumulation, structural adjustment, and surplus extraction have expanded considerably in recent years, while those concerned with popular rights and needs have clearly contracted. In addition to the military, the winners include state executives and bureaucracies, and departments of trade and finance, while ministries of labour or health and welfare institutions have atrophied. Something like a theory of the changing Third World state can therefore be inferred from the very negation of the state advanced by neo-liberal prescriptions, a theory which may be developed with the aid of eight closely related propositions:

1. *Markets, in a general and profound way, need states.* Without 'third-party enforcement' of contracts by the state and in the absence of the 'non-contractual elements of contract' such as infrastructure and enforcement, markets cannot flourish. New contract law, internationalized legal systems, appropriate judicial and enforcement agencies, and other state-backed instruments to encourage and interlink market forces, are essential here. Even multinational capital relies on a state-based system to ensure the predictability and reliability of transnational interactions. But, as Drache and Gertler write about market-driven change in general:

> The deeper reality is that the continuing drive for maximizing accumulation, whether for the few or in the name of national development, leads step by step to a crippling social dependency for the many. Liberal society has no way to redress the fundamental inequality in the transfer of power and wealth that results when private property is made sovereign. Thus at the centre of even a reborn, postmodern liberal society there remains a chronic, deeply rooted instability. Market rights work to suppress the democratic and libertarian possibilities inherent in liberalism.[28]

Thus states and markets are closely, almost symbiotically, bound together. The free market must, as it were, be planned for.

2. *Markets, in the Third World, must for the most part be established with state power.* To more fully align domestic markets with international markets, large parts of the state – mainly the agencies dealing with entitlements and enablements, or, as Willy Brandt once put it from a social democratic perspective, 'in the things that really matter . . . justice, education . . . health . . . and the environment'[29] – must be dismantled. Selective shrinkage of the social-needs and decommodified parts of the state can be accomplished most readily – that is, with least popular resistance – through the internationalization of the state on terms and conditions laid down by the dominant economic powers. The World Bank, IMF, GATT, certain UN agencies and the great array of IFI's (International Financial Institutions) and multinational corporations become a kind of transnational ersatz state in laying down the rules and regulations within which the local state is required to operate in the sphere of international capital accumulation. Indeed, transnational corporations, unable to achieve complete control over economic sectors and branches in countries of the South, may actually acquire a strong interest in the establishment of 'a

more bureaucratically capable, entrepreneurially oriented state apparatus'[30] to ensure that contracts are carried out and the regulations enforced in a reliable, predictable manner. A relatively – though selectively – strong state is needed, for instance, to vouch for loans made to domestic capitalists in joint-venture or compradore undertakings. Physical infra-structures, communications and a sense of continuity and stability must be present for transnational collaboration to succeed. Leo Panitch writes that capitalist globalization 'involves a shift in power relations within states that often means the centralisation and concentration of state powers as the necessary condition of and accompaniment to global market discipline.'[31] Thus, the 'relative autonomy' once ascribed to the Third World state becomes, in a period of recommodification, radical subsumption under the exigencies of the international marketplace, while its ruling groups more and more become the local (and subordinate) executive committee for administering the interests of transnational capital.

3. *The local state therefore becomes, more than hitherto, a law-and-order-state.* With the partial exception of perhaps a half-dozen states in Asia, Third World and ex-Second World states have enforced, or been forced to enforce, IMF conditionalities and GATT trade regulations at the expense of their poor underclasses, thus polarizing domestic politics even further. The ability to facilitate, and provide the institutional framework for international capital accumulation becomes the key to domestic public power, thus making local constituencies increasingly less relevant. For Latin America as for other areas of the South, the past two decades of IMF conditionalities have brought declines in living standards, per capita incomes, urban wages, state expenditures on health, and food consumption; only morbidity rates have risen.[32] A variety of oppositional movements have developed in response to deteriorating conditions, ranging from new social movements to peasant uprisings and urban revolts. Debt repayment and loan conditionalities reduce funds available for domestic (re)investment and bind Third World states to austerity programmes that both further enrich creditor institutions and impoverish populations in debtor countries. Since cheap labour is a principal compar-ative advantage in the Third Worlds, and since wages and benefits must be rolled back in order to maintain levels of extraction and, perhaps, attract more foreign capital, labour repression becomes increasingly important, even as declining living standards lead to further delegitimation. A, or perhaps the, primary task of the local state, in this context, is therefore to maintain law and order and ensure the continued reproduction of favourable conditions for capital both at home and in its transnational forms. This repressive-coercive function, of course, conflicts with the prescription for democratization, as has been shown above, but remains absolutely central to the changing role of the state in the Third World.

4. *The neo-liberal insistence on free trade, in particular, ensures the need for strong state authority.* To opt for an export-oriented strategy by definition means downplaying domestic concerns and popular needs. Driving down prices by reducing wages and benefits must create popular unrest, even while repealing state policies aimed at achieving economic stability and providing a 'buffer' against externally-induced economic fluctuations increases the need for political intervention to overcome the state of chronic vulnerability that necessarily develops. Furthermore, and as hinted at above, the pursuit of comparative advantage means overconcentration in a few, readily exploited, profitable sectors at the expense of balanced economic growth. Now mobile and flexible, transnational capital can sell off, de-emphasize or abandon unprofitable sectors or industries and move on to other parts of the globe. To forestall such actions, the local state is under pressure to offer tax write-offs, investment incentives, subsidized labour and a variety of other concessions, all of which further erode its autonomy, even while enhancing the centrality of its repressive domestic function. If the First-World state at the centre, particularly in the hegemonic countries, has the expansion of capitalism as its primary task, the peripheral state exists mainly to secure the conditions for world-market-dependent reproduction, and hence to facilitate penetration and extraction by international capital.

5. *The abiding 'structural heterogeneity' of Southern states – which neo-liberalism would absolutize – is a huge barrier to class compromise and regional alliances.* It reflects the contradiction between the transnational level at which capitalism operates and the national level at which political consent is organized.[33] Unable to control the processes of accumulation, the local state is left to maintain internal and external class domination. As such, it is the instrument of 'adjustment' to the demands of global accumulation. For this reason, as Samir Amin argues,[34] the projects of democratization and civil society are almost impossible to realize in the current conjuncture. Nef and Bensabat's picture of the 'receiver state' is most apposite here: the Latin American state in particular 'has become the executor and debt collector of a bankrupt economy on behalf of transnational creditors'. In fact, its central role has manifestly changed from that of promoting development and – and least in theory – protecting political and economic sovereignty, to that of 'facilitating surplus extraction and international subordination.'[35] And, paradoxically, because this is so, the neo-liberal ideology of anti-statism enjoys a wider resonance, as we have seen.

6. *The continued application of neo-liberal solutions simultaneously creates the need for a strong state while crippling the capacities that the state needs to carry out these solutions.* During the 1980s, the South managed to increase its exports in order to repay its debts to its Northern

creditors. It did so in the face of deteriorating terms of trade, as well as slow growth and rising protectionism in the North. These surpluses, exacerbated by capital flight from the South, resulted in a massive redistribution of wealth from South to North.[36] The trade-driven international economic system, one might conclude with C. Douglas Lummis, thus does not accidentally create inequality but produces it systematically. It is a system that 'generates inequality and . . . runs on inequality.' For this reason, he concludes, economic development is an antidemocratic force and as such primarily a political problem rather than an economic one[37] – soluble, if at all, within the purview of the state, not the international neo-liberal economy.

7. *Unequal competition and worsening terms of trade must in the long run become destabilizing and hence dysfunctional to capital.* Indeed, Samir Amin's 'Empire of Chaos' – his counterpoint to the New World Order – assumes that the South, under the conditions of the present global conjuncture, cannot continue indefinitely to reproduce on an extended scale.[38] Moreover, the continued polarization of classes into the extremely rich and secure and the extremely poor and insecure creates a growing legitimacy deficit. If not regulated and contained, the market will again work to suppress the limited democratic potential inherent in liberalism. Hence the globalized New World Order, like nineteenth century laissez-faire capitalism, will have to recreate the state or replace it with some other regulating mechanism in order, as it were, to save capital from itself. For the interests of capital as a whole, and of the hegemonic states that represent it, would certainly be 'better served by the existence of strong and internally stable and coherent allies, than by a proliferation of volatile and unpredictable dependencies.'[39] The exigencies of global accumulation, however, conflict here with political rationality.

8. *The neo-liberal project aims directly at discrediting and dismantling the state in the Third Word.* Indeed, as argued at the outset, anti-statism is what, in many ways, defines the neo-liberal project. While globalization in fact internationalizes many of the main functions of the Third World state – investment, production decisions, fiscal policies, etc. – and subordinates Third World economies to the international capitalist order which is dominated by the North, it simultaneously substitutes (also largely Northern-dominated) international agencies and organizations for the state. In these processes, a number of scholars rightly purport to see a form of recolonization via internationalization.[40] The neo-liberal project conceals its advocacy of massive state power behind an anti-state ethos. To discredit the state is to discredit the one agency capable of organizing and articulating nationalist aspirations in the South and of developing resistance to neo-liberal intrusions. It advances its prescription for weakening the Third World state both 'from above' where state policies are pre-empted and

state elites are co-opted, and 'from below' where organized labour is bypassed or declared irrelevant, and poor, marginal or oppositional groups are fragmented and set into competition with each other. Third World states so debilitated by competition and by surplus drainage are then less likely, and less able, to unite or combine against the forces of neo-imperialism.

This, then, is the anti-state project of neo-liberalism. Examined in context, it appears as remarkably simple, and in this simplicity lies much of its operational as well as ideological effectiveness. For instance, 'neo-liberal theory has no need for any knowledge about the demands and aspirations of the particular social groups affected in order to offer its solution. The medicine is supposed to work anywhere anytime. If not now, later.'[41] Neo-liberalism's reductionist certitude and assertive universality, made possible and lent legitimacy now by the absence of any threat from a competing anti-imperialist power bloc, lends it considerable force. To realize it, no qualitative transition is needed, no fundamental social change, but simply the 'abolition of as much state as possible.'[42] Yet even as it theorizes 'the' peripheral state away, the neo-liberal variant of globalization in reality makes it essential, if only to manage and execute its agenda. Vis-à-vis the North it prescribes globalization and 'complex interdependence' while for the South, having pre-empted (via internationalization) the crucial state functions, it prescribes a kind of internationalization that rests on state-level and inevitably state-centred solutions of recommodification and democratization.

State and Class

Even more than in the First World, the state in the Third World denotes a category of class power, namely the structural power of an (external and internal) capitalist class standing in a fundamentally antagonistic relationship to labour. Bearing in mind that 'class', like 'the state', has been pushed aside by the dominant paradigm and marginalized by the sub- and supra-state theories just mentioned, it is important, when 'keeping the state in' (which the following section advocates) to keep classes in too.[43] Class power in the Third World still stands in roughly isomorphic correspondence with state power; that is, the greater the control of a class, or class coalition, over state institutions, assets and revenues, the greater is its economic power likely to be – so much so that, in relation to the Third World state, one is justified in speaking, with Hartmut Elsenhans, of a 'state class'[44] – a class whose linkages and dependencies extend outward (in the form of economic and political dependence) and inward (as a relation of political domination) and who therefore operate 'their' state at the sub- and supra-national levels. Although globalization aspires to reduce the relative strength of state classes in favour of – postulated – commercial or industrial bourgeoisies, in reality the structurally given fusion of economic and political power in the Third World ensures that the respective dominant classes remain undifferentiated, at least in this respect.

Peripheral capitalist classes lack the socio-economic 'base' to sustain and develop a relatively autochthonous capitalism and so heavily rely on political means, in collaboration with their external class allies, to create the preconditions for, and to promote, private accumulation. The role of the state now, as before, is crucial and includes (a) harmonization of state policies and state institutions with the requirements and processes of international capital; (b) organization of distribution (because production is pre-organized and directed externally) in the interests of these endogenous and exogenous classes; (c) execution of the regulatory, disciplinary, and law-and-order functions described earlier; (d) mediation between fractions (or segments) of domestic capital, particularly arranging for the growing power of its middleman and compradore fractions and corresponding decline of its 'national bourgeoisies.' This state class, to follow Petras for a moment, is thus best conceived as a precarious coalition of 'collaborator classes' whose function 'is to organize the state and economy in accordance with core definitions of the international division of labour.' It assumes a 'double role - exploitation within the society and exchange outside the society.'[45] In a sense, therefore, the Third World state in the era of globalization has intensified its role in terms of what Miliband first identified as an ersatz 'means of production.'[46]

In terms of class (re-)formation this unmediated link between economics and politics is a major distinguishing feature of the peripheral state within the larger state system. If at the core, the state has managed to maintain some measure of 'relative autonomy' from the economically dominant classes and fractions within and without, even in the face of globalization, the peripheral state more than ever fuses class power and state power. The classical distinction between governing class and ruling class is rendered all but irrelevant where the 'governing class' amounts to the coalition of elite groups and segments (and their external collaborators) able to achieve hegemony over the state at a given time. These are, in the globalization conjuncture, those fractions that have a vested interest in surplus exportation and hence structurally perpetuated underdevelopment. The ongoing struggle for state power is therefore simultaneously a struggle for the means of distribution and consumption which only political domination can confer.

But the local elites at the periphery do not accumulate within the confines of the borders of the state. Peripheral (state) capital stands in a subordinate relationship to capital at the centre, and reproduction processes at the periphery, mediated by the world market, are overwhelmingly determined by valorization processes emanating from the centre. Peripheral capitalism, in a word, functions as an element of surplus production for the core. Neo-liberalism glorifies and vindicates this, and class formation in the South centres upon it. But the peripheral state elites must master the resultant conflicts between accumulation and legitimation and between the need for some degree of domestic political sovereignty and the fact of international economic dependency, and it is here that the contradictions between economic power and political power will have to be enacted and resolved. For the local ruling class, in the globalized economy, will always lack a firm basis of national legitimacy, since it owes its existence in large measure to an external bourgeoisie with whom it collaborates to the detriment of basic needs and popular interests. The one possibility for the state class to escape from this cycle of delegitimation – namely, to deliver material progress via economic development – is precluded by the fact of the dependent, externalized economy that expropriates and exports any surplus. The peripheral state class cannot ally itself, either totally or as a combination of segments, with the popular classes since any strategy promoting mass economic well-being or development would, *ipso facto,* undermine the basis and rationale of the peripheral state. The state class, in a word, has a vested interest in suppressing basic human needs and in perpetuating the existing international division of labour and of power.

Because this is so, and owing to this class's objective 'transmission-belt' functions vis-à-vis international capital, the state-compradore elites are growing progressively isolated from the societies they govern and repress, as their accumulation function more and more overwhelms their legitimation function. Here, the role of coercion remains central, despite the implementation of various liberal-democratic shells. The 'silent veto,' backed by their repressive power of the recivilianized militaries, therefore remains crucial to the successor elites who rule, in greater or lesser degree, at the military's pleasure.

This ruling coalition has been fortified, in the neo-liberal era, by the addition of many sectors from the middle classes. For, to the extent that the middle classes have not been decimated by austerity and conditionalities, they have in large measure, abandoned their former opposition to authoritarian military governments that led them to form alliances with labour and the poor, and have been coopted, via the provision of formal liberal democracy, into centrist and conservative parties where they have melded with the ruling coalition to preserve the existing distribution of economic power.[47] The defection from opposition of these sectors of the middle class may turn out to be one of the most salient developments in the era of globalization, and contributes further to the class polarization of the Third World state.

Keep the State In!

It is important, finally, to recall that there is nothing immutable, or even intrinsically sustainable, about the hegemonic ideology at a given time. Dominant paradigms do, after all, shift, and such shifts are themselves part of a political process relating to the constellation of power and conflicts at a particular historical moment. The specific conjuncture of forces and ideas of our time has produced neo-liberalism and globalization as the dominant paradigm. It is a mark of its universal acceptance that this paradigm, despite its mainly implicit concern with the state, has for the time being succeeded in banishing state theories from the mainstream of scholarly and political discourse, at the same time launching whole new areas of academic enterprise revolving around neo-classical economics, neo-liberal globalism, democracy and democratization, the revival of civil society and the prescription for good governance.

The interesting political theories to have emerged since the fall of state-socialist Communism in Central and Eastern Europe, among which I would include the new localism, certain kinds of concepts of civil society, most of the post-modernist variants (notably post-materialism, post-colonialism, post-structuralism, post-imperialism and post-modernism itself), new social movements, socialist and radical feminism and even post-Marxism, are in this sense also in accord with the Zeitgeist: *they remain at the sub-state level and therefore cannot point the way, either theoretically or practically, beyond the current neo-liberal globalist paradigm.*

To be sure, these theories are, in the main, important and innovative and do highlight many of the deficiencies of the centralized state, the arrogance of the paternalist world-view, the 'logocentricism' and Eurocentrism of existing and past development theories, the emancipatory and gender limitations of socialism, and much else that is wrong or misguided about state and supra-state theories. In their almost infinite variety and diversity they are evidence that globalization also begets heterogenization, at least at the sub-state level, and the multifarious search for niches, sub-group individuality, self-protection and self-affirmation that they embody, are surely the main fora for contemporary progressive social thought. By giving, or imputing, voice to hitherto marginalized groups and gender, they contribute in important ways to the assertion of identity, the search for alternative means of self-realization, and the possibility of a multiplicity of localized resistances and counteroffensives to hegemonic power. As such they may well hold the key to a future strategy of transforming domestic power in such a way as to overcome the problem of delegitimated, dysfunctional and effete elite rule in the Third World state, alluded to in the previous section. The 'postmodern rebellion' in Chiapas, for instance, aims not at taking state power and using it to transform the economy and society; it aspires instead to incite a broad popular movement that will somehow 'transform the country from the bottom up.'[48] But by failing to engage with neo-liberalism on its own terrain – a terrain which includes supra- and sub-state dimensions as well as the state itself – these theories, and the movements they depict, however internally consistent and politically sound they may be, abandon overall ideological hegemony to the currently dominant forces and discourses[49].

By the same token, standard supra- and inter-state theories (dependency and world-systems theory on the left, neo-realism and complex interdependence on the right) have not successfully probed and analyzed the sub-state level so essential to the explanation of state and supra-state phenomena.

The conceptual morass suggested here is well illustrated by a very recent work purporting to deal comprehensively and theoretically with the Third World state but which can only posit what the authors call a 'state-in-society' (as opposed to a more politically grounded state-against-society) perspective. They conceive of the Third World state as merely one social force among many, and not necessarily the dominant one, thus relativizing the role of the state and largely factoring out the part played by the international economy and transnational elite interactions.[50] Another fairly recent study of governance in Africa rightly observes that the African state centralizes and consolidates power and uses it to extract society's economic resources, 'yet it spends much of what it obtains on itself and lacks the capacity to spur the country's development as a whole'[51] – as if the state were able to control more than a fraction of the surplus so generated; as if, indeed, there were no 'external estate' guiding the international institutions and 'regimes' that – with the more or less willing assent of the local elite – *systematically* underdevelop the Third World State. These examples underline the point made at the outset, namely that an adequate theory of the Third World state is both a scholarly and practical necessity. Such a theory, if it is to stand against neo-liberal globalism, must be located 'at the intersection of external and internal dynamics, particularly in the operation of a world capitalist economy and in class conflict both at the world system and nation-state levels.'[52]

Although embedded in the same global economy as all the other component units of the international system of states, Third World states at the periphery of this system *are* differently affected and have different prospects and strategies than the dominant capitalist states. Neo-liberal theory ignores or denies this, preferring to conceive the Third World state as a homogeneous, proto-Western construct that need only follow the existing capitalist development model of free enterprise and individualism in order to achieve growth and development.[53]

To be sure, the *real* state in the Third World *is* in difficult straits. In Africa and parts of Latin America it has so decayed and contracted that the void is being filled in part by external agencies, especially NGOs and aid agencies, in part by incipient new social movements, and in part by informal and *ad hoc* vigilante and resistance groups, as well as organized crime. Third World societies, in the era of neo-liberalism, are increasingly polarizing into more and less powerful, rich and poor. The elites in such states are generally becoming more parasitical, more repressive and less 'attached' to the societies under their control, while their objective function of surplus extraction and hence of perpetuating underdevelopment hardly qualifies them as a progressive or visionary vanguard to guide the ongoing struggle for sovereignty, parity in the world state system, and economic development in the international economy.

Yet the 'failure of the Third World state' may not be a failure of state intervention *per se*. Perhaps 'the main problem was a lack of effective, coherent, nationally focussed and democratically controlled state intervention.'[54] This may or not be so; and much scholarly endeavour needs to be devoted to this question. But in any case there is no credible evidence that more market and less state is a viable prescription for the Third World. On the contrary, strong state power is likely to be needed to make the hard decisions of internal distribution and domestic power sharing arrangements while controlling and regulating the scope and scale of external investment and intervention, and maintaining sufficient sovereignty to control the recommodification pressures emanating from without.

Nowhere, in the past century or so, has any state actually 'modernized' or 'developed' in accordance with the neo-liberal prescription for a weak or invisible state. Quite the reverse: material development, as measured by various quantitative indices such as levels of production or amounts of consumption, has only been accomplished within the framework of development strategies in which the state's role has been determining. The observation applies to states as diverse in time and space as Bismarckian Germany, post-Meiji Japan, the Soviet Union and the 'Gang of Four' Newly Industrializing Countries in East Asia. In the competitive and unforgiving world economy of the nineties, concerted action, administrative competence and political will are prerequisites for development of any kind, and it is difficult to see any agency other than the state shaping and driving such an attempt. Nor, despite the pseudo-theories of the Huntingtons, Diamonds, Lipsets and di Palmas, does liberal democracy logically figure in such development except toward the end of the process, as a kind of top-dressing. The reality of the 'development state' has been an authoritarian allocation of investment and sectoral values, iron labour discipline, extensive social repression, and inequitable (though converging over time) distribution of intra-societal wealth in order to achieve effective capital accumulation and deployability. In his examination of 'developmental states' – states with consistent average economic growth of four per cent or more during the past three decades – Adrian Leftwich shows that they have concentrated political power at the top to achieve stability and continuity; are led by relatively uncorrupt and determined elites who rotate freely between government, the bureaucracy, military and business and remain relatively autonomous from special interests and groups whom they coopt or marginalize; impose discipline while disregarding liberal and human rights; and established their authority before foreign capital was able to penetrate decisively. He concludes that:

> The distinguishing characteristic of development states, then, has been that their institutional structures (especially their economic bureaucracies) have been developmentally-driven, while their developmental purposes have been politically driven. In short, fundamentally political factors have shaped the thrust and pace of their development strategies through the structures of the state.[55]

Today, the Third World state is diminished, and more subordinate than at any time since the colonial era. Its elites are more externalized and its hold on national sovereignty more tenuous than ever. Even so, the state remains by far the largest employer, at least in the 'formal' sectors of the economy, the primary location of class formation and domination – and the sole institution available with sufficient potential strength to negotiate, and if necessary to grapple, with international capital.

'The' real state in the Third World thus remains the major, and perhaps only, framework within which the important social and political issues can be dealt with in the context of a world system permanently stacked against peripheral societies and economies, while the theoretical state is probably the only conceptual framework capable of developing a counter-hegemonic project sufficiently comprehensive to challenge neo-liberal globalization. Without the state, therefore, there can be no large-scale, long-term emancipatory project for the South.[56] After all, 'insofar as there is any effective democracy at all in relation to the power of capitalists and bureaucrats, it is still embedded in political structures which are national or subnational in scope.'[57]

Only the state can offer a feasible *agency* capable of aggregating the multifarious counter-hegemonic forces in the peripheral state. Only state-economic power in the South has any prospects of standing up to, negotiating with or countering the pervasive economic power of international capital (and then only tenuously and probably necessarily in concert with other state capitals in the South). No doubt too, only the state, in combination with other states, can forge collective emancipatory projects directed against the hegemonic powers. And certainly any strategy for democratic or radical change, in a globalized world of states, must start from the state.

Without a real state, and a real state theory, then, the South would appear to have no way forward, out, or back. The question that needs to be posed, therefore, is not: state or market? but: what kind of state, and whose state?

NOTES

1. See Frans J. Schuurman (ed.), *Beyond the Impasse: New Directions in Development Theory* (London: Zed) 1993, esp. ch. 1.
2. See Fred Halliday, *Rethinking International Relations* (Vancouver: UBC Press) 1994, ch. 4.
3. See his *Politics and Markets: The World's Political-Economic Systems* (New York: Basic Books) 1977, esp. chs. 2 and 3. Time has, I think, shown the relative insignificance of his third category of social control, namely persuasion and preceptorial systems; in any case 'states' and 'markets' certainly constitute the perceived antinomy in which the globalization debate is at present conducted.
4. Peter Self, *Government by the Market? The Politics of Public Choice* (Boulder, Colo.: Westview Press) 1993, p. 63.
5. On this, see Gerald Berthoud, 'Market' in Wolfgang Sachs (ed.), *The Development Dictionary: A Guide to Knowledge as Power* (London: Zed) 1992.
6. See Philip G. Cerny, 'Globalization and the Changing Logic of Collective Action,' paper presented to annual conference of British International Studies Association, University of York, 19–21 December 1994, pp. 23–4 and pp. 19–20.
7. About 25% of such trade takes place within global companies, 25% is bilateral trade and 25% is barter trade; see Hans Glatz and Häas Moser, 'Der europaeische Integrationsprozess und die Rolle Oesterreichs' in H. Glatz & H. Moser (eds.) *Herausforderung Binnenmarkt: Kopfüber in die EG?* (Vienna: Fachverlag an der Wirtschaftsuniversität) 1989, p. 17.
8. Michael Valpy, *The Globe & Mail*, Toronto, 7 December 1994, p. 2.
9. Robert Cox, 'New Policy Directions for the State' in D. Drache & M. Gertler (eds.), *The New Era of Global Competition: State Policy and Market Power* (Montreal: McGill-Queens University Press) 1991, p. 340.
10. This is a quotation from Reich's contribution to the panel on 'Globalization and the Nation-State,' as edited and reproduced in *Review '90/Outlook 91* (Ottawa: North-South Institute) 1991, p. 18; for a more systematic account of his views of globalization, see his *The Work of Nations* (New York: Vintage Books) 1992.
11. John Keane, 'Introduction' to Claus Offe, *Contradictions of the Welfare State*, John Keane (ed.), (London, etc.: Hutchinson) 1984, p. 26.
12. Concerning which, see William D. Graf, 'Anti-Brandt: A Critique of Northwestern Prescriptions for World Order' in *Socialist Register 1981* (London: Merlin) 1981; or W. D. Graf, 'From Brandt to Brundtland and Beyond: Hegemonic-Ideological Aspects of the North-South Dialogue in the 1990's,' in *Journal of the History of European Ideas*, Vol. 15, No. 1–3 1992, pp. 399–406.
13. On which, see Nassau A. Adams, *Worlds Apart: The North-South Divide and the International System* (London: Zed) 1993, pp. 192–3.
14. Cox, *op. cit.*, pp. 338–9.
15. On this, see Manfred Bienefeld, 'Is a Strong National Economy a Utopian Goal at the End of the Twentieth Century?.' Carleton University School of Public Administration Working Paper Series 1994, pp. 15 and 35.
16. Richard Sklar, 'Social Class and Political Action in Africa: The Bourgeoisie and the Proletariat' in D. E. Apter and C. G. Rosberg (eds), *Political Development and the New Realism in Sub-Saharan Africa* (Charlottesville and London: University Press of Virginia) 1994, p. 123. For a further critique, see my review in *Candian Journal of Development Studies*, Forthcoming 1995
17. Jan Knippers Black, 'Elections and Other Trivial Pursuits: Latin America and the New World Order,' *Third World Quaterly*, Vol. 14, No. 3, 1993, p. 545.
18. Samir Amin, 'The Challenge of Globalization: Delinking,' in The South Centre (ed.), *Facing the Challenge: Responses to the Report of the South Commission* (London: Zed) 1993, p. 137.

19. Alicia Puyana, 'New Challenges for Developing Countries,' in The South Commission (ed.), *ibid.*, p. 284.

20. Black, *op. cit.*, p 547.

21. See Atul Kohli, 'Democracy amid Economic Orthodoxy: Trends in Developing Countries,' *Third World Quarterly*, Vol. 14, No. 4, 1993, p. 678.

22. Jorge Nef and Remonda Bensabat, "Governability' and the Receiver State in Latin America: Analysis and Prospects' in A. R. M. Ritter, M. A. Cameron and D. H. Pollock, *Latin America to the Year 2000: Reactivating Growth, Improving Equity, Sustaining Democracy* (New York, etc.: Praeger) 1992, p. 168.

23. Barry Gills & Joel Rocamora, 'Low Intensity Democracy,' *Third World Quarterly*, Vol. 13, No. 3, 1992, pp. 504–5.

24. A point made by S. Qadir, C. Clapham and B. Gills, 'Democratization in the Third World,' *Third World Quarterly* Vol. 14 No. 3, 1993, p. 13.

25. This point is made, in relation to the concept of good governance, by Adrian Leftwich, 'Governance, Democracy and Development in the Third World,' *Third World Quarterly, Vol. 14, No. 3, October 1994*, p. 369.

26. Bjorn Beckman, 'The Liberation of Civil Society: Neo-Liberal Ideology and Political Theory,' *Review of African Political Economy*, November 1993, p. 29.

27. On this see Leo Panitch and Ralph Miliband, 'The New World Order and the Socialist Agenda' and Robert Cox, 'Global Perestroika,' both in *Socialist Register 1992* (London: Merlin Press) 1992.

28. D. Drache and M. Gertler, 'Introduction' to Drache and Gertler (eds.), *op. cit.* p. xvi.

29. The full quote is: "People tend to think that [in Latin America] the state is too big. I believe that in the things that really matter, it is too small. In other words, justice, education and health – which are the real functions of the modern state – and the environment. Meanwhile, the state was too big in other areas.' See *Review 90/Outlook 91*, *op. cit.*, p. 17.

30. Peter B. Evans, 'Transnational Linkages and the Economic Role of the State: An Analysis of Developing and Industrialized Nations in the Post-World War II Period,' in P. B. Evans, D. Rueschemeyer and T. Skocpol (eds.), *Bringing the State Back In* (Cambridge, etc.: CUP) 1985, p. 199.

31. Leo Panitch, 'Globalisation and the State,' *Socialist Register 1994*, p. 64.

32. See Frans J. Schuurman, 'Modernity, Post-Modernity and the New Social Movements' in Schuurman (ed.), *op. cit.*, ch. 9.

33. The point is made by Ronaldo Munck, 'Political Programmes and Development: The Transformative Potential of Social Democracy' in Schuurman (ed.), *op. cit.*, p. 117.

34. Samir Amin, 'Preface' to Peter Anyang'Nyongo (ed.), *Popular Struggles for Democracy in Africa* (London: United Nations University and Zed Press) 1987, p.5.

35. Nef and Bensabat, *op. cit.*, p. 162.

36. For details see Michael Dolan, 'Global Economic Transformation and Less Developed Countries' in R. O. Slater, B. M. Schutz and S. R. Dorr (eds.), *Global Transformation and the Third World* (Boulder: Lynne Rienner) 1993, pp. 264–5.

37. C. Douglas Lummis, 'Development Against Democracy' in *Alternatives* 16 (1991), pp. 54 and 59.

38. Samir Amin, *Empire of Chaos*, trans. by W. H. L. Anderson (New York: Monthly Review Press), 1992.

39. Bienefeld, *op. cit.*, p. 5.

40. For instance, David B. Moore, 'Development Discourse as Hegemony: Towards an Ideological History – 1945–1995,' in D. B. Moore and G. G. Schmitz (eds.), *Debating Development Discourse: Institutional and Popular Perspectives* (London: Macmillan) forthcoming 1995, p. 10; and 'Commentary: States, Markets and Africa's Crisis,' *Review of African Political Economy* November 1993, p. 155 and ff.

41. Beckman, *op. cit.*, p. 25.

42. C. Colclough and J. Manor (eds.), 'Introduction' to *States or Markets? Neo-liberalism and the Development Policy Debate* (Oxford: OUP) 1993, p. 329.

43. Which the contributions to the much-cited P. B. Evans, D. Rueschemeyer and T. Skocpol (eds.), *op. cit.* (Cambridge, etc.: CUP) 1985 generally fail to do.

44. Hartmut Elsenhans, *Abhäginger Kapitalismus oder bürokratische Entwicklungsgesellschaft: Versuch über den Staat in der Dritten Welt* (Frankfurt: Campus) 1981, chapter 1.

45. James Petras, *Critical Perspectives on Imperalism and Social Class in the Third World* (New York: MRP) 1978, p. 36.

46. Ralph Miliband, *Marxism and Politics* (Oxford: OUP) 1977, p. 109.

47. Gills and Rocamora, *op. cit.*, pp. 516–7 (with special reference to their case-study countries of Argentina, Guatemala, the Philippines and South Korea).

48. Roger Burbach, 'Roots of the Postmodern Rebellion in Chiapas, *New Left Review*, No. 206, 1994, p. 113.

49. It is, however, worth stressing that the actual transformative potential of the new social movements and popular struggles has by no means been exhausted. An analysis of Carolyn Merchant's eco-feminist theory of women and ecological revolutions, Manuel Castell's theory of urban social movements, and James O'Connor's eco-Marxist theory of struggles relating to the conditions of production suggests that such sub-state groups have a strong and 'direct interest in preventing capitalist commodification of communal relationships, the environmental and public space' (Craig Benjamin and Terisa Turner, 'Counterplanning from the Commons: Labour, Capital and the 'New Social Movements'' in *Labour, Capital and Society*, 25:2 [1992] p. 222) and as such may be of incalculable importance in 'restructuring' the internal power relationships in Third World states.

50. See the (anonymous) 'Introduction,' Joel Migdal's 'The State in Society: An Approach to Struggles for Domination,' and Atul Kohli and Vivienne Shue's 'State Power and Social Forces: On Political Contention and Accommodation in the Third World,' all in J. S. Migdal, A. Kohli and V. Shue (eds.), *State Power and Social Forces: Domination and Transformation in the Third World.* (Cambridge: CUP) 1994.

51. Michael Bratton and Donald Rothchild, 'The Institutional Bases of Governance in Africa,' in G. Hyden and M. Bratton (eds.), *Governance and Politics in Africa* (Boulder and London: Lynne Rienner) 1992, p. 263.

52. Joel Samoff, 'Class, Class Conflict and the State in Africa,' *Political Science Quarterly*, Vol. 97, No. 1 (Spring 1982), p. 115.

53. The contributions to Colclough and Manor (eds.), *op. cit.*, and especially Manor's 'Politics and the Neo-liberals,' underline this point; see esp. p. 306 ff.

54. Manfred Bienefeld, 'Structural Adjustment: Debt Collection Device or Development Policy?' Carleton University School of Public Administration Working Paper Series 1994, p. 9.

55. Adrian Leftwich, 'Governance, the State and the Politics of Development,' *Development and Change*, Vol 25, No. 2, 1994, pp. 379–81.

56. The point has wider applicability. To follow Ralph Miliband, despite globalization and interdependence, 'the nation-state must remain for the foreseeable future the crucial point of reference of the Left. This is not a matter of clinging to an 'obsolete' notion of sovereignty but simply to assert the right of a government seeking to carry out a programme of radical social renewal not to be stopped from doing so by external forces.' *Socialism for a Sceptical Age* (Cambridge: Polity Press) 1994, p. 179. Clearly, the 'counter-hegemonic' power of the weak, whether of weak classes or weak societies and economies, is best served through the collective power of the state.

57. Panitch, 'Globalisation and the State,' *op. cit.*, p. 87.

THE 'UNDERCLASS' AND THE US WELFARE STATE

Linda Gordon

In the US as in Britain, conservatives – including those in the Democratic Party – repeatedly proclaim that the welfare state engenders dependency, laziness, and immorality, a new pauperism sometimes labelled with an old name – the 'underclass.' Under the force of that conservative attack, many liberals have joined in the clamour for or acceptance of cutbacks in social spending. Those on the Left who have resisted this moralizing against the very poor have been reduced to defending the puny and humiliating welfare provision we have in the US, so that our earlier radical critiques of the welfare system now seem frivolous and utopian. Even if one leaves aside questions of the accuracy and morality of this defence, it is not at all clear that it is instrumentally effective, because the negative consequences of the US welfare system are so palpably evident that our denial is transparently ideological.

Fifty years ago T. H. Marshall theorized a notion of a welfare state as a final, social, state of citizenship. His persuasive and optimistic idea arose in large part from the effort to make civil and political citizenship actual, acknowledging that poverty could effectively exclude people from actively exercising political rights or even defending their civil rights in a democracy.[1] Today it has become clear that not all versions of social citizenship are equally effective in providing a corrective to exclusion. It turns out that no type of citizenship is a binary, yes – or – no condition, free from stratification, and that certain constructions of soical citizenship, certain welfare states, even as they extend the theoretical reach of citizens' entitlements and relieve poverty, may also worsen the exclusion of the poor from all kinds of citizenship.

These exclusions rarely target 'simply' the poor; they do not follow 'pure' class lines. Indeed, there is no such thing as simple poverty or pure class because these abstractions cannot encompass the actual, historical construction and reproduction of social divisions. In the US as in all modern states, social citizenship is organised according to gender, racial and familial as well as class systems. In US history, for example, exclusions from first-class citizenship have affected not only those without property but also specifically American Indians, slaves, post-slavery African Americans, the Japanese during World War II, and women of all groups, to cite but a few examples.

I am interested here in a contemporary and expanding exclusion, that of an alleged 'underclass'.[2] I concentrate on one aspect of the construction of this 'class,' a paradoxical one. US welfare programmes, designed to alleviate poverty and even to mitigate inequality, ended by increasing inequality and exclusions from citizenship. Specifically, the Social Security Act of 1935 helped recreate the class structure in the US and in doing so promoted the development of an 'underclass.' The claim is not simply that Social Security's inequities and exclusions left some people economically disadvantaged, but that the legislation contributed also to civil, political and social inequities, exclusions from 'the edifice of citizenship,'[3] which rendered some of the poor an 'underclass.'

The particular kind of exclusion I am discussing arose as the US state began to expand in the 19th century to include measures for the public welfare. Exceptionally poor, stigmatized strata have long existed in a variety of societies, but a uniquely modern, and now perhaps postmodern, discourse about an 'underclass' developed in the last 150 years to describe those who were at once the targets but not the beneficiaries of that state development. The state constructs citizenship hierarchy as much by inaction as by action, and, as we shall see, as much through the construction of discursive categories as through unequal distribution of funds and privileges.

I want to argue, first, that such definitional questions – connotative as well as denotative – are significant because they tell us, if approached historically, something about the work of this pejorative concept, work which reinforces exclusions from citizenship and confirms regressive social divisions. Second, I argue that the alleged group was created not only by economic developments, but also by deliberate state action; and third, that the group only takes shape out of relation to other groups. This paper springs also from a theoretical or metahistorical project, an attempt to integrate structural analysis of social problems with critique of how their meanings were constructed, including the role of social policy in creating these meanings.[4]

The Historical Career of 'Underclass' Talk

There *is* a distinction, albeit not always easy to draw, between the poor in general and that portion of the poor engaged in antisocial, destructive, and self-destructive behaviour. 'Underclass' is not only a middle-class concept used to beat up on the poor. Poor and especially working-class people distinguish and condemn this bad behaviour. In the US today, where 'welfare dependency' has become a synonym for the 'underclass' condition, poor and minority people are often as quick as the prosperous to perceive those who rely on government 'hand-outs' as disreputable and lacking in morals, in contrast to the employed. While some romantic outsiders and militant insiders have at times glorified criminal, daredevil, and violent behaviour, these have usually been men, and only some men, while women, often the victim of underclass behaviour, as of poverty itself, have been more sceptical if not downright hostile. The problem for a critical observer is to distinguish what is antisocial, destructive and self-destructive from what is impoverished, angry, and out of the 'mainstream,' to use the currently fashionable American word, and to cut through the moralism to analyse how an 'underclass' was produced discursively and structurally.

'Underclass' talk leapt into popularity in the US soon after Ken Auletta's 1981 *New Yorker* articles on the subject.[5] If Auletta's usage hadn't grasped popularity, someone else's would have. The phrase attracts because it is so rich, encapsulating many escalating anxieties in the US – about increasing unemployment, continuing racial inequality and growing opposition to affirmative action remedies, women's changing sexual and reproductive behaviour and public participation, widespread use of hard drugs and dangerous weapons, highly visible homelessness, massive health problems and the near-collapse of public health facilities, the actual collapse of several state and local governments' ability to provide minimal services which are legally required, and the hegemony of a conservative agenda cultivating animosity to taxes.

'Underclass', like many politicized and moralized words, has fuzzy and often contradictory meanings. While social-science poverty experts have recently attempted to 'operationalize' a definition, popular usage only tangentially incorporates their instructions. Indeed, it is precisely the fuzziness of 'underclass' that gives the word its power. This particular word is one of a number of synonyms used widely in English for nearly a century and a half. Thus in the mid-19th century we meet 'dangerous classes,' 'outcast,' 'scum,' 'refuse,' 'residuum,' 'rough,' 'ragged,' '*lumpen*,' 'casual poor,' 'paupers,' and many others. In the historical discussion that follows, comments about 'underclass' refer to many of its synonyms as well.

Because the concept is rich, its meanings contain a number of paradoxes and subtexts. First, the concept arose from efforts to distinguish among the poor, to create a distinction slightly different from that between the deserving and undeserving: this new line was to separate the benign from the dangerous. Yet in practice the work of 'underclass' and its synonyms has been to blur that line of demarcation by making a broad segment of the poor generally threatening. Second, 'underclass' talk had a contradictory pity/revulsion/titillation effect. The earliest muckrakers, such as Henry Mayhew writing of the London poor beginning in 1849, often attempted to explain the bad conditions and behaviour of their objects of study in such a way as to excuse them on account of their very difficult environment and lack of choice. But the writers' attraction to extremely sensationalist, even disgusting stories of depravity, suffering, and stench stimulated more revulsion than sympathy. At the same time, especially in relation to women of the alleged 'underclass', the language contained strong pornographic undertones. Third, in this way as in others, 'underclass' talk has always contained subtexts about gender and often about race. Men, women, and members of different racial/ethnic groups gain the 'underclass' label in different ways, as we shall see. And fourth, in producing an 'othering' affect towards the 'underclass', making them appear alien in relation to readers, the rhetoric had the further effect of suggesting a fictive unity among the non-'underclass', among what in the 1990s US is often called the 'mainstream,'[6] as if there were no heterogeneity, immorality, and irresponsibility among the 'us'.

'Underclass' talk bears the marks of the specific historical context of its origin. The discourse arose with the growth of commercial and industrial *cities*. 'Underclass' is an urban concept.[7] (For example, while there is a veritable industry of experts studying the urban 'underclass' today in the US, most agree that virtually nothing is known about rural poverty.[8]) Poverty and behaviour reprehensible to the hegemonic culture was of course widespread in the countryside. But an 'underclass' was discovered only when great cities, such as London, Paris, and later New York, put the very poor and the privileged side by side; and only when these crowded cities transformed certain practices which had been typical and unremarkable in the countryside – such as disposing of garbage by throwing it into heaps – into life-threatening perils. 'The very condensing of their number within a small space, seems to stimulate their bad tendencies.'[9] 'Underclass' arose from a widespread but inadequately recognized historical phenomenon: the tendency of cities to attract more in-migrants than could be supplied with jobs.[10] These structural conditions were then partly explained in terms of cultural or psychological attributes of victims.

'Underclass' talk was equally tied to the expansion of *states*. It appeared from groups interested in government reform action. The British 'discovery' of an underclass arose from state reform initiatives and from journalistic sensationalism aimed at provoking state action. Chadwick wrote both of his influential reports (1834 and 1842) for parliamentary inquiries. Mayhew intended his 'yellow' series of letters to a daily paper in 1849-50 to encourage public health and welfare provision.

The journalists, reformers, and government experts who initiated an 'underclass' alarm began their investigations to reveal the conditions of the entire working class but ended, consciously or not, emphasizing only the most wretched. They hoped thus to shock the powerful into action. In this they had some success, but not only in reformist directions. Their stories were so horrifying that they diverted attention from more average proletarian conditions. The mental and behavioural depravity they found among the 'underclass' was so threatening that the perhaps more common balance between decency and nastiness that characterized the proletariat, as the middle class, went unnoticed. The rhetoric of horror was much louder than that of sympathy, the condemnation of immoral behaviour much more vivid than the analysis of structural causes.[11]

For example, the discussion of the Victorian 'underclass' often prioritized smell over the other senses.[12] (This consciousness of smell was equally important in constructing 'refinement' or 'gentility.') Several commentators wrote of the 'miasma' which emanated from the poor neighbourhoods, of 'putrefaction,' 'vapours . . . that blind and suffocate.'[13] The smells came from open cesspools, garbage and dead rats in the streets, the filth in the river and the 'sewage that passed as drinking water,' not from an 'underclass' itself.[14] But the people who lived in such conditions became themselves polluted, literally and figuratively, with the stench. And they became contagious: in mid-19th century medicine, bad air was itself considered to be the source of infection. American warrior against the 'underclass' Charles Loring Brace described his Children's Aid Society as 'a moral and physical disinfectant.'[15] The largest impact of these exposés of a mid-19th-century 'underclass' was to frighten and horrify, to make the objects of these writings appear dangerous, disgusting, and very likely irredeemable.[16]

The rhetoric about 'underclass' was above all moral, and structural explanations appeared as lame excuses. As Gareth Stedman Jones wrote about 'outcast London,' in the 'residuum the . . . psychological defects of individuals bulked even larger than before . . . The problem was not [perceived as] structural but moral, . . . not poverty but pauperism . . . with its attendant vices, drunkenness, improvidence, mendicancy, bad language, filthy habits, gambling, low amusements, and ignorance.'[17] We can see, in fact, a tendency of words originating in a variety of descriptive intents to converge in a moral register. For example, the 'miasma' caused by the waste-disposal practices of city dwellers – and the practices of the privileged classes were no better at this time, except that they had more space – soon became a personal characteristic of 'underclass' people, associated with their lack of individual hygiene. Or consider the term 'ragged,' which was first used literally to describe the clothing of the poor. Its usage became more and more metaphorical, and by the early 19th century one had 'ragged homes,' 'ragged Radicals,' and 'ragged schools' for the poor.[18]

Other words moved in a different, although not exactly opposite, direction: they began as condemnations of specific behaviour, but migrated to refer generically to entire groups whether or not all members of these groups exhibited such bad behaviour. Words such as 'dangerous classes,' 'disreputable,' 'underworld,' 'reckless,' and 'promiscuous' behaved this way.[19] Supporting this expansion of terms to encompass large groups was the biologistic language of the 19th century. Victorians, both in England and in the US, used 'race' in many absolutely vague senses: it could refer to a bewildering variety of ethnic groups, nations, religions. But it always had physicality in it, and was thus a group in which membership was inescapable, not chosen. In England the 'underclass' 'race' was further primitivized by being frequently called a 'tribe.' Thus the 'underclass' became in this rhetoric pre-civilized, at a lower level of human development.[20] An 1883 British journalistic series spoke of 'natural curiosities' akin to 'the Zenanas, the Aborigenes, and the South Sea Islanders.'[21] These 'outcasts' were a 'residuum' 'left behind by the mid-Victorian march of moral and material progress.'[22] Intermixed with this popular anthropology of the primitive was a discourse of exoticism, in which the titillation of fear and revulsion combined with that of sexual attraction. The depravity of the 'underclass' was formed of licentiousness, permissiveness, and lack of personal modesty. And of course wherever there was a sexual discourse there was a double standard and the complex mixed feelings so often directed by the elites towards the women of subordinated classes: attraction, hatred, and disregard.

'Underclass' depends for its meanings on a contrast with the respectable. All 'othering,' in fact, is produced by comparative, usually binary, assumptions and speech. The structure, membership, and values of the respectable were constructed by the contraposition. What is now in the US called the 'mainstream' (subsuming, as Christopher Jencks points out, both middle and working class) saw itself in the negative of the 'underclass'. Indeed, President Clinton's rhetoric in the US today contrasts welfare recipients with the 'middle class,' now defined as anyone with a job, thus liquidating the working class. This respectable majority became thus represented as homogeneous. This fiction was both self-fulfilling, as it pressured those who wanted to be 'mainstream' towards conformity, and also productive of hypocrisy, since it encouraged dissembling not only about behaviour but about wealth. In other words, the tendency to define an 'underclass' as an 'outcast' group supervises the behaviour of those who would be accepted as respectable; and then the spread of the term to take in more of the poor in general makes poverty itself disreputable and compels those who want to defend their respectability to separate themselves, both in public and in private consciousness, from the poor.

Separating the respectable from the disreputable is a highly gendered exercise. Men and women of the 'dangerous classes' were threatening in different ways. The emphasis on tramps and bums, refusal to work, criminality and violence apparently directed attention to men, as did working-class hostility to scabs. Anxieties about sexual promiscuity, prostitution, and reproduction focused on women. Women of 'loose' sexual behaviour were regularly labelled as 'underclass' and, conversely, 'underclass' women were expected to behave immorally and thus to have no claim to protection or sympathy if they were assaulted. Women were dangerous reproducers in several meanings of that term: biologically, because they brought unwanted, delinquent children into the world; socially, because as mothers they passed on a defective culture to the next generation. Moreover, in the Victorian gender system, 'underclass' women were in some senses responsible for men's sins, because they failed at their prescribed task of domesticating men and disciplining them to work.[23]

'Underclass' was also a racial term in the US. It soon became illustrated in the popular imagination by the immigrants who crowded the eastern cities after about 1880. Their otherness was in part religious, as antiCatholicism and antiSemitism characterized professional and upper-class Anglo-Saxon elites. The strange ways of the new immigrants, especially those from southern and eastern Europe and Asia Minor – their cuisines, drinks, dress, methods of child care and housekeeping – combined with their darker complexions to make them seem racially other. At the turn of the century fear of these poor strangers threatened to spread to the entire working class, now mainly immigrant, the disdain and revulsion usually reserved for the uniquely disreputable.

Starting in the mid-19th century there was also a counter-discourse about an 'underclass' that sought to defend the working poor. Marxist hostility to a *lumpenproletariat* expressed a common working-class perspective. 'Lumpen' means ragged too, but Marx and Engels hedged in their term with a more precise definition that did not spill over to stigmatize the poor in general. To the contrary, the heart of the lumpen-proletariat in the Marxist view was its propensity to attack the working class, the labouring poor, by prostituting itself to a threatened capitalist class. I use a prostitution metaphor deliberately, for the 19th-century Marxists shared with liberals a sense of the importance of sexual respectability to the proletariat and to a viable working-class consciousness. If there were aspects of 'underclass' behaviour that might be defended as Bohemian, antiauthoritarian, or pleasure-loving, Marx would have none of them.[24] His revolutionary followers were just as moralistic: Bukharin, for example, referred to the lumpenproletariat's 'shiftlessness, lack of discipline, hatred of the old, but impotence to construct or organize anything new, an individualistic declassed 'personality,' whose actions are based only on foolish caprices.'[25] His concept of the vices of the 'underclass' shared with that of liberals and conservatives a vision of a slippery slope to hell, with the first skid being decline in the work ethic; his greatest fear was that the slide led to loss of class solidarity, which liberals and conservatives were, of course, happy to dispense with. Not only Marxists but most unionists saw the 'underclass' as a breeding ground for scabs and, worse, mercenary thugs, goons, infiltrators and provocateurs used by bosses and the state against strikers, demonstrators, and revolutionaries. This was, to them, the rabble, the masses as opposed to the classes, and, later, along with the *petite bourgeoisie*, the storm troopers.

The New Left produced an alternative analysis which led to a marginal defence of an 'underclass.' In criticizing institutions of 'social control,' such as prisons, schools, and asylums, New Leftists often suggested that norms of respectability were imposed on the poor by the upper and/or middle classes.[26] Respectability was sometimes labelled 'bourgeois' by the New Left. In fact, there was a strong set of working-class norms of respectability which included hard work, cleanliness, religion or church attendance, and community or class solidarity, and a disapproval of disreputable behaviour which did not come from 'above.' Recognizing this is not incompatible with recognizing that middle class social control often functioned to change these norms and to divide poor communities by inducing intolerance.[27] But failure to recognize it has led to an opposite, often distinctly male, tendency to romanticize 'underclass' behaviour as rebellious, the opposite of 'uptight.' The attraction to vagabondage, irresponsibility, the street life, violence, was and remains highly gendered.

Marxists tried to integrate the concept into a class analysis by emphasizing its role in supplying a reserve army of labour. But this is not precise enough, for women have also functioned, Marxists argued, as a reserve army of labour without demonstrating the 'underclass' lifestyle that offended observers. Clearly 'underclass'ness always included lifestyle attributes, but for Marxists these were epiphenomena of structural locations. Moreover, a social class, as distinct from a stratum, is a relational concept; classes mutually produced each other through relations of production. By contrast in the common 'underclass' talk of the past or present, the group was defined in contrast to certain respectable classes, to be sure, but without suggestion that the respectable ones have produced the 'underclass' in the way that workers produce capitalists and vice versa.

Throughout the 19th century there was one dimension in which the 'underclass' appeared to arise from social-structural relations rather than individual character: this is the notion that public provision created an 'underclass'. Just as today's 'underclass' discussion focuses in part on the role of the welfare system so did that of the 19th century US, using above all the concept of pauperism. In the 16th century the term 'pauper' had meant simply a poor person. By the late 19th century, it took on a more restricted definition, denoting a new class of persons who chronically subsisted on poor relief, had lost commitment to the work ethic and personal independence; the concept became increasingly derogatory.

In the late 19th century US, the newly professionalizing field of social work developed a theory of 'scientific charity' to which 'pauperism' was central. Foreshadowing the concern of today's conservatives, these social workers criticized earlier and traditional public provision for encouraging 'dependence' and discouraging 'independence' by indiscriminate giving. Not only were some of the poor undeserving of help, but careless help could *create* papuerism. As geographer David Ward described the hegemonic attitude towards the early 20th century slums, 'in order to limit the presumably damaging effects of relief on able-bodied workers, much attention was given to the size of a morally delinquent residuum.'[28] Thus pauperism was sharply distinguished from poverty. Theoretically one could be poor without being a pauper, if one was hard-working and hopeful; indeed, in theory one could be a pauper without being poor, if one related to society as a sponger, although in practice such a usage of 'pauper' – which would have stigmatized many in the upper class – never caught on. Rather what happened, as with the language of 'dangerous classes,' is that the stigma of pauperism spread to include more and more of the poor, making the possibility of an honourable poverty disappear. Perhaps nothing expressed the horrifying stigma of pauperism as much as the possibility of being without a proper burial and ending up in a pauper's grave.

Politically, 'pauperism' became not only an argument against generosity towards the poor but also an early 'culture of poverty' analysis. Help could create pauperism not only in individuals but in groups and for generations. Charity leaders and social workers feared that social provision could accustom the poor to expect handouts without working and thus create a culture of pauperism which, once developed, could become self-perpetuating. This fear was not exclusive to one side of the political continuum. Although conservatives usually expressed themselves with more animus towards the poor in their characterizations of 'underclass' behaviour, socialists condemned the same behaviours. The 19th-century working-class mutual benefit societies that proliferated among virtually all ethnic groups in the cities also distinguished between the deserving/undeserving poor and carefully reviewed claimants of benefits to make sure that they were honest and upright.[29] Right through the Progressive era in the US, social workers and activists continued to express anxiety that a too-good welfare system could pauperize unless accompanied by moral reform of the poor.[30]

But the 19th and early-20th-century discourse about pauperism did not create an 'underclass' alarum in the US. The poverty, crime, and deviance that reformers saw in the immigrant ghettos of the early-20th-century US cities was integrated into a context of general optimism about these poor newcomers' possibilities of upward mobility. Not even the African-American ghettos resulting from the Great Migration into eastern and midwestern cities produced an 'underclass' discourse because these migrants, too, appeared to be on their way up.

'Underclass' warnings began to appear sporadically in the US between 1930 and 1970, mainly from the political Left.[31] The Depression, of course, did not tend to provoke these fears because poverty was so widespread that its stigma decreased. Nevertheless, some observers began to observe long-term, structural changes within the economic emergency. Rexford Tugwell, for example, Franklin Roosevelt's Secretary of Agriculture, aware of the large-scale evictions of sharecroppers (induced by New Deal policies), predicted in 1934 the development of an 'underclass.' Revealingly, it was in the officially prosperous 1950s and 1960s that close observers of economic trends became aware of the problems identified by the label 'underclass' today. In an essay published in 1947 sociologist August Hollingshead discussed the 'scum of the city.'[32] By 1966 sociologist David Matza wrote about the 'disreputable poor,' astutely concluding that the future development of this stratum depended on the outcome of the 'Negro mobilization,' i.e. the civil rights movement.[33] Socialists Michael Harrington and Stanley Aronowitz raised the spectre of a hereditary 'underclass' in 1963.[34] The Department of Labor began to report on 'Men in Poverty Neighborhoods' affected by residential segregation, unemployment, low pay, and high rates of marital breakup, although it used no synonym of 'underclass'.[35] The most important of these prede-cessors of the contemporary debate was, of course, the 'Moynihan Report' of 1965, to be discussed below. The term may have been slow to become common in the US because of lingering notions that it was a classless society; a 1977 *Time* article attributed the concept of an 'underclass' to 'class-ridden Europe.'[36] Examining this semantic history, we see that it was not until after several decades of increasing immiseration and its attendant demoralization that the concept of 'underclass' reached popular usage.

Welfare Constructs an 'Underclass'

The Great Depression of the 1930s and the US version of a Popular Front government – the New Deal – created a more democratic political culture, lessened the stigma on poverty and unemployment, and gave rise to the first major federal government programmes against poverty since Reconstruction and the Freedmen's Bureau. Nevertheless, the 'underclass' that was harvested in the 1980s had been fertilized in the New Deal.

In 1934 and 1935 when the Social Security Act was debated, there was no fear of long-term labour redundancy or overpopulation. No one considered the massive unemployment rates of the Depression to be permanent. Just a few years previously, southern landowners had been struggling to insulate their sharecroppers from the call of northern industrial jobs. President Franklin Roosevelt's social policy-makers focused not on an 'underclass' but on mass unemployment affecting even the previously stable and prosperous working class and lower middle class. Influenced by some Keynesian ideas, Roosevelt wanted to relieve the unemployed (particularly those who were Democratic voters), pump up the economy with new consumer spending power, and erect permanent barriers against another such terrible collapse.

When Roosevelt established a Committee on Economic Security to draft a welfare bill for him in 1934, he opened the door to a small but passionate stream of welfare thought that had been growing in the US since at least 1890. This stream had two tributaries, about which I have written at length elsewhere, but which must be reviewed here.[37] One was identified with the notion of 'social insurance,' had been much influenced by European, particularly German, proposals, and focused on programmes to replace wages lost through unemployment, disability, or death. An earlier enthusiasm for health insurance provoked such opposition from the American Medical Association, the physicians' guild, that social-insurance proponents dropped it in favour of proposals more likely to succeed. A second branch of welfare thought had grown from the charity and then social work tradition. It focused on helping the most needy, notably women, children, and the infirm. This group of social workers believed strongly that the injuries of poverty were not only economic, and that the poor needed not only money but also other kinds of help, including medical care, education, counselling, for example.

The class and race standpoint from which these two approaches arose were similar – virtually all the influential welfare proponents were white and from privileged families and most were Protestants. But they differed sharply by sex. The social-insurance group was almost exclusively male and its perspective showed this. At the turn of the century, women alone with children were disproportionately impoverished as they are today, but social-insurance writings almost never mentioned the needs of women or children. Social insurance was designed in part to regulate the labour market and in part to maintain male breadwinners as heads of families and households. The recipient of social-insurance aid was envisaged as a male head of household and a prominent part of this vision was to provide payments in ways that did not reduce his dignity and authority. Thus the social-insurance planners designed programmes in which the receipt of help would be a dignified entitlement, ensuing automatically from a contractual position. In the two major programmes they created in the

Social Security Act (old-age pensions and unemployment insurance), they devised special, earmarked forms of taxation so that the benefits would appear to be independent of traditional government relief.[38]

Meanwhile, by the turn of the century the strong US women's movement, making its influence felt through the many women active in charity, social work, and social reform, had given rise to a distinctly female approach to welfare.[39] The social-work profession and its associated social-reform network were feminized, imbued with the maternalist views of several generations of social reformers. The greatest lasting victory of this group was in the mothers'-aid laws, programmes passed by most states in the US between 1910 and 1930 providing public aid to some needy single mothers with children, usually widows but sometimes also including deserted wives and unmarried mothers. Indeed, it is a measure of the strength of this women's welfare network that these mothers'-aid laws were the only area of welfare state development in which the US did not lag behind European countries.

By the Depression, the Left edge of the women's/social work coalition was proposing a truly progressive approach to welfare, breaking with both the charity tradition and with the social-insurance model. Leaders such as the social-democratic-leaning Edith Abbott and the Communist-leaning Mary Van Kleeck proposed programmes of universal government support for those who were, for whatever reason, un- or under-employed. And, like other New Dealers, they counted on public medical insurance and public jobs when necessary. There was substantial support for these proposals, particularly from unions.

But Roosevelt did not believe that his Democratic Party coalition, resting as it did on conservative southerners as well as the white working class, would support such a turn and instead appointed a far more cautious group to write his welfare legislation, which was to become the Social Security Act. The drafting group rejected the more generous and universal proposals coming from the Left, male and female, and sought participation only from the more mainstream social-insurance and charity/social work tendencies. Then, instead of choosing between these two historically different approaches, the group compromised in typical Rooseveltian fashion, giving each tendency several programmes of its own. In fact the social insurance proponents were dominant, but precisely because they believed their programmes to be the wave of the future, and public assistance programmes would become increasingly marginal, they did not see that their compromise would create a lasting stratification.

In the resultant legislation, two major new social-insurance programmes, unemployment compensation and old-age insurance, were written by social-insurance men. The social-work women who wrote Aid to Dependent Children did little new conceptualization at all but merely added federal money to existing state and local mothers'-aid programmes. In fact, the eleven titles of Social Security installed at least five different programme models. But for the sake of my argument here, about the construction of an 'underclass,' one dichotomy looms particularly large – that between social insurance and Aid to Dependent Children (ADC).[40] Let me enumerate some of these contrasts.

(1) While social insurance coverage was not reserved for the poor but based on employment factors – e.g., employment by employers of a certain size, steady employment for a certain length of time – ADC was exclusively for the very needy. It was means-tested so as to prevent those not in need from collecting, and those with any substantial personal resources, such as home-ownership, were excluded. ADC recipients were often required to divest themselves of resources, such as a house, in order to receive aid.

(2) While social-insurance benefits were paid in such a way as to preserve a claimant's privacy, ADC benefits included supervision. A man receiving unemployment compensation or old age insurance could spend his entire benefit on opium, liquor, or gambling and live in a pigsty, with the clerk who administered his payment being none the wiser. A woman receiving ADC would be assigned an individual caseworker who would require her to prepare a weekly or monthly budget to make sure that the stipend was being properly used; she would receive home 'visits' by caseworkers to evaluate her standards of housekeeping, child-care, and domestic morality. To receive benefits, the ADC applicant had to position herself as a supplicant requesting help, one who might be refused, while the social insurance recipient merely claimed his rights.

(3) Social insurance went to the covered person as an individual. Although the justification for these programmes sometimes dwelt on the plight of the worker's dependents should he fail to bring home wages, in collecting his benefit his entitlement was as an individual. He received the same amount regardless of his number of dependents, and they could leave or he could cut them off without losing his benefit. ADC by contrast was doled out in differential amounts according to need. ADC was officially not a payment to an adult individual at all but to the support of children in the care of their mother. Since the mother had no individual entitlement, her receipt of a stipend was dependent on her proving that she was spending it on her children and not on herself.

(4) Social insurance payments were designed to be big enough that a recipient and his family might live on them, and they soon became indexed to inflation. ADC was never sufficient to support a family, rarely even an individual, and it shrank with inflation.

(5) Social insurance was designed to prevent poverty with money. Its assumptions were that this was what men needed to retain their health,

dignity, citizenship, and family authority, and it self-consciously broke with the charity legacy of suspicion that the poor lacked character. ADC, by contrast, denied that money alone could solve the problems; it rested on the conviction that poor single mothers also needed counselling, rehabilitation, guidance.

(6) Social insurance was based on the workplace – eligibility was defined in terms of certain standards of employment, and some of the money was collected as an employment tax. This was deemed essential by its designers, not technically but politically. Social insurance could have been as easily paid for from taxes, and entitlements attached to citizenship; in practice, for example, old-age insurance funds were used by the US government for other expenditures, and the stipends were not in fact directly connected to employees' contributions. The creation of apparently separate contributions was designed to make social insurance *appear* an entitlement which could not be abrogated and thus to separate it from poor relief. Public assistance, by contrast, appeared as charity, paid for by others, unconnected to work or to any other kind of contribution to society made by its recipient.

All these differences were fundamentally gendered. The supervision inherent in the ADC model assumed a subordination of the client that was culturally acceptable for women but not for men.[41] Its smaller stipends were understood as appropriate because their recipients – single mothers – were not 'real' heads of households but only temporary caretakers during men's absence. Furthermore, even those policy-makers who had observed the considerable numbers of single mothers saw that phenomenon as dangerous and disorderly, and insisted that public provision not function to encourage it. Gender norms of the time did not include imagining women as supporting families. Even women alone were conceived to need less to live on than single men.[42] Citizenship and its entitlements were still conceived primarily as male. After all, most of the mothers'-aid laws on which ADC was based were passed before women could vote, and woman suffrage was still a new innovation in the 1930s. Men had rights, women had needs. And men particularly had a right to personal privacy, while it was acceptable for women to plead for help and to be supervised. All these distinctions were naturalized by the association of social insurance with the workplace, which remained a predominantly male sphere.

The agreement to include two kinds of programmes was in part a political compromise, giving two groups each a plum. It was also a compromise based on a mutually accepted division of labour, between male-style and female-style programmes, and that division in turn was acceptable because it rested on considerable agreement. Both groups considered social insurance the master plan. It was a set of programmes designed to rescue male family heads from undeserved destitution, and to support these men's dependents indirectly. The women accepted the theory that women and children would be adequately provided for as dependents of male breadwinners. Both groups understood that some individuals would not be covered by a family head's entitlement, such as unmarried mothers, but both expected these groups to be small. One figure may provide a vivid example: the first appropriation asked for by the women who designed ADC, reflecting their sense of the size of the problem, was $25 million, to provide for an expected 288,000 families. Moreover, they expected the need to *decline* over time, because more women and children could collect benefits as the dependents of social-insurance beneficiaries, and because amelioration of poverty and unemployment would reduce the number of single mothers. They could hardly have been more wrong. In fiscal year 1991 the total spent on ADC was $20.3 billion, serving 4,362,400 families – and this was after amendments had shifted many of these single-mother families to the social-insurance programmes.

Except for a few radical feminists, both male and female welfare advocates assumed the same gender system. Their joint premise was the family wage, the belief that men should be the sole breadwinners for families. This premise was also the source of the ADC authors' gross mistake in estimating the need for ADC. So strong was their belief in the family-wage *norm* that it blinded many experts to the *reality* about how many single and working mothers there were. (As many children lived with single mothers in 1930 as in 1960 – about 9 percent; the majority of working-class men could not support their families single-handedly but relied also on women's and children's earnings.) So strong was their belief in the family-wage *rule* that many welfare advocates were reluctant to subvert it by making it too easy for single mothers to maintain themselves as heads of families.

Recently feminist scholars have sometimes conceptualized these gender norms and rules as imposed by men on women. On the contrary, the fundamental determinants of the gender/family system were widely, almost universally, supported by both men and women welfare reformers. It was not until the 1960s that most feminists began to question the necessity of male-headed families. The maternalist feminists who wrote ADC believed that close supervision was important to poor single mothers, whom they believed to be in need of encouragement, education in rational and modern housekeeping and child-care methods, and protection from immoral temptation.[43]

If the first reason for the two-track welfare system was the intersection of economic need with the gender system, the system was soon influenced even more powerfully by the racial system. Let us recall the racial construction of citizenship in the US in the 1930s. Blacks remained concentrated in the South where they were almost entirely disfranchised and deprived of most rights pertaining to citizenship; white southerners and many northerners simply did not perceive Blacks as full citizens. The South was a one-party Democratic region and it was an essential part of FDR's electoral coalition. Because southern politicians were uncontested in elections, they acquired seniority in the Congress, and seniority within the majority party was at the time the only principle determining Congressional leadership. Southern Democrats thus controlled powerful Congressional committees which had to approve legislation before it could reach the floor, and they knew that a federal government welfare programme would loosen the stranglehold that southern landowners maintained on their low-wage agricultural labour force, notably share-croppers but also urban workers and domestic servants.

So key Southern Congressmen and Senators insisted on crucial amendments to the Social Security Act, and Franklin Roosevelt and his advisers believed that surrender on these amendments was the price of getting Social Security passed. First, they eliminated agricultural and domestic workers – most Blacks, Latinos, Asians and American Indians – from the social insurance programmes. More minority and white women workers – usually employed by small businesses, often dropping in and out of the labour force – were also excluded. Second, amendments to the public assistance programmes, which were operated on the basis of joint federal-state funding, eliminated federal controls which might have prevented southern states from discriminating. State and local authorities were thus left free to determine eligibility for public assistance, and they systematically excluded most minorities.

The groups left out – Blacks and other poor minorities, white women, single mothers especially – are precisely the core of the 'underclass' today. Since then, most readjustments of the US welfare system have given more to those in its upper strata programmes and reduced the value of benefits to those served by the inferior programmes.

The terms of social citizenship installed or confirmed by Social Security had consequences for civil and political citizenship. ADC recipients often found their civil rights curtailed – denied the right to interstate travel (by state residency requirements), to due process (by administrative procedures allowing for termination of benefits *before* a hearing and long delays in holding hearings), to privacy (by constant means- and 'morals'-testing), to protection from unreasonable search and seizure (by unannounced home inspections, the famous 'midnight searches').[44]

But perhaps most consequential among these restrictions on citizenship was the message that receipt of ADC constituted a type of 'dependency,' a parasitism, that was incompatible with the honourable status of citizen. The issue is not just unequal stratification. It is that these programmes solidified a distinction already present embryonically – that some government provision is an entitlement while some is charity; that some is earned and deserved, while some is not. We see this in American usage today: the good programmes are called by specific names – Social Security or Unemployment Compensation; the main second-class programme, ADC, is called 'welfare,' a last resort and mark of shame. The nature of the second-class programmes steadily escalates resentment: the supervision is costly to taxpayers, the means-testing keeps alive a fear that recipients are cheating, the morals-testing stimulates a sense of widespread immorality at government expense. Small wonder that the recipients hate the programme as much as do wealthier taxpayers. While recipients of Social Security old age insurance feel as entitled as veterans, accepting their payments almost as a symbol of citizenship, ADC recipients are likely to experience their payments virtually as proof of noncitizenship. They receive so many messages in which they are described as parasitical, dependent, disreputable, immoral, and greedy that it is a wonder that any are able to value themselves and their parenting work. It is not surprising that so many studies show that the poor share some of the same hostility to 'welfare' that the middle class do. Today to most Americans the 'underclass' *is* the welfare class.

Contemporary 'Underclass' Talk

'Underclass' rhetoric in the US today carries some of the same charge as that of Victorian England. The discourse is almost entirely urban and state-centred, dwelling on state responsibility in the past or future. It often appears in the most liberal discourse, aimed at securing more resources for social benefits. Thus a liberal child-welfare scholar refers to a 'new class of 'untouchables' . . . emerging in our inner cities . . . young people who are functionally illiterate, disconnected from school, depressed, prone to drug abuse and early criminal activity, and eventually, parents of unplanned and unwanted babies.'[45] A lawyer in a 1982 Saul Bellow novel, well-meaning but despairing, explains:

> Your defendant belongs to that black underclass everybody is openly talking about, . . . economically 'redundant,' . . . falling farther and farther behind the rest of society, locked into a culture of despair and crime – I wouldn't say a culture, that's a specialist's word. There is no culture there, it's only a wilderness, and damn monstrous, too . . . a people denuded. And what's the effect of denudation, atomization? . . . just a lumpen population . . . nothing but death before it . . . They kill some of us. Mostly they kill themselves.[46]

Metaphors of primitivism, ugliness, redundancy, and sexual license proliferate. As in the last century, the word attempts to distinguish the respectable from the disreputable poor but in practice stigmatizes all the urban and especially the minority poor. Print, broadcast, and movie exposés of ghetto life, drugs, and drive-by shootings evoke and escalate the combined pity/revulsion/titillation effect, as in the 19th century. The 'underclass' concept remains fundamentally moral despite the continued attempts of experts to define it objectively. Indeed, working-class and poor people often use the 'underclass' concept to place themselves in the 'mainstream' by distinguishing themselves from the disreputable. And the 'underclass'/'mainstream' dichotomy offers a binary taxonomy of 'class' which substitutes for a more complex analysis and deflects attention from the actual distribution of resources and power.

The gender, racial and familial meanings are abundantly clear, in the professional as in the popular discourse. Today in the US the dominant scholarly definition of 'underclass' employs four indicators: chronic joblessness or 'weak labour-force attachment', welfare 'dependence,' social isolation in ghettos, and several kinds of social deviance. Experts argue that these are objective and sex- and race-neutral. Let us consider these claims. For example, what does chronic joblessness, or 'weak labour-force attachment' as it is often called, mean for women? 'Weak labour-force attachment' was the preferred normative behaviour for the majority of US women until a generation ago, and labour-force discrimination along with responsibility for children combine to concentrate women in unstable jobs. Moreover, women's responsibility for raising children makes it difficult for many women to hold jobs that do not allow them to meet children's needs (such as medical insurance, sick leave, parental leave, flexible hours, ready access to telephone for personal conversations). Defining 'underclass' in terms of welfare 'dependence' is equally problematic. Women's responsibility for raising children is the main reason most of them collect 'welfare;' caring for dependents makes them 'dependent.' Moreover, 'dependence,' too, has been part of the female norm; what is different, in terms of 'dependence,' between a woman raising small children on a husband's allowance and a woman raising small children on a government allowance?[47] Behavioural definitions are equally problematic in the absence of gender analysis. Women are less often active in crime and drug-selling, and when they are they are often tools, frequently involuntary, of men. Many women could be said to become 'underclass' because of their dependence on 'underclass' men, just as many women enter the middle class because of their dependence on men. Indeed, many husbands and boyfriends react aggressively, even abusively, precisely when women show signs of gaining independence. Women who seek escape from their dependence on unreliable men, thus becoming single mothers, end up in the same 'underclass' by a different route. A central 'deviance' which defines the 'underclass' today is by definition female – teenage pregnancy and out-of-wedlock childbirth. In the standard discussion of these censured behaviours, men are so absent that one might assume the conceptions were immaculate. Thus we read that 'women who start their families before marriage and before the end of adolescence [are] the main engine propelling the underclass disaster.'[48] Out-of-wedlock fatherhood is out of sight. So inadequate parenting is an exclusively female deviance; fathers are virtually never charged with child neglect.[49]

Racial structures, equally, underlie 'underclass' talk. What does 'weak labour-force attachment' mean for minorities? Discrimination always created disproportionate levels of unemployment and underemployment among them. As late entrants into the industrial economy many migrated from the agricultural South or Southwest, or into the US from Mexico, just as the long expansionist phase of US industrial production ended. In shop closings, labour-force reductions and other manifestations of deindustrialization, minorities were often the last hired and thus the first fired. Forced onto reservations, American Indians were often far from available jobs. Measuring weak or strong labour-force attachment does not make useful distinctions between the ordinary poor and the 'underclass' poor among young minorities who are chronically jobless. Nor is 'social isolation in ghettos' a sharp discriminating measure given patterns of residential segregation which affect many employed and even middle-class as well as poor minority people. Out-of-wedlock childbearing has considerably different meanings for poor Blacks and middle-class whites. Not only is disapproval of out-of-wedlock childbirth and female-headed households less in African American than in European American family culture. In addition, Black female-headed households are often extended, taking non-nuclear family members and non-kin as an antipoverty strategy. (From the 1940s through 1980, female-headed households were twice as likely to be extended as male-headed households.)[50] Furthermore, teenage childbearing is less costly to poor women, whose chances of escaping poverty are not significantly reduced by early motherhood.

Welfare 'dependence' among minorities also has had historically different meanings. We have seen that racial minorities were originally excluded from most programmes of government provision. In the 1950s and 1960s, poor minority mothers took the lead in asserting their rights to receive welfare aid. Claiming welfare was an economic strategy developed in adaptation to a severely discriminatory labour market; using it as a criterion for 'underclass' membership ignores the ways in which it was precisely part of an effort not to be 'underclass.'[51] The welfare-rights movement that grew in the late 1960s was at once a part of the civil-rights and women's movements. Its members saw 'welfare' as a citizenship entitlement not unlike education and suffrage for which they were simultaneously struggling. Equally important, they enunciated a more dignified image of the work of poor single mothers; their rhetoric prefigured 'wages-for-housework' analyses of domestic labour. In the late 1960s they mobilized progressive lawyers who helped force the courts to restrict some of the infringements of their constitutional rights that ADC had created: they stopped unwarranted searches of their homes, won the right to *prior* hearings before termination of benefits, and stopped residence requirements.[52] Seen historically, rising welfare claims were in some ways a sign of increasing resourcefulness and self-esteem among poor and especially minority single mothers, a step towards first-class citizenship, and not necessarily a sign of impoverishment or character flaw.

That 'underclass' definitions are not sex- or race-neutral is not marginal but central to the problem, because minority men and women and white women are so disproportionately represented in the 'underclass.' Current estimates calculate that the 'underclass' is 60 percent Black, 20 percent other minority, and 20 percent white. At least 60 percent of 'underclass' families are headed by single mothers.[53] These groups are prominent among those excluded from the better Social Security programmes.

Moreover, US welfare programmes constructed social citizenship from two sides – that of the poor and that of the non-poor, those excluded and those included. Social Security built entitlements and a sense of membership in the polity for some even as it denied citizenship to others.[54] Its benefits to middle-class and upper-working-class men and their dependents were greater, absolutely and proportionately, than its contributions to the poor. In the 1980s, eighty percent of the US social welfare budget flowed to the non-poor.[55] These welfare benefits accounted for a larger share of the economic advancement of the middle class over time than income. That is, more employed people would have been poor had it not been for government provision. Even the War on Poverty contributed more to the non-poor than to the poor.[56] In the last fifty years, the 'good' Social Security programmes got steadily better. Old Age Insurance benefits were increased, protected against inflation, and extended to more beneficiaries, especially dependents. By contrast, the real value of AFDC and other public assistance programmes fell and through 1970s eligibility criteria began to exclude more of the poor.[57] And these benefits, unlike those of social insurance, were unreliable: millions of recipients were at times cut off because of administrative errors, caseworkers' judgements, or client errors in filling out paperwork. Moreover, AFDC regulations created disincentives to upward mobility: for example, extended family strategies, so common among the poor and especially the Black poor, conflicted with welfare requirements and often led to suspension of benefits.

Unequal citizenship was reinforced by the social and cultural meanings constructed around Social Security's tracking system. The dynamic in which the well-off got more and the poor got less accelerated over time within the Social Security system. For example, the fact that recipients of old-age insurance were labelled as entitled by Social Security strengthened their lobbying power, which in turn strengthened their identity as entitled still further. Public assistance claimants, meanwhile, identified as parasites, grew poorer and more stigmatized, which in turn undercut their ability to organize to create political pressure, and their lack of organizational strength then further weakened their ability to offer a counter-discourse. Nothing illustrates this better than the substantial gains welfare claimants made during the period in which they built the National Welfare Rights Organization, and their losses since the decline of that organization in the 1970s.

As a result, even during periods defined as prosperous, the 1950s and 1960s, relative indicators for stigmatized groups moved downward. For example, even while Black employment and income was growing, Blacks' *share* of unemployment steadily increased. And the numbers of the poor who were marginally employed also increased, notably those who could not get into full-time major industry jobs but depended on service-sector, seasonal, temporary employment.

Some qualifications must be reemphasized: of course the Social Security Act was not the only social policy that contributed to creating an 'underclass.'[58] Nor was Social Security's influence all in the direction of inequality. But opposite trends were developing even in these decades usually labelled prosperous. For these the state must share responsibility with the society. Still, understanding the contribution of the welfare system to the politics of resentment of the poor, and resultant hatred of 'welfare,' is an important historical lesson in the context of today's backlash against social citizenship.

Indeed, because that backlash is by no means confined to the US, it would seem useful to internationalize scrutiny of the negative effects of the design of welfare programmes. The US experience suggests that welfare structures themselves have been important components in the erosion of popular support for the welfare state and for the possibility of ending poverty and reducing inequality. Words and meanings are very important here: a New York Times poll recently showed that almost half of Americans support cutbacks in 'welfare' but oppose cutbacks in support for poor children! Since the New Deal, polls have suggested that the public strongly supports those welfare programmes it benefits from, while welfare that is 'targetted' (a revealing metaphor) on the poor quickly loses popularity among the nonpoor. Moreover, the public supports government programmes that produce visible, tangible goods, such as good schools, safe and clean neighbourhoods and parks. By contrast, welfare that is so stingy and underfunded that it cannot reduce poverty, crime and filth loses popularity. Thus stigmatization, fragmentation, stratification and stinginess of welfare provision erodes support for welfare.

Such stratification also undermines possibilities for unity or even solidarity among the working class. Historical inquiry into the roots of an 'underclass' demonstrates the severe and lasting costs of sex and race inequalities within the working class. We face today a bitter contradiction: although women's and civil rights movements of the last thirty years have had some success in delegitimating sex and race prejudice, the welfare state has institutionalized and perpetuated discriminations based on the prejudices of sixty years ago. New Deal welfare programmes took differences then widely perceived as natural and gave them materiality and endurance by institutionalizing them in the state. Welfare stratification created by past forms of domination increases the obstacles to challenging other forms of domination today. Welfare structures not only carry the dead weight of the past into the present but provide rallying points for dangerous hate-mongering along new lines, demonizing single mothers, gays, the poor. While prosperous women and minority men have improved their positions considerably, the poor are harvesting rather a renewed stigma. Resentments against women and minority men sowed by the structures that consigned so many to second- or third-class citizenship are pushing many constituencies formerly central to the socialist or social-democratic projects far to the Right.

If we are to struggle against this new 'class' ideology that pits the 'middle class' or 'mainstream' against the poor, it is important to take careful note of how much of this ideology arises from definitions of welfare state activity. The questions of what counts as 'welfare,' as 'dependency,' as 'entitlement,' and as 'work' need to be contested. The decisions taken by the Democratic Party in the US and the Labour Party in Britain to pander to reactionary definitions of these concepts, and to join in the scapegoating of single mothers and the very poor, can only further erode the political possibilities of the Left.

NOTES

1. Nancy Fraser and Linda Gordon, 'Contract Versus Charity: Why Is There No Social Citizenship in the United States?' *Socialist Review* 22 #3, July-September 1992, pp. 45–67; idem, 'Civil Citizenship against Social Citizenship?' in *The Condition of Citizenship* ed. Bart van Steenbergen (London: Sage, 1994), pp. 90–107.
2. In fact the word 'underclass' was more common in the US ten years ago – even in 1991 when I began this research – than it is today. Nevertheless, the numbers of people included by the concept, and the pejorative discussions of them, have continually grown.
3. Ralf Dahrendorf, *Law and Order* (London: Stevens & Sons, 1985), p. 98.
4. See my *Pitied But Not Entitled: Single Mothers and the History of Welfare* (New York: Free Press, 1994).
5. Published as Ken Auletta, *The Underclass* (New York: Vintage, 1983).
6. E.g., Ricketts, Erol R. and Isabel V. Sawhill, 'Defining and Measuring the Underclass,' *Journal of Policy Analysis and Management* vol. 7, No. 2 (1988), pp. 316–325; Barbara Schmitter Heisler, 'A Comparative Perspective on the Underclass: Questions of Urban Poverty, Race, and Citizenship,' *Theory and Society* 20, 1991, pp. 455–483; 'Defining Help for the Underclass,' *America*, vol. 155, Oct. 11, 1986, pp. 177–178; William Julius Wilson, 'Cycles of Deprivation and the Underclass Debate,' *Social Service Review*, Vol.

59, No. 4, (December 1985), pp. 541–559.

7. L. Chevalier, *Classes laborieuses et classes dangereuses a Paris, pendant la premiere moitié du XIX siècle*, Paris 1978.

8. Rural Sociological Society Task Force on Persistent Rural Poverty, *Persistent Poverty in Rural America* (Boulder, Colorado: Westview Press, 1993).

9. New York Children's Aid Society, *2nd Annual Report* (NY, 1855), p. 3.

10. Stanley Aronowitz, *False Promises: The Shaping of American Working Class Consciousness* (NY: McGraw Hill, 1973), considers the underclass a 'result of the disparity between the historical tendency of capitalist production to require less labor for the production of commodities and the urbanization of the whole population,' p. 11.

11. Gertrude Himmelfarb, *The Idea of Poverty: England in the Early Industrial Age* (New York: Knopf, 1984), pp. 328–29; Himmelfarb, *Poverty and Compassion: The Moral Imagination of the Late Victorians* (New York: Knopf, 1991), p. 11.

12. E.g., Ladies of the Mission, *The Old Brewery and the New Mission House at the Five Points* (NY: Stringer & Townsend, 1854). There is a brilliant description of the stench of the cities in Patrick Suskind's novel *Perfume: The Story of a Murderer*, trans. John E. Woods (NY: Pocket Books, 1987).

13. *The Old Brewery*, p. 20; Children's Aid Society, *2nd Annual Report*, p.5.

14. Himmelfarb, *The Idea of Poverty*, pp. 356–57.

15. Quoted in Robert H. Bremner, *American Philanthropy* (Chicago: University of Chicago, 1960), p. 60.

16. I do not mean to imply that sensationalist writing inevitably produces such moralistic responses. Some socialist writers, such as Upton Sinclair, sensationalized the depravities of the capitalist class, thus positioning poor workers as victims.

17. Gareth Stedman Jones, *Outcast London: A Study of the Relationship between Classes in Victorian Society* (Oxford: Oxford University Press, 1971), p. 11.

18. Jones, pp. 371–2.

19. Jennifer Davis, 'Jennings' Buildings and the Royal Borough: The Construction of the Underclass in mid-Victorian England,' in *Metropolis-London: Histories and Representations Since 1800*, ed. by David Feldman and Gareth Stedman Jones (London and New York: Routledge, 1989).

20. Linda Gordon, *Woman's Body, Woman's Right: Birth Control in America* (New York: Viking/Penguin, 2nd. ed., 1990); Himmelfarb, *The Idea of Poverty*, p. 324.

21. George Sims quoted in Himmelfarb, *Poverty and Compassion*, p. 58.

22. Davis, 'Jennings' Buildings,' p. 11.

23. Thanks to John Clarke for explaining this important point.

24. Indeed, Marx did contest with a more positive and romantic view of the underclass, that enunciated by Max Stirner in the 1840s, against which Marx and Engels wrote their *German Ideology*.

25. Nikolai Bukharin, *Historical Materialism* (New York: International Publishers, 1925), p. 284 and p. 290, quoted Matza p. 291.

26. See my introduction to *Women, the State, and Welfare*, ed. Linda Gordon (Madison: University of Wisconsin Press, 1990).

27. E.g., Judith Walkowitz, *Prostitution and Victorian Society: Women, Class, and the State* (New York: Cambridge University Press, 1980).

28. David Ward, *Poverty, Ethnicity, and the American City, 1840–1925: Changing Conceptions of the Slum and the Ghetto* (Cambridge: Cambridge University Press, 1989), p. 97.

29. David T. Beito, 'Mutual Aid, State Welfare, and Organized Charity: Fraternal Societies and the 'Deserving' and 'Undeserving' Poor, 1890–1930,' *Journal of Policy History* 5 #4, 1993, pp. 419–434..

30. Linda Gordon, 'Social Insurance and Public Assistance: The Influence of Gender in Welfare Thought in the United States, 1890–1935,' *American Historical Review* 97 #1,

February 1992. David Matza speaks mistakenly of fear of pauperization as exclusive to conservatives; see David Matza, 'The Disreputable Poor,' in Bendix and Lipset, eds., *Class, Status, and Power: A Reader in Social Stratification* 1966, p. 296.

31. June Axinn and Mark J. Stern, *Dependency and Poverty: Old Problems in a New World* (Lexington: Lexington Books, 1988), pp. 97–99.

32. August B. Hollingshead, 'Selected Characteristics of Classes in a Middle Western Community,' *American Sociological Review* 12 (1947), pp. 385–95, reprinted in Reinhard Bendix and Seymour Martin Lipset, eds., *Class, Status, and Power: A Reader in Social Stratification* (Glencoe, Illinois: Free Press, 1953), p. 222.

33. Matza, 'The Disreputable Poor,' p. 302.

34. Michael Harrington, *The Other America: Poverty in the United States* (NY: Macmillan, 1963); Stanley Aronowitz, *False Promises*, p. 11. Aronowitz discussed the development of 'a substantial underclass . . . [unlike] a reserve army of labor since it is characteristically not employed in the expansion of capital but enters the labor market only in the most marginal service occupations or as seasonal agricultural laborers.'

35. Hazel M. Willacy, 'Men in Poverty Neighborhoods: a status report,' *Monthly Labor Review*, Feb. 1969, pp. 23–27.

36. 'The American Underclass,' *Time* Aug. 29, 1977, pp. 14–27, this usage from William J. Wilson, 'Introduction to the Wesleyan Edition' in Kenneth B. Clark, *Dark Ghetto: Dilemmas of Social Power*, 2nd. ed. (Middletown, CT: Wesleyan University Press) xix.

37. Gordon, *Pitied But Not Entitled*.

38. Jerry R Cates, *Insuring Inequality: Administrative Leadership in Social Security, 1935–54* (Ann Arbor: University of Michigan Press, 1983).

39. A divide between women primarily oriented towards social work and those committed to societal reform did not materialize in the US as it had in England.

40. The programme was later amended and renamed Aid to Families with Dependent Children, and is thus called AFDC today. I have retained the earlier historical name. To name just a few of the other distinctions of note: that between the long-term old-age insurance and time-limited unemployment insurance; that between ADC and the very worst programmes of general assistance for childless adults; the somewhat better terms of public assistance for the disabled.

41. Although there are today welfare programmes that provide counselling for men, such as drug addicts or the homeless, these have developed in the context of several decades of the legitimation of psychotherapy and psychological modes of thought. In the 1930s prescribing counselling for poor men would have been perceived as undercutting their manliness and politically unacceptable.

42. Alice Kessler-Harris, *A Woman's Wage: Historical Meanings and Social Consequences* (Lexington, Kentucky: University Press of Kentucky, 1990).

43. Moreover it was significant that Social Security was written during a relative lull in the women's-rights movement. The mothers'-aid model, which was relatively progressive in 1910, was rather conservative by 1935, given how much had changed for so many women. Still, the social-work network of the 1930s did retain some of their maternalist-feminist heritage in their commitment to helping those women and children left out of family-wage support. Their programme expressed both their residual feminism and their own agenda for power in an expanded federal government. Like British women reformers of the early 20th century, they were concerned to get some help directly to women as mothers, and thereby to protect their custody rights and their authority as mothers. By working in a public-assistance framework they resisted making the workplace the only source of welfare entitlements (as unemployment compensation and old-age insurance did). At the same time the public-assistance framework provided, they hoped, an institutional need for trained welfare caseworkers. By focusing on single mothers they kept alive the awareness that not all women and children were supported by men. And by focusing on single mothers rather than a universal children's allowance they could do so

without challenging male economic dominance.

44. Fraser and Gordon, 'Contract versus Charity.'

45. Joy Dryfoos, *Adolescents At Risk: Prevalence and Prevention* (New York: Oxford University Press, 1990), p. 3.

46. Quoted by Michael Katz in his introduction to *The 'Underclass' Debate* (Princeton: Princeton University Press, 1992), p. 3.

47. Nancy Fraser and Linda Gordon, 'A Genealogy of 'Dependency': A Keyword of the US Welfare State,' *Signs* winter 1993.

48. John Leo, 'The High Cost of Playing Victim,' *US News and World Report* Oct. 1, 1990, p. 23.

49. Linda Gordon, *Heroes of Their Own Lives: The Politics and History of Family Violence* (New York: Viking/Penguin, 1988).

50. 'Underclass' definitions tailored, albeit perhaps unconsciously, to describe Black poverty may not fit other racial minorities. A recent study of poor Mexican Americans in California is instructive. High proportions are indeed extremely poor, educationally deprived, and their young men display some of the gang and criminal behaviour associated with an 'underclass.' But these Latinos have fewer health problems than the Black *or Anglo* poor, are nearly twice as likely to live in two-parent nuclear families, and less likely to collect welfare. California Latinos have higher life expectancies and lower infant mortality rates than Blacks or Anglos; Latina women are less likely to be smokers or alcohol and other drug abusers. That so many of them remain extremely poor suggests what's wrong with behavioural theories of the 'underclass'; as one scholar put it, they do everything 'right' but remain poor. Karen J. Winkler, 'Researcher's Examination of California's Poor Latin Population Prompts Debate over the Traditional Definitions of the Underclass,' *Chronicle of Higher Education* Oct. 10, 1990, pp. A5–A8.

51. Kathryn M. Neckerman, 'The Emergence of 'Underclass' Family Patterns, 1900–1940,' in Katz, *The 'Underclass' Debate*, pp. 194–219.

52. Martha F. Davis, *Brutal Need: Lawyers and the Welfare Rights movement, 1960–1973* (New Haven: Yale University Press, 1993).

53. Ricketts and Sawhill, p. 322.

54. During the Depression, emergency government relief and public works had a bigger impact than long-term welfare programmes. New poor – those only temporarily disadvantaged – and old poor often collected from the same programmes; but after World War II brought back prosperity, the differential effects of the Social Security Act were felt keenly.

55. James T. Patterson, *America's Struggle Against Poverty* (Cambridge: Harvard University Press, 1981), pp. 76, 92–4; Sheldon Danziger, Robert Haveman and Robert D. Plotnick, 'Antipoverty Policy: Effects on the Poor and the Nonpoor,' in Sheldon H. Danziger and Daniel H. Weinberg, eds., *Fighting Poverty: What Works and What Doesn't* (Cambridge: Harvard University Press, 1986), pp. 66–7. The US spends, for example, approximately $25 billion on the major public-assistance programme for the poor, AFDC, and $200 billion on old-age insurance, which goes mainly to the nonpoor.

56. Thomas F. Jackson, 'The State, the Movement, and the Urban Poor: The War on Poverty and Political Mobilisation in the 1960s,' in Katz, *The 'Underclass' Debate*, pp. 403–439.

57. Michael R. Sosin, 'Legal Rights and Welfare Change,' in Sheldon Danziger and Weinberg, eds., *Fight Poverty: What Works and What Doesn't*, p. 276.

58. For example, housing policy, public and private, raised walls around ghettos which concentrated the minority poor. Transportation policy, public and private, increased the difficulty the poor faced in commuting to jobs. Police policy, from discriminatory harassment to gross brutality, added to the despair and bitterness of racial minorities. Education policy, public and private, deepened existing inequality. Economic policy which made capital flight easier contributed.

'CLASS WAR CONSERVATISM': HOUSING POLICY, HOMELESSNESS AND THE 'UNDERCLASS'

Joan Smith

The degree of autonomy which the state enjoys for most purposes in relation to social forces in capitalist society depends above all on the extent to which class struggle and pressure from below challenge the hegemony of the class which is dominant in such a society. Where a dominant class is truly hegemonic in economic, social, political and cultural terms, and therefore free from any major and effective challenge from below, the chances are that the state itself will also be subject to its hegemony, and that it will be greatly constrained by the various forms of class power which the dominant class has at its disposal. (Ralph Miliband,1982)[1]

Fifteen years of Conservative rule in Britain have born out Ralph Miliband's argument. Since Free Market Conservatism (which Miliband described more accurately as 'Class War Conservatism') captured Parliament and the State, nine 'employment' acts, the abolition of wage councils, and unemployment rates that were the highest in Europe in the 1980s, have crystallised into a low wage economy where workers face ever increasing productivity demands, real wage cuts and worsening conditions. Anti-union legislation, centralised control over local and regional administrations and, most recently, the Criminal Justice Act of 1994 curtailed political opposition, anti-government strikes and demonstrations. Welfare programmes with popular support, such as health and education, had the 'market' introduced into them, and less popular programmes were reduced, means-tested and, in the case of social housing, almost destroyed.

Some writers have argued that Conservative administrations failed to impose their welfare agenda because welfare expenditure has continued to rise.[2] This misses the point. The most important principle of Class War Conservatism has been the removal from public life of any *alternatives* to free market capitalism and a centralising authoritarian state. Not only have welfare recipients been increasingly impoverished through benefits being indexed to prices rather than wages, but *alternative* welfare strategies, both municipal Keynesian and municipal socialist, have been shut down or prevented. Oppositional local authorities were shackled and, in the case of the Greater London Council, even abolished. Publicly accountable bodies have been replaced with quangos that now control £60 billion of public

188

money per year but are unaccountable to Parliament, or indeed to anyone except the businessmen and Conservative supporters who have been appointed to run them. Rising unemployment has been used as a weapon in the control of labour, while alternative ownership patterns have been obliterated. National industries that provided cheap utilities and were prevented from disconnecting some consumers on social grounds, have been sold off and their workforces axed.

Other guiding principles of British New Right welfare policies have been: the rejection of government responsibility for maintaining national minimum standards; the replacement of earnings related and universal welfare rights based on national insurance principles with targetted means tested benefits of low value; increasing bureaucratic controls over the recipients of welfare; raising the cost of the welfare state to the bottom half of society in a fiscal redistribution of income from poor to rich; redistributing welfare responsibility from the state to the family through programmes of community care and abolition of income support for young school-leavers; and removing protective programmes for women and children in the name of 'family values'. The New Right has successfully used welfare policies and fiscal measures to create rather than prevent a divided society: income inequality is now at a level comparable to the end of the 19th century.

With wage councils abolished and the alternative of a national minimum wage rejected, income support and social housing provision are the two programmes that have prevented the final construction of an 'underclass', a socially excluded group of the poor, disempowered and low waged. Yet the Cabinet have set their sights on undermining both programmes through a concerted attack on 'welfare dependency' before the end of the Conservatives' fourth administration, and their possible electoral defeat. In November 1994 the Chancellor of the Exchequer, Kenneth Clarke, and the Minister for Social Security, Peter Lilley, announced the establishment of a new 'job-seekers allowance' to replace both unemployment benefit and income support in April 1996. In a re-enactment of the 'genuinely seeking work' clause of the 1930s, the unemployed will have to have the appropriate appearance and the appropriate attitude towards job-seeking in order to qualify for benefit; and the benefit stop has been increased from two weeks to six months for those who don't comply.[3]

Unwaged single mothers are also to be removed from Income Support and Housing Benefit through the implementation of the Child Support Act. From 1993 the state has enforced its own assessment of maintenance payments, over-riding previous court settlements, for all single parents living on Income Support. The funding formula has been designed to extract maximum payments from even the poorest absent fathers in order that all welfare support should be clawed back. The assessment process has left many women dependent on erratic maintenance rather than weekly state support. Some women have preferred to risk a twenty percent reduction in state income support rather than go through the maintenance process.[4] Beside attempting to reduce Treasury support for the unemployed and for unwaged single parents, the Government also proposes to repeal all homeless legislation under which most single mothers have been rehoused, and to cap the level of housing benefit that a household can claim.

Many writers have assessed the effects of income support cuts and fiscal redistribution of income on the poorest. Equally important is the assessment of the effects of the growing crisis in the provision of social housing. This article is about the effects of fifteen years of Conservative housing policy and the importance of ongoing social housing provision for the prevention of an even more unequal and divided society in Britain. It outlines first the particular context of housing in Britain and the decline of social housing provision, second the rising problem of homelessness, and third the relationship between the New Right's construction of the idea of an underclass and the proposed repeal of homeless legislation. In conclusion it is argued that the clarity of purpose with which Class War Conservatism has sought to dismantle the Keynesian Welfare State should be matched with clarity of purpose towards the welfare state from the socialist movement. At the heart of the welfare state is the provision of shelter as well as the provision of income.

1. The British Housing Market and Conservative Housing Policy

The British housing market has a quite particular structure compared with its European neighbours or other English-speaking countries. In Australia, Canada, New Zealand and the USA, a large proportion of households live in owner-occupied housing (60–70%), a smaller but important proportion live in private rental housing (25–35%) and public sector housing provision is very limited. Among European countries there is a wide range of home-ownership (30–85%) and private rental provision, and social housing/cost-rental schemes are provided by non government organisations financed by the government. Britain has been unique in developing a housing tenure pattern with a very small private rental sector (10%), a large local authority rental sector (34% in 1979, now down to 24%) and a large home ownership sector (55% in 1979, now 66%). The non-government social housing sector (housing association) has a small share of the market.[5]

The origins of this particular tenure pattern can be found in the early municipal socialist programme of Independent Labour Party leaders like John Wheatley. Wheatley's scheme for £8 a year rental cottages to be provided for workers in Glasgow by the Glasgow Corporation was the foundation of ILP success on Red Clydeside, and local authorities were encouraged to build houses when he became Minister of Housing in the 1924 Labour Government. The model of local authority low cost rental provision was well established by the Second World War, and after 1945 the predominant private rental tenure was replaced by local authority and new town social housing, on the one hand, and private home ownership on the other.[6] From the 1960s, housing associations provided social housing through government-funded but non local authority organisations. Together local authorities and housing associations provided 100,000 social housing units in 1979. From 1979, however, local authority housing has been sold off to provide windfall political and economic gains for New Right Conservatives. The sale of local authority housing and the destruction of local authority plans for new social housing have provided both huge gains in revenue and huge savings in capital expenditure;[7] while the promotion of a home-owning society through the 'right to buy' campaign was the first pro-privatisation campaign and created an audience for the argument that individuals, rather than society, were to be responsible for their own and their family's welfare.

During the first two Conservative administrations the central feature of housing policy was the encouragement of home-ownership including tenants' 'right to buy' their local authority house at a discounted price, a policy pioneered by some Conservative local authorities before 1979. The argument for home-ownership and against renting was already popular with householders who had lived through two bouts of house price inflation in the 1970s. Home-ownership came to be seen as the only safe hedge against inflation, an investment that also had a use-value (you could live in it) and much preferable to paying rent; home-ownership also gave householders freedom to alter the property as they wished. For all these reasons the right to buy policy was popular with working class people,[8] and Labour-controlled authorities who continued to evade the sale of their housing stock lost votes to the Conservatives. Council house sales provided the bulk of home-owner expansion under the Conservatives; home ownership rose from 55% of households in 1979 to 66% in 1990.

The other side of Conservative housing policy was hostility to any expansion of local authority social housing provision. Receipts from council house sales were ring-fenced so that the capital could not be used to build new houses, and the cuts in housing budgets gave the first Conservative administration three quarters of its social welfare savings between 1979–82. The result has been a catastrophic decline in local authority and new town housing completions, from 85,000 completions in 1979 to 19,200 in 1988 and 2,000 in 1992.[9] In order to disguise their opposition to social housing provision the government argued they were funding new provision through Housing Associations: thus associations which previously had provided for specialist housing for the elderly or for single people, became promoted as the providers of family social housing. In 1986 the Conservatives made their first attempt to remove the remaining 4 million local authority houses from local authority control when the Housing and Planning Act first allowed for the sale of local authority housing to private developers and other landlords, including Housing Associations. In 1986 the discount for tenants was raised to 50% off the market price after two years' tenancy.

Whereas in their first two administrations, the Conservatives sought popular support for their housing policies, from their victory in 1987 they used their increasing hegemony to *impose* their welfare agenda. For social housing this meant that all local authorities that were not processing 'right to buy' applications were forced to comply. Some Conservative-held local authorities interpreted the policy as allowing them to sell off local authority housing to whomever they selected. The London Borough of Westminster even adopted a policy of selling local authority housing to non-local authority tenants in order to ensure Conservative majorities in marginal wards. In the 1988 Housing Act it was proposed that housing trusts should take over existing local authority housing, and tenants could only reject such trusts if two-thirds of all tenants actually voted against it; abstentions were to be counted as being in favour. Despite these wildly undemocratic procedures, in many areas tenants voted against the proposals. Nevertheless there was a new wave of council house sales to anxious tenants who would rather buy their property than be placed under a new landlord. Over a million council houses were sold by 1989, for a gain of £17,580 million, providing 43% of the receipts from all privatisations in the ten years 1979–89.[10]

From 1987 the government also shifted its emphasis from the right to home-ownership to the right to rent, but the right to rent at *market* level rents. It was argued that the housing benefit system (introduced in 1982 to replace the previous rent and rate rebate scheme) was already available for the support of all unwaged tenants, both those in the private rental market and the 4 million households still in social housing, and that housing benefit 'subsidised people rather than buildings'. The low-cost rents of local authorities which allowed low paid workers to live relatively cheaply were to be abolished. The 1989 Local Government and Housing Act prevented all local authorities from subsidising council rents out of other revenues. This policy did not represent a great gain in revenue for local authorities, because with rising unemployment, an ageing tenancy, and greater numbers of single parent families in tenancies, the majority of tenants were entitled to housing benefit paid by the local authority. For the minority of working tenants, however, the policy represents a real decline in living standards and the policy of subsidising people not buildings has produced the most extreme welfare trap in Europe; local authority tenants have to find a job with high wages to pay market level rents. This is also true of Housing Association tenants whose rents rose when the government changed their funding formula by decreasing central government support; rents for newly built units doubled to £40–50 a week from a previous average of £25–30. In the private rental market the 1988 Housing Act allowed short-hold and assured tenancy agreements for all private renting tenancies as well as for new-build private tenancies; this was designed to give landlords greater flexibility to change tenants and increase rents. The purpose of all these policies was to establish rents at equivalent and higher levels in local authority tenancies, housing association tenancies and private tenancies.

Local authority tenants are paying higher rents for ever worsening conditions as all local authority estates suffer from lack of investment and impoverished tenants. Many local authority estates that once housed both the employed and unemployed, youth and elderly, couple households and single parent households, have been turned into high-crime, low employment, dilapidated 'residual' housing. Over the next five years local authority tenants will face new housing management regimes; all local authority housing departments will have to tender competitively for the contract to manage the local authority housing stock. Some local authorities, particularly in rural areas where a higher proportion of smaller numbers of units have been bought, have already made over the control and management of their remaining stock to Housing Associations.

Underlying these changes in the provision of housing has been a systematic drive to replace the attitudes and values of the Keynesian Welfare State with that of a Free Market privatised society. T. H. Marshall's social citizen must be replaced by the privatised individual. Each person's safety net is to be individualised through ownership of housing, an individual pension plan, and, preferably, an individual healthcare plan. With soaring house prices in the second half of the 1980s many workers bought into the vision of a home-ownership society where they could reap untaxed capital gains for their retirement. Wealth was, in John Major's terms, to 'cascade down the generations' from home-owner parents. The actual language changed: in government documents householders owned a 'home' but they rented a 'house'.[11] Society became divided by home-ownership, and a new version of the 19th century division between the 'respectable' working class and the 'rough' emerged in Britain: respectable people made sacrifices to buy their own 'home', while the rough could be found renting on local authority housing estates. For those households whose owner-occupation dream turns sour and whose house is re-possessed the alternatives are bleak. With an ever-diminishing stock many local authorities are finding it harder and harder to rehouse.

From the perspective of 1995 the rush to home-ownership does not look as individually attractive as it did in the mid 1980s. Some local authorities have been forced to buy back houses that were structurally unsound when they were sold; and the government's latest scheme for selling council houses, from 'rent to mortgage', has attracted only two buyers. Following real falls in house prices, 1 million households 'own' houses worth less than their mortgage and with high unemployment, repossessions by the building societies and banks are increasingly commonplace; repossessions particularly affect ex-local authority council tenants. By 1989 the repossession rate rose to 70,000 units a year and is still 50,000 a year. Yet, 85% of all young people in Britain aspire to own their own house. They know they have little alternative: in 1979, four out of ten newly-built housing was social housing, now it is only one out of ten. Owner-occupation is no longer put forward as a positive choice, as in the early stage of Conservative 'free market' rule, but as an *only* choice for most households; the government's target for home-ownership is 80% of all households. As a sole option there is now no need to provide incentives to encourage owner-occupation, and from 1992 there has been a systematic erosion of tax relief on mortgages and no support for programmes to prevent repossessions. In 1995 income security support will be withdrawn for interest payments on mortgages for new borrowers who become unemployed.

It has become apparent that the promised 'cascade of wealth' has not happened for many new home-owners and for council tenants who bought their houses and flats (apartments) on poor quality estates. Nor is this cascade a reality for families whose elderly relatives require long-term residential care; from 1986 the government has taken home-owner equity belonging to a surviving spouse to pay residential care fees, replacing social security support.[12] The popular support home ownership bought for the New Right's privatising and tax cutting message is now eroded by the reality of high indirect taxation, low wages and proposed wage cuts, crumbling health and education services, and falling house prices. The major utilities have been sold off, and the windfall gains for small investors, although not for large corporations, have ended. Alongside all this there is a feeling of dismay at the society which Britain has become, and a fear of the social consequences of so much poverty and public disinvestment. The New Right is now reduced to seeking support through its negative programme, the control of crime and disorder, the ending of 'welfare dependency' and the promise of future tax cuts. As well as the successful introduction of an appalling Criminal Justice and Public Order Bill, the early 1990s has seen an extraordinary rise in vituperative outbursts against the unemployed, single mothers, and homeless 'beggars' who, both John Major and Peter Bellamy claimed, were not really homeless and were making a lot of money out of begging. Throughout the early 1990s right-wing ideologists have been hard at work adapting Charles Murray's thesis on the United States 'under-class' to the British experience of a large local authority housing sector. Welfare dependency, it is argued, is to blame for three clearly identifiable tendencies – the 'residualisation' of local authority housing, the rise in unemployment and the rise in numbers of never-married single mothers.

The 'residualisation' of council housing during the past fifteen years is a result of two processes: the best houses, semi-detached and terraces, have been sold, and the remaining four million units have become increasingly inhabited by those in the bottom fifth of income distribution, claiming income support and housing benefit.[13] Housing association property has also been 'residualised'; as associations have been required to provide housing for homeless families at lower building standards and ever higher rents, only those on benefits can afford to become new tenants. The result is that nearly two out of three single mothers live in social housing, and only 41% of heads of households in social housing have jobs compared with 69% living in other tenures.[14] A new welfare trap has been established where workers living in social housing cannot take jobs because they cannot afford to pay the market rents being charged in the social housing sector.[15] Market level rents imposed on local authority and housing associations tenants have meant that central government expenditure on housing benefit was £8,000 million pounds in 1992 while expenditure on capital was £6,000 million. The response of Government ministers, particularly Peter Lilley and Michael Portillo, has been to launch an attack on housing benefit, the subsidy to people promoted by the Conservatives as an alternative to subsidising housing.

The fourth Conservative administration, presented in the 1992 General Election as a caring alternative to Thatcherism, has produced the most thorough-going assault on social housing yet seen. First, in January 1994, the 'Access to Housing' consultative document was released by the Department of the Environment, foreshadowing legislation which would overturn all Homeless Persons legislation. Second, Michael Portillo, then speaking as Chief Secretary to the Treasury, outlined procedures to restrict the level of Housing Benefit being paid to new claimants, which have now been enacted in the November budget. Third, John Major launched a spiteful attack on young beggars at the same moment as the government announced the shutting down of its own 'Sleeping Rough' initiative which had provided an additional 1600 hostel places for rough sleepers from the winter of 1992 to the summer of 1994. The final retreat from the provision of social housing is the complement to new jobseeker allowances intended to drive people to work for any wages, or to drive them off benefit, and to the Child Support Act intended to enforce the family wage system for single parents previously dependent on state benefits.

2. The Rise of Homelessness in Britain, 1979–1994

The existence of a large local authority social housing sector in Britain has been the backbone of one of the genuine social reforms of the last Labour Government in Britain, the 1977 Homeless Persons' Act. This Act, which was relentlessly lobbied for by four housing charities, and followed two Royal Commissions, on One Parent Families and on Domestic Violence, made the provision of housing a statutory duty for local authorities. Local Authority Housing Departments were instructed to provide permanent accommodation for the homeless in priority need, i.e., for families with dependent children and for homeless elderly aged 60 or over. Applicants had to prove that they were unintentionally homeless, living in accommodation from which they were asked to leave or evicted (the parental home, for example) or where they had no actual right of abode (as in temporary accommodation with friends or relatives), or they were the victims of domestic violence. Local authorities then had a statutory duty to rehouse them in *permanent* accommodation i.e. in the local authority cost-rental sector of social housing. Prior to this Act local authorities were only obliged to rehouse in temporary accommodation, the situation since 1948.

Following fifteen years of New Right policies and world wide recession, *statutory homelessness* has reached heights undreamed of in 1977. The number of households accepted as homeless by local authorities per year rose from just over 53,000 in 1978 to nearly 149,000 in 1991; every year 400,000 persons are accepted as homeless including nearly 200,000 children.[16] However, *statutory homelessness* only shows *part* of the homeless picture among couple-parents and single-parents; on average local authorities in England reject 40% of homeless applicants.[17] Many households have to wait in temporary bed and breakfast accommodation until increasingly scarce housing becomes available, and in some local authorities the housing system has all but broken down. More and more couple households are also living in their own temporary accommodation. In the 1991 Census 198,000 households were found to be sharing house-keeping at the same address and 95,000 households were living in non-permanent accommodation such as caravans and mobile homes; both these figures have increased by 17% compared with the census of 1981.[18]

Although the 1989 Children Act for the first time included some statutory duty to rehouse 16 and 17 year olds, especially young people leaving local authority/social services care, young people have not been included as a priority need group in the legislation. They are the largest group of *non-statutory homeless*, alongside those rejected as homeless by the local authorities. The most visible sign of increasing homelessness among young people has been the rising incidence of *rooflessness*. However, young rough sleepers represent only a fraction of the number of young people living in hostels, shared housing, squats, bed and breakfast, and insecure accommodation who have swollen the numbers of non-statutory homeless. In 1990 John Greve reported estimates of up to 120,000 young single homeless in London from the National Federation of Housing Associations and between 64,500 and 78,000 by the London Boroughs Working Party. Nationally the guess was up to 180,000 young single homeless.[19]

Successive Conservative governments have responded in two different ways to the increase in young single homelessness. First, in 1985 the 'board and lodgings' allowance for young people looking for work away from home was repealed, and in 1988 income support payments for sixteen and seventeen year olds were abolished; the full adult rate is only paid at age twenty-five. These measures were designed to keep young people at home, in their families, and to force sixteen and seventeen year olds to enter the youth training schemes set up by the Government. Second, in the face of increasing street homelessness, in 1984 funds were released for a new wave of hostel building and refurbishment of old dwellings for hostel use; and in 1990, following the House of Commons All-Party report on homelessness, new money went into homeless hostels. These measures were clearly aimed at taking young people off the streets into *temporary* accommodation, especially in London, and were accompanied by police use of the Vagrancy Law of 1824 to arrest and harass beggars.

Government ministers have ignored existing definitions of homelessness when creating policy for young people and described only those without a roof as homeless; once the young person was re-housed in a hostel or other temporary accommodation they were no longer homeless. This re-definition of homelessness as rooflessness is one that the Conservative Government now intends to apply to the statutory homeless, those families who have a right to permanent social housing under 1977 legislation as amended in 1985. The Department of the Environment consultative document, 'Access to Housing', argues: 'someone accepted as homeless is in fact occupying accommodation of some sort at the time he or she approaches the authority . . . Indeed the largest single category of households accepted as statutorily homeless are people living as licensees of parents, relatives or friends who are no longer willing or able to accommodate them.'[20] The argument that anyone staying in accommodation with friends or relatives is a licensee in the same way that private tenants are licensees under new legislation shifts the duty to support from the state to private individuals and charities with a vengeance.[21] The Government is seeking a situation in which families would have to obtain an eviction order in order for young people to be rehoused in temporary accommodation, and any friends and relatives who had taken in young people in an emergency situation would be expected to continue to house them until temporary accommodation was made available.

The heart of the new proposals is a return to the pre-1977 policy of providing temporary accommodation for homeless families. Under these new proposals local authorities would only have a duty to house for a limited period those in 'priority need, in an immediate crisis that has arisen through no fault of their own, and who have no alternative accommodation available.'[22] This reverses all current practice derived from the 1977 and 1985 Acts and effectively ends the provision of permanent housing to priority homeless cases. The housing applicants who will be most affected by this change are single mothers. In acknowledgement of this, the document even suggests the possible return of mother and baby homes for single mothers, demonstrating the government's deliberate identification of all single mothers as never-married teenagers. In fact, of course, only a minority of single mothers are never married; the majority of single mothers are women left to raise their children alone.

Sir George Young defended this policy in seminars and on radio programmes using the argument that single mothers and others are 'jumping' the housing queue through the homeless applications procedure. He presented the White Paper as a proposal for 'integrated waiting lists'; the waiting list would be the sole route through which housing applicants could be allocated a secure local authority tenancy or nominated by a local authority for a housing association tenancy.[23] Even some homeless people were misled into agreeing that integrated waiting lists would be a 'fairer' way to allocate a scarce resource because they did not want to 'jump the queue'. However, without the statutory need to rehouse homeless people there need be no provision of permanent social housing at all. The London Borough of Wandsworth, the original proposers to the Department of the Environment of the new 'Access to Housing' proposals, was taken to court because its policy of disposing of all local authority housing has led to insufficient permanent accommodation for its own homeless families, and the rejection of homeless applicants with a clear statutory right to housing. In the future it would be impossible to take such local authorities to court. Moreover, without priority need status single mothers would be further down the waiting list than couple parents, because one adult gains fewer housing points than two. Despite 9,000 organisations and individuals writing in to oppose the new proposals, and only two organisations supporting them (including the London Borough of Wandsworth), the government is still determined to go ahead. In fact it needs to go ahead; there is so little new social housing stock available and the need for social housing is so great that if it fails to repeal the Homeless Persons legislation many more local authorities will not meet their statutory duty.

For the young single homeless the government has also reversed its previous policies, closing down its 'Rough Sleepers' initiative in Central London with the loss of 1600 bed spaces and launching another police offensive against begging under the 1824 Vagrancy Act. The Criminal Justice and Public Order Act also gives the police sweeping powers to deal with squatters and with travellers, many of whom now include homeless young people especially from the rural areas. Trespass is now a criminal and not a civil offence, giving land-owners and others new powers to use the police to 'protect' their property. It also gives the police powers to suppress spontaneous demonstrations against government policy.[24]

These political attacks on both the statutory homeless and the non-statutory homeless reveal the importance of housing to the renewed agenda of the 'New Right' in Britain, particularly that of the 'No Turning Back Group', whose members include the Cabinet Ministers, Michael Portillo and Peter Lilley. In their eyes social housing is part of a state welfare system that is *creating* dependency among the poor and unemployed, while home-ownership is part of a private welfare system through which *families* take more responsibility for their own and their children's welfare. The virulence with which they have pursued this agenda is the result of two conflicting beliefs within the New Right. First, Class War Conservatism is feeling more and more confident, not merely 'free from any major and effective challenge from below' but also free from any effective alternative abroad with the world-wide collapse of Communism. The ideologists of the Institute of Economic Affairs and the CPS have been emboldened by international adoption of privatisation programmes, including that of public housing in Russia and elsewhere in Eastern Europe.[25] The rule of private property and private economic man and woman appears unstoppable. The return of the New Republicans in the United States under Newt Gingrich, the shutting down of homeless provision in New York and the serious proposals for mother and baby homes, all give confidence to the New Right agenda in Britain. Second, however, in Britain popular support for the New Right is now unravelling; they may only have two years of government left in which to put in place a social order which cannot be reversed. The assault on social housing and income support is part of the construction of a new social order designed to create and control an 'underclass' which the Conservatives have already named as being the *result* of 'welfare dependency' but which an even further shrunken welfare net has helped to create. In an economy that was no longer 'mixed', where public good had been sacrificed to private profit, there would exist a workforce compelled to accept work at any price.

3. Housing, the Underclass and Single Mothers

From 1989 many households living in social housing and dependent on income support and housing benefit have been increasingly labelled as an 'underclass' in speeches by Ministers and pamphlets from the right think-tank, the Institute of Economic Affairs. In Britain the idea of an 'underclass' was popularised for the right by the American Charles Murray through articles in the *Sunday Times*, an Institute of Economic Affairs Seminar in 1990, and an IEA pamphlet.[26] Murray's pamphlet was followed by others including *Families without Fatherhood* by Norman Dennis and George Erdos, written, they claimed, from the standpoint of 'ethical socialism'.[27] In *The Sunday Times* in 1994 Charles Murray described this underclass as a 'new rabble' unfavourably comparing its claimant members with the hard-working, home-owning, two-parent families of the 'new Victorians' of respectable society.[28] The primary cause of the rise of this 'New Rabble', he argued, was rising numbers of single mothers. It was they who were responsible for the rise in numbers of unemployable young men and never-married daughters. Only through denying single mothers benefits and using the savings in public funds to support adoption and fostering services could the vicious circle be broken.[29]

The argument that state welfare actually creates dependency distinguishes current theories of the underclass from previous theories of the culture of poverty (Oscar Lewis) and the cycle of deprivation (Keith Joseph).[30] Both Gilder and Murray have argued that the benefit system in the United States creates an underclass because claimants can live better on welfare than working.[31] This is therefore a *structural* rather than cultural version of the underclass thesis.[32] It is the right's answer to liberal and left arguments that their free market policies are creating an underclass through the deregulation of labour and rising unemployment. In the United States, Wilson argued, with the rise of male unemployment and crime, the 'marriageable pool' has shrunk for young black women in urban areas, leaving women to raise children alone.[33] Now Wilson's liberal explanation for the rise of poverty has been turned on its head by Murray in both the United States and in Britain.[34] In Britain David J Smith has followed Murray and re-defined the composition of the underclass: he argues that the underclass is not comprised of unemployed or criminal individuals but families living on welfare:

> Hence the underclass is not individuals who have no stable relationship with legitimate gainful employment, but members of family units that have no such relationship. It follows that the structure of family units must have far-reaching consequences for the size and nature of an underclass. There will be a strong tendency for single parents of young children to belong to the underclass. Single parenthood is not part of the suggested definition of the underclass: many single parents would not be members of the underclass, and many members of the underclass would not be single parents. On the other hand, a growth in single parenthood could well be an important explanation of a growth in the underclass.[35]

The provision of social housing, income support and housing benefit is now being identified by Murray as the *cause* of rising numbers of single mothers and therefore of a rising underclass, just as the existence of Aid to Dependent Families is being identified as the 'cause' of the 'underclass' in the United States. The vision of welfare systems creating 'dependency' has been accepted by both right-wing Democrats in the United States and members of the Labour Party Shadow Cabinet in Britain. There has been little resistance to measures that subject the unemployed to a barrage of 'personal independence planning' schemes – job cuts, jobstart, restart, job interview guarantees – nor to the proposals to vet the personal appearance and attitude of the unemployed when the 'jobseeker's allowance' replaces income support and unemployment benefit in 1996. Personal independence planning and youth training schemes (which neither train nor lead to permanent jobs) have drastically reduced the statistics of the unemployed who now officially number two and a half million.

Personal independence planning has also been introduced in a different way for single mothers. Proposals for job retraining for women have a hollow ring in a country with one of the lowest rates of child care provision for under-school age children in Europe. Instead of personal independence the government is intent on encouraging old forms of dependence. The family-wage system is now to be enforced for single mothers through the Child Support Agency, which has begun its work of collecting child care maintenance from fathers by targetting the fathers of all children whose mothers are on Income Support. Through a complicated formula the government is seeking not a proportion of a father's wages to support the child but sufficient income to replace state payments, even if this reduces the father's income to Income Support levels, while mothers who do not cooperate with the agency can have their benefit reduced by 20%. The proposal to repeal homelessness legislation and to place single mothers on integrated housing waiting lists will also remove single mothers' source of independent shelter, placing them behind couple parents on housing waiting lists because one adult does not attract as many points in the system as two adults. It is actually designed to force women to stay in relationships with men – no matter how abusive or criminal. As Dean and Taylor-Gooby note: 'Ironically, therefore, those who are dependent on collective provision by an impersonal state have become *independent* of the wage relation and/or of the family'.[36] It is this independence, not dependence, that the New Right seeks to reverse.

4. Conclusion

Although many of the policies and ideas of the New Right have been imported from the United States, British Class War Conservatives have been innovative adaptors and successful implementers.[37] Their approach to the privatisation of social housing has been reimported into the United States, exported to Eastern Europe, and privatisation of housing is now on the agenda for Western Europe. From this review of the undermining of social housing provision in Britain it is clear that the irreversibility thesis is simply not true for this particular programme, nor will the continuation of a steady-state welfare system be allowed. With the collapse of Communism and the adoption of privatisation policies in Eastern Europe, Western Europe and New Zealand, the New Right in Britain, as in the United States, have moved their welfare objectives further and further to the Right.

Financially the renewed assault on social housing in 1994 is important for the British Conservatives because of their commitment to reduce the cost of the provision of all welfare. Privatising social housing also would provide one of the last great cash bonanzas. In the long-term, of course, enforced owner occupation brings other benefits: home-owner equity is available to support residential care, domiciliary care and/or private health care.[38] *Ideologically*, it is also important for a deeply unpopular government that its policies should not be held responsible for the deterioration in the living conditions of a large and growing minority of the British population.[39] The responsibility for poverty and homelessness must be placed elsewhere, either on the individuals themselves or on their family structure. This is the purpose of the attempt to generate a moral panic over rising numbers of never-married single mothers, the rise in lone parent households, and of young unemployed. So far the British New Right have been less successful in their attempts to blame the poorest in society than the American New Right,[40] and with increasing parliamentary crisis it is still possible that further dismantling of social housing provision can be prevented. So far, however, the Labour Party has proved totally inadequate as an opposition when faced with welfare cuts, new employment and anti-trade union legislation, and threats to civil liberties.[41]

For socialists it is important that the clarity of purpose and comprehensive agenda with which the New Right has tackled the dismantling of the Keynesian Welfare State should be matched by an equal clarity of purpose and a principled agenda. Linda Gordon's discussion of socialist feminist perspectives on welfare in *The Socialist Register 1990* argued that the defence of existing welfare programmes against cuts had suppressed discussion about the possible shape of socialist welfare programmes and that it is important for socialists to consider this because it is clearly not the case that all welfare problems would be solved under socialism. Gordon makes the important observation that most welfare need is due to a failure of the family wage-labour system rather than to 'natural' events such as death and disability. She argued that most of this discussion is coming from feminists because women constitute the majority of the recipients and the providers of welfare.[42] In Ramesh Mishra's review of the differences between New Right and Social-Corporatist responses to the crisis of the Keynesian Welfare State, he argues that the welfare state is a product of democratic class struggle.[43] Although Mishra is concerned to differentiate this perspective from those Marxist perspectives on the welfare state which stress the limits to class struggle and working class power under capitalism, his work shares with many Marxist perspectives the central weakness of not adequately acknowledging social-feminist and feminist perspectives on welfare.

Integrating all these perspectives would mean that a socialist-feminist perspective on welfare would begin from four fundamental principles: first, support for welfare measures that shift the balance of class forces in favour of working class struggle and prevent the development of fragmented interests within the working class; second, support for welfare measures that undermine inequality of gender relations and provide support for women and children independent of family structure; third, support for welfare measures that prevent and reverse the oppressed status of any ethnic minority group; fourth, support for welfare measures that provide diverse welfare packages giving control back to the individuals who require the welfare support. It is also apparent that the breadth of welfare must be redefined. Beveridge wrote of the five great Wants in society to be dealt with by five great services: idleness or unemployment was to be covered by unemployment insurance; want or poverty to be covered by income support; squalor to be covered by housing services and town planning; sickness to be covered by a national health service; ignorance by the education services. All of these services, however, also assumed that there were women, at home, available to undertake the 'care' service supported through the family-wage system. Children could leave school at 3.30 p.m. because mothers were there for them; there was no need for nursery provision; sick people could return to their homes to be nursed; men were to have the tenancies, and women's income needs were to be covered by their husbands' employment or income support/unemployment benefit. It is extremely important that a sixth great Want should be acknowledged, that of care, and that care services should have an equal priority.

The New Right in Britain has worked particularly hard to exacerbate the internal contradictions of welfarism and differential interests within the working class. It has sought to blame the rise of unemployment and single parenthood on welfare dependency rather than on its own economic and social policies and the ongoing individualisation and atomisation tendencies of capitalism. As poverty triples and the distribution of incomes in Britain edges closer and closer to Victorian England, the New Right has been determined to enter the 21st century with a work-force whose employment rights are the least in Europe and whose citizenship rights are the least in the English-speaking world. In this way they hope to continue to manage Britain's 'uncompetitiveness' in a global capitalist order. Those parts of the welfare state that prevent abject dependence on the market and the family-wage system, housing provision and income support, have to be not just eroded but transformed, while entry to the new provision will depend, as in the 19th century, on appearance and morality, a servile attitude and proper behaviour. Many will not object because they do not believe they will be part of the bottom third who face unemployment and the job-seeker's allowance, house re-possession and temporary accommodation, continuing care at home rather than in a medical facility, and old age pensions at the lowest level relative to average wages since the 1940s. The development of a socialist-feminist welfare agenda is an important part of the argument for the socialist democracy that Miliband urged the Left to develop as the alternative to the dominance of capitalist democracy presented today as the 'end of history'.[44]

NOTES

1 R. Miliband, 'State Power and Class Interests' reprinted in *Class Power and State Power*, (Verso, London 1982).

2 This is an argument that R. Mishra terms the 'irreversibility thesis'. See R. Mishra *The Welfare State in Capitalist Society*, pp. 32–42, Harvester Wheatsheaf, UK *1990*. Mishra particular identifies writers like Le Grand, Offe, Therborn and Piven and Cloward with this thesis. He himself rejects the thesis, because, although spending has risen, the defining characteristic of the welfare state, 'the institutionalisation of government responsibility for maintaining national minimum standards', has been reversed.

3 The newly unemployed will also not receive help with their mortgage payments for the first nine months.

4 Many feminists have supported the Child Support Act, seeing its measures as a process through which women can leave Income Support and live at standards of living more comparable to those of their previous partners. However, the assessment formula adopted by the Government was clearly punitive at the lowest income scales, in order to remove the mother and child from Income Support. The government has also not guaranteed the regularity of maintenance payments themselves. See The Child Poverty Action pamphlet, *Putting the Treasury First: The Child Support Act*, London, 1993, which includes examples of the funding formula in its appendix.

5 See J. Doling, 'Encouraging Home Ownership', in C. Jones *New Perspective on the Welfare State in Europe*, Routledge, UK, 1993, pp. 71–3.

6 See P. Malpass and A. Murie, *Housing Policy and Practice*, MacMillan, London, 3rd Edition 1990; D. Clapham, P. Kemp and S. Smith, *Housing and Social Policy*, Macmillan, London 1990, for histories of housing policy and the current situation of housing tenure in Britain.

7 See P. Malpass and A. Murie, as above p. 93. The total exchequer subsidy to local authority housing in England fell from £1,393 million in 1980/81 to just £342 million in 1984/5, but then began to rise again.

8 See P. Saunders, *A Nation of Home Owners, 1990*, pp. 341–343 for the results of his survey into attitudes towards council house buying. Saunders presents an extremely pro-home-ownership position, but there is no reason to doubt his argument that the policy was most popular with working class people.

9 Housing Association new build was only 11,000 units in 1992, and the Government were forced to change policy and promise increased support for Housing Association new build, up to 26,000 units this year.

10 See P. Malpass and A. Murie, *op. cit.*, pp. 88–94 for a review of government housing policy.

11 See S. Watson and H. Austerberry, *Housing and Homelessness: A Feminist Perspective*, Routledge 1986, for the different construction of the terms 'house' and 'home'.

12 With the transfer of responsibility for continuing care from the health authorities to social services, the service for the long-term sick has also been transferred from a universal service to a means-testing one.

13 John Hills in *The Future of Welfare*, Joseph Rowntree Foundation, York, 1993, has demonstrated the increasing shift into home-ownership of all income groups except the bottom one fifth (p. 70), quoting his own joint article in J. Hills, ed. *The State of Welfare: the welfare state in Britain since 1974*, Oxford, Clarendon Press 1990. Much of Alan Murie's work has also concentrated on the residualisation process in social housing in Britain, see P. Malpass and A. Murie above.

14 See J. Hills, *ibid.*, p. 71. In 1979 59% of head of households in social housing had jobs, compared with 73% in other tenures.

15 See J. Hills, *ibid.*, pp. 23–27 for estimates of net income required from employment to compensate for combined loss of benefits.

16 See G. Bramley, 1994, 'The affordability crisis in British Housing: Dimensions, Causes and Policy Impact', *Housing Studies*, Vol. 9, No. 1, 1994; and Greve, J. and Currie, E., *Homelessness*, Joseph Rowntree Foundation, 1990.

17 See A. Evans and S. Duncan, *Responding to Homelessness: Local authority policy and practice*, Dept. of the Environment, HMSO, 1988, p. 13.

18 See *Roof*, May–June 1994. *Roof* is the journal of SHELTER, London.

19 See J. Greve and E. Currie, *op. cit.*, 1990, p. 10.

20 Department of the Environment, 'Access to Local Authority and Housing Association Tenancies', Consultation Document, 1994, Section 2.8.

21 This policy is weirdly reminiscent of Russian state policy where a young person's 'right' to their bedroom within their parents' flat was and is frequently enforced by law. The difference is that in Russia the state owned the flat, but in Britain the policy was to be applied in a 'property owning democracy'.

22 *Ibid.*, section 3.2.i.

23 *Ibid.*, section 3.2.ii.

24 The new socialist monthly *Red Pepper* has covered the issue of the Criminal Justice and Public Order Bill in the most detail, from the perspective of its political implications. The implication of the Bill for Criminal Justice itself is also quite horrendous.

25 See R. Desai, 'Second-Hand Dealers in Ideas: Think-Tanks and Thatcherite Hegemony' *New Left Review*, No. 203, 1994, for a history of the IEA and the Centre for Policy Studies.

26 Charles Murray, *The Emerging British Underclass*, Institute of Economic Affairs, London 1990, in which the articles from the *Sunday Times Magazine* of November 1989 are reprinted.

27 N. Dennis and G. Erdos, *Families without Fatherhood*, I.E.A., 1992. See also J. Davies, ed. *The Family: Is it just another lifestyle choice?*, I.E.A., 1993.

28 *Sunday Times*, May–June 1994.

29 Such ideas could be dismissed if the proposal for increased funding of mother and baby homes had not also surfaced in the 'Access to Housing' consultative document that is proposing the withdrawal of rights to permanent accommodation for single mothers.

30 See Hartley Dean and Peter Taylor Gooby, *Dependency Culture. The explosion of a Myth*, Harvester Wheatsheaf, UK, 1992, Chapter 2 for a summary of contributions to these debates in the USA and UK.

31 See C. Murray, *Losing Ground: American Social Policy 1950–1980*, Basic Books, New York, 1984.

32 Therefore the recent study by Hartley Dean and Peter Taylor Gooby, above, which successfully undermines arguments for the existence of dependency culture, can't itself invalidate the underclass thesis.

33 Willetts in D. Smith, ed. *Understanding the Underclass*, Policy Studies Institute, 1992, p. 49; see W. J. Wilson, *The Truly Disadvantaged: The inner city, the underclass and public*

policy, University of Chicago Press, 1987. See also C. Jenks, ed. *The Urban Underclass*, 1991, for research papers summarising the results of US research programmes to test W. J. Wilson's underclass thesis. An important and interesting collection of papers that throw doubt on even Wilson's thesis, e.g. Robert D. Mare and Christopher Winship's paper 'Socio-economic Change and the Decline of Marriage for Blacks and Whites' argues that Wilson's concept of the marriageable pool only explains 20% of the decline in marriage rates for young black people.

34 Murray and others consistently fudge the boundary between all single mothers and never-married teenagers. In Britain never-married mothers equal 29% of all lone mothers; 44% of lone mothers are divorced, 19% are separated, 8% are widowed.

35 See D. Smith, *op. cit.*, p. 5. The culture of dependence, according to Smith, may or may not exist. The structural argument for the existence of an underclass identifies three key groups as likely to be dependent on income support and therefore likely to be members of the underclass: the long term unemployed, unskilled workers in erratic employment and young single mothers: and then asks the question is there any link between them?

36 Dean and Taylor-Gooby, above, p. 48.

37 Joel Krieger, 'Social Policy in the Age of Reagan and Thatcher', *Socialist Register*, 1987. In this paper Krieger discusses the proportion of Reagan's legislation that he was able to get through. This, of course, is not a problem for Conservative governments in the United Kingdom with no elected second chamber and no constitutional rights for regional and city government.

38 This would overcome the problem that John Hill described in *The Future of the Welfare State*, 1993. How do you force one generation to fund both present welfare expenditure and their own future provision?

39 See V. Kumar, *Poverty and Inequality in the UK. The effects on children*, National Children Bureau, 8 Wakley Street, London EC1V 7QE, for detailed estimates of the rise in poverty in the United Kingdom from 1979–1992 which included a tripling of the numbers of children living in poverty.

40 Each annual *British Social Attitudes Survey*, from Social and Community Planning Research, London, has found that a majority of the British Public are prepared to pay more taxes for higher welfare. In the early 1980s the area of welfare spending least in favour was housing, but since then the rise of homelessness support for spending in this area has risen. The two *International Social Attitudes Survey* reports of 1986 and 1992 clearly demonstrate that the majority of British people have attitudes towards welfare and social citizenship rights closer to those in Europe than those in the US or Australia.

41 The independent Labour Commission for Social Justice has also been pulled into discussing welfare issues in the language of dependence and independence.

42 L. Gordon, 'The Welfare State. Towards a Socialist Feminist Perspective', *Socialist Register*, 1990, pp. 171–200.

43 R. Mishra, *The Welfare State in Capitalist Society*, Harvester Wheatsheaf, 1990, p. 11.

44 R. Miliband, 'Fukuyama and the Socialist Alternative', *New Left Review*, No. 193, 1992.

CAPITALIST DEMOCRACY REVISITED

John Schwarzmantel

The purpose of this paper[1] is to offer a tribute to the work of Ralph Miliband by examining the concept of 'capitalist democracy', a concept which played a central part in his work, and which forms the title of one of his books, *Capitalist Democracy in Britain*[2]. The critical analysis which follows is in memory of Ralph Miliband as an inspiring teacher; for all too short a time a stimulating colleague; and a warm-hearted and generous friend. Whatever criticisms are raised are made as contributions to a debate which Miliband himself inspired and greatly developed – a debate about state power and class power, probing the limits of Marxist theories of politics.

The intention is to give an exposition of the term 'capitalist democracy', to examine its meaning, and to see what problems there are in the concept. By 'problems' is meant here the question of whether the term provides a useful means of understanding the nature of democracy in the contemporary world and of analyzing the structure of power in those systems which call themselves democracies. This involves discussing what light the label of 'capitalist democracy' casts on the problems facing those societies.

It should be made clear at the outset that the term 'capitalist democracy' is applied in the work of Ralph Miliband, and in this paper, to a certain kind of political system and its social context, and it may be useful to indicate briefly the characteristics of such systems, before giving an extended exposition and 'deconstruction' of the term. 'Capitalist democracy' is used in Miliband's work to describe a particular type of state, which could be also called liberal-democratic. Miliband uses the term capitalist democracy to refer, as he says, to 'the political system which has gradually developed in Britain since the passage of the Second Reform Act of 1867, and particularly since the suffrage came to include all adults by virtue of the Acts of 1918 and 1928'.[3] This form of state is marked by a plurality of political parties competing for political or state power; such competition takes the form of electoral rivalry, settled by popular vote in regular elections open to all parties. This state form is also characterised by a separation of powers in the state itself. The state apparatus in such systems of capitalist democracy has a number of branches which to some extent check and control each other. Among these elements of the state apparatus there is a representative assembly or parliament, which functions as a forum for examination and discussion of government policies, and acts as a central focus for political life. Such a system also possesses what could be called an independent and active 'civil society', which is marked by a range of pressure groups and associations of various kinds. This constitutes what C. Wright Mills called a 'society of publics', on the surface at least contributing a diversity of voices to an active public opinion and forming the source of various pressures on the holders of state power.[4] So far in this description there is nothing that could not be equally well described by the term 'liberal democracy', or 'pluralist democracy', but the idea of 'capitalist democracy' is meant to suggest that this state system, with the characteristics described above, exists in a particular social framework or context, which is one of capitalism, and that this fact has decidedly important implications for the working of such political systems of capitalist democracy, whose main features have now been delineated.

We can note here that 'capitalist democracy' is to be distinguished from what Miliband referred to as systems of 'capitalist authoritarianism', of which fascism would be one, though by no means the only, variant. Such systems of 'capitalist authoritarianism' (overlooking specific differences between them) have the characteristics that they abolish the rights and liberties afforded by systems of capitalist democracy. They represent forms of strong state (what Poulantzas calls *l'état d'exception*) which limit, or destroy altogether, the power of criticism of the representative assembly.[5] They severely restrict, to the point of annihilation in regimes of fascist totalitarianism, the 'space' of civil society and its independent groups and associations. In short, the term 'capitalist democracy' has built into it, so to speak, a contrast with forms of state which also exist within a capitalist context and which override or smash the degree of pluralism and autonomy of civil society from the state which exists in these systems of capitalist democracy. The point is very important, and is one which Miliband himself makes at several points.[6] Criticism of the limitations imposed on capitalist democracy by its social and economic context should not blind one to the crucial differences between such systems and authoritarian forms of the capitalist state.

One other preliminary point may be worth noting too. In the present age these systems of 'capitalist democracy' appear to be dominant, at least in the sense that some of the chief rivals to these systems, which in the 20th century were fascism on the one hand and communism or Soviet-type systems on the other, seem to have disappeared as rivals to the capitalist democratic or liberal-democratic systems of what used to be called the

West, but which now have been eagerly accepted and taken up in Eastern and Central Europe, the countries of ex-Communism. This does not mean one has to endorse Fukuyama's famous claim, in *The End of History and the Last Man*, that 'we have trouble imagining a world that is radically better than our own, or a future that is not essentially democratic and capitalist', or his assertion in the same book that 'there is now no ideology with pretensions to universality that is in a position to challenge liberal democracy'.[7] It does however mean that it seems a task all the more urgent to investigate the critical edge and explanatory use of the concept of 'capitalist democracy', since those systems to which the term is applied are held up, at least by some, as the only valid and desirable model for a modern political and economic system. It should be clear by the end of this paper that whatever else the term 'capitalist democracy' has to offer, it does serve as a critique of modern liberal democracy, and, at least in the work of Ralph Miliband, there is not only an implicit contrast with systems of 'capitalist authoritarianism' but also with a potential alternative, 'socialist democracy', and this too must be evaluated.

Part One: the term explained and expounded

It is necessary to give a fuller exposition of the concept of 'capitalist democracy' before seeking to assess its limitations and its use as a tool for explaining the reality of modern democracy. First, the term 'capitalist democracy' can be taken to highlight a central tension in those societies marked by the characteristics listed above, and which are often referred to as 'liberal democracies', or even 'democratic societies' *tout court*. That tension is between the democratic ideal of equality, of all citizens having certain basic rights of political participation, rights which are held equally by all citizens, and the pervasive structure of inequality in the social and economic context of these systems of capitalist democracy. The democratic ideal, simply put, is one of inclusion and equality, of 'everyone counting for one and no one for more than one', as Bentham expressed it. Over a certain minimum age, and this restriction presumably rests on an idea of common rationality, all people in the national territory are assumed to have the rational capacity of knowing their interests, of being able to assess competing political programmes, of having an equal right to stand for office and engage in the struggle for power through election. There is thus an idea of equality here, which is central to democracy, and which is seen as entailing that differences of wealth, intelligence, ethnic identity, gender, to take only the most obvious, should not count with respect to the rights of citizenship. Those citizenship rights involve the ability to participate, whether directly or through representatives, in the making of the society's collective decisions. In turn these decisions affect the way in which the society is governed, and hence help to determine the structure or framework within which people's lives are conducted. Robert Dahl formulates what he calls a strong principle of equality, which he sees as a fundamental principle of democracy, in the following words:

> All members are sufficiently well qualified, taken all around, to participate in making the collective decisions binding on the association that significantly affect their good or interests. In any case, none are so definitely better qualified than the others that they should be entrusted with making the collective and binding decisions.[8]

Dahl also writes of the idea of inclusiveness as a criterion for the democratic process: 'The demos must include all adult members of the association except transients and persons proved to be mentally defective'.[9] The democratic ideal rests on these twin ideas of people being *equally* qualified to take part in the collective decision-making process, whether directly or through representatives, and on an idea of inclusiveness, that the demos should include all those supposedly rational beings living within the territorial area of the democratic community.

The concept of 'capitalist democracy' suggests that there is a tension between the democratic idea of equal citizenship rights and the structure of inequality that exists in 'civil society', or rather in the capitalist economy within which democratic political institutions are situated. This tension is seen as significant for various reasons. In the first place social inequality may place a strain on civic or political equality. The greater command over economic and social resources which stems from a structure of social inequality, and which gives some individuals considerable power over others, can be translated into superior political resources or political influence. All citizens are equal at the polls, according to democratic theory. The vote of the rich person counts the same as the vote of the poor person. Without falling into too simplistic an analysis, social and economic inequalities can erode this democratic equality in at least two ways: one, in terms of influence over the holders of state power, since those who command substantial economic resources have more bargaining power over the state elite; two, in terms of 'agenda setting', of putting issues on the agenda and mobilising support and moulding consciousness. These tasks require economic resources, which are unequally held in this kind of society. Especially in an age of sophisticated information technology leading to the possible manipulation of consciousness, the greater such resources individuals hold, the more effectively they will be able to perform this task. The agenda of issues discussed, and equally important the issues *not* discussed, in a democratic society, are therefore determined, though not exclusively, by those who stand at the top of the economic and social scale. This obviously oversimplifies the issue, and the question of the relationship between capitalism and democracy is analyzed further below, but the critical thrust of the term 'capitalist democracy' is to contrast the sphere of political equality with that of social and economic inequality, and to suggest that the latter has an impact on the former, and that this impact is a negative one. In this sense capitalist democracy satisfies the demand of R. H. Tawney for a term which describes what he called 'a type of society which combines the forms of political democracy with sharp economic and social divisions'.[10] These social and economic divisions stem from a context of class power. Such class power is not the only significant dimension of power. However, it clearly has serious implications for the functioning of democracy.

Secondly, the idea of 'capitalist democracy' as developed by Miliband operates with an idea of 'containment', or the limiting of popular pressure or influence 'from below'. In Miliband's words, 'Democratic institutions and practices provide means of expression and representation to the working class, organised labour, political parties and groups, and other such forms of pressure and challenge from below; but the context provided by capitalism requires that the effect they may have should as far as possible be weakened'.[11] This too can be explained with reference to classical democratic theory. The democratic aspiration is to a situation of popular power, in which the demos or people collectively, through established mechanisms and procedures, implement their will, or effectively exercise sovereignty. These formulations give rise to huge problems, some of which were classically dissected by Schumpeter in his famous critique of what he called 'the classical doctrine of democracy' in his book *Capitalism, Socialism and Democracy*.[12] Is there such a thing as the popular will, how can it be formulated and discovered? If it can, is it 'one' or 'multiple'? Surely unanimity is impossible to expect in any complex modern society, and there is no such thing as 'the will of the people'; there are sectional and fractional interests or aspirations which are contradictory to each other. Even if this problem of discovering what the people's will is, or wills are, can be solved, through what mechanisms could it, or they, be realised? These are all key problems of the democratic project, seen as an 'unfinished journey', an attempt to realise something which can never be definitively or finally realised.[13]

However, the thesis of capitalist democracy involves the suggestion that systems of liberal or capitalist democracy are well endowed with a range of structures and devices which seek to limit or contain the effective power of the people, and that such a politics of containment derives, again, from the capitalist structure within which liberal democracy is situated. In this sense the politics of capitalist democracy can be seen as a constant struggle on the one hand to extend democracy, to realise ideas of popular sovereignty, and, on the other, the countervailing pressure by holders of economic and social, as well as of political power, to push back such democratic advance, to maintain a space free from the intrusions of popular power. Thus the paradox or contradiction of capitalist democracy is that for all the invocations of freedom and the people, popular power in practice is feared. The power holders in such systems seek to maintain a distance between their exercise of power and their accountability to the people, and to restrict the active involvement of the people in public affairs. Here too there are a number of issues which should be probed. In the words of Miliband, writing in his book *Capitalist Democracy in Britain* of the British political system, this system proclaims itself as democratic. It promises to realise what Miliband calls 'popular participation in the determination of policy and popular control over the conduct of affairs'. Yet the reality of British politics, so Miliband argues, is rather to limit and contain the exercise of popular power, so that 'Democratic claims and political reality do not truly match'.[14] This is not to deny that there are in the British system, as in other similar capitalist democracies, a number of features which make it possible for the citizens to express their views, and for those to impinge on decision makers. Indeed, as Miliband points out, the fundamental fact of elections may mean that power-holders lose their hold on state power as a result of shifts in opinion as expressed in an election. Nevertheless, the term 'capitalist democracy' is meant to suggest that the pressures from below and demands for popular involvement in politics are contained and checked, for reasons which need to be explained.

The picture thus emerges of a movement for extending and deepening democracy, a movement which in societies like Britain has a long history, but a movement which power-holders in state and society have succeeded in limiting and controlling. The analysis of capitalist democracy promises to be an analysis of the institutions and structures which succeed in this task of neutralising public pressure. No less importantly, the analysis of capitalist democracy is meant to suggest, at least in general terms, ways in which these limitations or imperfections could be removed. We have here a set of hypotheses concerning 'the future of capitalist democracy' in Britain, or any other such society, which point to a number of possibilities for the development of such systems of power. To anticipate the argument, the perspective offered by Miliband is one of a class-based movement which would seek to remove the capitalist shackles (or fetters?) holding back the democratic participation of the citizens of such a society. Capitalist democracy therefore promises more than it delivers, it invokes the aspiration to rule of the people but cannot deliver anything remotely approaching this goal. The thesis of capitalist democracy suggests that the main reason for this is, to put it crudely, the fear that popular pressure would lead to demands which contradict the interests of the holders of economic and social power, the ruling class in Marxist language. There is thus a standing tension within liberal democratic societies, namely the fear that if such societies lived up to the principles of popular rule which they proclaim, this might be threatening to the inequalities of economic and social power, the capitalist context within which the liberal-democratic state is situated. Let us now probe some of the implications of this idea of the 'politics of containment', taking starting points from Miliband's work.

There are two aspects to the question worth stating. First, this idea of capitalist democracies as systems of 'containment' rests on an assumption which is by no means a new one, but which has been articulated for as long as mass pressure was a feature of politics, i.e. it is concomitant with the political age of modernity inaugurated by the French Revolution. That assumption can be called the assumption of the radicalism of democracy, or the idea that democratic deepening and extending popular involvement in politics would in fact lead to demands for greater social equality or control over the private ownership and disposition of economic forces. In other words, the assumption is that there is a link between *political equality*, or the greater realisation of democratic demands, and *social equality*. This assumption is if not exactly as old as the hills then at least as old as the French Revolution and the onset of modern politics, and was, and indeed still is, shared both by those who welcomed the coming of democracy and those who feared it. Historically, one could cite Engels' exultant cry of 1843 that 'Democracy, nowadays that is communism', or the Duke of Wellington's fears that democracy would declare war on property, or the liberal de Tocqueville's prediction that when the people is sovereign it is rarely miserable.[15] To take a more contemporary example, the late Friedrich von Hayek writes as follows in his essay *Whither Democracy?*, expressing his fears about democracy:

> Agreement by the majority on sharing the booty gained by overwhelming a minority of fellow citizens, or deciding how much is to be taken from them, is not democracy. At least it is not that ideal of democracy which has any moral justification. Democracy itself is not egalitarianism. But unlimited democracy is bound to become egalitarian.[16]

Indeed, Hayek goes on to write of 'the fundamental immorality of all egalitarianism' and its incompatibility with individual liberty:

> While equality before the law – the treatment of all by government according to the same rules – appears to me to be an essential condition of individual freedom, that different treatment which is necessary in order to place people who are individually very different into the same material position seems to me not only incompatible with personal freedom, but highly immoral. But this is the kind of immorality towards which unlimited democracy is moving.[17]

His proposed solution was to make a separation between a governmental assembly and a legislative assembly. The power and policies of the former would be subject to the laws laid down by the latter, and such laws could only be 'universal rules of just conduct', implying that the governmental assembly, bound by rules passed by the legislative assembly, would not be able to pass specific acts of redistribution or expropriation. Hayek writes that

Arbitrary oppression – that is coercion undefined by any rule by the representatives of the majority – is no better than arbitrary action by any other ruler. Whether it requires that some hated person should be boiled and quartered, or that his property should be taken from him, comes in this respect to the same thing.[18]

In order to make the legislative assembly, whose laws restrict the power of the governmental assembly, sufficiently remote from popular pressure, Hayek suggested that it should be composed of men and women independent of political parties, above a certain age and of a certain respectable social condition and status, and free from any possible wish for re-election. In his words,

I imagine for this reason a body of men and women who, after having gained reputation and trust in the ordinary pursuits of life, were elected for a single long period of something like 15 years. To assure that they had gained sufficient experience and respect, and that they did not have to be concerned about securing a livelihood for the period after the end of their tenure, I would fix the age of election comparatively high, say at 45 years, and assure them for another 10 years after expiry of their mandate at 60 of some dignified posts as lay-judges or the like.[19]

This suggestion may strike one as somewhat extreme, but it well illustrates the classical liberal fear of democracy as leading to egalitarianism in the social field, and the desire to contain it, in this instance by the 15 year-long tenure of office, in the legislative assembly, of middle-aged men, and, it must be said, women too.

This fear of democracy and the desire to contain it has been classically expressed by some liberals. But let us return to the concept of capitalist democracy. The argument here is that it rests on an assumption which was shared by those (like Hayek) who would be most unsympathetic to the use of the term, and that assumption is that the consequence of extending democratic participation would be radical in the sense of posing a challenge to the existing structure of wealth and privilege. The question that this assumption raises is whether it was right to assume, whether in hope or fear, that democracy and democratic pressures would be 'revolutionary', or at least radical in the sense of offering opposition to capitalist power and to a deeply unequal distribution of economic resources. Of course this assumption was shared by both friends and foes of the process of the democratisation of the liberal state, but with the benefit of hindsight one may ask 'what did the ruling classes have to fear?' Why was 'containment' a necessary strategy on their part? For example, the movement to extend democracy in the USA does not seem to have unleashed demands of a socialist kind for restructuring of the social hierarchy. A recent study of *The Radicalism of the American Revolution* by Gordon S. Wood seems to suggest that its radicalism took another form, one of individual advancement, the idea that everyone's interest was as good as anyone else's and that the political system could be the vehicle for individual achievement rather than for a collective attempt to challenge the social structure. Wood writes that the radicalism of the American revolution came to differ from the austere and rather elitist vision of the founding fathers:

A new generation of democratic Americans was no longer interested in the revolution-aries' dream of building a classical republic elitist virtue out of the inherited materials of the old world. America, they said, would find its greatness not by emulating the state of classical antiquity, not by copying the fiscal-military powers of modern Europe, and not by producing a few notable geniuses and great-souled men. Instead it would discover its greatness by creating a prosperous free society belonging to obscure people with their workaday concerns and their pecuniary pursuits of happiness – common people with their common interests in making money and getting ahead.[20]

In other words, the creation of a working democracy, and a democracy of working people, was quite compatible with the absence of any socially radical movements challenging disparities of wealth and economic power.

Alternatively, if the strategy of 'containment' was indeed necessary because of the socially radical implications of democracy, then in what ways, through what strategies, and for what reasons, has it been so successful, in the societies of 'capitalist democracy'? This raises another related theme, which is central to the work of Ralph Miliband, and linked with the idea of capitalist democracy as a system strongly protected by institutions which ward off the potentially radical challenges of democracy and, linked with those challenges, of socialism. This theme is that of parliamentarism, of the use of parliament or representative institutions in general as a means of conciliation, of absorbing or defusing radical protest, while at the same time paying lip-service to the democratic ideal of popular participation. In Miliband's words:

In conditions of capitalist democracy, with universal suffrage, political competition, the capacity of the working class to exercise different forms of pressure, the crucial problem for the people in charge of affairs is to be able to get on with the business in hand, without undue interference from below, yet at the same time to provide sufficient opportunities for political participation to place the legitimacy of the system beyond serious question. The point is not to achieve popular exclusion altogether; that would be dangerous and ultimately self-defeating. The point is rather to give adequate and meaningful scope to popular participation; but to 'depopularize' policy-making and to limit strictly the impact of the market-place upon the conduct of affairs. Parliamentarism makes this possible: for it simultaneously enshrines the principle of popular inclusion *and* that of popular exclusion.[21]

It should be made clear that 'to limit strictly the impact of the market place', in the sense of curbing popular power and containing the weight of public opinion, is quite compatible with increasing the impact of the 'market' on politics, in terms of letting the supposedly impersonal processes of the market carry on free from the dangerously egalitarian impact of popular pressure. However, the central point is that 'parliamentarism' here means the use of representative assemblies as devices to neutralise and contain conflict. Parliament is a central institution for practising the 'politics of containment' necessary to ensure the stability of liberal-democracy.

Two points can be made in this context: one, the idea of containment or 'deradicalisation' seems bound up, at least to some extent, with the very nature of representation, of representative democracy as such, within which parliament has such a central role to play. This point has been made from a variety of theoretical perspectives, ranging well beyond Marxism, to elitism and even anarchism. As Przeworski well puts it, incidentally referring to Miliband's book *Marxism and Politics*, 'workers can process their claims only collectively and only indirectly, through organisations which are embedded in systems of representation, principally trade-unions and political parties', adding later on:

> . . . relations within the class become structured as relations of representation. The parliament is a representative institution: it seats individuals, not masses. A relation of representation is thus imposed upon the class by the very nature of capitalist democratic institutions . . . Masses represented by leaders: this is the mode of organization of the working class within capitalist institutions. In this manner participation demobilises the masses.[22]

One way of drawing the consequences of this is an elitist one: there will always be an elite, distanced from and superior to the rank and file, because of the very structure of representative institutions.

The other point to be noted is of course that this 'deradicalising' effect of parliament, or representative institutions in general, does not signify that such institutions have no importance as elements which distinguish forms of capitalist democracy from forms of capitalist authoritarianism. It suggests, however, that parliamentary confrontations often take the form of ritual occasions (think of Question Time in the British case) which do not really contribute to one of the tasks which representative assemblies are supposed to fulfil, the education of public opinion.

Part Two: examining the theory of capitalist democracy

The democratic institutions and practices of the liberal-democratic state are thus limited and constrained by a system of social inequality which undermines democratic equality. It means that popular involvement in politics is contained by a network of institutions which distance the public from the effective exercise of power. But this thesis raises many large questions, two of which will now be discussed. First, assuming the thesis of capitalist democracy is correct in suggesting the large gap which exists between the democratic rhetoric of 'people power' and the reality of the effective exercise of power by a state elite, the question arises of explaining this gap. Is it the capitalist structure of social inequality which is the chief cause of the limited degree of popular participation in liberal-democratic societies or are other factors more significant? Secondly, what alternatives are there to capitalist democracy, or how can the constraints which limit it be removed? These are large questions indeed.

We have seen from the Przeworski quotation that the lack of popular participation may be due to some extent not to the fact of capitalist power, but to the very nature of representation itself. Various theorists from Michels onwards, not to speak of earlier ones such as Rousseau, have suggested that the very process of representation creates an elite often different from the represented in their interests and concerns. Is 'containment' a result of the inevitable processes of representative democracy rather than of capitalist power as such?

Furthermore, the idea of capitalist democracy suggests that 'capitalism' and 'democracy' are in an antagonistic relationship, that it is the existence and power structure of the former which constrains and impedes the latter. This touches on one of the key debates in the currently growing field of the study of democratisation. As David Beetham suggests in his useful review of 'Conditions for Democratic Consolidation', 'The relationship (i.e. of capitalism and democracy) . . . is an ambiguous one, and both positive and negative aspects need asserting together'. Beetham notes that the hypothesis that 'a market system is a necessary, though not sufficient, condition of democracy' is usually formulated as 'a relationship between *capitalism* and democracy'.[23] On the one hand, capitalism has a strongly anti-paternalist thrust. Ideas of consumer sovereignty and individual rights as a consumer suggest ideas of voter sovereignty and competition for political power. We noted above the existence of a sphere of civil society as a crucial feature of liberal-democratic (or capitalist democratic) regimes. Such a sphere of civil society is fostered by a system of economic power (i.e. the market) separate from the state. In this sense, the defenders of capitalism can point to the fact that taking the sphere of production decisions outside the sphere of the state creates preconditions for centres of power in civil society which are independent of the state, and can function as sources of opposition and pluralism.

Of course, as Beetham also points out, the problem here is one noted above in this paper, that, in his words, 'The inequalities of wealth which come with market freedom tend to prevent effective political equality'. The holders of economic and social power have greater resources with which to influence the workings of democratic politics, and with which to penetrate the preserves of the state elite. One can also endorse Beetham's formulation that 'The experience of being treated as a dispensable commodity in the labour market contradicts the publicly proclaimed idea of the democratic citizen as the bearer of rights in a context of social reciprocity'.[24] What all this suggests is that the idea of 'capitalist democracy' contains a number of ideas which need careful probing. There is the connection, central to Miliband's work, between what he calls 'class power' and 'state power'. In other words, how exactly does the power of an economically dominant group translate into political power? Or, to put it in Therborn's words, how does the ruling class rule?[25] In what ways does the privileged economic position of those who control the productive resources of society erode or threaten to undermine the equality of citizens in a democratic society? And finally, what are the alternatives to capitalist democracy, how can its limitations be transcended? Mindful of the character Morris Zapp in David Lodge's novel *Changing Places* who (rightly) thought that 'any damn fool could think of questions', the real point was to come up with answers, the aim here is to try and suggest some answers to these questions, at least in terms of the problem of the alternatives to capitalist democracy.

There are two alternatives to capitalist democracy which are sketched out in Miliband's work. These are, on the one hand, what he calls 'capitalist authoritarianism', and on the other what he refers to as 'socialist democracy'. The former has been referred to earlier. It differs from 'capitalist democracy' in that the institutions and rights which offer the chance of 'pressure from below' are annihilated, whether by a monopolistic state party as in the case of fascism, or by military rule in cases of military dictatorship, or versions of clerical conservatism (like in Dolfuss's Austria) and other types of authoritarianism which do not aim at mass mobilisation (such as Portugal under Salazar and Caetano). The chances of such regimes being installed seem higher where the parties of the Left are divided, where parties or movements of the Right (or military leaders) can claim to be preventing a threat from the Left, real or imagined, and where the support for democracy is eroded by economic crisis, social dislocation, and deep uncertainty. These conditions all provide fertile ground for demagogic leaders and movements which promise the false solution of some kind of 'strong state' which will do away with the divisions and conflicts of liberal democracy and the opportunities it affords for 'pressure from below'.

In terms of the relevance of 'capitalist authoritarianism' to the situation of contemporary politics, there is one sense in which this scenario of the transition from capitalist democracy to capitalist authoritarianism is less likely, another sense in which it is still highly relevant to contemporary politics. The chances of this happening in contemporary systems of 'capitalist democracy' seem diminished to the extent that the fear of the Left and of socialism is reduced, though it should not be imagined that this is a permanent condition. On the other hand, it is dislocation, disruption and economic and social uncertainty which provide fertile breeding ground for movements of the extreme Right and demands for a strong state of capitalist authoritarianism. Such conditions may well arise where market relations are introduced by executive imposition, rapidly and without heed of the social consequences, in societies which were formerly Communist.[26]

The analysis of the possible development, or rather degeneration, of capitalist democracy into capitalist authoritarianism is by no means a scenario remote from the politics of our own day.

Finally, to turn to what Miliband suggested was a feasible and possible alternative to capitalist democracy, which he labelled 'socialist democracy'. This was defined by him in no uncertain terms as totally distinct from what he called the 'anti-model' represented by Soviet-type one-party systems, which were notable of course for their denial of democratic rights, not least because of the lack of any genuine and effective controls over the leaders of the single party. Socialist democracy is defined by Miliband as 'an *extension* of capitalist democracy, and at the same time a *break* with it'.[27] The problem here lies with specifying the nature of this socialist democracy and discussing the likelihood of it coming into existence – by what means, through what agency, through what policies?

Clearly, socialist democracy in this model differs, as Miliband also makes clear in his study *Marxism and Politics*, from the (classically Marxist?) model of the Paris Commune of 1871, in which the parliamentary state is smashed and replaced by an extreme, almost direct, form of popular democracy. We all know what happened to this model when it was introduced, very briefly, it must be said, in Russia in 1917. The claims for this model, that it was far superior to representative government of the parliamentary type, are well described by Neil Harding:

> For a brief period of perhaps nine months after the October Revolution in 1917, the Bolsheviks committed themselves to the most audacious attempt at transforming the vocabulary and the practice of politics since the French Revolution of 1789 . . . The idea of soviet democracy was directly counterposed to that of 'bourgeois', 'liberal' or 'parliamentary' democracy. It signified the direct, unmediated participation of the people in the administration of all public affairs.[28]

We know that this version of direct participation was in practice short-circuited by the continued dominance and reinforced grip of the single (Bolshevik) party. However, leaving aside the special conditions of Russia after 1917, such a model of popular power is hard to apply in conditions of complex advanced modern democracies, not least because of the heavy demands it would make on the citizens of such a participatory democracy. This 'Paris Commune' model rests on an assumption of the 'transparency' of public affairs and politics which seems highly unrealistic.

However, Miliband's picture of, or aspiration to, a state of 'socialist democracy' is one which, as he says

> would embody many of the features of liberal democracy, including the rule of law, the separation of powers, civil liberties, political pluralism, and a vibrant civil society, but it would give them much more effective meaning . . . In short, it would give the notion of citizenship a far truer and larger meaning than it could ever have in a class-divided society.[29]

Miliband also suggests that there is a tension in this model between the need for a state in a socialist society, to steer the whole enterprise through, and at the same time a vigorous and independent civil society, to prevent the distortions of 'statism' which in the Soviet model (or rather anti-model) have crippled the socialist project. This makes the idea of a socialist democracy a difficult enterprise indeed, steering between Scylla and Charybdis, the Scylla being excessive state power and the danger of an all-too strong state, and the Charybdis being an excess of popular power, or rather a fragmentation which gets out of hand. The crucial dilemma is that the state may need to be strengthened in order to achieve changes in capitalist democracy, but the danger is that this 'transformatory state' may itself assume undemocratic features and escape accountability to the people. This dilemma of the 'transition' has been all too real a problem in the past history of the socialist project.

The idea of capitalist democracy has thus built into it some statement or view of a possible alternative to it, socialist democracy, which for Miliband has to be clearly distinguished from the model (anti-model) of Soviet Communism. This socialist democracy is seen as an extension of, as well as a break with, capitalist democracy, but there are two questions that badly need answering: first, in what ways is this extension-cum-break to be envisaged, what would it actually mean in practice? Clearly it does not mean 'smashing the state', it means complementing the representative parliamentary system by a network of associations of popular power, but this raises the question of how this is to be achieved. There is indeed a literature on 'democratic deepening' which Miliband does not take fully into account which addresses some of these questions. Such books as those by Benjamin Barber on *Strong Democracy*, Jane Mansbridge's, *Beyond Adversary Democracy*, and Paul Hirst on *Associative Democracy* seek to give from a range of different perspectives some realisation of the idea of extending participation.[30] The problem is one of creating what Barber calls a situation of 'strong democracy', different from, in his phrase, 'politics as zoo-keeping'. Politics as a minimal activity to do with defence of one's interests is replaced by a form of democratic politics which develops people's horizons, knowledge, and civic capacities. But what is noticeable about at least some of this literature is that there is no explicit connection between the extension of this democratic participation and anything that is recognisably socialist. Indeed Paul Hirst in his book *Associative Democracy* announces that the Left-Right struggle is irrelevant, and that 'socialists have written themselves out of the task', in this case of helping the underclass, because (he argues) 'they have abandoned the task of building security and welfare through mutual institutions in civil society'.[31] This is a highly contestable judgement, but the general point that emerges is this: there is no guarantee, so to speak, that the democratisation of civil society will contribute to a socialist democracy, since the space opened up by this revived civil society may be used for a whole range of purposes, some of which do not contribute to the democratic control over the productive resources which is at the heart of the socialist project. Democracy and socialism need not necessarily go together. 'Democratic deepening' may not lead to the establishment of a socialist democracy.

Conclusion

By way of concluding remarks, it can be said that we live in a world where 'democracy', without any qualification, is exalted, where democracy and the associated ideas of popular sovereignty are saluted as the highest good. The concept of 'capitalist democracy', used by Miliband in a number of his books, serves excellently as a critical tool in deflating the pretensions, not of the democratic ideal, but of what could be called 'real existing democracies'. The concept highlights the crucial importance of the economic and social context in which the institutions of the liberal-democratic state are situated. Liberal democracy is indeed stunted by the inequalities which stem from its capitalist context, inequalities of class which give more effective power to men and women who control the resources of the economy. This power lies in their agenda-shaping role, as witnessed by the power of a Berlusconi or a Murdoch, and in their privileged access to the state elite. (Indeed, for a while, Berlusconi as Prime Minister *was* the leader of the state elite.)

However, there are problems with the concept of capitalist democracy. Used uncritically, it suggests that class is the only or main source of constraint on the realisation of popular power. It risks the underestimation of other limitations on democracy, whether they stem from gender divisions, ethnic and national divisions, or international factors (globalisation), all of which have proceeded apace in the very recent period. There is also the problem that the containment of popular pressure may be a feature not just of capitalist democracy, but of any system of representation. If a socialist democracy were to be achieved, which itself is of course an unlikely achievement in the present situation, it too would have to grapple with many of these problems which concern the implementation of popular power. There is also the key problem that the relationship between capitalism and democracy, or between the market and democracy, is more problematic than some uses of the idea of capitalist democracy allow. Under certain conditions, the growth of capitalism can stimulate demands for democratisation of hitherto non-democratic systems, and assist the development of a democratic civil society. There are thus three problems with the concept of capitalist democracy: one, it gives explanatory primacy to capitalism, and its associated class inequalities, in terms of explaining the defects of what could be called 'real existing democracy'. The danger is of overlooking other dimensions of inequality and sources of 'democratic deficit', including the structure of representative institutions as such. Two, the concept of capitalist democracy, associated with the alternatives of capitalist authoritarianism and socialist democracy, risks a too rigid classification of forms of state, including a whole range of different types of capitalist democracy. The concept of capitalist democracy itself requires sub-divisions, applications to particular cases, as of course Miliband himself exemplified in his work on the British state. And three, the relationship of capitalism and democracy is itself problematic, and, as suggested above, capitalist pressures can in certain circumstances be seen as democratising ones. However, at the same time capitalist democracies do seek to deradicalise and contain democratic pressures, fearful that these may turn out to be socially radical. Yet this assumption too, the radicalism of democratic pressure, is something, as we have seen, that is not true under all circumstances.

Finally, there is the question of the alternative to capitalist democracy. This was posed by Miliband in two ways, one involving the possibility of a resort to capitalist authoritarianism, the other leading to moves towards a form of socialist democracy. The former possibility remains real enough, if not in the societies of Western Europe then in those of Central and Eastern Europe where over-enthusiastic imposition of a market society can set off dislocation and social misery which find expression in support for movements promising a strong state and which seek a scapegoat in whatever targets lie to hand. However, the huge problem remains of the vision of a socialist democracy, building on and extending the liberties of liberal–democracy, yet destroying the class constraints of this latter mode of democracy. The problem is that in the popular consciousness, and in large part because of the Soviet experience, socialism and democracy have become disassociated, socialism has come to be linked with ideas of a strong, not to say all-powerful, state and with centralised regulation of all aspects of social life. The fundamental problem remains one of combining democracy with social control and coordination over the productive resources of society. Miliband's vision correctly points out the limitations of liberal–democracy, and his agenda does remain our agenda, posing the question of how such a model of socialist democracy could get popular support, and how it could be implemented, without falling prey to the distortions which have crippled socialist movements in the past.

NOTES

1. An earlier version of this paper was given to a seminar on 'Democracy and Democratisation' at Leeds University, and I am very grateful to the participants in that seminar and to John Saville for helpful comments.
2. Ralph Miliband, *Capitalist Democracy in Britain* (Oxford University Press, Oxford, 1982).

3. Miliband, *Capitalist Democracy in Britain*, p. 1.
4. C. Wright Mills, *Power, Politics and People* (Oxford University Press, New York, 1967), p. 35.
5. Nicos Poulantzas, *Fascism and Dictatorship. The Third International and the Problem of Fascism* (New Left Books, London, 1974).
6. For example in his *Marxism and Politics* (Oxford University Press, Oxford, 1977), p. 75 and p. 83.
7. Francis Fukuyama, *The End of History and the Last Man* (Hamish Hamilton, London, 1992), pp. 45–6.
8. Robert Dahl, *Democracy and Its Critics* (Yale University Press, New Haven and London, 1989), p. 98.
9. Dahl, *Democracy and its Critics*, p. 129.
10. R. H. Tawney, *Equality* (Allen & Unwin, London, 1964), p. 78.
11. Miliband, *Capitalist Democracy in Britain*, p. 1.
12. Joseph Schumpeter, *Capitalism, Socialism and Democracy* (Unwin University Books, London, 1965), Chapters XXI and XXII. For an interesting discussion of Schumpeter, see George Catephores, 'The Imperious Austrian: Schumpeter as Bourgeois Marxist', *New Left Review* 205, May/June 1994, pp. 3–30.
13. See John Dunn (ed.), *Democracy, The Unfinished Journey 508 BC to AD 1993* (Oxford University Press, Oxford, 1992).
14. Miliband, *Capitalist Democracy in Britain*, p. 1.
15. Engels' statement comes from his report on 'Das Fest der Nationen in London', in Karl Marx and Friedrich Engels, *Werke*, (Dietz, Berlin, 1970), Vol. 2, p. 611; see also R. N. Hunt, *The Political Ideas of Marx and Engels* (Macmillan, London, 1975), Vol. 1, p. 135; for Wellington's prophecies see R. J. White (ed.), *The Conservative Tradition* (A. & C. Black, London, 1964). More generally see Charles S. Maier, 'Democracy Since the French Revolution', in John Dunn (ed.), *Democracy, the Unfinished Journey*.
16. F. A. Hayek, 'Whither Democracy?', in *New Studies in Philosophy, Politics, Economics and the History of Ideas* (Routledge & Kegan Paul, London, 1978), p. 157.
17. Hayek, 'Whither Democracy?', p. 157.
18. Hayek, 'Whither Democracy?', p. 154.
19. Hayek, 'Whither Democracy?', p. 160.
20. Gordon S. Wood, *The Radicalism of the American Revolution* (Alfred A. Knopf, New York, 1992), p. 369.
21. Miliband, *Capitalist Democracy in Britain*, p. 38.
22. A. Przeworski, *Capitalism and Social Democracy* (Cambridge University Press, Cambridge, 1985), p. 11 and p. 14.
23. David Beetham, 'Conditions for Democratic Consolidation', *Review of African Political Economy* 60, pp. 157–172.
24. Beetham, 'Conditions for Democratic Consolidation', p. 165. For other perspectives see *Journal of Democracy*, Vol. 3, No. 3, July 1992, special issue on 'Capitalism, Socialism, & Democracy'.
25. G. Therborn, *What does the ruling class do when it rules? State apparatuses and state power under feudalism, capitalism and socialism* (New Left Books, London, 1978).
26. On these issues see *Journal of Democracy* Vol. 5, No. 4, October 1994, special issue on 'Economic Reform and Democracy', notably the article by Leszek Balcerowicz, 'Understanding Postcommunist Transition', pp. 75–89.
27. Ralph Miliband, 'The Socialist Alternative', *Journal of Democracy*, Vol. 3, No. 3, July 1992, p. 123, and see also Ralph Miliband, *Socialism for a Sceptical Age* (Polity Press, Cambridge, 1994), pp. 71ff.
28. Neil Harding, 'The Marxist-Leninist Detour', in John Dunn (ed.), *Democracy, the Unfinished Journey*, pp. 164–5.
29. Miliband, 'The Socialist Alternative', p. 123. These ideas are further developed in

Socialism for a Sceptical Age, especially Chapter 3, 'Mechanisms of Democracy'.

30. Benjamin Barber, *Strong Democracy* (University of California Press, Berkeley and London, 1984); Jane J. Mansbridge, *Beyond Adversary Democracy* (University of Chicago Press, Chicago and London, 1983); Paul Hirst, *Associative Democracy* (Polity Press, Cambridge, 1994). In *Socialism for a Sceptical Age*, pp. 88–90 Miliband does refer to Barber's book and suggests that a socialist democracy would combine representative with participatory democracy.

31. Hirst, *Associative Democracy*, p. 10.

PARLIAMENTARY SOCIALISM REVISITED

John Saville

The years which followed the end of the second world war were notably deficient in critical socialist writing. The radicalism of the war years, which had produced the massive swing to the Labour Party in the general election of July 1945, weakened steadily after about 1948, and this for several reasons. One was the revival of the Conservative Party and their success in exploiting the middle class dislike of austerity produced by rationing and the continuation of wartime controls; another was the failure of the Labour government to develop further its own radical programme; and a third was the marked complacency which was beginning to be exhibited, notably by the intellectuals of the Fabian Society, about what had been achieved in terms of social change. The background was the rapidly worsening international situation and the hardening of attitudes between the western powers and the Soviet Union. Stalinism inside Russia was exhibiting the intellectual stupidities of Lysenko and Zhdanov, and outside its national boundaries, the brutalities and terror of the regimes on its western borders were provoking vigorous anti-Soviet reactions. The complexities of the Cold War, which involve a recognition of the major responsibilities of Britain and the United States for much of the deterioration of international relations, were greatly simplified and were to be subsumed beneath a widespread anti-communism and anti-Sovietism that led to the hysteria of McCarthyism in the United States and a pervasive Cold War mentality in western Europe: much colder in countries like Britain than is commonly appreciated.

The Conservative Party came back to power in Britain in the latter months of 1951 although the Labour Party polled its highest ever total of votes. For the rest of the decade the Labour Party was faction ridden, and by 1959 it had lost three general elections in succession: 'the fifties' Ralph Miliband wrote in the concluding pages of *Parliamentary Socialism* 'have often appeared to lack the political instrumentalities of radical change. And to this impression, a consolidating Labour Party, revisionist in practice if not in theory, has greatly contributed. If politics in the fifties have seemed a decreasingly meaningful activity, void of substance, heedless of principle, and rich in election auctioneering, the responsibility is not only that of the hidden or overt persuaders: it is also, and to a major degree that of Labour's leaders'.

Parliamentary Socialism was the first major critical analysis of the Labour Party in Britain since the end of the war in 1945, and its intellectual impact was considerable. Miliband's opening words justified the title of his book. In a comment that has been widely quoted he wrote:

> Of political parties claiming socialism to be their aim, the Labour Party has always been one of the most dogmatic – not about socialism, but about the parliamentary system. Empirical and flexible about all else, its leaders have always made devotion to that system their fixed point of reference and the conditioning factor of their political behaviour. This is not simply to say that the Labour Party has never been a party of revolution: such parties have normally been quite willing to use the opportunities the parliamentary system offered as one means of furthering their aims. It is rather that the leaders of the Labour Party have always rejected any kind of political action (such as industrial action for political purposes) which fell, or which appeared to them to fall, outside the framework and conventions of the parliamentary system. The Labour Party has not only been a parliamentary party; it has been a party deeply imbued by parliamentarism. And in this respect, there is no distinction to be made between Labour's political and its industrial leaders. Both have been equally determined that the Labour Party should not stray from the narrow path of parliamentary politics.

It was the incisive analysis of the history of the Labour Party since the formation of the Labour Representation Committee in February 1900 that caught the imagination of the younger age groups within the Labour movement. Most had read nothing comparable. Earlier generations had available accounts such as Egon Wertheimer's *Portrait of the Labour Party* first published in German in May 1929 with an English translation in the following month – a somewhat neglected text, although Wertheimer had only the 1924 Labour government on which to rest any serious observations about Labour in power. In 1937 Allen Hutt published for the Left Book Club the nearest equivalent to Miliband's analysis in *The Post-War History of the British Working Class* although Hutt omitted any appraisal of the serious mistakes the Communist Party had made at certain times: notably the 1929–1931 Class Against Class period of malignant sectarianism. Hutt was especially critical of the pusillanimity of the Labour leadership and their accommodation to capitalist society. There was also much to be learned from the biographies of prominent figures, both of the Right and the Left: of the former *From Workman's Cottage to Windsor Castle* (1936) – a revealing title – and the latter Fenner Brockway's *Inside the Left* (1942) with its illuminating examples of the Labourist traditions within the years of the 1929–31 Labour government. But no one had unravelled in the way that Miliband did the strands of liberalism and reformism that came together to provide the leading ideas of the British Labour Party.

There are some general points that need to be made arising out of

Miliband's analysis over the decades he covered. One, which in the light of the subsequent history of the Labour Party after 1961, needs further emphasis, is foreign affairs and Labour's policies. Before 1939, although there were examples of the acceptance by the Labour leadership of the Conservative Party's approach – the issue of Non-Intervention in the first eighteen months of the Spanish Civil War is one of the most scandalous – nevertheless within the body of the Labour movement and often also within its leadership there was a long-standing tradition of a radical critique of government, that is, of Conservative, foreign policies. The influence of the Union of Democratic Control, and the pacifism which came out of the years of butchery of the first world war, remained important influences during the whole of the inter-war years. The widespread confusion over support for a rearmament programme in the second half of the nineteen thirties is an example of the struggle of powerful political ideas at all levels of the movement. It was accepted as axiomatic that the activities of the armament manufacturers were obscene, and the acquiescence in the most recent decades of armament sales as a necessary and useful contribution to the British balance of payments would have been unthinkable in the years before the second world war. Ralph Miliband recorded the widespread opposition to the rearming of Germany during the 1950s although the Labour and trade union leadership were able to use the block vote in its support; and to the Suez debacle, against which there was a vigorous opposition, although, as he notes, once the military operations ceased so did the Labour leadership's campaign.

If *Parliamentary Socialism* had been written two decades later the pervasive influence of the Cold War would have been given a great deal more emphasis. Since he wrote the archives of the Foreign Office and other departments have shown the anti-Soviet and anti-communist policies of the Labour Government after 1945 from the very beginning of its term of office. The Foreign Office, with Ernest Bevin as their powerful spokesman, was more single-minded in the first months than the United States. The starting point was Empire and the central aim the preservation of the pre-war colonies as an integral part of Britain's status in the world as a major power alongside the United States and the Soviet Union. Such a place in the world power system was not possible for Britain without American dollars and this involved, among other requirements of the so-called special relationship, a high level of defence expenditure – well beyond the resources of the United Kingdom – from the end of the second world war until the present. Labour in office and Labour out of government accepted levels of defence costs which throughout the whole postwar period were higher in proportion of its national income than any western European country; undoubtedly one of the important factors in the relative economic decline of Britain by comparison with other advanced industrial societies.

These continuities were explicit as well as implicit in *Parliamentary Socialism*. The most important single issue in the late 1950s and early 1960s, when the manuscript was being completed, was unilateral nuclear disarmament. The 1960 Labour Party Conference declared in favour of a unilateralist defence policy by not quite 300,000 votes: a decision reversed the following year after a vigorous mobilisation of supporters by Hugh Gaitskell. But Gaitskell had lost his attempt to revise Clause IV of the Party's constitution: the clause which formally committed the Labour Party 'to secure for the workers by hand or by brain the full fruits of their industry and the most equitable distribution thereof that may be possible, upon the basis of the common ownership of the means of production and the best obtainable system of popular administration and control of each industry and service'. Gaitskell had begun and lost his campaign for constitutional revision soon after the defeat at the 1959 General Election, but the Party Conference of 1960 was asked to accept a general statement of aims which embodied the aims of Gaitskell and the Right wing of the Party and which was a clear enough indication of the route that Gaitskell, had he lived, would have consciously followed. The statement adopted at the Conference, as a clarification of its basic economic policies, accepted that the Party's

> social and economic objectives can be achieved only through an expansion of common ownership substantial enough to give the community power over the commanding heights of the economy [and] recognising that both public and private enterprise have a place in the economy it believes that a further extension of common ownership should be decided from time to time in the light of these objectives and according to circumstances, with due regard for the views of the workers and consumers concerned.

This attempt by Gaitskell to weaken the principles embodied in Clause IV has been matched by the statements of Tony Blair after he became leader of the Labour Party in the summer of 1994, and the promise of a Conference in the spring of 1995 to find acceptance of a new form of words which will embody the basic principles of the Labour Party in the future. It is really very odd that revisionist Party leaders feel it necessary to change the text of the Constitution when throughout the whole history of the Labour Party the leadership has without scruple ignored both Constitution and Party Conference decisions when it suited their purposes. It is perhaps just as odd when for so many in the Labour Party the wording of the original Clause IV is appreciated as a necessary symbol of aims and policies when all are aware that in most elections, both before 1979 and certainly after, Clause IV has been absent from any serious political strategy. But the opposition to change in this context is that the Labour leadership can never be reminded too often of what the post-1918 Constitution involved; and there are, after all, quite a large number of ordinary members of the Party who still call themselves socialists.

The particular historical circumstances in which the Party leaders feel it necessary to set down their revisionism upon the Mosaic Tablets have some important features in common. In the 1950s the Labour Party had lost three successive elections; in the 1980s and early 1990s four general elections had gone to the Tories; in both periods the economic and social background was believed to have changed in ways that demanded a radical re-thinking of Labour's approach. In the fifties, in addition to the faction fighting within the Labour Party – an important electoral consideration – there were two rather contradictory matters that together helped to persuade many voters either to abstain from voting Labour or to support the Tories. The first was the point made by Ralph Miliband in the opening words of Ch. 10: 'The Labour Party' he wrote 'accepted its loss of office in 1951 with a certain complacency. This was partly due to a feeling that so much had been accomplished since 1945 that a breathing space had become natural and inevitable'.

This belief that 'so much had been accomplished' was both an important statement of fact and a figment of the imagination of Fabian intellectuals. The nationalisation programme and the social reform measures, with the creation of the National Health service as its most important single achievement, were regarded by Labour leaders not as the beginning of the social revolution, but as *the* social revolution. There would be some Labour ministers who might agree that there was still much to be done to consolidate the social revolution, but their own intellectuals were in no doubt about what had been accomplished. In *New Fabian Essays* published in 1952 Crosland argued that we were no longer living in a capitalist society but rather in a half-way stage to socialism, and in the same volume John Strachey, the former Marxist from the 1930s, was of the opinion that 'the Labour Government between 1945 and 1951 did in fact appreciably modify the nature of British capitalism'. In his abridged and revised version of *The Future of Socialism* (1964: originally published in 1956) Crosland was still writing that 'the distribution of personal income has become significantly more equal; and the change has been almost entirely at the expense of property incomes'. Full employment, of course, was the central factor in the rise of living standards, but to speak of anything approaching a fundamental change in the nature and working of capitalist society was implausible. It was to be demolished in economic and statistical terms in the 1960s by Richard Titmus and others, but the observant worker only had to look about him/her to appreciate that the evidence of a massive shift in income distribution was not exactly unmistakable.

And this was the second of what was described above as the two contradictory factors which influenced voting patterns by the end of the nineteen fifties. On the one hand the Labour Party managers were much concerned with those they called the 'floating voters', those, that is, who were supposedly no longer tied to their class position in society because of increasing affluence; and on the other, there was the estimate that by 1960 there were between seven and eight million persons living below a defined 'national assistance' standard. During the nineteen sixties the inequalities of income began to widen; not on the scale that occurred in the 1980s but still observable and measurable. As in the Thatcher years the Labour leaders in the late 1950s began to shift away from their obvious constituency – the wage earners of the traditional kind, much more numerous than they were two decades later – and their social policies became less radical and more blurred in their impact. In the Thatcher decade the Labour leadership, especially when Kinnock assumed the position of Leader of the Opposition, became wholly bemused with consumerism and the workings of the market, entirely supportive of the Conservative Government's foreign policy, notably in support of the Falklands War and the Gulf War, and running away as fast as was politically practicable from Labour's historic alignment with trade unionism and the concepts of collectivism and egalitarianism. These were changes and developments, given the difference of two decades, comprehensively in line with the analysis that over twenty years earlier suffused the pages of *Parliamentary Socialism*.

The publication of *Parliamentary Socialism* was widely acknowledged. R.H.S. Crossman in the *New Statesman* discussed the work in a long hostile review of three columns which seriously distorted the main lines of Miliband's analysis. His exposition, wrote Crossman, was 'grotesquely one-sided' but Crossman nevertheless recommended that the Labour leadership, 'determined to rebuild the Party's morale', should be ready to study carefully an account of the present 'crisis of confidence, even when it is presented in the form of partisan history'. And he continued:

> If it is horrifying to see how unfair some of these charges are, it is important to remember that Dr Miliband is speaking for a horrifyingly large number of active Party workers.

The main theme of Miliband's analysis according to Crossman was that the 'real fight' against Toryism required direct action, a 'semi-revolutionary demand for strike action' which the greater part of the Labour movement 'instinctively shies away from'. *Parliamentary Socialism* was, of course, arguing a much more subtle understanding of the history of the Labour Party. Ralph Miliband was certainly not against direct action where the circumstances demanded an intervention by the organised working class, as in the years immediately after world war one. But situations such as opposition to the military support for the anti-Soviet forces in the immediate aftermath of the war occur only seldom. What Miliband was arguing was that the struggle for elementary rights or against reactionary policies cannot be confined to Westminster but that a wide range of options is available to popular movements in order to express their political will. Thus support for Republican Spain between 1936 and 1939 evoked an extraordinary range of political and social activities, from large demonstrations in the major cities to collection of foodstuffs and the provision of humanitarian aid. Spain is notably relevant to the central thesis of *Parliamentary Socialism* given the utterly shameful support for the policy of Non-Intervention by the official Labour movement for the first eighteen months of the war: a support for the British Government which encouraged the fascist powers in their large scale assistance to Franco. But there are so many other examples, whether in the years of unemployment during the thirties or the more affluent decade of the fifties. It was the passivity of the Labour and Trade Union leadership that formed a central part of the analysis of Labourism by Miliband: his emphasis upon the narrow constitutional parameters that the Leadership accepted from the beginning of the century; their deference to the established order and their fear of any upsurge of militancy from below.

But to return to Crossman in the *New Statesman*. He was answered in the week immediately following (27 October 1961) by the present writer in a letter which the editor placed at the beginning of the correspondence columns; and I reproduce some parts of my letter here as an example of one expression of the political sentiments of the Left of those days. My letter began:

> I was delighted to read Mr Crossman's review of Ralph Miliband's book on parliamentary socialism. Mr Crossman has long been my favourite example in British affairs of the Kansas politician who sat securely on the fence with his ears to the ground on both sides; and that Miliband has helped to push him off the fence is a considerable achievement. For what Crossman's furious review amounts to is a firm commitment to the existing Labour leadership and its practices that is, in the context of Mr Crossman's own political history, little short of heroic.

The remainder of my letter was concerned to provide Crossman with the opportunity to state his own analysis of the historical record of the Labour Party:

> It is widely believed [I wrote] that in this last decade the Labour Party, inside and outside Westminster, has been inept and incompetent, devoid of ideas, drained of political passion, regarded with derison by the Tories and by their own supporters with, at best, an apathetic acquiescence. Three general elections in a row have been lost. Labour Party politics are not even radical politics, and the generations under 30, not to put too fine a point on it, can hardly be said to be enthusiastic in their support for Mr. Crossman's colleagues on the front bench. Is this a wild exaggeration, and if it is why do so many who are far beyond the ranks of Socialists believe it to be true? Anyway, let us have a pithy statement from Mr. Crossman which sums up the record of these last ten years.

My letter ended with a reference to Crossman's accusation of 'a degree of tendentious distortion and misquotation which no journalist or politician would dare to use'. After noting that I could not share Crossman's faith in journalists and politicians, I accepted that the matter of 'distortion' was always capable of being argued about in a serious historical work; but that 'misquotation' was a matter of fact and Crossman was invited to produce his examples. He replied the following week (3 November 1961) and again it was the first letter in the correspondence columns. He began by making such an absurd mistake that it confirmed how superficially and/or hurriedly he read the books he was offered to review, for he began by apologising for not having included me as one of the authors of *Parliamentary Socialism*. What he was referring to was the generous acknowledgement of my help at the drafting stage by Ralph Miliband; but as to authorship, I pointed out in a letter the following week, Crossman had only 'to look at the dust cover, the publishers blurb, the title page, the list of acknowledgements and the heading of his own review to see that the author is in fact Ralph Miliband'.

Crossman in the 3 November letter listed his own diagnosis of what had gone wrong in the 1950s:

(1) The fundamental reasons for Labour's failures in the 1950s were economic and social – in particular the development of an affluent society, which made it extremely difficult to arouse popular enthusiasm either for a Socialist analysis or for Socialist measures. This situation was exploited with great skill by British Conservatism.

(2) It is probably true that once Lord Attlee had made the fatal decision to go to the country in the autumn of 1951, Labour had no chance of regaining office during this decade, whatever we said or did.

(3) In these circumstances it is my belief – argued at length in a Fabian Pamphlet, *Labour and the Affluent Society* – that our wisest course would have been to behave not as *the alternative government*, but as a *fighting opposition*, prepared to remain in the wilderness until events undermined popular faith in the Establishment and confirmed our radical criticisms. What we should have concentrated on between elections was not propaganda to the apathetic voter, but the education of a cadre of active Socialists who really understood the contradictions of the affluent society, and who could explain to the electorate how those contradictions can and must be overcome by the next Labour government.

Crossman then continued to make the extraordinary statement that the Left did not seem to believe in the need for political education; and then apologised for the accusation of misquotation which he had made in his first letter. But much more important than these matters of detail, which are certainly not unimportant, was the general political attitude that Crossman displayed. These were clearly dominated by the improvement in living standards – the 'affluent society' – although it never occurred to him that full employment due to a world boom was the most important single factor and that there were very large social groups in society still living on what for advanced industrial societies were conditions of poverty. The high levels of defence expenditure were not considered worth remarking on, Mau Mau and the Cyprus crisis were just coming to an end, the entrenched conservative institutional structures of British society were still in place, and all Crossman could suggest was to wait until the electorate came to appreciate the 'contradictions' in a society of affluence.

There followed the publication of *Parliamentary Socialism* two decades during which the Labour Party were in government for more years than the Tories, although at the beginning and the end their majorities were insecure. But the sixties, as we all know, were years of vigorous debate – so very different from the fifties – when many matters hitherto regarded as being confined to the closet were brought out into the open and vigorously debated. By the end of the decade the Vietnam War agitation had crossed the Atlantic, and the events of May 1968 in Paris had passed over the English Channel. There was a serious interest among the younger age-groups in socialist theory, often it must be acknowledged, of the esoteric kind that occupied so much time on the Left Bank. The output of socialist books in the sixties and seventies certainly filled the empty shelves of the nineteen fifties which had been much commented on. But the intense and serious discussions of the 1968 generation began to run into the sands during the next decade. The Labour governments from 1964 were not without some social advances, but their incompetent handling of the economy and the absence of anything approaching an imaginative understanding of the changing problems of British society, founded as they were upon encrusted conservative administrative and constitutional structures, steadily alienated the various parts of their native constituencies. In the general election of May 1979 there was a massive swing of 2.2 million votes to the Conservatives, and this included an eight per cent swing among skilled industrial workers.

The election defeat of 1979 was followed by a decade of major retreat for the whole Labour movement. Continued de-industrialisation steadily reduced the number of trade unionists in the old established unions which drew their membership from the manufacturing sectors. The sharp recession of the early eighties, which might even have been capitalised on by the shambling leadership of Michael Foot, was countered by the Falklands War which Labour supported and from which Thatcher reaped an electoral benefit. And then there came Kinnock, after the general election of June 1983 which had left Labour with only 28.3 per cent of the national vote (against 36.9 per cent in 1979).

The political Left inside the Labour movement had advanced its positions in the late 1970s and early 1980s, and when Kinnock was elected Leader it was this Left he had to defeat before he could seriously remould the Labour Party in a new image. This process was interrupted by the most important single political issue for Labour during the whole of the decade: the miners' strike of 1984–5. The strike, it must be emphasised again, was the key political question for Britain in the 1980s. A miners' victory would have had profound consequences for politics in general and naturally for the Labour movement itself. There was a remarkable response from the grass roots of the movement by no means limited to groups of unionists and Labour Party members of the left. There was an understanding at the base of the movement that the miners had to be supported against the Thatcher government, buttressed as she and her government were by the media and supported on the ground by physical violence from the police. In December 1984 – the strike began in March 1984 – the government cut social security benefits for the families of striking miners, and the shadow Cabinet refused all demands from back bench MPs to raise the issue in the Commons. During the first ten weeks of the strike, after which the Commons went on holiday for a fortnight, there was no debate initiated by the Labour front bench. Discussion had always come as a result of initiatives from backbenchers. The Labour front bench continued throughout to regard the strike as damaging to their standing in the opinion polls. On 31 July 1984, after the strike had lasted 21 weeks, it was Opposition Day in the Commons when Labour could choose the subject of the main debate. The miners' strike continued to dominate the media. The motion which Kinnock spoke to was one which condemned the general industrial and employment policies of the Thatcher government, and he made only a brief reference to the miners' strike towards the end of his speech; and this, let it be repeated, at a time when there was only one issue that everyone in the country was talking about.

The miners' strike was not only a turning point for the Labour Party, it was also a central question for the Thatcher government, and we now know the extraordinary lengths to which the Government employed its intelligence services to undermine the position of the NUM leadership. The Labour front bench certainly underestimated the importance of the miners' strike, but this was not a mistake the Tory government were ever going to make. The propertied classes always have a very clear appreciation of *their* enemies, and matters of constitutional propriety are never allowed to interfere with their plans. All this was clearly understood by the author of *Parliamentary Socialism*, and what happened to the Labour movement in the 1980s was wholly in line with his analysis of both the unemployed nineteen thirties and the more affluent nineteen fifties. His book *Socialism for a Sceptical Age*, published a few months after his death at the end of May 1994, takes forward a number of important themes already considered in his first work. He was concerned especially to emphasise the problems that would always be encountered in parliamentary democracies by social movements engaged in serious reform of one kind or another: not, he emphasised, necessarily of a direct socialist kind. As he noted in *Socialism For a Sceptical Age*, there was

> a general failure on the part of many writers on the Left to take seriously the existence of a formidable structure of power in capitalist democratic regimes, and the lengths to which

people will go in order to preserve it. To ignore this allows any amount of model construction; but the construction, however attractive, lacks any basis in reality. Revolutionaries may have tended to under-estimate what is possible within the compass of capitalist democracy; but social-democrats have tended to be blind to the severity of the struggle which major advances in the transformation of the social order in progressive directions must entail. Of course, all such warnings can be airily dismissed as left-wing paranoia, but this is to fly in the face of extensive experience. (p. 163)

There have been other trends in the years since *Parliamentary Socialism* was written that confirm the analysis it offered. The failure to develop new directions of a radical kind has meant that the sober judgements of the closing pages of the 1961 volume – summed up in the title of the closing chapter, 'The Sickness of Labourism' – have been further augmented. Miliband had emphasised the importance of the trade union relationship, and when full allowance is made for the political character of much of the union leadership the argument for the close connection between the organised working class and the Labour Party remains unaffected; except that it was precisely the trade union connection that Kinnock was anxious to weaken, and there is little evidence that the post-Kinnock direction of the Labour Party is moving in any other way. Miliband's last book, *Socialism for a Sceptical Age*, is in a number of respects a further development of *Parliamentary Socialism*, although it was not planned or written as a continuous history. Inevitably, of course, since the volume had two main purposes, one, the argument for a socialist society in contemporary terms, and two, an examination of the many political problems that would be encountered in achieving a democratic socialist objective the history of the radical movements of the twentieth century formed the backcloth for the elaboration of his analysis. The exposition is grounded in historical experience, and again and again reference is made, has to be made, to the politics of the past and their relevance, whether qualified or not, to the present and future. Throughout this final volume Miliband relates what has gone before to an understanding of the present and what might develop in the future. The quotation which follows is an example. He is asking the question whether there would appear to be any prospect of the existing social-democratic parties moving towards more radical policies, and he notes that history does not offer much consolation to those who look for change. But he continued:

Against this, there are a number of different factors to be taken into account. One of the most important of these is the end of the Cold War, which has lifted the immense burden it had placed on the Left ever since 1945. Social democratic leaders had played a major role in the containment of left militancy in the interwar years, particularly when it was Communist-inspired or led. This role became ever more pronounced after World War II; and it turned social-democratic parties into invaluable allies of conservative parties. On all major issues, notably over foreign policy and defence, there existed in fact a fundamental consensus between social democratic leaders and their conservative opponents*. The Communist bogey was a most valuable weapon in the hands of social democratic leaders.

Its elimination does not mean that their struggle against critics on the Left is now over; but it removes from the reckoning an argument against left critics that was used to great effect. 'Trotskyite' and other derogatory labels do not have quite the charge which 'Communist' and 'fellow traveller' once had. (p. 146)

These passages were followed by a discussion which Miliband emphasised was the most important factor in the future development of social democratic parties, and this was the failure of market economies 'to tackle effectively a vast range of massive problems, from unemployment to the deterioration of public and collective services': in general the deterioration in the quality of life for the mass of the people. He accepted that the outlook in this context was somewhat bleak at the time of writing, but he insisted that at some time in the future the problems and difficulties of capitalist society would provide serious opportunities for parties of the Left. Whether those opportunities would be taken would depend upon the ways in which Left politics had been developing over the previous years. He noted that the decline of the Communist Parties 'for all their weaknesses and derelictions' had represented a marked impoverishment for the Left in general; and he could have gone on to remark that in the British case the 1980s represented the first decade in the twentieth century when there was no effective political organisation to the left of the Labour Party that was developing a distinctive socialist perspective, and at the same time creating the organisational channels through which ideas and policies could be transmitted into the main groupings of the Labour Party.

There was one particular matter in this context that was taken for granted in *Parliamentary Socialism* but which received important emphasis in his last book. The early history of the socialist movement in Britain centred upon the propagandist activities of groups of devoted socialists in different towns and regions. Political education was the key to the spread of socialist ideas. The street corner meeting, the production and sale of pamphlets, the distribution of leaflets and the door to door canvassing of socialist candidates in elections, local and national: these were the recognised activities of socialists, and they educated, agitated and organised. It has always been accepted that socialist propaganda is a central necessity of the socialist movement. The forms of propaganda change, and the radio, cinema and especially television have ended most of the forms of political activity that were typical of the past. The matter was not commented on in any marked degree in *Parliamentary Socialism*, being taken for granted, but *Socialism for a Sceptical Age* made the point several times that political

---

*In a footnote to the text quoted above was written: 'The consensus also applied to the bitter and bloody struggle against movements of colonial liberation in former colonial possessions; and this struggle too was waged against 'Communism'. The French Socialist Party in particular was implicated after World War II in the savage wars waged by the French Republic in Algeria and Indochina; but other social democratic parties in colonial countries, for instance the Labour Party in Britain, were also involved in such wars.'

parties of the Left have an indispensable role in the creation and development of a counter-hegemonic culture to that of the dominant groups in society. He emphasised how crucial it was for the success of any reforming government to have prepared the ground well; to have brought together the economic and social grievances and to have presented the alternatives: 'how much . . . its philosophy and its policies have come to be part, again in Gramsci's terms, of 'the common sense of the epoch', at least for a large part of the population; and how much in consequence the vote which brings it to office is not only a vote against hitherto governing parties, but a positive vote for what the government proposes'.

Parliamentary Socialism was a key text in the revival of socialist ideas in the 1960s and 1970s. It offered for the first time an extended analysis of why the great hopes of 1945 had so quickly evaporated into the dull conservative decade of the nineteen fifties; and it fitted the great stirrings of political conscience which came with the nuclear debate at the end of the decade. Most of Ralph Miliband's writings in the three decades which followed were concerned with the class nature of society and the role of the State. It was his last book, *Socialism for a Sceptical Age,* that brought together much of his thinking about the manifold problems of agency and power for a more progressive future, and his analysis needs to be read together with the historical understanding of his first major work.

BIBLIOGRAPHICAL NOTES

The first requirement is obvious: to read, or re-read, *Parliamentary Socialism*, first published by Allen and Unwin in 1961 and then re-issued by Merlin Press in 1964, and in a second edition, with a postscript, in 1972. As indicated in the text, the historical background that Ralph Miliband analysed down to the end of the 1950s has a central bearing on the arguments of his latest work, *Socialism for a Sceptical Age,* (Polity Press, 1994).

The flow of writing on socialist history and socialist themes that began from around the time that *Parliamentary Socialism* was first published has continued to our own day. For the political developments which followed the revelations of Khrushchev in 1956 about Stalin's regime, and the invasion of Hungary which came eight months later, there is a solid account in Lin Chun, *The British New Left* (Edinburgh University Press, 1993) although it can be expected that a good many other analyses will follow. David Coates, *The Labour Party and the Struggle for Socialism* (Cambridge, 1975) covers the same ground as did Ralph Miliband – and is much influenced by him – but continues the story into the 1970s. Later the same author published *Labour in Power? A Study of the Labour Government 1974–1979*. There are two other important marxist analyses, both published in 1976: David Howell, *British Social Democracy* (Croom Helm) and Leo Panitch, *Social Democracy and Industrial Militancy* (Cambridge). A less politically committed text but useful for its careful documentation is Patrick Seyd, *The Rise and Fall of the Labour Left* (Macmillan, 1987). There are four books for the 1980s that are required reading. The first two are concerned with the politics of the Labour Party. Gregory Elliott's *Labourism and the English Genius: The Strange Death of Labour England?* (1993) provides a well-written historical background to the 1980s; and Richard Heffernan and Mike Marqusee, *Defeat from the Jaws of Victory: Inside Kinnock's Labour Party* (1992) offers a devastating critique of the whole decade and most particularly after Kinnock's assumption of leadership of Labour in 1983. Both books are published by

Verso, as is one of the most important books ever published concerning the machinations of those who control state power, Seumas Milne's *The Enemy Within: M15, Maxwell and the Scargill Affair* (1994), is a closely documented analysis of the infamies of British Intelligence operating at the behest of their political bosses – of whom Margaret Thatcher was chief – a campaign of lies, distortions, disinformation and surveillance against Arthur Scargill and the National Union of Mineworkers that matches the worst accounts of the FBI under Hoover. This decade of the 1980s was not only a period of marked political backsliding from even the moderation of previous decades, it was also one in which many of the intellectual Left, much influenced by Paris, moved away from classical marxism to various forms of intellectual and political agreement with the existing order of society. Ellen Meiksins Wood, *The Retreat from Class. A New 'True' Socialism* (Verso, 1986) provided a succinct, adroit analysis of these new intellectual trends which remains the best introduction we have to date.

HAROLD LASKI'S SOCIALISM*

by Ralph Miliband

Editor's note

*This essay, originally commissioned in 1958 or 1959 for a Fabian Society pamphlet but never published, offers unique insights into the influence of Laski on Miliband's thought. It reveals much about Miliband's own thinking in the late 1950s just as he was writing *Parliamentary Socialism*. Reading it today demonstrates, moreover, considerable parallels in many aspects of both their approaches to socialism over the course of their lives. In addition to so many of the themes and ideas in this essay having direct relevance for contemporary debates, the publication of Miliband's manuscript on Laski at this time contributes to the revival of interest in Laski occasioned by the two biographies published in 1993 (I. Kramnick and B. Sheerman, *Harold Laski: A Life on the Left* and M. Newman, *Harold Laski. A Political Biography*, both of which were reviewed by Miliband in *New Left Review* 200, July/August, 1993). For reasons of length, and in light of matters covered in the recent biographies, a brief biographical sketch, near the beginning, and a section on 'Russia, America and World Peace', towards the end, have been omitted from Miliband's original manuscript.

I. Introduction

There are many different facets to Harold Laski's life. He was a teacher and a scholar; a political theorist who was also deeply involved in the politics of his day; a pamphleteer and a practical reformer; the friend and counsellor of the powerful and eminent, and also of the humble and the anonymous.

Laski brought to these activities an encyclopaedic learning, a vivid imagination and a tireless industry, the force of a warm and generous personality, an impish sense of humour and a sharp wit.

These gifts and the manner in which they were exercised have already been depicted, most notably in Mr Kingsley Martin's memoir of Laski's personal and public life.[1] It is not my purpose in this essay to tell that story once again. Nor am I here concerned with a detailed analysis of all of Laski's writings.[2] My object is to examine Laski's main ideas on Socialism.

Laski was an immensely prolific writer. The books, essays, pamphlets and articles which flowed from his pen ranged over a wide field of history and jurisprudence, political theory, social philosophy and public administration. Yet, whatever the subject which Laski was discussing at any particular moment, it is social change and socialism which form, directly or by implication, the underlying themes of most of his writings, just as the cause of socialism provided the impulse for most of his activities.

It is his treatment of these themes which gave Laski so remarkable an influence on the intellectual configuration of his times. For a period of some twenty-five years, Laski contributed more to the discussion of the meaning and challenge of Socialism than any other English Socialist. From 1925, when his *Grammar of Politics* was published, until his death in 1950, countless men and women were given a new insight into the problems of their times because they heard or read Laski.

Much of Laski's most important work was deeply influenced by the sombre events of the nineteen thirties, and that grim decade, together with the ideas and attitudes which it engendered, now appears scarcely less remote than many earlier periods of history. Every generation tends to view its problems as wholly new and therefore incapable of understanding, let alone of solution, in terms of a diagnosis fashioned for an earlier era. The reaction to the thirties, which has been much enhanced by the propensity to breast beating of many who were intellectually alive at that time and who are still alive today has now been in full swing for a number of years. As part of that reaction, it is now fashionable to believe that Laski's writings are mostly irrelevant to the problems we ourselves now confront. I believe this to be a mistaken view.

In essence, Laski sought throughout his life to explore the conditions in which fundamental social changes which he deemed urgent and desirable in our society might be realised without the obliteration of freedom; how, furthermore, socialism as a form of economic and social organisation might be combined with political democracy. These questions remain of central importance in our own day. Compared to them, the controversy between socialists and the various schools of conservative thought assumes an air of even greater futility. For, in intellectual terms at least, the question is no longer whether we are, or should be, moving towards some form of socialist society, but how best it should be brought about.

This is why, now more than ever, socialists need to understand the meaning of their purpose and the implications of their aims. To such an understanding, Laski's writings make a substantial contribution. To none of these questions did Laski provide a final or conclusive answer. Nor, let it be said at once, are his writings free from ambiguities and contradictions, the more so since his views evolved substantially over the course of the years. Laski's supreme merit was to ask uncomfortable questions and to provide an illuminating commentary on problems to which no Socialist can afford to remain indifferent . . .

II. The Nature of Socialism

Two dominant convictions were expressed in Laski's early writings, on which the impact of World War One is easily discernible. The first was that concentration of power in the state was fatal to liberty; the second was that the War had made more urgent than ever the achievement of large scale social and economic reforms.

The War's first effect was greatly to enhance the suspicion Laski had learned to harbour of the State's claim to the undivided allegiance of its citizens. Despite the variety of their subject matter, the essays which make up his first books are mainly concerned with a refutation of doctrines of allegiance based upon the view that the State had any inherent, prescriptive or even prior claim to obedience. In accordance with the political pluralism to which he was then committed he insisted that the State was only one association among many; whatever its legal right to enforce obedience, that right, as such, was devoid of any ethical validation. Like every other association, the State was always in competition for the allegiance of its members. It was always on trial. There was nothing to warrant the assertion that the verdict must necessarily be rendered in its favour. The nature of that verdict must always depend on its performance and on its ability to convince its members that their own good was involved in their acceptance of its commands. The price of freedom was contingent anarchy.

In a sense, Laski remained a political pluralist all his life. 'I confess to a frank fear', he said in 1949, 'of what I used to call the monist state'. He never ceased to view the Great Leviathan as a dangerous beast, never to be trusted, whatever its announced intentions.

Yet, he soon came to believe that political pluralism, in its insistence that the State was only one association among many, was entirely inadequate as a realistic description of the State's real nature. However much it might be necessary to refuse to the State the exalted status it claimed, its nature could not be determined by the mere denial of that status. Something else was needed.

But there was, he perceived, another grave flaw in the pluralist theory. For it made impossible the recognition of the fact that the State alone was capable, in the world of the twentieth century, of serving as the instrument of fundamental social and economic reform.

The War, besides enhancing Laski's distrust of the State, had also given a much sharper edge to his conviction that there was an imperative need for vast improvements in the condition of the working classes. 'The main result of the recent conflict', he wrote, 'will be to bring the working classes to a new position in the State.'[3] That new position, Laski did not doubt, would find political expression in the growing importance of the Labour Party, which he had immediately joined on his return from the United States. The Labour Party had, in 1918, declared itself a Socialist party, bent upon the transformation of Britain into a Socialist commonwealth. A new social order was to be built upon the ruins of the old. What was to be the nature of that social order? How was it to be achieved? These are the questions which form the underlying themes of Laski's major theoretical work of the twenties, the *Grammar of Politics*, which was published in 1925.

The *Grammar of Politics* is one of the most comprehensive attempts ever made by an English Socialist to give concrete meaning to the ideals of the Labour Party. Sidney Webb, who was not given to exuberant praise, called it a 'great book'.[4] The modern reader is unlikely to go quite so far, not least because so many of the ideas of the *Grammar* have now been accepted as part of the common currency of contemporary thought. But there can be no doubt that it remains one of the few fundamental 'texts' of English Socialism.

The basic postulate from which Laski starts is that the purpose of social organisation is to secure to each member of society the fullest opportunities for the development of his or her personality, subject only to the impediment of natural aptitude and ability.

Such a society presupposes the recognition of rights to each of its members. Among those rights, the right of free speech and of assembly, of equality before the law, irrespective of race, colour and creed, must obviously figure high. But, Laski insisted, to these must be added other, scarcely less important rights, such as the right to work and to earn an adequate wage, to leisure and to education, to protection against insecurity, sickness and old age, as well as the right of the workers to share in the management and control of their enterprise.

Freedom, in any positive sense, has no meaning without rights. But neither freedom, nor rights, said Laski, could have more than a formal and contingent meaning in a society fundamentally divided between those who lived by their ownership of the means to life and those whose livelihood was wholly derived from their labour. In such a society, reward must, in the main, depend upon ownership and not function, upon property and not service.

In such a society too, the use of material resources must depend upon their owners' decisions; and those decisions were based on the search for profit, and not on considerations of public welfare. The conclusion was inescapable that so long as the ownership and control of property remained concentrated in private and irresponsible hands, so long must the lives of the vast majority remain stunted and mean, whatever their formal rights.

The good society must be based on an 'approximate economic equality' between its members. 'It is only by making identity the basis of our institutions, and differences an answer to the necessities of social functions that we can make our society call into play the individuality of men.'[5] This was impossible as long as the existing system of property remained unaltered.

At the time he wrote the *Grammar of Politics*, Laski was still extremely cautious in his approach to the reform of that system. 'I do not', he wrote, 'envisage anything like the disappearance of private enterprise'.[6] He was then content to advocate the nationalisation of 'obvious' monopolies and the rigorous control by the State of the operation of private enterprise. 'But', he said, 'Men will still be able to make fortunes', 'although they will be subject to heavy taxation upon income, and still heavier duties upon their estates at death.'[7] And the product of that heavier taxation would be used by the State for a wide extension of social services.

'The achievement of greater economic equality would involve', said Laski, 'slow and painful experiment'. No doubt, the men of property would bitterly resent the erosion of their rights and privileges. But the gradual nature of the change and the persistent pressure of the working classes, speaking through the Labour Party, upon the democratic state guaranteed ultimate success. The road might be long and the journey slow but that the destination would be reached was not in doubt.

The optimism which pervades the *Grammar of Politics* stems in a large measure from the view Laski then took of the nature of the State. 'The State', he said in the *Grammar*, is 'the organisation for enabling the mass of men to realise the social good on the largest possible scale';[8] it is 'the final depository of the social will'.[9] Given this view there was no good reason to suppose that the State would fail to respond to the demands of the majority of its members.[10] It is only incidentally that a different note is allowed to creep in. One of the major results of an economically unequal society, Laski suggests, is to gear the State's purpose to the interest of those who hold economic power. The State, in such a society, 'is compelled to use its instruments to protect the property of the rich from invasion by the poor.' But the implications of this notion which were so greatly to concern Laski in later years, are not explored in the *Grammar*.

The political problem which worried Laski at the time was of a different order. The realisation of the social good, in the sense in which it is defined in the *Grammar*, must obviously lead to a vast increase in the State's power. To deny the State that increase of power was to deny the possibility of reform. The question was how both to grant the State the powers it needed and yet to control the exercise of that power.

Laski sought the answer in the notion of power as federal. Authority, in the growingly collectivist society, must be widely dispersed. The State must allow and indeed encourage the widest possible degree of popular participation in the exercise of power and responsibility. Ordinary men and women must be called upon, through a multiplicity of associations, to share in the making of decisions which affected them as producers, as consumers and as citizens. In this sense, democratic pluralism must be a fundamental feature of any society based on freedom and equality. Laski could only take that view because he deeply believed that ordinary people were capable of making a significant contribution to the shaping of their own destinies. At the root of his thought, there is a profound conviction that there existed in society reserves of civic responsibility and talent which it would be one of the major purposes of a new social order to release.

Laski remained faithful throughout his life to the ultimate objectives he had set out in the *Grammar of Politics*. But there was also much about the book which he found increasingly inadequate as a realistic description of the political processes as the twenties gave way to the thirties.

Until the late twenties, Laski was a Fabian Socialist; from then onwards, he considered himself a Marxist. So much confusion has come to surround that last label that some precise explanation of what it involves in relation to Laski is essential if one is to understand what he was about.

A great deal too much can be made of Laski's 'conversion' to Marxism. Laski did not suddenly 'discover' Marx at the end of the twenties. He had wrestled with him as early as 1921 and found his system unattractive and unconvincing.[11] But the bitter social and industrial climate of the twenties, allied to the failure of the first Labour Government and the experience of the General Strike, led him to a progressively more favourable view of Marx's diagnosis. By 1927, he was describing Marx as the most powerful social analyst of the nineteenth century.[12]

The Great Depression completed the process. To Laski as to countless other critics of capitalism, the Great Depression seemed to offer conclusive proof of what had hitherto been little more than a plausible hypothesis. The intensity and the duration of the Depression appeared to confirm the Marxist prediction that the capitalist system was inherently incapable of overcoming its contradictions. It was now demonstrating, at the price of fearful human suffering, its inability to make use of the formidable productive power it had itself brought into being. Capitalism had become an intolerable drag upon the use of capital. Laski was careful to point out that the failure of the system 'would not be dramatic enough to have an intense or wide effect in a short space of time';[13] in fact he considered that its decline might be appreciably slowed down by the kind of State intervention, of which the New Deal in the United States was an early example. But, he maintained, though the decline might be slowed down, the trend itself was unavoidable.

Laski's Marxism involved much more than a simple acceptance of the validity of Marx's prediction of the inevitable decline of capitalism. On the other hand, it involved much less than the acceptance as scientifically true of that vast, all-embracing structure known as dialectical materialism. In that sense Laski was never a Marxist at all.[14] In essence, what Laski took from Marx is contained in one single passage of the latter's writings, which so deeply coloured Laski's later thinking that it is worth quoting in full. I refer to the famous passage of Marx's Preface to *A Contribution to the Critique of Political Economy*:

> In the social production which men carry on they enter into definite relations that are indispensable and independent of their will; these relations of production correspond to a definite stage of development of their material powers of production. The totality of these relations of production constitutes the economic structure of society – the real foundation, on which legal and political superstructures arise and to which definite forms of social consciousness correspond. The mode of production of material life determines the general character of the social, political and spiritual processes of life. It is not the consciousness of men that determines their being, but on the contrary their social being determines their consciousness. At a certain stage of their development, the material forces of production in society come in conflict with the existing relations of production or – what is but a legal expression for the same thing – with the property relations within which they had been at work before. From forms of development of the forces of production, these relations turn into their fetters. Then occurs a period of social revolution.[15]

These formulations of course represent the essence of the Marxist interpretation of history. 'No serious observer', Laski said about it in 1948, 'supposes that the materialist conception of history is free from difficulties, or that it solves all the problems involved in historical interpretation. But no serious observer either can doubt that *it has done more in the last hundred years to provide a major clue to the causes of social change than any other hypothesis that has been put forward.*'[16]

These lines, as so much else which Laski wrote on Marxism, show well enough that he was not a convert to a new secular faith. Historical materialism to him was a supremely useful tool of analysis, not a mental straight-jacket.

It could hardly be doubted that Europe and the world *had* by the early thirties entered upon an era of crisis. The implications of that fact could not be other than immense and we shall see presently how Laski sought to define them. But the first consequence of his acceptance of historical materialism as a fruitful hypothesis was to give far greater precision to his view of what the achievement of a socialist order entailed.

The ownership and control of property had long occupied a place of importance in Laski's thought. He now placed property at the centre of the social equation. For, if it was indeed true that the factor which basically determined the character of society was its mode of production and its

property relations, it logically followed that any Socialist seriously interested in really changing the social order must, above all else, seek the
socialisation of the means to life. Without that socialisation, the evils in
capitalist society which Socialists condemn might be attenuated, but they
could not be abolished. Without it too, the property relations of a capitalist
society might be mitigated, but they must continue to exercise a predominant impact on the character of society. Socialism, in other words,
required the socialisation of property; on any other view, it amounted to no
more than social reform.

This is not to say that Laski, by the end of the twenties, had become the
prisoner of an all-or-nothing, apocalyptic mentality, the most obvious
consequence of which is always romantic futility. What he was concerned
to stress was that Socialists and the Labour Party must cease to delude
themselves with the belief that specific measures of social reform were
synonymous with Socialism. Unless these measures formed part of a
broader strategy designed to achieve the transfer of the means of
production from private into social ownership, they must fail to eliminate
the waste and inefficiency, the social inequality and the spiritual meanness
of a capitalist order of society.

Such an assertion, it is worth noting, was entirely consistent with the
Labour Party's own doctrine, since the constitution it had adopted in 1918
made the 'common ownership of the means of production, distribution and
exchange' the basis upon which was to be secured 'for the workers by hand
or by brain the full fruits of their industry and the most equitable distribution thereof that may be possible.'[17]

But the experience of the first two Labour Governments had shown the
width of the gulf which separated theoretical intent from actual practice.
Their history, said Laski, could be defined as a determined attempt to evade
'the problem of the ownership and control of economic power which is the
root problem of equality';[18] 'the whole burden of its (Labour's) experience
since 1924 has been the inadequacy of any policy which leaves untouched
the fundamental basis of class relations.'[19]

It is of course true that the Labour Governments of 1924 and 1929 were
minority governments whose power of socialist initiative was narrowly
limited by the constricting mathematics of parliamentary strength. What
Laski was condemning was not their failure to achieve socialism, but their
obvious unwillingness even to begin the attempt. No doubt, they would
have suffered defeat had they done so, but their failure would have been far
less ignominious and debilitating than the defeats they suffered in any case.
Socialists who had no intention of acting upon Socialist principles should
leave the administration of a capitalist state to those who believed in the
virtues of capitalism.

By the end of the twenties, Laski had arrived at the view that Socialism, in any meaningful sense, meant the disappearance of existing class relations and that their disappearance was impossible without the socialisation of the means to life. Much of his thinking in the thirties was devoted to an exploration of the momentous implications of that view.

III. Capitalism and the Socialist Challenge

With the Great Depression, the collapse of the second Labour Government in 1931 and the rise of Nazism, Laski ceased to feel the confidence in the inevitability of a gradual evolution towards socialism, which had been at the core of the *Grammar of Politics*. The constitutional crisis of 1931, he believed, had raised in a dramatic form the question whether 'evolutionary socialism (has) deceived itself in believing that it can establish itself by peaceful means within the ambit of the capitalist system'.[20] The task which Socialists set themselves, he now insisted, was one of immense difficulty. 'To transform the ultimate economic foundations of society', he wrote in 1932, 'is the most hazardous enterprise to which men can lay their hand.'[21] Nor, obviously, was he referring to the multitude of problems connected with the creation of a new system of economic organisation. These problems, though real and grave, were, in any adequate perspective, much less formidable than the political hazards which the attempt to transform capitalism out of existence must entail.

The one sure lesson of history, Laski now said, was that violence had always been the midwife of fundamental social change. Faced with a resolute challenge to those of their privileges which they deemed beyond surrender, ruling classes had always sought to meet that challenge by suppression. The English, the French and the Russian revolutions were only the most conspicuous examples of a pattern to which there had so far in history been no exception. New systems of class relations had always been born amidst the smoke of battle and christened in human blood.

The thirties of the twentieth century hardly suggested that our own epoch was destined to inaugurate a new pattern of social change. For, when all else had been said about the specific characteristics of Italian Fascism and German Nazism, the fact remained that both Mussolini and Hitler had only been able to hoist themselves to power because of the support and encouragement they had received from Italy and Germany's respective ruling classes. And they had received that support because the essence of their programme was the destruction of democratic institutions, the functioning of which had come to present to those ruling classes a threat of social subversion they no longer felt capable of meeting within the framework of democratic institutions.

Both Fascism and Nazism might assert the need for a new social order. Yet, as Laski pointed out, 'the suppression of democratic institutions, both in Italy and in Germany (had) been accomplished without any alteration in the economic relationship of classes in either country.'[22]

Other instances of the same process were not lacking in the Europe of the 1930's. The special brand of Catholic authoritarianism which Franco sought to impose upon the ruins of the liberal Spanish Republic showed well enough that different countries might develop their own national forms of conservative reaction. But, in Spain as in Germany and Italy, it was the privileged interests who had eagerly welcomed the suppression of political democracy because of the challenge to property which it made possible. Nor was it possible to explain in any other terms the eagerness with which, some years later, so large a segment of the French ruling class had welcomed defeat and accepted collaboration with an enemy who might hold France in subjection but also offered a guarantee against social subversion.

Fascism, whatever its peculiar national variants, was everywhere the enemy not only of Socialism but of political democracy. The sympathy which it had encountered among the privileged orders the world over underlined the dangers which democracy, everywhere, confronted in the epoch of capitalist decline. More clearly than any other phenomenon, the emergence and spread of Fascism betokened the fact that political liberalism and parliamentary democracy were a luxury which a contracting capitalist order could ill afford.

Both, Laski argued in one of his most scholarly studies in the history of ideas,[23] had been the product of an attempt on the part of a nascent capitalist class to wrest from a landed aristocracy at least a share of political power. 'New material conditions ... gave birth to new social relationships; and, in terms of these a new philosophy was evolved to afford a national justification for the new world which had come into being.'[24]

The thesis was of course not new. The real interest of *The Rise of European Liberalism* lay in Laski's brilliant demonstration of the manner in which liberalism, as the ideology of the middle classes, had been used as a justification for the removal of the multitude of barriers which prevented them from taking advantage of new economic opportunities.

The spokesmen of liberalism had preached individualism and freedom against the antiquated claims of frozen hierarchies; they had upheld reason and tolerance against superstition and prejudice; they had glorified progress against stagnation, enterprise against custom, scientific enquiry against consecrated ignorance, constitutionalism against arbitrariness.

The triumph of their ideas, said Laski, had represented 'a real and profound progress.'[25] Without that triumph, 'the number of those whose demands upon life would have been satisfied must have remained much smaller than it has been'; 'that', he added in a significant phrase, 'is the supreme test by which a social doctrine must be judged.'[26]

Liberalism had, of course, undergone profound modifications in the course of its long evolution. Initially grounded in the denial of the State's responsibility in economic life, it had moved to a more positive view of limited State action. Starting with a narrowly restricted concept of political participation, which excluded from effective citizenship the vast majority of those devoid of property, it had come to include universal suffrage as a vital part of its meaning.

But liberalism had never ceased to retain the essential stamp of its origin. The political democracy it helped to foster, said Laski, 'was established on the unstated assumption that it would leave untouched the private ownership of the means of production.'[27] That assumption had, save marginally, remained unquestioned so long as capitalism had seemed to be synonymous with economic growth and material progress. Once that ceased to be the case, political democracy must increasingly be used as a means of seeking to effect a radical change in capitalist class relations. Political democracy, in other words, must, by the law of its own being, seek the achievement of social and economic democracy. But in doing so, it was driven to invade an area of life which liberal doctrine had always held to be sacrosanct. Thus must the fears which had haunted so many of the intellectual progenitors of liberalism come to be realised. Property must, to an increasing extent, become a major target of attack on the part of those devoid of it. What this meant was that the men who had controlled the purpose of the State by virtue of their ownership of property would be required to surrender that control, so that their power and privilege might be taken from them.

The State, Laski now stressed, was not a neutral institution standing over and above contending economic classes within the social framework. It was the supreme coercive agency for the maintenance of a given set of class relations.[28] In every instance where a ruling class had been threatened in its fundamental privileges, it had sought to use the State to repel the threat; where it had failed, it had always sought to recapture the State power by the organisation of counter-revolution. In either case, the result had always been violence. 'A social order whose way of life is challenged will not easily accept the methods of a debating society.'[29]

In such a perspective, the most vital question which confronted a party bent on a radical transformation of class relations was whether such a transformation could in fact be achieved by peaceful means.

To that question, Fascism had, in a number of countries, already provided an emphatically negative answer. But in none of the countries where it had prevailed had parliamentary government and democratic institutions been more than relatively recent acquisitions.

Unlike those countries, Britain had a unique record of parliamentary

continuity and government by discussion. With, and through, her political
system, she had weathered acute social, political and economic storms.
What was the secret of that achievement? And how likely was it to be
repeated in the age of capitalist decline? These are the fundamental
questions Laski had already asked some years earlier[30] and which he asked
again with even more anxious insistence in his *Parliamentary Government
in England* (1938).

It is, I think, true to say that until the publication of *Parliamentary
Government in England* no-one since Bagehot had seriously sought to
relate the English Constitution and its workings to Britain's social and
economic system. Its uniquely successful power of adaptation to changing
conditions had been variously ascribed to the national genius for
compromise, to the rule of law and the independence of the judiciary, to the
existence of a constitutional monarchy or to the harmonious combination
of Cabinet rule with parliamentary control, and so on. Laski started from
different premises. All these features of the Constitution, he suggested,
were more in the nature of results than of causes. For the causes of the
Constitution's adaptability, one must look deeper into the foundations of
society of which the Constitution was the expression.

Britain had not been a political democracy until the first decades of this
century. From the end of the seventeenth until this time, the foundations of
society had never been seriously called into question. Echoing Lord
Balfour's famous words, Laski argued that 'until our own day we have
been governed in all fundamental matters by a single party in the state
since 1689.'[31] That party was the party of property.

It had not, obviously enough, been an homogeneous party. Its diverse
groupings had often been locked in conflict, even bitter conflict. Issues like
the Reform Bill of 1832 and the Parliament Bill of 1911, both of which
represented a real shift of power within the propertied classes, had strained
the Constitution to breaking point. In one fairly recent instance, that of
Home Rule and the fate of Ulster, one section of the party of property had
even been willing (and the willingness was not without ominous significance) to encourage preparations for armed resistance and civil war against
the constitutionally elected government of the day.[32]

Yet, it remained true that none of these issues, however violent the
passions they had temporarily aroused, had ever brought into question the
private ownership of property. The contending factions had always found
that, however real their divergences, they were fundamentally agreed on
that issue, which, as Harrington and Madison had said long before Marx,
was the greatest of all sources of faction in society. Beyond its divisions,
the party of property had always found unity in the perception that,
transcending its own quarrels, there loomed a far more serious conflict
with the unprivileged masses who remained excluded from the area of

economic, social and political power it itself occupied. That unity of those who ruled Britain had, above all other factors, been the secret of Britain's success in the maintenance of constitutionalism and government by discussion.

Even so, the achievement this represented was not one which Laski sought to minimize nor was he in the least blind to the importance of the political tradition which has thus been bred in British political life.

Nor did he underestimate the capacity, amounting to genius, which Britain's ruling classes had shown in acceding to the demands for social, economic and political reform with which they had been confronted. However reluctantly, they had always in the past had enough political sagacity to pay what Joseph Chamberlain had bluntly called ransom as the necessary price for the maintenance of their essential power and privilege.

There were, of course, many factors which had gone into the willingness to pay that price. But the most important of these, said Laski, had been the existence of an enormous fund from which to draw. Economic expansion had always provided the necessary reserves with which to buy off social discontent and to breed that sense of security which makes for generosity in politics.

The situation Laski held was now vastly changed. In a period of progressive decline, British capitalism was now less and less able to satisfy expectations which had, however, grown greater and greater. Here lay the seeds of social conflict far more acute and deep-rooted than any since the period of primitive capital accumulation which had straddled the decades of the Industrial Revolution, and during which the working classes had been far too weak to make an effective challenge to the power of property.

Now, however, the decline of British capitalism had led to the emergence of the Labour Party as a major political force. And, unlike the two parties which had traditionally alternated in office throughout the nineteenth century, the Labour Party was not agreed with its rivals on the fundamental issue of property. 'Between the frontiers of Conservative thought and those of the Labour Party in Great Britain, there is, in fact, a doctrinal abyss now unbridgeable in terms of the old continuity of policy.'[33] The two main parties, Laski claimed, were now divided by a fundamental antithesis of ultimate purpose. What was at stake was not a peripheral difference over specific policies, but the very essence of social and economic life.

In such a situation, 'the temptation to a party of property to use all its influence, direct and hidden, to rid itself of its opponents in an epoch of challenge appears to be immense.'[34] And, as the crisis of 1931 had already shown, its power to do so would be proportionate to the temptation. As he saw it, a Labour Government elected on a programme, the main feature of which would be proposals for extensive socialisation, would find mobilized against it powerful economic and financial interests, ready, by virtue of their power, to threaten it with economic dislocation and national bankruptcy. The press these interests controlled would be shrill in its denunciation of the Government and its single-minded endeavour would be to sow fear and mistrust among the people. Nor, he insisted, was it possible to ignore the likelihood that the party of property would seek to use whatever organs of the State power were amenable to its influence for the purpose of destroying the Government. The influence of a Court deeply steeped in conservatism might be invoked; the House of Lords would be relied on to use all of its remaining powers to thwart the loyalty to the government of the day of the higher Civil Service and of the upper reaches of the Army. Nor did the social background and political leanings of their personnel make it wildly improbable that these attempts would meet with success.

At the end of that road, there clearly lay conflict of a kind which must rapidly make impossible the continuation of the normal processes of constitutional government.

Laski did not suggest that the fears he expressed, and which were widely shared in the Labour movement during the thirties, were bound to be realised. But he certainly thought at the time that the likelihood of their being realised was extremely high. In the light of history and contemporary experience, they were at any rate not fears which Labour could afford to disregard.

Before proceeding further, it is necessary to look at some of the objections which, in the light of subsequent developments, have been raised against the whole of the foregoing analysis.

Without a doubt, much of that analysis, as presented here, without the refinements Laski brought to its support, strikes a jarring note on the contemporary ear. What was unorthodox but arguable in the very different climate of the thirties now tends to appear unreal. How unreal is it in fact?

The question is best considered by reference to three distinct and fundamental objections to Laski's analysis.[35]

There is firstly the objection that the economic view upon which the whole argument rests is entirely unsound. Capitalism, we are told, is not in decline; on the contrary, it has discovered the secret of perpetual expansion which Jeremiahs like Laski deemed to be entirely beyond its resources.

It is certainly true that Laski – like Marx before him – gravely underestimated the vitality and power of adaptability of the capitalist system of production.

It is of course equally true that capitalism has bought viability at the price of massive State intervention in the economic process. No Government, however much it might be wedded in theory to the 'free enterprise' system would now dare to put to the test the claim that capitalism functions best without State 'interference'. And it is no less important to note that the capitalist system has yet to prove that it can maintain a continuous level of effective demand without the massive military expenditure which has been such an important form of pump-priming in the post-war era.

Even so, it remains the case that, however wastefully, capitalist societies have been able – so far – to prevent the recurrence of the mass unemployment of the inter-war years. And, more positively, there can be no doubt that the growth in power and influence of the Trade Union and Labour movements have been such as to enable them to obtain within the ambit of capitalism, concessions substantial enough to lead to real improvements in the conditions of life of the working classes.

But, to take Britain alone, it surely requires heroic faith to maintain that the real social and economic advances of the post-war years have even begun to resolve the deep-seated economic ills which caused Laski to speak of capitalist decline. If anything, the economic sickness of our society has grown worse rather than better.

The impoverishment caused by the War, the post-war burden of military expenditure; the progressive disappearance of the colonial empire, the competition of more powerful capitalist economies and the emergence as new competitors of countries in the Communist bloc, the loss of British influence in Asia and the Middle East: these certainly tend, in a global perspective, to accentuate even more sharply the decline of Britain's economic status in the world. To check, even more, to reverse, that decline will be a back-breaking task. There is so far nothing to suggest that our present social and economic arrangements will be adequate to it.

Post-war capitalism has shown itself incapable of more than a partial and precarious resolution of the cycle of crises which have punctuated the years since the war. It has failed to remedy the technical obsolescence characteristic of much of British industry and it is clearly significant that where technical progress has been real, it has been, for the most part, the result either of nationalisation or of extensive state help to private industry. But it has, above all, failed to generate the kind of disciplined cooperative effort which can alone save Britain from the status of an impoverished client state, living on memories and interested charity.

The implication of all this is simple and obvious. It is that, though Laski's timing was faulty, his diagnosis was accurate enough. The decline of which he spoke may be much more protracted and its consequences therefore even less dramatic than he himself envisaged. But the decline itself can only be denied by a resolute escape from reality.

It has secondly been argued, among others by R. T. McKenzie, that Laski fundamentally misunderstood the nature and aims of the Labour Party.[36] The Labour Party, McKenzie contends, is in no sense that revolutionary intruder upon the British political scene which Laski's 'romantic view' had conjured up. He vastly exaggerated the ideological gap between the parties; he 'seemed somehow to have convinced himself that the Labour Party after its nominal conversion to Socialism in 1918 had become a militant political force determined, as he put it in 1938, "to launch a direct parliamentary attack upon the central citadel of capitalism"'; and equally determined, if that parliamentary attack were frustrated, to fulfil its purpose by other means.

The charge that Laski misunderstood the character of the Labour Party is easily refuted by his own writings on the subject. In truth, few people have so incisively condemned Labour's failure to distinguish social reform from socialism.[37]

Nor was Laski a remote observer, spinning utopian fantasies in an academic void. He was a member of the National Executive Committee of the Labour Party for some twelve crucial years. From his election to the N.E.C. in 1936 until he left it in 1948, he was in semi-permanent opposition to the orthodox majority within the directorate of the Labour Party.[38] More than most, he had ample opportunity to discover, as he often told his friends, that the conversion of a majority of the electorate to the support of fundamental social change would be a relatively easy task compared to the task of converting to Socialism many of the Labour Party's leaders.

In fact, what Laski argued was that, given capitalist decline, the Labour Party could not indefinitely postpone the choice of renouncing its principles or seeking to translate them into practical policies. In the first case, it could not avoid disruption, inside and outside the House of Commons. In the latter, it must expect capitalist resistance of a kind which would make the continuation of parliamentary government difficult in the extreme.

But, he also argued, the burden of extra-constitutional and anti-democratic action must be squarely laid at the door of the party of property. In the event of such action, the Labour Party must further choose between abdication and self-defence, which must clearly involve the suspension of the normal processes of constitutional government.[39] How he viewed that prospect we shall consider later.

The third objection to Laski's thesis rests on the belief that the Labour Party has already achieved a substantial part of its aims and that it has done so without any of the grim political consequences against which Laski warned the Labour Party in the thirties. The Conservative Party, in the period of Labour rule between 1945 and 1951, did not seek to upset the verdict of the electorate by anti-constitutional means; the House of Lords was not obstructive; on the contrary, it helped to improve Labour's legislative proposals; the Higher Civil Service and the Army served their

Labour masters with loyalty and devotion. Nothing, in other words, seriously disturbed the even tenor of British political life. For Laski's most stringent critic to date, the experience of those years conclusively proves 'a serious, if not fatal, blow to Laski's fundamental thesis – that the capitalist class will not allow the instruments of democracy to be used to effect a transformation of the property system.' Indeed, says Deane, 'the failure of this prediction shatters the whole structure of his political thinking,'[40] no less.

Writing in 1935, Laski had said that 'if a socialist government in Great Britain or France or the United States were peacefully to transform the basis of the property system from private to public hands the argument that fundamental changes could be accomplished by democratic means would be immensely strengthened.'[41] But 'that evidence', he had added, 'does not exist.'[42]

Deane's suggestion that it now does rests on an obvious misreading of Labour's achievements between 1945 and 1951. These achievements were real and Laski himself described them in 1949 as 'outstanding'.[43] But they are not the 'fundamental changes' of which Laski spoke and which define the meaning of socialism. Nor indeed does the Labour Party itself claim that they are. 'We are still two nations economically as well as socially' states one of its latest policy statements; 'half the nation owns little more than their personal and household effects; one per cent of the nation owns something like half the nation's private wealth.'[44] So much for Deane's Socialist revolution.

A Labour Government was able, in the propitious climate engendered by the war, to bring into public ownership the mines and a number of public utilities without encountering the kind of resistance which would have made parliamentary government impossible. But these enterprises were, by the time they were nationalised, at the periphery and not at the centre of capitalist power.[45] And it is certainly worthy of consideration that when Labour sought, somewhat half-heartedly, to move inward from that periphery by nationalising part of the steel industry, it immediately faced, inside and outside Parliament, opposition of an entirely different kind.[46]

The cooperation which a Labour Government can expect from private industry largely depends on the maintenance of a coincidence of interests. There is no good evidence to suggest that, if that coincidence did not exist, a Labour Government would not be faced with the bitterest hostility on the part of industry and its political spokesmen. There is, in fact, nothing to suggest that Laski was mistaken in warning, in the last months of his life, that:

> if there is a danger ahead, it seems to me to lie in the use of great financial and industrial power to prevent the will of the electorate being made effective by the government of its choice . . . in a period of rapid social change, it is a risk that might easily become a grave

one, for it represents the effort of men, who though small in numbers, have the immense powers great wealth confers, to challenge, by means outside the ordinary conventions of Parliamentary life, the right of the House of Commons to support the Government of the day, and put its measures upon the Statute book. That is the method which invites all parties to a disrespect for constitutional tradition.[47]

To transform the ultimate economic foundations of society remains 'the most hazardous enterprise to which men can lay their hands.' The experience of the post-war years does not 'prove' the willingness of the capitalist to abide by the verdict of the electorate when that verdict affects them deeply in their property and privileges.

What encouragement there is to be drawn from the experience of the post-war years derives from different factors. It derives primarily from the fact that Labour's power and influence in the country are immeasurably greater than they were in the 1930s. Given that power and influence, a Labour Government, carried to office by the support of the Labour movement and a majority of the electorate, and determined to carry out its announced programme, *might* be able to convince its opponents that resistance to its purposes was doomed to failure. And this was a possibility which Laski, even in the very different climate of the thirties, always refused wholly to discount. The fact of that refusal, and the reasons for it, are of central importance in Laski's thought.

IV. Socialism and Democracy

After the turn of the twenties, Laski was wont to proclaim himself a Marxist. But he was not at any time a Leninist, notwithstanding his admiration for Lenin's genius. He never accepted Lenin's assertions of the inevitability of violent revolution or his insistence that the most imperative duty of Socialists was to hasten its occurrence. Laski viewed Marxism, as I have suggested earlier, as the most useful of all tools of historical and social analysis; Leninism, on the other hand, he believed to be Marxism's strategic corollary in certain *specific* circumstances. As far as Laski was concerned, there was, so to speak, much more than a hyphen separating Marxism from Leninism.

Lenin's whole strategy, he held, was the outcome of the circumstances which must prevail in any society characterized by the absence of democratic habits and institutions. In such societies, it might well be true that the achievement of fundamental social change was inseparable from revolutionary violence.

But from the twenties onwards, Laski consistently condemned the attempts of the Third International to bind all working class parties to the acceptance of a strategy, the essential implication of which was that Bolshevik experience and Bolshevik practice were the only possible models for parties committed to the achievement of Socialism. Such uniformity, he predicted as early as 1927, could only be self-defeating; its price must be the stifling of political creativeness; its result must be failure to gain any insight into the specific needs and traditions of any particular country. The Communist strategy, he wrote some years later, was gravely deficient because it failed to take into account British differences from Russia or Germany or France. Long before the present Russian leaders began to speak of the possibility of reaching Socialism by roads other than that travelled by the Soviet Union, Laski was insisting that 'we shall wear our revolution with a comprehensive difference' and that 'the profound immersion of the British and American peoples in bourgeois liberalism has built a system of habits of which grave account will have to be taken.'[48] 'We cannot', he said again in 1947, 'escape from our own history any more than the Russians can escape from theirs ... we shall have to build on over our foundations and recognize that whatever lessons we apply from the experience of Russia, both the method of applying them, and the outcome of their application will seem British or French or American when our task has been accomplished.'

It is this insistence which often gives to Laski's writings on social change an appearance of contradictoriness and ambiguity. It would no doubt have been easier for him piously to avert his gaze from the real world in which class conflict and violence gave the lie to his earlier optimism that the inevitability of gradualness was the magic formula of social change; or, alternatively, to declare, with equal dogmatism, that only through revolutionary violence was the new social order to be brought into being. In taking up either of these positions, he would have run less risk of being misunderstood. He would also have been a much less interesting thinker. For the position he did take up made him, to a unique degree, the mirror of dilemmas and doubts which confronted a whole generation, and which have not ceased to be relevant to our own. What Laski asserted was that Leninist conclusions did not necessarily and inevitably follow from Marxist premises and that the achievement of fundamental social change could not therefore solely be viewed in a Bolshevik perspective. Ambiguity arose because he felt it necessary to argue at one and the same time against 'reformist' complacency and 'revolutionary' rigidity. Complacency might spell disaster; reliance on rigid formulae must result in divorce from living reality.

Laski never ceased to hold the view he expressed in 1933, that 'in a constitutional state, based upon universal suffrage, it is an obligation upon any party which proposes to disturb foundations to do so upon the basis that the will of the electorate favours its innovations.'[49] That obligation, in his view, did not merely stem from motives of expediency. Parliamentary democracy, as far as he was concerned, was not merely a convenient weapon to be used until it was possible to discard it. It was a system of government which Socialists, in the context of British institutions, must make it one of their principal aims to preserve. Socialists, he argued, must not delude themselves into thinking that its breakdown would represent anything but a tragedy.

Laski believed this because of the intense suspicion with which he always viewed the notion of the dictatorship of the proletariat.

Dictatorship must always rest on the employment of arbitrariness as an habitual mode of government. Repression, albeit in the name of the proletariat, could not be selective and discriminating. The iron fist of the dictatorship must crush all those (and the number was unlikely to be small) whose actions and speech either did not, or appeared not to, coincide at any particular moment with the immediate purposes and policies of the holders of power. Many years before Khrushchev admitted to the XXth Congress of the Bolshevik Party the magnitude of the 'mistakes' which had characterised the Stalin era, Laski was asserting that those 'mistakes' were implicit in the doctrine of the dictatorship of the proletariat. Laski was a libertarian to the root of his being. No-one who attended his lectures on the history of political ideas at the London School of Economics could fail to see that to him the drama of history was the struggle for toleration, for the exercise of reason in human affairs, for the extension of individual freedom.

It might well be that, if there was to be a Socialist regime in Russia at all, it must inevitably take the form of Police Socialism. But Russian experience itself was the best argument for seeking, in a country like Britain, to achieve fundamental social change by other means, which would make possible the preservation of liberties and political habits, the value of which it was blind folly for British Socialists to underestimate. This is why Laski was ready to see a Labour Government go to the utmost limit to conciliate its opponents, so long as conciliation did not involve a betrayal of its purposes. For, he said, 'to seek the maximum of consent on reasonable terms is to make the task of one's opponents a far more difficult one ... when a party puts its policy into operation in terms of an obvious effort to do all possible justice to those whose rights it proposes to redefine, the latter are deprived of an emotional support of high importance. It is one of the supreme virtues of parliamentary democracy that it offers, as no other system, the opportunity to create this atmosphere'.[50]

A Socialist government, said Laski, must not only govern *for* the people, but also *with* the people. It must, in other words, encourage that flowering of popular responsibility and initiative which are essential to the development of personality.

Much more clearly than in the twenties, Laski, in the last decade of his life, saw that the new social order would necessitate planning on an extensive scale and that the powers which a Socialist government must possess in the economic field were even vaster than he had earlier visualised. But the powers and controls which were essential to its purposes, he also saw, offered a fertile soil for the proliferation of power hierarchies, for whom the abuse of power must be a permanent temptation. Nor would abuse of power be less noxious because of the admirable intentions of those responsible for it.

In an increasingly scientific and technical age, moreover, it was inevitable that the expert should exercise an ever widening degree of influence in society. But, said Laski, 'no society ought to leave to experts the definition of its ends';[51] 'the problems which the statesman has to decide are not, in the last analysis, problems upon which the specialisation of the expert has any peculiar relevance.'[52] Power, in fact, must be responsible. And it would be responsible only in the degree to which it was widely shared and dispersed.

Returning in his later writings to a theme he had already explored in the *Grammar in Politics*, Laski insisted that authority in a Socialist society must be federal in character and combine the maximum amount of administrative decentralisation compatible with the necessary minimum of uniformity. Responsibility must be delegated to that multitude of organisations which, over the course of the years, had provided so large a training ground in the habits of democracy. A Socialist government must rely on the Trade Unions, the Cooperative societies and a multiplicity of similar popular institutions for the implementation of purposes the people themselves had had a share in defining. It must allow adaptation and experimentation, variety and initiative for, in the ultimate, 'authority . . . lives not by its power to command but by its power to convince.'[53]

No less, it must seek to create an alert and informed public opinion. It must tell the truth, and allow the truth to be told, even when that truth was unpalatable to those in authority. 'We must not play tricks with the proletariat', Jaurès once said in answer to George Sorel's elaborate plea for ideological mystification. This was a sentiment which Laski wholeheartedly endorsed. Nor was there anything in the history of the British working classes, he said, which suggested that trust and truth would not evoke the kind of response which would immeasurably strengthen the government which relied upon them. On the contrary, the talent for disciplined initiative and the civic devotion which they had so often shown in the past gave Britain an outstanding chance to fashion a social order that was both socialist and free.

All democrats are not – unaccountably – Socialists. And all Socialists are not necessarily democrats. Laski was both, out of a belief that, only the marriage of Socialism and democracy gave their full meaning to either term .

V. Socialism and the Intellectual

No academic intellectual of his time was more profoundly involved in the world of politics than Laski. Most of the time that he did not spend in strenuous academic work was devoted to political activity, whether for the Labour Party or for a variety of other political and semi-political organisations.[54] As a speaker of quite outstanding powers and as one of the most articulate spokesmen of Socialism, 'the Professor' was in constant demand. And the quite astonishing rapidity with which he could turn out a pamphlet, draft a memorandum, or set out a statement of policy, led to innumerable calls being made upon him – seldom in vain. Few men have ever been so generous with their gifts in the service of good causes.

To many people – and not least to many of his fellow academics – an involvement in vulgar politics as deep as that of Laski always seemed in exceedingly bad taste. And their antipathy was not diminished by the fact that he chose to be involved in a brand of politics they found particularly uncongenial.

Others, on the other hand, felt, for different reasons, that Laski was dissipating his gifts and energies in directions which left him too little time for scholarly reflection.

Whether this be so or not is not a question which admits of any conclusive answer. It is, in any case, of far greater interest to ask why Laski felt driven to involve himself as deeply as he did.

In that involvement, there certainly entered a personal eagerness to play a direct part in the shaping of events and to be near the centre of political power. But only mean minds will find such an explanation in the least sufficient. For, besides much else, it leaves out of account the fact that Laski consistently refused to grasp the many opportunities he had of embarking on a political career that would have given him far greater power than he could otherwise ever have hoped to achieve.

The explanation, I have no doubt, lies in a different direction. It lies, above all else, in the view which Laski took of the role of the intellectual in an age such as ours.

Laski's supreme conviction was that we had entered, from the time of the First World War and the Russian Revolution, upon a period of crisis in our civilisation greater than any since the long drawn out conflicts which had marked the end of the Middle Ages and the emergence of the modern world. The root of that crisis, he held, lay in the clash between those who sought to perpetuate an increasingly inadequate economic and social system and those who saw in its transcendence the promise of a more civilised social order.

As in other ages of revolution, one crucial expression of that crisis was the breakdown in our traditional system of values, and the doubt, pessimism and despair which so deeply coloured the mood of our epoch.

In such an age, the intellectual, be he scholar, novelist, poet or playwright, could not, in the nature of his vocation, remain outside the area of conflict. He might dearly wish to seek aloofness; but the aloofness he sought inevitably ranged him on the side of the *status quo*, however real his distaste for its values. He might seek refuge in a private universe which shut out 'the crude and angry problems of the real world.' But he could only do so at the price of a divorce from reality which must spell triviality. Nor was it enough that he should be willing to denounce the sickness of our society unless he was also willing to base his denunciation on the affirmation of positive values. For without that affirmation, his protest, however angry or anguished, must merely swell the chorus of those who insist that our predicament, which is real, is also insoluble.

As Laski was at pains to make clear, his plea was not for the intellectual to turn himself into a party man 'addressing envelopes in the committee room of his party.' Nor was he even concerned to suggest that the intellectual must necessarily play an active role in politics.[55] He meant something far larger than narrow party identification.

What he meant was that the intellectual could only play a fruitful role in his society if he sought to help in the creation of a social order based upon the proposition that civilisation, in the twentieth century, required, not the perpetuation of property and privilege, but the enhancement of the dignity and the welfare of the common people.

The dangers to human values in an age of crisis, he said, were immense. 'The responsibility of the intellectual who sees the drift of his time towards the abyss is to mitigate its dangers by seeking, through the profundity of his alliance with the masses, to make their dreams and hopes seem practicable and legitimate. To stand apart from the danger as a neutral, even more, to lend his aid, when he has awareness of it, to the oligarchy in power, is a supreme betrayal of his function.'[56] 'In an age which like our own, is shaken to its foundations', he added, 'the intellectuals must have a sense of the urgency of the times if their work is to be creative.'[57]

It was above all this 'sense of the urgency of the times' which impelled Laski as a theorist, as a teacher and as a member of the Socialist movement, and which made him refuse to abdicate the responsibility he felt, as an intellectual, to understand and to make understandable to others both the nature of our predicament and the means to its civilised solution.

The manner in which he sought to fulfil that responsibility well entitles him to the claim that he was, in a phrase of Heine he liked to quote, 'a soldier in the liberation army of mankind'. As such, he will be remembered with as much gratitude by the men and women of the Socialist society of tomorrow as he is remembered today by those whom he taught, by precept and example, that life is a mean and pitiful adventure if it is not lived in the service of a great cause.

NOTES

1 K. Martin, *Harold Laski* (1893–1950). A Biographical Memoir, (London, 1953).
2 Such an analysis has been attempted by an American political scientist, Herbert Deane. (H. Deane, *The Political Ideas of Harold J. Laski*, New York, 1955). I have tried to indicate what appear to me to be some of the major shortcomings of Deane's book in the *Stanford Law Review* for December 1955.
3 'The State in the New Social Order' in *Studies in Law and Politics* (London), p. 21.
4 In a letter to the author, K. Martin, op. cit., p. 71.
5 *Grammar*, op. cit., pp. 160–161.
6 Ibid, p. 437.
7 Ibid, p. 437.
8 Ibid, p. 21.
9 Ibid, p. 25.
10 Ibid, p. 176.
11 See Laski's amusingly supercilious view of Marx at this time in the M. DeW. Howe (ed) *Holmes-Laski Letters* (1953). Also his Fabian pamphlet on Marx, published in 1922.
12 See *Communism* (London, 1927).
13 *The State in Theory and Practice* (London, 1935), p. 299.
14 Nor, it might well be argued, was Marx himself.
15 T. B. Bottomore and M. Rubel, *Karl Marx, Selected Writings in Sociology and Social Philosophy* (London, 1956), pp. 51–2.
16 *Communist Manifesto. Socialist Landmark* (London, 1948), p. 71.
17 Labour Party Constitution. Clause IV.
18 *Democracy in Crisis* (London, 1933), p. 35.
19 *The State in Theory and Practice*, p. 148.
20 For Laski's interpretation of the crisis and the lessons he drew from it, see *The Crisis and the Constitution: 1931 and After*, (London, 1932).
21 *Liberty in the Modern State* (London, 1932), p. 37.
22 *The State in Theory and Practice*, op. cit., p. 133. The passing years, it may be added, have richly confirmed Laski's insistence on the counter-revolutionary character of Nazism and Fascism. In 1945, after twelve years of Nazi rule, the single facet of German life which the Allies found basically unimpaired in Germany was its social and economic structure. The Nazi 'revolution', whatever else it had tried to achieve, had not sought to alter the broad contours of German class-relations. The same holds for Fascism in Italy, with an even longer period of undivided rule.
23 *The Rise of European Liberalism* (London, 1936).
24 Ibid, p. 13.
25 Ibid, p. 13.
26 Ibid, p. 18.
27 Ibid, p. 243.
28 For a detailed discussion of the nature of the State, as Laski saw it in the thirties, see *The State in Theory and Practice* (London 1935), Ch. II.
29 'The Decline of Liberalism' (Hobhouse Memorial Lecture, London 1940).
30 *Democracy in Crisis* (London, 1934), Ch. II.
31 *Parliamentary Government in England* (London, 1938), pp. 105–6. 'Our alternating Cabinets', Lord Balfour had said, 'though belonging to different Parties, have never differed about the foundations of society'. (Introduction to Bagehot's *The English Constitution* (World's Classics Edition, London, 1928, p. xxiv)).
32 For some recent evidence of the Tory party's attitude in the Ulster crisis and of the willingness of its leaders to press matters to the point of civil war, see R. Blake, *The Unknown Prime Minister: The Life and Times of Andrew Bonar Law 1858–1923*, (London, 1955), Ch. IX, X, XI.

33 *Parliamentary Government in England* (London, 1938), p. 185.

34 Ibid, p. 28.

35 Laski himself sought to deal with the more general objections to the formulations of historical materialism. As I am not concerned in this essay with Marxism as such, I must refer the reader to Laski's own attempts to meet these objections. See, e.g. *The State in Theory and Practice*, Ch. II.

36 R. T. McKenzie, 'Laski and the British Constitution,' *British Journal of Sociology*, No 3 pp. 260–263 (1953).

37 See, *inter alia, Parliamentary Government in England*, op. cit., pp. 185 ff and *Marx and the Present Day* (London, 1943), pp. 3 ff.

38 For a detailed account of Laski's political activities on the left of the Labour Party, see K. Martin, op. cit., pp. 102–122.

39 Laski's acceptance of the possibility that parliamentary government might break down and his discussion of the Labour Party's attitude in that event led to one of the most spectacular libel actions of the post-war era. Laski sued the *Newark Advertiser* for reporting him as saying at a meeting in Newark during the General Election of 1945 that if Labour could not obtain what it needed by general consent, 'We shall have to use violence even if it means revolution.' Laski denied ever having used those words. The action was tried before a special jury on the 26th, 27th, 28th and 29th November, and the 2nd December 1946. Laski lost the case. Special juries were abolished shortly afterwards. For a verbatim report of the action, see Laski v. Newark Advertiser Co. Ltd. & Parlby. (Published by the Daily Express, London, 1947). The costs of the case, which were awarded against Laski were in the region of £15,000. The Labour Party opened a fund to cover that sum. The fund was oversubscribed with donations from all over the world.

40 H. Deane, op. cit., p. 290.

41 *The State in Theory and Practice* (London, 1950), op. cit., p. 146.

42 Ibid, p. 146.

43 *Trade Unions in the New Society* (London, 1950).

44 *Towards Equality. Labour's Policy for Social Justice* (London, 1956), p. 19.

45 See, e.g. A. A. Rogow and P. Shore, *The Labour Government and British Industry 1945–1951* (London, 1955). This is an admirable case study which ought to be required reading for anyone who would be tempted to take Deane's argument seriously.

46 Rogow and Shore, op. cit., Ch. VIII.

47 *Reflections on the Constitution* (London, 1951), p. 93.

48 *Democracy in Crisis*, op. cit., p. 254.

49 Ibid, op. cit., p. 249–50.

50 Ibid, op. cit., p. 252.

51 Ibid, op. cit., p. 177.

52 Ibid, p. 172.

53 *Trade Unions in the New Society*, op. cit., p. 42.

54 Not the least important of which was the India League. The cause of Indian independence was extremely close to Laski's heart and he was tireless in his efforts to help in its achievement.

55 Faith, Reason and Civilisation (London, 1943), p. 137.

56 Ibid, p. 133.

57 Ibid, p. 137.

HOW IT ALL BEGAN: A FOOTNOTE TO HISTORY

Marion Kozak

The *Socialist Register* was conceived on an exceptionally sunlit Sunday, April 7 1963, over lunch. Sitting round the table were John Saville, Lawrence Daly, Edward Thompson, Ralph and I. To an outsider it was evident that Lawrence Daly in some ways dominated the group. Daly, who had once been a working miner in Fife and later became a trade union leader, had been part of John and Edward's circle in the course of their break with the Communist Party in 1956–57 and after, and they considered him a most remarkable working class intellectual. He had attracted considerable attention in the 1959 general election campaign when he had beaten the official Communist candidate into third place in Willie Gallagher's old constituency – a traditional stronghold of Communism. But what sticks out in my memory is not the politics but that Edward wanted to talk to him about poetry and that the afternoon concluded with a discussion about Shakespeare's sonnets which Lawrence had been reading.

In their different ways, all the individuals at our little meeting were among the first wave members of the British New Left, and represented various aspects of a revived Marxist culture whose immediate antecedents were the revelations of the 20th Party Congress. On the one hand, Khrushchev's speech to the Congress of the CPSU had exposed the crimes of Stalinism as well as the fallibility of the Communist project as exemplified in the Soviet suppression of the Hungarian revolution. On the other hand, the broad Left and even the centre of the political spectrum in Britain had demonstrated widespread disillusion with Cold War politics, in the protest against the colonialism of the Suez invasions and in the growing movement against nuclear weapons. It was the coming together of personalities and groupings which included the left of the Labour Party and young intellectuals in the universities who previously had never had a political affiliation, which gave the New Left a coherent point of reference for political action later on. Two journals, *The New Reasoner* and *Universities and Left Review* supplied an intellectual link for disparate individuals and endowed the project with genuine excitement.

International links were formed with dissidents in the East and West long before the birth of the New Left in the USA. In 1957 Ralph was sending copies of both journals to C. Wright Mills and had organised a meeting of the New Left group with the Polish dissident philosopher Leszek Kolakowski in 1958.

I sometimes mentioned that glowing afternoon of April 1963 to Ralph, but he didn't have the same memories – he certainly did not remember that we had kebabs for lunch and that he had thought that they were too 'chi-chi'; or that all four of them had just returned from an acrimonious meeting with the editorial team of *New Left Review* – which had taken up Saturday the 6th and part of the Sunday, and whose outcome had stimulated them into setting up not an 'alternative' but 'another' socialist journal to which they could give their energies.

The first memo about starting the *Socialist Register* was written by Ralph on that sunny Sunday, April 7 1963, on my portable Olivetti which he had adopted after discarding his own very noisy Remington Quiet Writer – a little fact so anachronistic in the days of the super-speed computer. How the *Register* was set up, its political purpose and its evolution, is inseparable from my own and Ralph's lifelong intellectual and emotional involvement with John Saville, helped along by gallons of strong black tea. Its birth is the subject of this brief aide-mémoire.

The fizz and determination to do something that very afternoon of April 7, 1963 arose from a gradual estrangement between the 'old new left' Board of *New Left Review*, which happened to have been of the *New Reasoner* vintage, and the new directorate, or editorial committee, of *New Left Review* Mark II as Thompson called it, who included Perry Anderson, Tom Nairn and others. Briefly, and without reproducing the careful analysis documented by Lin Chun in *The British New Left*[1], a thumbnail sketch of the history of the two journals is in order. *The New Reasoner,* a quarterly established in 1957, had merged with *Universities and Left Review* in 1959 to establish *New Left Review*. The Board, whose role was advisory, represented most of the left currents of the time under the then editor, Stuart Hall. The new editorial Committee with Perry Anderson at its head took over in May 1962. Several different strands of the left were therefore struggling unsuccessfully to establish a peaceful transition to the *New Left Review*.

First, there was the *Reasoner* and the *New Reasoner* generation which represented a roll-call of well-known ex-Communists who had either left the Party or been expelled from it in 1956. The history of the Party in the UK had been punctuated by milestones of doubt and disaffection but not by mass resignations or expulsions. The 'fifty sixers' were different; they had put up with the 1939 Hitler-Stalin Pact and the absurd notion of the 'imperialist' war against the Nazis, the Slansky trials, the Soviet break with

Tito, the 'doctors plot' of 1953 as well as the suppression of the Berlin rising of the same year, but were incensed by the obduracy of the Party to open up the debate after Khrushchev's revelations to the Twentieth Party Congress. The issues at stake were not only the perniciousness of Stalinism but the brutal suppression of the Hungarian uprising and the uncertainty as to what would happen in Poland. The refusal to discuss these openly in a democratic spirit was ultimately the cause of 10,000 resignations and expulsions. John Saville and E P Thompson who had started *The Reasoner* in 1956, were later joined by an editorial Board which included Ken Alexander, Doris Lessing, Ronald L Meek, Randall Swingler, and subsequently Derek Kartun, Peter Worsley and Malcolm McEwen. Thompson symbolised the growing dissent and revulsion in his article 'Through the Smoke of Budapest' in the final issue of *The Reasoner* (November 1956). When the editors were forced to leave the Party rather than accede to the journal's suppression, it became the quarterly *New Reasoner* in the summer of 1957.[2]

Parallel to the ferment spilling out of the British Communist Party, the *Universities and Left Review* simultaneously provided a forum for younger left academics and students, some of whom were Labour Party members. Under the leadership of Raphael (then known as Ralph) Samuel, Peter Sedgwick, Stuart Hall, Rod Prince, Charles Taylor, Alasdair McIntyre and other writers and academics most of whom had never been Communists, the *ULR* provided a lively forum for the independent and activist left. Some *NR* people like Thompson and Miliband maintained contacts and wrote for both journals. Raymond Williams, who had left the CP in 1941, was close to Thompson and Miliband in age, but was not close to the *New Reasoner* people or the maelstrom of their debates in the 1950s. Although he thought the *New Reasoner* was 'a much more solid journal', he was more attracted to *ULR* by virtue of addressing itself to problems of popular culture and 'the extraordinary transformations of scene in England'.[3]

The reason for the amalgamation of *New Reasoner* and *Universities and Left Review* was that both journals seemed to be reaching out to the same constituency and both had administrative and business burdens. In particular, Thompson bore the strain of housing the editorial offices of *The New Reasoner* in his own home in Halifax. *New Left Review*, under the editorship of Stuart Hall and a large editorial board, seemed the answer to the problem, with the first issue appearing in January 1960. At first, *New Left Review* was a quarto bi-monthly with a magazine format using photographs, drawings and a mixture of long and short articles, reaching out to a committed but not exclusively academic audience of activists. The new editor, Stuart Hall, had a hard time with the heavy weight of left gurus on his Board and on his back. He left in January 1962 and was succeeded by the new editors Gabriel Pearson, Denis Butt, Raphael Samuel and Perry

Anderson.

The character of the new *NLR* or *The Review*, as it became known, gradually changed. It became a much heavier read, with fewer but longer articles, designed in an altogether more abstract style. It was a book-size journal and meant to be used as such, with no concessions to those who wanted light relief together with the serious stuff. Whereas the *NLR* Mark I used its editorial columns to address readers on current issues of British politics, *NLR* Mark II desisted from a preachy approach or political counsel. From a magazine of 60–70 pages *NLR* became a 120 page journal, and its only concession to 'popular' taste were its 'Scanner' columns, brief reviews or highly intellectual analyses of rock music which will undoubtedly one day find their way into academic books on the sociology of music. A new 'cultural' analysis was initiated by Raymond Williams. His *Culture and Society* and *The Long Revolution* (1961) were very influential texts, paralleled by theoretical perspectives on the political front led by Anderson and Nairn.

The setting up of *New Left Review* signalled a break from the participation of the non-academic left in the politics of a journal like *The New Reasoner*. That journal had continued to integrate active members of trade unions and grass roots 'movements' because of their common history in the Communist Party which had laid considerable stress on day to day collaboration with the industrial working class. In 1958, John Saville was enthusiastically planning a series of popular, *NR* sponsored lectures at the LSE which would be both 'academic and polemical' (JS to RM 25.6.58). However, neither *New Left Review* or for that matter *The Socialist Register* ever succeeded in providing a forum for the non-academic, working class audience. Some of those lost included prominent ex-CP activists greatly admired by John Saville and others such as Jim and Gertie Roche (Leeds), both ex-CP members; Walt Grenald (Hull), later President of the TGWU, Colin Barnet (Sheffield), H. W. Wynn, President of Derbyshire Miners, Reg Parker (Leeds), Harry Wright, Don Major, President of Hull Trades Council – all of whom attended an *NR* and *ULR* Industrial Weekend School in November 1958 in Leeds. (*Minutes*, 16–17 December 1958). The New Left Clubs, which also represented the activist wing of *The New Reasoner* and *Universities and Left Review*, also gradually disappeared from view in the new *NLR*. (A good few of the Left Clubs' secretaries have since become honoured academics, one a Vice-Chancellor of a University, another a Fellow of All Souls.)

Ralph had joined *NR* later than the ex-Communist members, in April 1958, and strongly opposed the merger that occurred between *NR* and *ULR*. Ralph's opposition to the merger was well known. In a letter to John and Edward he wrote that he met with Charles Taylor to discuss the project of the new consolidated journal and expressed profound doubts about its political consistency. He wanted a journal with a 'clear political line . . . I am sure we shall come to look back on the last two and a half years as a useful preparation for something a good deal more oriented' (RM to JS and EPT 18.2.59). The relationship that had been forged by Miliband with both Saville and Thompson during the years of the *New Reasoner* had given Ralph a sense of 'socialist comradeship', an experience which he had missed since his student days and which he articulated in an uncharacteristically effusive letter to Edward and John on 5.12.59:

A letter of thanks

I have just finished reading through the editorial and the Letter to our Readers in *NR* 10, received this morning, and I feel like sending a letter to the editors. It's an awkward letter to write in some ways, but I want to do it, even if it sounds a bit embarrassing . . . Actually it's just to say a personal thank you to both of you. What you have done for me needs saying now. In effect you have given me the sense of socialist comradeship (I said it would be embarrassing) which I have not had before, save perhaps in early student days. You have both made me feel that, beside the sense of belonging to a movement, I was also involved in a personal comradeship with people who had more experience than I, who could share in a direct way the political worries I have, who spoke my language and who also welcomed me as one of their number. This last point is something I do want to stress. I have felt deeply involved with *NR* (which is perhaps one reason why I have fought so stubbornly again its disappearance) and you have both given me a measure of confidence I might make a contribution to what you were trying to do. Assertiveness, in this context, is not the same thing as assurance; and both your praise, often to my mind over generous, and your criticism, has helped me more than I can possibly tell you. I find that you have both become part of an inner forum in why I write and what I think – not inhibiting but stimulating, and formative. I hope you will believe that it is no false pathos which makes me say that whatever I can do for *NLR* and for the kind of movement we want in the next few years will be better done because of what you have done for me in the last two years. So – thank you, comrades.

Both Edward and John responded to this letter in generous terms and John spoke of 'an elation that I certainly did not feel for most of this miserable decade we have just lived through'. Saville also described the goals of the *New Reasoner* as a way of developing 'our theoretical work as Marxists and really to build a marxist tradition in the Anglo Saxon countries and . . . to develop in our localities a lively political tradition'. (JS to RM 7.12.59) Both John and Ralph had found EPT an inspirational figure whom they admired intensely. In 1960 John and Ralph were exchanging letters confirming their appreciation of how much Edward had given to 'the movement'.

There is clearly a way in which the *New Reasoner* gave Ralph what he had been looking for in terms of group affiliation after abandoning the Tribunite Left and Victory for Socialism – two left groups active inside the Parliamentary Labour Party which Ralph had joined briefly in 1956 and which had included major Labour Party personalities such as Barbara Castle, Michael Foot, Stephen Swingler, Konni Zilliacus, Ian Mikardo and Jo Richardson. Ralph was an exception in the *New Reasoner* circles because he had never belonged to the Communist Party – and always knew that he would never join despite the fact that in moments of political gloom he sometimes wished he could bring himself to give the Party his allegiance. Very much later, he partly explained his inhibition about becoming involved with the Communist Party by the fact that at the age of about eighteen or nineteen he had read Jan Valtin's *Out of the Night* (1941)[4] – a book of disillusionment with Communism which had sowed serious doubts in his mind about practices in the Soviet Union and the Comintern. In notes for a political autobiography he prepared in 1983, he wrote: 'Jan Valtin's *Out of the Night* left me with a serious question mark about the Comintern and the reality of Communist politics and a certain scepticism about total and unqualified commitment, or so I think in retrospect' (RM 22.5.83).

There had been various troubling aspects of Soviet politics which worried Ralph when he arrived in England in 1940: the Hitler-Stalin Pact and the assassination of Trotsky. When he was at the LSE, which was evacuated to Cambridge during the war, he was close to many Party members, got involved in hosting a visit by fraternal delegates from the Soviet army during the war but never affiliated. After the war he continued to argue with his Communist friends about issues of freedom of expression and civil rights and he retained a commitment to 'communism' but not to the Party or the Soviet State and its politics.

After 1956 the process of destalinization was painfully slow inside the CPGB, the French Communist Party and to a lesser extent even inside the Italian Party (PCI), which had the reputation of being the most democratic of all European Communist Parties. In the 1960s the CPGB adamantly refused to engage in meaningful debate with people outside the party, particularly former members, while continuing to interpret the Soviet example as the only valid route to reaching the Holy Grail. Ralph found it difficult to condone the wooden debates in the *Morning Star*, daily newspaper of the CPGB, which continued broadly speaking to put a positive gloss on the Soviet experience and to use the epithet 'Trotskyist' and 'nihilist' as an expression of opprobrium until well into the 1970s. He always agreed to enter into dialogue with Communist Party officials on public platforms. He poured scorn, however, on the politically correct concepts of 'bourgeois art', and 'bourgeois science' and the fossilised attitude to Marxism in the Soviet Union which he described as 'la pourriture du Marxisme Officiel' (RM to Marcel Liebman 28.5.67). Ralph was also scathing about the level of intellectual debate: 'vocables passe-partout tels que classe ouvrière, aliénation dont les social scientists sovietiques sont pleins' (RM to ML 24.11.67).

It is certain that in some way *The New Reasoner* compensated Ralph for not having a political home. It provided him with a forum to discuss and to publish on issues relating to the Labour Party and western capitalism. In the late 50s, as he was writing *Parliamentary Socialism* (a work which provided him with an inexhaustible seam relating to Labour politics), it was clear that his association with *The New Reasoner* helped unlock his writing talents by giving him not only a place to publish but also a group of people who shared his concern for current politics. This stood in contrast to his working environment at the LSE. John Saville, in particular, and to a lesser extent Thompson, were the ones who took the keenest interest in the new interpretation of Labour Party politics which Ralph was formulating at the time. Saville made an enormous contribution to a critique of *Parliamentary Socialism*, as it came off the typewriter. It was the tradition of *New Reasoner* partnership, lost in the *NLR*, which Ralph tried to recreate subsequently in the *Socialist Register*.

The break between the Board and the editorial team of *NLR*, which occurred at the acrimonious meeting on April 6–7, 1963, was the culmination of a long history of strain. Relations between the old Board and new Team were edgy and had to do with divergent perspectives and ideologies. Apart from particular disagreements on issues of principle and theory, the new *Review* was criticised for standing aside from contemporary politics and putting too much emphasis on the intellectual task of 'deepening the analysis and theory available to the left', as a memo (undated) from the editorial team, sent out in the months before the break, put it. This memo had set out the work plan for forthcoming issues in a take-it-or-leave-it manner, and while it invited Board members to attend, it did so without naming any time or place. John had expressed the division as 'the old guard and the young guard' with Edward as the Chair bearing the burden of bridging the gap. *NLR* Mark II had rejected articles on economic issues relating to the Common Market by members of the old Board, about which Edward still remained angry ten years later (EPT to RM and JS 20.6.73). While everyone from the *New Reasoner* team was clear, as a result of bitter experience in the early days of the merger in 1960 between *NR* and *Universities and Left Review*, that the new Team had to have the independence which had been denied to Stuart Hall, the previous editor, they felt a sense of frustration about being unwanted, about disagreements with the editorial policies of *NLR* and feeling redundant. There was a lot of nostalgia for the days of the *New Reasoner*, especially from Ralph.

Before the final break, the increased alienation between the Old Board and the new editorial committee found expression in the prodigious memo writing talent of Edward Thompson. On April 3, 1963, just before the meeting of April 6–7, he wrote 15,000 words straight onto the skins of his old Gestetner entitled 'Where are we Now?' which was distributed to all the members of the Board and the new editorial committee. In this memo he magisterially took the new editors to task on various issues of substance, which he expressed at length and with superb elegance, echoing some of the criticisms of Ralph and John. Edward was harsh with the 'deraciné' element of the new *NLR*, the lack of knowledge or interest among the new editorial committee in British politics, and even more emphatically their denigration of British empiricism. While the new editorial committee avowed an interest in 'intellectual work', Edward detected in their interest an 'abrupt shift to new themes and preoccupations. This is not consolidation it is rejection'. Much of the memo dealt with his concept of internationalism as opposed to the new ideas of 'Third Worldism' as propounded at the time by Fanon, Sartre and less so by Che Guevara, which were echoed in the pages of *NLR*. Edward's memo attacked their analysis of imperialism which neglected to highlight indigenous British struggles waged against it. Edward cited his own father as well as E.D. Morel, other left labour intellectuals and working class and trade union activists who had all vigorously opposed imperialism. He contrasted these activities with the 'Neo-Sorelian mystique of violence', which was becoming fashionable in the 1960s.

Ralph had expressed similar views in March 1963 in a letter to Perry Anderson about an article published in *NLR* No 18 – 'The Third World' by Keith Buchanan – referring specifically to the charge of imperialism against the First World's working classes as the chief beneficiaries of colonialism:

> Buchanan's appeal for aid to the Third World is the worst kind of misleading liberal claptrap. If ever a country has dished out aid on a global massive scale it is the US in Vietnam, Korea, Greece and most countries of the Third World. 'Aid' is one of those notions which has to be interpreted and handled with care. Otherwise it is just cheap, heart warming rubbish, which conceals the fact that what the underdeveloped countries need is social revolution, to make aid fruitful. Following from this failure of understanding stems the worst feature of the piece, (a) the assumption that the Western proletariat would have to forego affluence to provide 'aid' to the underdeveloped world; this is one of those nice catch notions that warms the heart of liberals. (b) It is monstrous and grotesque to argue or rather it is monstrous and cowardly to say that in the opinion of Moussa (and Buchanan?) these efforts of Western workers to raise their standard of living have contributed more to the deterioration in underdeveloped countries than has the profit motive of industrial and commercial leaders. If you are to say such a thing, it is absolutely incumbent upon you to give some evidence . . . this is hardly a minor point; what it means, simply is that the working classes bear a larger share of guilt for poverty in the underdeveloped countries than capitalism. (RM to Perry Anderson 9.3.63).

The official break between the Old Board and the editorial Committee of *NLR* was formally announced on the last page of issue no 24 (April 1964) which boldly stated that the editorial team had asked the Old Board to transfer to itself the entire legal, financial, as well as editorial responsibility for the Review. 'The Review is therefore now owned by the editorial team and the New Left Board has been dissolved. It is hoped that former Board members will have close informal relations as contributors to the

Review.'

Considering the strains of those years in which *NLR* Mark I became Mark II, the correspondence of the *Socialist Register* editors from April 1963 indicates almost no bitterness towards the editorial committee of *NLR* Mark II, except for occasional references that dwelt on a sustained criticism of the contents of the new *NLR*. Despite Ralph's loyalty to his comrades on the Board, there is no evidence in his bulging files of disputations on paper with members of the new *NLR* and certainly nothing but a courteous reply from Tom Nairn about the criticism Ralph had aimed at the Buchanan article in March 1963. And even after the *Socialist Register* was initiated, there were exchanges between John and Ralph in 1965 about plans to invite Tom Nairn to review Deutscher's biography of Trotsky and to do a critical essay on *The New Statesman*.

The break had occurred because of a basic difference in style and philosophy. The new *NLR* was beating a new style among left journals from which the 'Old Board' was brusquely excluded, and the editors of the *SR* were therefore losing their political home. The fact that the new team had never been through the school of party-based Communism was also a factor. Neither Anderson, Nairn, Mitchell nor subsequent editors of *NLR* had ever been touched by the agonies of belonging to the Communist Party or its ideology. For a long time *The Review* remained resolutely non-aligned and untouched by the need to be identified with a cause.

Subsequently, the contents of *NLR* became increasingly academic and remote from contemporary British politics.

Fortunately, as they decided to set up the *Socialist Register* its editors set aside these old controversies and succeeded in carving out a new and independent, socialist path for themselves which was different from the old *New Reasoner*, different from *NLR*, but not in opposition to it. They published articles which were critical of the work of *NLR*, notably by Thompson and Kolakowski, but avoided sectarian mud-slinging. Although *NR* names were relied on, Ralph did mention that he would 'like to strike out a bit from *NR* circles (!)' (RM to JS 31.5.63). Edward described *The SR* subsequently as 'the last survivor in the direct line of continuity from the Old New Left'.[5] Indeed, one of Ralph's proudest moments was to receive two letters written on the same day from Thompson and Anderson, both congratulating him on the contents of the 1974 *Register* and on his two articles in that issue (PA and EPT to RM 25.1.74).

Everyone in the New Left had enough of editorial Boards, and in the initial stages of the *SR* it was envisaged that the three editors would be responsible for different sections. By April 29, 1963 it was clear that Thompson would not agree to be an editor although he intended to contribute to the first issue. It was Edward who introduced Ralph to Martin Eve who became the *Register's* publisher and godfather. The production costs were estimated at £660 for 2500 copies which if sold at 30/- (at today's prices, £1.50) for a hardback and 15/- (75p) for a paperback, would have made some profit. The editors both made a financial contribution through standing orders to get things started.

John was very keen to enlist the support of Michael Foot and the Tribunite Left which he thought might benefit from having a new Left Journal, which could provide intellectual underpinning for that wing of the labour movement. Foot was at the time regarded as an ally of the independent left, deeply involved in CND and working outside the mainstream of Labour party politics. Ralph went to see Foot who was 'enthusiastic about the annual. Like everyone else he could not think why anybody had not done it before. He is most willing to write a piece on the last years of the Labour Government. All we must hope for is that he will come up with decent stuff' (RM to JS 30.5.63). That article did not materialise because of Michael Foot's terrible car accident in 1963.

The original concept of the *Register* differed appreciably from the final product. Ralph visualised a broad based content which included articles of up to 15,000 words(!) on 'socialist theory and practice', labour history, the labour movement and aspects of 'capitalist society', 'agencies of historical change'. John was very keen on an 'international chronicle of events' and a round up of books (JS to RM 20.5.63), documents from labour history, for example Luddite documents (proposed by Edward), obituaries and an article marking the centenary of the formation of the First International in 1864. The Annual Chronicle of Events did not materialise in the end, nor did the obituaries or book reviews in a regular fashion. After six months of toying with various titles for the new Review, in November 1963, Martin Eve came up with *The Socialist Register: A Survey of Movements and Ideas*, after Cobbett's *Register*, which had figured prominently in Thompson's *Making*. Everyone thought that this was a perfect idea, with just the right, evocative tinge of radical historical perspective about it and much superior to *The Socialist Annual* which had been the working title until then.

By December 1963 the editors began work on the forthcoming issues. Ralph had been attending meetings between Harold Wilson and the National Peace Fellowship and wrote to John and Ernest Mandel on the hopeless prospects for a left Labour Party policy. There was strong agreement that something had to be carried about the welfare state, which finally materialised in volume 2 as 'Facts and Theories of the Welfare State' by Dorothy Wedderburn. Deutscher promised an article and wanted someone to review his Trotsky trilogy. Ralph began a fruitless search for a suitable candidate to review Sartre's *Critique de la Raison Dialectique*. He wrote in 1964 and 1965 to Leszek Kolakowski who had been seriously ill, in political difficulties and having problems in being published in Poland.

In an essay published in the 30th anniversary issue, *The Socialist Register 1994*,[6] Ralph wrote that at no time did he and John 'devote any time to the discussion of the ideological and political direction of the prospective publication', given their in-depth discussions and agreement on questions of socialist theory and practice over the previous years. They both took it for granted that it would be broadly within the Marxist tradition but certainly without a 'party line'. In writing to Ernest Mandel, Ralph defined the SR as 'une sérieuse revue de l'Année, d'un nombre de points de vue. J'aime dire que l'orientation politique de l'Annual sera fort générale – all the way from Michael Foot leftwards'. (8.7.63). He sometimes teased John about being 'a bit too Bulletin of the Society for Labour History oriented', but there were no ideological disagreements on issues to do with the *Register*.

Ralph still missed not being in a Party, but the *Register* became a substitute by providing a formal renewal of his collaboration with John, after an interval of three years, since the demise of *The New Reasoner*. Ralph saw their new publication as a vehicle, speaking to the world with one voice about the things that they wanted, particularly on issues affecting contemporary politics in Britain:

> You make me weep Saville. When I said I thought the article on Labour's 100 days should be an inside job, I meant of course that it should be done by both of us or if not by both, just me. Your suggestion that we might entrust the job to . . . is cretinous, ditto for . . . . Jeeeeesus, . . . I simply would not consider going outside the editorial board, so to speak. (RM to JS 3.7.64)

The *Socialist Register* became their joint 'political' voice, which they had lost as members of the Board of *New Left Review*. There were, however, differences in style and articulation, if not on substantive issues, which separated Ralph and John on the one hand and Edward on the other. In retrospect, it may have been certain differences about the starting point of socialist engagement, allied to the pressure of work, which prevented Edward from joining the editorial Board of the *SR* in April 1963. (EPT to JS and RM, 13.3.65). At that time Thompson was completing his magnum opus *The Making of the English Working Class* published in November 1963 to great public acclaim – selling 1700 copies in the first four months. Although Edward supported the establishment of the *SR*, and so did Dorothy Thompson, he had feared 'differences over editorial policy' although not 'serious political disagreement' between the editors and himself. In fact, he offered to write an article on 'The Marxist Tradition' which both editors supported enthusiastically but which did not materialise until the second issue of the *Register* under the title 'The Peculiarities of the English'. Writing in March 1965 about the contents of that article, Edward stressed his commitment to 'socialist humanism' which required a regular attack on Stalinism or post-Stalinism and admitted that his decision not to join the Board of the *SR* stemmed partly from the fact that 'R. and I do have a different attitude on this point'. Differences had arisen when Ralph had criticised an attack on Communism which could have been construed as 'Encounterish'. But in the end Thompson agreed to excise it from his final version and accepted other editorial suggestions (EPT to JS and RM, 13.3.65).

Various aspects of these differences surface in their correspondence over the years. Part of the tension arose in the course of trying to link the ex-Communist tradition of the *NR* and independent left socialism – a strand represented by Ralph as someone who had not been a member of the CP but who was strongly committed to 'digesting the Soviet experience' rather than just rejecting it. An early sign of the tension with Edward in this respect arose in the context of Ralph's closeness to Mills and Deutscher, both of whom, in their different ways, had some positive messages about the Soviet Union at the beginning of the 1960s. When both Edward and Dorothy Thompson questioned this Ralph responded:

> I too have been thinking a great deal about the evening with Mills and the talk then, [which] has crystallised . . . some sharp unease I have had for sometime about much of the New Left and Russia, or rather NL vis à vis Russia. Look, whether we call it the transition to communism or the transition to socialism does not matter a bugger. Deutscher the night before had made the point that they were in fact only at the first stage, just. The real point is whether the kind of society they are creating looks like approximating to something we think is socialism and whether in the development of socialism in the world they are or are not a hopeful, indeed the most hopeful factor. On both counts my answer is yes, with all the qualifications, ambiguities, hesitations and this and what you will. It may well be that they are adrift to hell on old people's homes, boarding schools, Pasternak, culture and much else. . . And I feel that so long as this is not resolved in our own minds, we are going to be weak, theoretically and practically . . . The fact is that the New Left just hasn't digested Russia, or still suffers from an indigestion which affects the whole system. Please let's not talk about pro-Soviet or anti-Soviet. (RM to Dorothy T 31.5.1960).

Ralph was always openly critical of the politics of the Soviet State and the Communist Parties. In essence, *The Socialist Register's* relationship to Communism continued to be the litmus test, as it had been for the *New Reasoner*, for evaluating its political message. (Indeed, the correspondence about the first volume reveals worries about contributors writing too enthusiastically about the PCI.) Whatever ambiguity he may have felt about 'real' Communism, Ralph was always ultra-sensitive to any Stalinist tendencies among contributors, or any use of CPSU-speak, such as 'petty bourgeois anarchism' in relation to a critique of an article on Soviet art in *SR* 1965: 'After all we have to speak for the Yevtushenkos and others who work still under highly restrictive conditions. This is also why I write with some heat.' (RM to JS 27.11.64).

Nevertheless, at that point Ralph did not, despite his doubts, write off the Soviet project or Soviet reality; and, at the same time he was very sensitive to avoiding the kind of argument or terminology that might be taken as evidence of anti-communism. His own attitude to 'Communism' was ambiguous to this extent, and it must be said that although he remained openly critical of the Soviet Union's politics in the 1960s, he did not think at the time that the project was so fundamentally flawed as to be irretrievable. The sixties encapsulated for Ralph the grossest forms of American imperialism abroad and racism at home, in contrast to what appeared as slow progress in the 'Eastern' bloc, allied to the Soviet Union's apparent support for anti-imperialist struggles, particularly in South Africa, Cuba and, to a lesser degree, in Vietnam. This was not a view universally shared. When Ralph went to the Soviet Union in April 1961 for an extended trip he consulted Thompson about issues to raise with his hosts. His advice was 'Ask them why they are such terrible liars'.[7]

A second, albeit related, aspect of the difference with Edward concerned 'socialist humanism'. *The New Reasoner* bore the subtitle 'A quarterly journal of socialist humanism', and Edward had emphasized socialist humanism in his 20 page 'Where are we Now?' memo to the NLR Board in April 1963. Addressing the younger comrades (itself an expression with a slightly archaic ring today), he wrote: 'I doubt whether socialist humanism can be usefully defined but the attempt must be made again and again . . . if we abandon the effort for one moment we fall victims to the realpolitik of determinism'. What bothered Ralph about such expressions as 'socialist humanism' or 'socialist morality' was not what they conveyed about the necessity for criticism of realpolitik or determinism, but rather the sloppy writing about Marxism that often went under their rubric, the kind of writing for which C. Wright Mills had coined the pithy phrase 'lyric upsurge'. In the draft preface to the *SR* 1965 Ralph wrote about 'a deeply felt need among socialists everywhere for the kind of strict, undogmatic and committed socialist writing'. Commitment included serious reappraisal of the Communist project. But this should not leave the way open to vague moralising which sometimes reflected the abandonment of the critical faculty. This was a style of writing that he was concerned to avoid in the *Socialist Register*.

Throughout the first decade of the *SR*'s existence, Ralph's letters show an insistence on the need for a 'hard analysis', 'rigorous thinking', 'analysis and interpretation, summation of trends and events, with appropriate facts and figures e.g. strike movements in Western Europe . . . hard, factual even statistical information'. All this was seen as sustaining what he approvingly referred to as 'intransigence of belief' – which he contrasted with Edward's doubts 'about identifying himself as a Marxist without important qualifications on essential matters' (RM to EPT 31.10.1963). There are references in Edward's letter to a lost 'moral vocabulary' in the Marxist tradition which he subsequently described as having 'no defences against reasons of power' (letter from EPT to Saville and Miliband, 20.6.73 concerning 'Open Letter to Leszek Kolakowski').

The issue of 'power' had, in fact, been the subject of correspondence between Ralph and Edward ten years earlier. Edward had written a critical review of C. W. Mills' *Power, Politics and People* (which he had offered to *Peace News* and not *SR* out of respect for Ralph's feelings for Mills, who had been one of his closest friends). Edward had doubts about all of Mills' work after *The Power Elite*, particularly *Listen Yankee, Causes of World War Three* and *The Sociological Imagination*; and he sent Mills a strong critique of *The Marxists,* especially in respect 'of the philosophical dimensions of Marxism which went with the dismissal or even discussion of the early Marx writings' (EPT to RM 5.10.63). Ralph's response to this critique was sharp:

> There was, as you say, . . . 'real ambiguity in his attitude to power'. For Christ's sake. Don't you feel ambiguous to power? Doesn't every serious socialist feel ambiguous to power? Isn't that exactly the underlying tension in all the stuff we are talking about, and that serious socialists have been talking about since the year dot? Wasn't Marx ambiguous about power? And even Lenin, at least in his last years? How is it possible to be anything but ambiguous about power? (RM to EPT 7.10.63)

This concern about power was central to Ralph's attempt to rescue Marx from his so-called disciples in the Soviet Union. In responding to Edward's letter about his article on 'The Marxist Tradition', Ralph wrote: 'You say "I don't for example, feel happy about identifying myself as a Marxist without important qualifications on essential matters". My God, isn't that exactly my own position? . . . That is exactly the kind of piece which is most wanted in the Annual. And giving these postgrad lectures has made me the more aware of this' (RM to EPT 29.10.63). Ralph's notes for a lecture on 'The Relevance of Marxism Today' given to the LSE Students Union and Research Students' Association (Margate, 26.4.63) confirm that he was wrestling with the concepts of Marxism, with its emphasis on class struggle, but also its 'morality, a message, a call, a vision of human regeneration'.

All this formed an essential part of Ralph's vision of 'socialist democracy'. But it was significant that it was this term which Ralph very much preferred to 'communism with a human face' or 'socialist humanism' of earlier vintage vocabulary among left dissidents both East and West. Writing to John in 1963 about the contents of the first volume, Ralph stressed this: 'an article on the Moral Basis of Socialism is an utterly lousy idea. The subject does not appeal to me and the author . . . even less. It is exactly the kind of waffle which this sort of piece always produces which I should like to see avoided.' (RM to JS 25.5.63). John replied by trying to steer Ralph back to the idea of 'The Morality of Socialism': 'I still think therefore that this is a subject that needs full discussion for every generation of socialists – and I will grant immediately that it is so easy to write crap'. John suggested that the author in question be asked to do a piece which would include 'the moral basis and necessity of political commitment' (JS to RM 24.5.63). Ralph agreed that 'I may have been too sweeping about the Moral Basis of Socialism – the thing is that I cannot remember anything worthwhile on this subject for years . . . My objection is not aesthetic but intellectual and practical'. Finally, the editors of the *SR* compromised on the need for a contribution on the loosely defined theme of morality and invited Donald C. Hodges to put forward a highly critical analysis of Eugene Kamenka's *Ethical Foundations of Marxism* (1962) – a book which stressed the importance of the ethical vision of Marx's early writings.

The concern to interpret anew, but rigorously and relevantly, the politics of Marx became the hallmark of the politics of the *Register*: theory, by all means, but theory that bore relevance to the editors' preoccupations with contemporary politics. *The Register* was a journal which, among others, contributed to reviving a meaningful debate about Marxist theory away from the old calcified base-superstructure debates, while expressing scepticism about new 'structuralist' interpretations which soon became fashionable. Rediscovering the theoretical Marx especially preoccupied Ralph from the early sixties until the late seventies. The deformations of 'official Marxism' in the Soviet Union, and 'Marxism-Leninism' in general, were the object of his disdain. 'There is more than a hyphen which separates Marxism from Leninism'[8], was how Ralph put it in an article in *Tribune* on November 20, 1964. Just a week before, he had communicated in a letter to John Saville a sense of excited discovery as he worked on his essay on 'Marx and the State' for the 1965 volume of the *Register*:

> I have some sensational stuff for 'Marx and the State' which should set the cat among the pigeons. Nothing less on the basis of massive internal as well as external evidence, than that the whole notion of the dictatorship of the proletariat in Marx has been completely misintrepreted, from Engels onwards. You will be properly sceptical, but wait till you have seen the texts and the argument. (RM to JS, 14.11.1964)[9]

Ever since Ralph first became a student at the LSE at the age of 18, Marx and Marxism were the subject of long term academic interest which he continued to develop throughout his life. (In 1942 he wrote to his father that Laski had assigned him an essay on Marxism: 'Ce n'est pas facile mais ca m'interesse' – RM to Samuel Miliband 11.10.1942). The early Marx and late Marx, Marx and the State, Marx and Engels, dialectical materialism were all part of the background for Ralph's work on *The State in Capitalist Society* (1968) and for the first ever lecture series on Marxism in the LSE Political Science Department. Yet Ralph's subsequent work on Marxism bears out his determination to steer clear of any particular emphasis on Marx's early work, in particular the 1844 manuscripts which became so widely read in the 1960s, and the espousal of the alienation theory as a tool of analysis. Ralph was not a philosopher by training; he was much more interested in class conflict as the yeast of social action than in alienation, which does not feature at all in his *Marxism and Politics* (1977). Ralph was preoccupied with an analysis of capitalism and the agencies of change which worked to reform it or destroy it. He took his cue from Marx in refusing to speculate on what a 'truly human' society would look like. 'Marx's first concern is with the material, concrete reality which lies hidden, as he believes, behind the religions, the ideologies, the moralities, which men create for themselves and for others out of ignorance, fear or design'.[10]

The Socialist Register's contribution to the revitalisation of Marxism was much enhanced by the resolute internationalism that characterized the project. In its gestation period *SR* benefited to some extent from contacts with contributors to the *International Socialist Journal*, a venture initiated by Lelio Basso (a socialist member of the Italian Senate based in Milan), and with Jon Halliday as its English language editor. Ralph attended meetings in Paris at the beginning of April, 1964 where he met some of those who became future contributors to the *Register*. These contacts, as well as old friendships with Leo Huberman, Paul Sweezy and Harry Magdoff of *Monthly Review*, K. S. Karol, André Gorz and other French intellectuals, Rossana Rossanda in Italy were essential to the development of the *Register*. Marcel Liebman, one of Ralph's oldest friends and a former student, and Ernest Mandel in Belgium kept him in touch with events there and in West Germany, as well as with writers in France. The fact that he was bilingual in French and English made it easier for Ralph to use material he had picked up from *Temps Modernes, Nouvel Observateur* and other sources, and also to write for French journals, such as *La Gauche*, which he did regularly in the mid to late sixties. The fact that Ralph had never been a communist had provided him with opportunities to travel to the United States in the days when the aftermath of McCarthyism still made things difficult; and he had many American friends from the late 1940s as well as New Left acquaintances he had met through C. Wright Mills, such as James Weinstein of *Studies on the Left*. The *Monthly Review* editors put him in touch with subsequently prominent Latin American intellectuals. A very different set of contacts was represented by the Poles whom Ralph had met on a trip there with C. Wright Mills in 1957, including Kolakowski, Schaff and Lange. He took delight in the seamless internationalism of the *Register* whose contributors were seemingly unaffected by longstanding ethnic conflicts even between Arabs and Israelis (RM to JS 7.6.63).

By 1963 the focus of attention for the editors of the *Register* was not only the Soviet Union but also China, the Sino-Soviet split, Tibet, and the

Indian dispute which were coming into prominence. Deutscher was at the time the expert on Russia and even China and was held in great respect by both Ralph and John, who both took enormous care to show him utmost personal courtesy. Deutscher was a good bit older than Ralph and according to John had not been treated well by the New Left. (This might have been a reference to a rejection by *NR* of a review of *Dr Zhivago* which was first published in *Temps Modernes* in 1959. Both Peter Worsley and EPT independently refused to use it on the grounds that the review did not deal with the book's literary or artistic merits but only with its politics as if it were a book of history.) Deutscher became an invaluable contributor to the *SR* until his tragically early death in 1967 at the age of 60. Unfortunately, there is no record of his exchanges with Ralph on issues of Communism and the Soviet Union, because he lived practically next door, with the result that the discussions were never put on paper.

Apart from the articles that were featured in the 1964 edition, other issues which preoccupied the editors included a socialist critique of the Robbins Report published in 1963. At the time the Report was regarded as a major advance towards increasing the number of entrants into British universities, opening up additional places outside the prestigious Oxbridge and London elite institutions. In fact, although the number of university students doubled by 1967, the Robbins reforms did not fulfil their democratic promise of providing a place for all A-level qualified students. The editors also pursued their political project in wanting to reappraise milestone texts by focusing on John Strachey's *The Coming Struggle for Power* which had such a deep resonance when it was first published in 1932. Nasserism, Cuba, a critique of the *New Statesman*, to parallel John's piece on *Encounter* scheduled for issue No 1, were all part of the diverse menu in preparation. One is also glad to see that 'the woman question' was on the agenda. Ralph had approached Dorothy Thompson for a contribution and John suggested MacGregor (now Lord MacGregor), who had published a pioneering bibliography of writing on women's issues for the *British Journal of Sociology*, and Griselda Rowntree as alternatives, but clearly nothing came of it until the 1976 issue with, rather typically, an article entitled 'Marxist Women versus Bourgeois Feminism' by Hal Draper and Anne Lipow. But *The Register* was in its first decades never comfortable with debates about the politics of feminism, except within the confines of a classical left framework.

Other central issues which were discussed but did not find their way into the first issue were the Viet-Nam (sic) war and the 'negro' (sic) movement, which James Weinstein perceptively recognised as central to American politics. Ralph wrote to Bayard Rustin seeking a contribution on the 'Negro' movement but various names including Wilfrid Burchett's, suggested by the *Monthly Review* people, for an article on Vietnam were rejected. In the end there was nothing on issues of race in the first *Register.* Because of the pressures of political activism, Bayard Rustin apologised for not doing his piece on notepaper headed 'The March on Washington'. By November 1963 President Kennedy had been assassinated and the 'Negro Movement' at the time had other priorities. The burgeoning Civil Rights struggles signalled the beginning of the New Left in the USA. No article on black people's struggles in the USA was published until 1968 although the debate on Third World issues was well represented in articles by Alavi, Abdel Malek and Victor Kiernan.

The first issue of *The Register* was launched at a dinner at Schmidt's Restaurant in Charlotte Street on April 29 1964, with Deutscher and Michael Foot present. Schmidt's, like the Budapest in Greek Street, was one of those cheap but satisfactory restaurants patronised by the left where you could always fill up on goulash or pancakes. I don't remember whether Lawrence Daly came to the launch dinner which cost 12/6, including the speeches, but certainly Shakespeare was back on the agenda. In January 1964 Ralph had written to John 'What about a piece on Shakespeare – socialist view for 1965, certainly I would like to jazz the thing up somewhat – you know, Culture, Freud and all that jazz'. Victor Kiernan was asked to do something for Shakespeare's 400th anniversary but he refused and that suggestion was never revived.

After the successful launch of the first issue of *The Register*, and with all sorts of luminaries lined up for the 1965 volume, Ralph jokingly suggested to John: 'Now that we have Lukàcs, O'Brien, Deutscher and Foot for 65, I think we should aim to have an article/essay on the Monarchy from the inside by HM Queen for 1966' (RM to JS, 23.5.1964). But however luminous their list of contributors, their main concern, as they planned future volumes, remained to make a political impact:

> I still think there may be something to be said for a piece on the Labour Government and the Left. I am impressed with the fact that this conference last Saturday was a *direct* result of our piece in *The Register* and there may be a lot to be said for a repeat performance with an analysis of this particular version of Labourism, which is what the Government is about, on the basis of the performance in the '100 days' . . . I want to say very loud that one of the things the left must do is to begin working on the programme for the next election and the election after that. (RM to JS 11.11.64)

The partnership of John and Ralph continued until 1990, with Marcel Liebman and Leo Panitch co-opted in the interim. Despite the hard work and regular annual outbursts, mostly from Ralph, which were always about missed deadlines rather than issues of substance, the partnership continued with John showing remarkable, almost saintly, understanding and tolerance, never nurturing resentments – at least not for long. Ralph relied on this moral support whenever – as often happened – he got despondent, about the *Register* not being 'good enough': 'We shall survive, provided,

repeat provided, Hull – [the town where John lived] radiates encour-
agment, cooperation, patience etc. I have no call to say this at the moment
but I do get anxious about the bloody *Register* and it is important this
volume should be very good. If it is we shall have established the venture
very firmly' (RM to JS 11.11.64).

A difficult question arises as to who were the *Register's* editors and
authors and where they stood politically? The successful publication of
annual volumes was largely due to an unspoken agreement between the
editors as to what constituted 'being on the Left' – an agreement which had
already integrated unequivocal opposition not only to Stalin but to
Stalinism of every kind, as well as an overall acceptance of the basic tenets
of socialism/communism and a clearly Marxist perspective. They were not
Communists with a capital C. Their commitment to civic freedom and
serious doubts about the insurrectionary model of 1917 put them beyond
the pale of some left revolutionary groups. And yet, the *Register* was an
open forum for many socialist thinkers of different persuasions, with the
editors participating frequently in debates with the Communist Party as
well as the Trokskyite groups. The *Register* consequently attracted some
world famous socialist theorists who were politically homeless. *The
Register* became one of the havens, a sort of missing persons' bureau, for
the non-aligned Left. K. S. Karol or it may have been Rossana Rossanda
coined in the 1960s the homely concept of a left 'Swiss Community' – a
neutral, welcoming but somewhat exclusive land of debate for independent
socialists. From then on Ralph and Karol would classify their acquaintances as full, potential or aspiring members of the Swiss Community. The
passport into the Community was an independence of mind allied to a
commitment to socialist values. The correspondence between Ralph and
Karol was peppered with references to Swiss Community opinions on this
or that world event, while playing the lighthearted power game of
excluding this or that person for expressing views that ran contrary to
Swiss Community canon.

It is comforting to see that even in the far-off 1960s there was uncertainty among people who thought of themselves as being socialists, about
the relevance of Marxism, 'the left' and socialism. Nevertheless, the first
issue of *The Register* was widely reviewed in the mainstream press and
reviewers correctly perceived that the editors were 'influenced to a great or
lesser extent by Marxism' (Robin Gollan in the *Australian* 9.1.1965). It is
also surprising that most reviews of the *Register* were favourable, except
for the one in *The Daily Worker* which complained that there was no article
by a Communist writer in the whole volume and criticised Deutscher for
offering 'a one sided, distorted approach'.[11] Elsewhere, there was recognition that the *Register* deserved praise for taking up a world-wide compass
and that its Marxist approach was not equated with 'dogmatism and sectar-

ianism which has for so long characterized the "Marxism" of Communist parties'.[12] In a *Spectator* review by Walter Laqueur there was an implicit recognition that the *Register* represented a new type of left with positive features – later to be dubbed the 'Old New Left'.[13] There was a respectful review in *NLR* in August 1964 by Tom Wengraf who praised the editors for breaking out of the 'theoretical and cultural parochialism of the British Left'. [14] Some articles in the first issue became classic texts; indeed, there were requests to reprint Hamza Alavi's article 'Imperialism Old and New' by *Temps Modernes*, as well as from as far away as Buenos Aires and Delhi (RM to JS, 3.7.64).

After the first six years, the editors embarked on one of their 'taking stock' sessions aimed at agreeing a clearer political perspective. In June 1969 Ralph reviewed the editorial policy as it had evolved over the years as 'being fairly eclectic and let a hundred flowers bloom' and concluded that this was the reason why the *SR* had not made a greater impact:

> I would not want a rigid line but I think the time is long overdue for something a good deal more specific . . . Ideally this would require a review of the year from the editors and an editorial essay, an assumption of a position . . . Assuming this cannot be done there would still be much to be said for something less amorphous. We live too negatively in the *Register* and this makes each volume an agglutination of articles without backbone . . . We stand somewhere between ultra-leftism and left labourism; between Maoism and Brezhnevism; between undialectical opposites in the world socialist movement . . . we ought to stand for something apart from the presentation of interesting material. (RM to JS June 1969)

Ralph believed that he and John should call together a group of people who would provide feedback and inject fresh thinking into the enterprise: 'We are playing this too close to our chests and have carved out a little enterprise for ourselves without asking anyone to react to it'. He had made similar suggestions in 1965 to Ken Coates (now Member of the European Parliament) to set up a left forum discussion group 'without the parliamentarians' (RM to Ken Coates 6.8.65). In 1966 he suggested monthly Saturday meetings to John (RM to JS 24.7.66).

However, John's response to this call in 1969 for a change in direction was a sober appraisal of what was possible and what was desirable: 'The more journals a movement has the more volumes of essays, the more socialist literature generally the better. It doesn't of course give you a political movement but in advanced industrial countries you are not likely to get a "movement" without vigorous political discussions . . . I am not sure you are right to suggest that our line has been all over the place . . . I should have thought our place in the spectrum is fairly well defined but I can see the point you are making.' The suggestion about having an advisory group meet three times a year would have meant an awful lot of correspondence and effort and far too great a commitment of time which John could not make. John responded that he had a full timetable and was unable to devote more time to correspondence and arrangements, and if this was Ralph's wish, he could proceed without him. However, Ralph replied: 'I have no wish to carry on the *Register* without you'. That was the last discussion of substance about the way in which the *Register* was going or about its 'political' administration. They continued thereafter their kitchen cabinet meetings, in London, Leeds or Hull, sometimes by phone, but mostly by letter, to agree themes and contributions. The editors sometimes called on others to evaluate specialist materials, with Martin Eve, their publisher, an ever helpful presence when they wanted another opinion.

Ralph's worry about undue eclecticism was not shared by other readers, sympathizers and colleagues on the Left. Steven Lukes, writing in the *New Statesman* in 1975, celebrated the fact that there was no 'correct line' in the pages of the *Register* and that on every theme – Maoism, Leninism, the Labour Party or Colonialism – there were at least two different, if not opposing, viewpoints. Lukes remarked on 'the high level of argument . . . somehow managing to avoid both sectarianism and eclecticism'. Clearly the editors had hoped for more. Perhaps they visualised that the *SR* might have given expression to a political movement in the way that the Left Book Club had done in the days of the struggle against fascism. However, the *Register* provided a forum for the independent, non-Communist, Marxist movement that had sprung out of the discredited and linear CP straitjacket, publishing contributions that were unafraid to criticise the Soviet Union and showed a high degree of commitment to civil liberties.

In some ways the 1980s and 1990s provided even tougher challenges for a distinctly disoriented Left, although Ralph might have denied that anything was worse than the coldness of the Cold War. But one cannot help feeling on reading the files that to its initiators and editors the *Register* embodied a political project which was separate from their academic work although influenced by it, but with a coherent intellectual agenda of its own. Its editors had always hoped that the magazine would continue to provide alternative perspectives for troubled times. The annual sold well; the first volume almost sold out by the end of 1964 (JS Memo to contributors for the 1965 edition) and so did the 1973 edition with Thompson's 'Open Letter to Leszek Kolakowski' which was reprinted. Neither Ralph nor John, nor later Marcel Leibman and Leo Panitch, ever lost the sense of reaching out beyond the present. Yet whatever the message, Ralph remained slightly deprecating about the *Register's* achievements: 'has done well, could do better', as he wrote in the last edition which he helped to edit.[15] This verdict belied the endless care over commissioning articles, corresponding with authors about the texts, over the minutiae of translations, which often required re-translating, and the agonies about misprints. *The Register* owed its success to the fine-tuned collaboration between the editors and to the generosity of its contributors whose reward did not represent publication in a 'refereed' journal but participation in a political project. This is also a belated homage to them all.

NOTES

Warm thanks to my friends who made such valuable suggestions about this text: John Saville, Leo Panitch, Linda Gordon, Wendy Levitt-Kristianasen, Martin Eve, David and Edward Miliband, Lesley Johnson and Dorothy Wedderburn. I am grateful to Dorothy Thompson for permission to quote from letters and documents written by Edward Thompson and for pointing out several inaccuracies in an earlier draft.

ABBREVIATIONS:

RM   Ralph Miliband
JS   John Saville
EPT Edward Palmer Thompson
PA   Perry Anderson
ML   Marcel Liebman

1. Lin Chun, *The British New Left*, Edinburgh University Press, 1993.
2. John Saville, 'Edward Thompson, the Communist Party and 1956', *The Socialist Register 1994*.
3. Raymond Williams, *Politics and Letters*, London: Verso, 1979, p. 362.
4. Jan Valtin, *Out of the Night*, New York: Alliance Book Corporation, 1941. Having lost his original copy of this book, Ralph was extremely grateful to receive the gift of a replacement copy in 1984 from Mordechai Bubis (Benjamin Books, Ottawa), an outstanding socialist bibliophile.
5. Lin Chun, p. 64.
6. Ralph Miliband, 'Thirty Years of the Socialist Register' *Socialist Register* 1994, p. 2.
7. Personal communication, RM to MK.
8. Ralph Miliband, 'Voices of Socialism; Karl Marx', *Tribune*, London, 20.11.1964.
9. John Saville disagreed with Ralph's intrepretation of Marx's concept of the State (*Socialist Register 1965*) which argued that Marx was anti-Statist and that his thought had been misintrepreted. (JS to RM, 29.12.1964).
10. *'Voices of Socialism' Tribune*, 20.11.1964
11. *Daily Worker*, London, 28.5.1964.
12. *Times Literary Supplement*, London, 18.6.1964.
13. Walter Laqueur 'Confusion Compounded', *The Spectator*, 22.5.1964.
14. Tom Wengraf, 'The Socialist Register' *New Left Review*, no 26, August 1964.
15. 'Thirty years of The Socialist Register', p. 19.

RALPH MILIBAND: A SELECT BIBLIOGRAPHY IN ENGLISH

Books

Parliamentary Socialism; A Study in the Politics of Labour, London: Allen and Unwin, 1961
Parliamentary Socialism; A Study in the Politics of Labour second edition, with postscript: London: Merlin Press, 1972
The State in Capitalist Society, London: Weidenfeld and Nicolson, 1969
Marxism and Politics, Oxford: Oxford University Press, 1977
Capitalist Democracy in Britain, Oxford: Oxford University Press, 1982
Class Power and State Power, (Essays), London: Verso, 1983
Divided Societies; Class Struggle in Contemporary Capitalism, Oxford: Oxford University Press, 1989
Socialism for a Sceptical Age, Cambridge: Polity Press, 1994
Doctoral Dissertation, University of London, 1956, *Popular Thought in the French Revolution 1789–1794*

Essays and articles

'Harold Laski' *Clare Market Review* Vol 26, No. 1, Michaelmas 1950
'The Politics of Robert Owen', *Journal of the History of Ideas,* Vol 15, No 2, April 1954
'The Politics of Contemporary Capitalism', *NR* 5, Summer 1958, 'The Transition to the Transition', *NR,* Autumn 1958; subsequently published in an abbreviated version in *MR* Vol 10 No 10, Feb 1959 as 'The Politics of the Long Haul'
'The New Capitalism; a View from Abroad', *MR* Vol 11 Nos 3–4, July–Aug 1959
'A Rethinking Sermon', *New Statesman,* 7.11.1959
'The Battle for the Labour Party', *MR,* Dec 1960
'Bold but Sound', *New Statesman,* 20.8.1960
'The Sickness of Labourism', *NLR* 1, Jan/Feb 1960
'Footnote to Labourism', *NLR* 8, March/April 1961
'C. Wright Mills', *NLR* 15, May/June 1962
'The People's Militia in the Soviet Union', *MR,* vol 13 No 12, April 1962
'If Labour wins . . .' *MR,* vol 15 No 6, Oct 1963
'Harold Laski', *Tribune,* 12.6.1964
'Labour's Framework of Policy', *International Socialist Journal,* vol 1 No 3, June 1964
'Socialism and the Myth of the Golden Past', *SR* 1964
'Voices of Socialism: Karl Marx', *Tribune,* 20.11.1964
'Mills and Politics', in I. L. Horowitz (ed), *The New Sociology,* Oxford: Oxford University Press, 1964

'Marx and the State', *SR* 1965, reprinted in *Class Power and State Power*, 1983
'What does the Left want', *SR* 1965; abbreviated version in *Tribune, 28.5.1965*
'The Labour Government and beyond', *SR* 1966
'Marx and Contemporary Capitalism', *New Knowledge*, 17.10.1966
'Vietnam and Western Socialism', *SR* 1967
'Professor Galbraith and American Capitalism: The Managerial Revolution Revisited', *SR* 1968
'The Problem of the Capitalist State' *NLR* 58, Nov/Dec 1969
'Lenin's *The State and Revolution*', *SR* 1970
'Marxism' in *Colliers Encyclopaedia*, New York, 1981
'The Capitalist State: Reply to Nicos Poulantzas', *NLR* 59, Jan/Feb 1970, reprinted in *Class Power and State Power*, 1983
'Barnave: A Case of Bourgeois Class Consciousness', in I. Meszaros, (ed) *Aspects of History and Class Consciousness*, London: Routledge and Kegan Paul, 1971
'Poulantzas and the Capitalist State', *NLR* 82, Nov/Dec 1973, reprinted in *Class Power and State Power*, 1983
'The Coup in Chile', *SR* 1973
'Is Disruption on the Campus ever justified?', *THES*, 10.5.1974
'Marxism: Looking Backward and Forward', *MR*, vol 26 No 2, June 1974
'Politics and Poverty' in D. Wedderburn (ed) *Poverty, Inequality and Class Structure*, Cambridge: Cambridge University Press, 1974
'Marxist Theory and the Modern State', *Arena*, No 39, 1975
'Political Forms and Historical Materialism', *SR* 1975
'Teaching Politics in an Age of Crisis', Inaugural lecture, University of Leeds delivered on 7.10.1974, *The University of Leeds Review*, vol 18, 1975
'The Smiles on the Face of Labour's Right', *The Guardian*, 19.9.1975
'Moving on', *SR* 1976
'The Future of Socialism in England', *SR* 1977
'Constitutionalism and Revolution: Notes on Eurocommunism', *SR* 1978
'A State of De-Subordination', *BJS*, Vol 29 No 4, December 1978
'A Commentary on Rudolf Bahro's Alternative', *SR* 1979
'John Saville: a Representation' in D. Martin and D. Rubinstein (eds), *Ideology and the Labour Movement*, London: Croom Helm, 1979
'Military Intervention and Socialist Internationalism', *SR* 1980
'Political Action, Determinism, and Contingency',in M. Zeitlin (ed), *Political Power and Social Theory*, Research Annual, Vol 1, Greenwich, Conn: JAI Press Inc, 1980
'Class War Conservatism', *New Society*, 19.6.1980
'Power and Responsibility', *THES*, 22.5.1981
'Socialist Advance in Britain', *SR* 1983
'State Power and Class Interests', *NLR* 138, Mar/April 1983
'Why Labour must not retreat from the Politics of Radical Renewal', *The Guardian*, 27.2.1984
'The Politics of Peace and War' in Martin Shaw (ed) *War, State and Society*, London: MacMillan, 1984
'The New Revisionism in Britain', *NLR* 150, March/April 1985
'Why the Left has fallen on Hard Times', *The Guardian*, 22.4.1985
'A Road to take the Left inside Labour', *The Guardian*, 5.8.1985
'State Power and Capitalist Democracy' in S. Resnick and R Wolff(eds), *Rethinking Marxism; Essays for Harry Magdoff and Paul Sweezy*, New York: Autonomedia, 1985
'Activism and Capitalist Democracy' in Carol Harlow (ed), *Public Law and Politics*, London: Sweet and Maxwell, 1986
'Class Analysis', in A. Giddens and J. Turner (eds), *Social Theory Today*, p325–34,Cambridge: Polity Press, 1987

'Class Struggle from Above' in W. Outhwaite and M. Mulkay (eds) *Social Theory and Social Criticism; Essays in honour of Tom Bottomore*, Oxford: Basil Blackwell, 1987
'Freedom, Democracy and the American Alliance', *SR* 1987
'Old Labour Sickness', *The Guardian*, 14.9.1987
'Reflections on the Crisis of Communist Regimes', *NLR* 177, Sep/Oct 1989
'Counter-hegemonic Struggles', *SR* 1990
'What comes after Communist Regimes?', *SR* 1991
'Socialism in Question', *MR* March 1991
'Fukuyama and the Socialist Alternative', *NLR* 193 May/June 1992
'The USSR used to work', *Workers' Liberty* 16, March 1992
'The Example of Harold Laski', *NLR* 200, July/Aug 1993
'The Socialist Alternative' in L. Diamond and M F Plattner (eds), *Capitalism, Socialism and Democracy Revisited*, Baltimore and London: The Johns Hopkins University Press, 1993
'Ethnicity and Nationalism: a View from the Left', *Socialist Alternatives*, Vol 3 No 1, 1994
'Reclaiming the Alternative' in A. Callari, S. Cullenberg, and C Biewener (eds) *Marxism in the Postmodern Age*, New York: The Guildford Press, 1995
With Marcel Liebman:
'Reflections on Anti-Communism', *SR* 1984; reprinted in *MR* vol 37 No 3, July-Aug 1985
'Beyond Social Democracy', *SR* 1985/6
With Leo Panitch:
'The New World Order and the Socialist Agenda', *SR* 1992
'Socialists and the 'New Conservatism'', *SR* 1987; reprinted in *MR* vol 38 No 8, Jan 1987
With John Saville:
'Labour Policy and the Labour Left', *SR* 1964
With John Saville and Leo Panitch:
'Problems and Promise of Socialist Renewal', *SR* 1988
Contributor to: Tom Bottomore (ed)
A Dictionary of Marxist Thought, Oxford: Blackwell, 1983

Reviews

'Popular Sovereignty and the French Constituent Assembly 1789–1791', *The Cambridge Journal*, Vol 6 No 12, September 1953
'Deane: The Political Ideas of Harold J Laski', *Stanford Law Review*, vol 8 No 1, December 1955
'Progress in the Age of Reason', *PQ*, Vol 28 No 3, July-Sept 1957, p 298–300
'Freedom and Coercion', *BJS*, Vol 9 No 1, March 1958
'Party Democracy and Parliamentary Government', *Political Studies* Vol 6 No 2, June 1958
'Who governs Britain', *ULR*, 3, winter 1958
'Power at the Top', *ULR* 7, Autumn 1959
'Revolutionaries by half', *NLR*, 11, Sep/Oct 1961
'The French Revolution from its Origins to 1783', *PQ* Oct-Dec 1962, p 430–1
'The Reluctant Rebel', *Bulletin of the Society for the Study of Labour History*, No 6, Spring 1963; reprinted in *MR*, vol 15 No 7, Nov 1963
'The Man on Horseback . . .', *PQ*, April-June 1963, p219–20
'Parties and Politics', *Tribune*, 31.1.1964
'Accountable Power', *Tribune*, 13.3.1964
'The Moderates', *Spectator*, 27.3.1964
'Firing from the Left', *Tribune*, 4.6.1965
'Three Faces of Fascism', *PQ*, April-June 1966, p221–2
'Isaac Deutscher – an appreciation', *Tribune*, 1.9.1967

'A Study of Graduate Work at the London School of Economics', *Cambridge Review*, 10.6.1967

'Castro. A Political Biography', *PQ*, Oct-Dec 1969, p513–7

'In Place of Revolution', *Sunday Times*, 16.3.1969

'Against Dogmatism', *Tribune*, 13.2.1970

Review of studies of Marx by Jean Hyppolite, Robert C Tucker and J. B. Sanderson, *PQ*, vol 41 No 3, July-Sept 1970, p 353–5

'Marxist Sociology in Action', *PQ*, vol 42 No 3, July-Sept 1971, p 341–343

'The Hurdles are getting Higher', *The Guardian*, 19.8.1971

'On the Trot', *The Guardian*, 2.9.1971

'Coups for Beginners', *TLS*, 28.4.1972

'Selections from the Prison Notebooks', *Society for the Study of Labour History Bulletin*, No 25, Autumn 1972

'Stalin's Blight', *TLS*, 16.6.1972

'White Hopes', *TLS*, 1.12.1972

'Situating Marx', *BJS* vol 24 No 3, September 1973

'Stalin and after', *SR* 1973

'Reflections on the Causes of Human Misery' *BJS* Vol 25 No 3 September 1974

'Bettelheim and Soviet Experience', *NLR* 91, May/June 1975

'Kolakowski's Anti-Marx', *Political Studies*, vol 29 No 1, March 1981

'The Forward March of Labour Halted?', *Marxism Today*, April 1982

'Who Rules Britain', *AJS* Nov 1992

Abbreviations

AJS American Journal of Sociology
BJS British Journal of Sociology
MR Monthly Review
NR New Reasoner
NLR New Left Review
PQ Political Quarterly
SR Socialist Register
THES Times Higher Education Supplement
TLS Times Literary Supplement
ULR Universities and Left Review